Uzawa Hisa. Shite (Yorikaze). Photo: Jonathan Wolff.
鵜沢久、シテ頼風、写真、ジョナサン・ウルフ。

The Noh *Ominameshi*:

女郎花

A Flower Viewed From Many Directions

edited by Mae J. Smethurst
co-edited by Christina Laffin

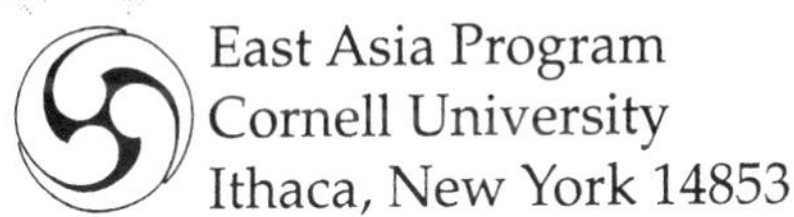

East Asia Program
Cornell University
Ithaca, New York 14853

The Cornell East Asia Series is published by the Cornell University East Asia Program (distinct from Cornell University Press). We publish affordably priced books on a variety of scholarly topics relating to East Asia as a service to the academic community and the general public. Standing orders, which provide for automatic billing and shipping of each title in the series upon publication, are accepted.

If after review by internal and external readers a manuscript is accepted for publication, it is published on the basis of camera-ready copy provided by the volume author. Each author is thus responsible for any necessary copy-editing and for manuscript formatting. Address submission inquiries to CEAS Editorial Board, East Asia Program, Cornell University, Ithaca, New York 14853-7601.

Number 118 in the Cornell East Asia Series

ISSN 1050-2955
ISBN 1-885445-18-0 pb
Library of Congress Control Number 2003107104
Printed in the United States of America
18 17 16 15 14 13 12 11 10 09 08 07 06 05 03   9 8 7 6 5 4 3 2 1

COVER DESIGN BY KAREN K. SMITH

⊗ The paper in this book meets the requirements for permanence of ISO 9706:1994.

Contents
目　次

Illustrations and Photo Reproductions
図版・複写

The editors and publishers thank those listed below who kindly gave permission to reproduce the images on the following pages.

資料の複写に際しご協力くださった方々に感謝申し上げる。

Contributors
執筆者紹介

Amano Fumio 天野文雄, Professor at Osaka University within the Graduate School Department of Theater Studies. His publications include 岩波講座能・狂言I（能の歴史), co-authored with Omote Akira (Iwanami Shoten, 1987), 翁猿楽研究 (Izumi Shoin, 1995), and 能に憑かれた権力者－秀吉能楽愛好記 (Kodansha Sensho Mechie, 1997).

Monica Bethe, Professor of Theater and Literature at Otani University, is a practitioner and scholar of noh. Her books include *Nō as Performance* (1978) and *Dance in the Nō Theater* (1982), co-author, Karen Brazell (Cornell, East Asia Program), and *Patterns and Poetry: Nō Robes from the Lucy Aldrich Collection,* co-author, Nagasaki Iwao (Rhode Island School of Design, 1992).

Steven T. Brown, Associate Professor and Chair of the Department of East Asian Languages and Literatures at the University of Oregon, works in the areas of Japanese literature, popular culture, and critical theory. He is the author of *Theatricalities of Power: The Cultural Politics of Noh* (Stanford, 2001), and co-editor of *Performing Japanese Women* (*Women & Performance*, vol. 23, 2001).

Susan Blakeley Klein, Associate Professor of Japanese Literature and Culture at the University of California, Irvine, specializes in Japanese theater, premodern religion, and literature. Her publications include *Allegories of Desire: Esoteric Literary Commentaries of Medieval Japan* (Harvard, 2002) and "Woman as Serpent: The Demonic Feminine in the Noh Play *Dōjōji*" (in *Religious Reflections on the Human Body*, ed. Jane Marie Law, Indiana, 1995).

Christina Laffin, a Ph.D. candidate in East Asian Languages and Cultures at Columbia University, specializes in diary and travel literature. Her current research is on women and travel in medieval Japan.

Publications include "Inviting Empathy: *Kagerō Nikki* and the Implied Reader" (in *Gender and Japanese History*, ed. Wakita Haruko, et al., Osaka, 1999).

William R. LaFleur, the E. Dale Saunders Professor in Japanese Studies at the University of Pennsylvania, has written on Japanese religion, ethics, and literature. His books include *The Karma of Words: Buddhism and the Literary Arts of Medieval Japan* (California, 1983) and *Liquid Life: Abortion and Buddhism in Japan* (Princeton, 1992), for which he was the first non-Japanese to receive the Watsuji Tetsurō Culture Prize for scholarship.

Susan Matisoff, Professor of Japanese and Chair of the Department of East Asian Languages and Cultures at the University of California, Berkeley, specializes in medieval Japanese narrative and dramatic literature. Major publications include *The Legend of Semimaru, Blind Musician of Japan* (Columbia, 1978) and "Barred from Paradise? Mount Kōya and the Karukaya Legend" in *Engendering Faith: Women and Buddhism in Premodern Japan*, ed. Barbara Ruch (Michigan, 2002).

Carolyn A. Morley, Professor of Japanese Language and Literature at Wellesley College, is the author of *Transformations, Miracles, and Mischief: The Mountain Priest Plays of Kyōgen* (Cornell, East Asia Series, 1993), as well as a number of articles on noh and *kyōgen*. She is presently researching the role of the *kyōgen* interlude in noh.

Nishino Haruo 西野春雄, Professor of Literature and Director of the Hōsei University Institute for Noh Studies at Hōsei University, has worked on performances of noh such as *Kanemaki* and conducted surveys of European noh mask collections. Major publications include 新訂増補 能・狂言事典 (Heibonsha, 1999), 新日本古典文学大系『謡曲百番』(Iwanami Shoten, 1998), and 岩波講座 能・狂言 III 能の作者と作品, co-authors, Yokomichi Mario, Hata Hisashi (Iwanami Shoten, 1987).

Mae J. Smethurst, Professor of Classics at the University of Pittsburgh, specializes in comparative Greek and Japanese drama and poetics.

Her publications include *The Artistry of Aeschylus and Zeami: A Comparative Study of Greek Tragedy and Nō* (Princeton, 1989), (also in Japanese, Osaka University, 1994), and *Dramatic Representations of Filial Piety: A Translation of Five Noh* (Cornell, East Asia Series, 1998).

Takemoto Mikio 竹本幹夫, Professor of Literature and Vice-Director of the Tsubouchi Memorial Theater Museum at Waseda University. Major publications include 観阿弥・世阿弥の能楽 (Meiji Shoin, 1999), 早稲田大学演劇博物館蔵特別資料目録5貴重書 能狂言篇 (Theater Museum at Waseda University, 1997), and 能楽の伝承と芸論, co-author, Omote Akira (1988, rep. 1992).

Arthur H. Thornhill III, Associate Professor of Japanese at the University of Hawaii at Manoa, specializes in medieval Japanese literature and religion. His publications include *Six Circles, One Dewdrop: The Religio-Aesthetic World of Komparu Zenchiku* (Princeton, 1993), and "*Yūgen* After Zeami" (in *Nō and Kyōgen in the Contemporary World*, ed. James R. Brandon, Hawaii, 1997).

Uzawa Hisa 鵜沢 久, a Kanze school *shite* actor, began her career at the age of three under the tutelage of her father, Uzawa Masashi. Upon graduating from the Tokyo University of Fine Arts, she continued her studies under Kanze Hisao and after his death under the late Kanze Tetsunojō. A full-fledged member of the Kanze Tessenkai troupe, she performs and teaches both in Japan and abroad.

Wakita Haruko 脇田晴子, Professor of Cultural History at the University of Shiga Prefecture, specializes in medieval history. Her recent publications include 女性芸能の源流－傀儡・曲舞・白拍子 (Kadokawa Shoten, 2001), *Gender and Japanese History* (ed., vol 1–2, Osaka University Press, 1999), and 中世京都と祇園祭 (Chuōkōronsha, 1999).

Preface

Mae J. Smethurst

In the winter of 1996, during a snowstorm, several scholars met in New York City at Columbia University to discuss the content and the format of a conference on the subject of noh. After much discussion, it was decided to limit the conference to one play and have the participants prepare themselves for the conference by becoming well-versed in various aspects of that noh and then presenting their ideas in a way that reflected their research interests. Setting up the conference in this way ultimately proved successful. It resulted in a collection of scholarly contributions, this volume, that, by concentrating on the one noh, *Ominameshi*, attempts to show some of the breadth and depth that is available for the study of Japanese literature and drama both in Japan and abroad.

The noh *Ominameshi* was chosen as a play that we thought likely to provide ample material for discussion among the participants. There were many questions related to this noh which had not been granted the scholarly attention in print that seemed appropriate for one of the two hundred noh in the regular repertory of the Kanze school today. To be sure, publications had appeared on the subject of *Ominameshi*, for example, work by Omote Akira and Itō Masayoshi.[1] The written views of a panel discussion in which Konishi Jin'ichi and Sakakura Atsuyoshi, among others, participated after a visit to the area of Otokoyama, the setting of the noh, were printed in *Kanze*.[2] And yet, it seemed that the play might deserve even more consideration than it had received to date.

Many of the reasons for choosing this noh were tied directly to the question of how a study of *Ominameshi* can be instructive to the study of noh in general. For example:

[1] Omote Akira, "*Ominameshi* no furuki utai kō," *Kanze* (July 1974): 4–11, and Itō Masayoshi, ed., *Yōkyokushū* in vol. 57 of *Shinchō Nihon koten shūsei* (Tokyo: Shinchōsha, 1983).
[2] *Kanze* (July 1966).

1) In spite of its importance within the history of the genre, the play has not been published recently in translation into English. Therefore, questions of translation of noh in general can be treated with a fresh viewpoint untainted by recent attempts to translate this play.
2) *Ominameshi* contains a large number of poetic allusions and quotations and lends itself to a reading in the light of earlier medieval poetry commentaries. Because the play appears in the wake of a rich tradition of poetry and legends about the *ominameshi* figure, including what is considered an earlier version of the noh itself, the play provides an important analogue for the study of the use of literary precedents in noh, for readings of the language and the special use of paronomasia made within noh plays, for reconstructing the way in which noh are composed out of earlier versions of legends and stories, and for placing a text into its proper place within the canon of noh and the history of dramatic literature.
3) The *ai-kyōgen* section provides an example of how important these sections can be to an appreciation of the action of a noh as a whole.
4) Because *Ominameshi* is a *mugen* noh and yet shares features of *genzai* noh, that is, some of the language is down-to-earth and the main characters are not part of the high nobility, a close analysis of *Ominameshi* in the light of other noh of both types is crucial to an appreciation of the play.
5) *Ominameshi*, like other noh, provides a window into the socio-political forces of those times during which it was popular.
6) Because many have thought that the plot of the play involves a man's apparent slight of a woman, her subsequent suicide, his suicide, and then his punishment in hell, for them an interpretation of *Ominameshi* entails questions of women's roles within and without noh. Both new historicist and gender-oriented readings of the play have been applied to shed light on these issues.
7) The play, set at Iwashimizu Hachiman Shrine/Temple and strongly religious in its provenance, including a scene of "hell" at the conclusion and reference to the Hōjōe rite, invites an analysis that brings with it a knowledge of Shinto and Buddhist religions and institutions as they apply to noh.
8) Since the author of *Ominameshi* is unknown, studies of the play

allow the scholar to use works by various noh playwrights to determine who the author was.

9) Other noh written on the subject of *ominameshi* provide valuable material for an interpretation of our *Ominameshi*.

10) *Ominameshi* is in the repertory of plays being performed regularly today and available for viewing on videotape, for example, at the library of the National Noh Theatre in Sendagaya. Thus the performance and musical elements can be examined critically. This is important inasmuch as the choice of costuming, including the masks, and of dance movements for the main actor differ from one noh school to another. An understanding of what is appropriate to a performance of this play depends both on one's interpretation of the play and on a knowledge of the performance of other noh.

These and other considerations provided compelling reasons for bringing together a group of scholars and discussing this particular noh, first at a workshop and then at a conference.

Over a warm summer weekend in 1996, eight American scholars of noh met in Ithaca, New York, at Cornell University, to discuss *Ominameshi* and to determine whether it could sustain a full-scale conference. Each scholar spoke about this play, named after the flower, now called *ominaeshi*, from different points of view. The group's presentations included a detailed account of the possible choices for costume and mask and diagrams of the movements on stage; an explanation of how the author of the play, replete with poetic allusions and quotations, used poetry from earlier works/collections; a survey of the musical patterns; an interpretation of the relevance of the medieval commentaries to a reading of the play; an analysis of the meaning of the final scene; a comparison of the play to other noh, especially those in which *ominameshi* figures; the relevance of the *kyōgen* section to the structure of the noh and to an audience's appreciation of the noh in the Edo period when the play was popular; and comments on the importance of the *waki* as a dramatis persona. Two of the participants performed parts of the play in the styles of the Kanze and Kita schools in order to demonstrate the differences in performing styles between them. On the basis of this workshop, it was decided that the play as the sole focus could sustain a conference, one which included six scholars and a performer of noh from Japan and an additional two participants from the United States.

The conference was held at the University of Pittsburgh in October, the month in which *ominaeshi*, one of the seven autumn grasses in Japan, normally bloom. None of the participants presented a paper. Instead the play was divided into as many sections as there were scholars and after each passage was read and viewed on videotape a discussion open to everyone followed. Since all participants had studied the play from their own points of view, the discussion, always informed, remained lively. In addition to the roundtable discussions, Uzawa Hisa performed the second half of the play with the assistance of Richard Emmert and Uzawa Hikaru at the City Theatre of Pittsburgh. For the students and faculty of the University of Pittsburgh, Wakita Haruko performed parts of *Izutsu*; Richard Emmert introduced the various instruments used in noh performances.

After the conference, most of the participants wrote articles on some aspect of the play, each from a different point of view. This volume, the product of their work, illustrates some of the many questions that can be raised about *Ominameshi* and how varied the answers can be. As the editor, I made no attempt to alter these articles, except to make a few minor suggestions, nor did I attempt to standardize their format throughout. Some of the authors used footnotes, others did not; some included illustrations, others did not; some summarized the play and translated lines, others did not; some were very speculative, others were not; some worked from a base of familiarity with a large body of early documents related to the play, others did not. This editorial decision of mine reflects a desire to present to the reader without interference the vantage points and approaches of scholars in both Japan and North America and of scholars on both sides who had different fields of expertise, all relevant to the study of noh. These various approaches influenced my decision not to include a bibliography separate from citations within the articles themselves. It is my hope that readers will be able not only to enjoy new insights into reading, interpreting, and appreciating the noh *Ominameshi* in particular, but also to appreciate anew some of the problems and pleasures that surround the study of noh in general.

序

メイ・スメサースト

1996年冬、大雪のなか、ニューヨーク市のコロンビア大学に数人の研究者が集い、能を主題とする学会の内容と形式について話し合った。その結果、本学会では話題を一つの能にしぼり、参加者には事前にその一作品をさまざまな面から調査してもらい、かつ各人の研究目的に沿って発表してもらうかたちをとることになった。実際学会を終えてみて、こうした形式は成功だったと言える。この学会の集大成である本書は、能「女郎花」に関する論文の集積であり、日本国内外における日本文学および演劇の学術的分析を可能にするさまざまな方法を明らかにすることを意図している。

能『女郎花』は、議論するにあたり必要な資料を十二分に用意しうる作品である、という理由で選ばれた。この能は、観世流の能二百番の一つでありながら、研究対象としてはそれほど注目されてこなかったようである。『女郎花』関連の文献としては、たとえば、表章氏、伊藤正義氏の各著書[1]、小西甚一・阪倉篤義各氏ほかによる座談会の記録（『観世』[2]）——能の舞台である男山を訪問したのち開催されたもの——などがある。が、これらの議論にとどまらず、『女郎花』はまだなお研究する余地が多く残されていると思われる。

この能が本学会のテーマに選ばれる経緯において、『女郎花』の研究が能全体の研究にどう寄与するか、という点がもっとも考慮された。たとえば、

1）『女郎花』は、能で歴史的重要性を有しているにもかかわらず、近年、英訳の出版がない。こうした状況により、翻訳に左右されずに、能の翻訳全般に関する問題を新鮮な視点から扱うことができる。

[1]表章「女郎花の古き謡考」『観世』1974年7月、4～11頁、伊東正義、編『謡曲集』新潮日本古典集成、第57巻、新潮社、1983年

[2]『観世』1966年7月

2)『女郎花』には多数の本歌取りや引用があり、それ以前の中世詩歌の注釈を視野に入れた解釈が有益である。この能およびその古形と考えられている作品には、オミナエシに関する詩歌や伝説のさまざまな型が豊富に見いだせる。したがって『女郎花』の作品研究は、能における文学的イメージの取り込み方や、掛け詞の特殊な使用法を知り、あるいは能が前代の伝説や説話を素材として作り出されていく過程を再構築し、能を古典文学および演劇文学の歴史のなかに的確に位置付けるためにも、重要な意味を持つと思われる。
3)『女郎花』の間狂言は、能全体の筋・構想を認識するうえでいかに間狂言が重要なものか、その重要性を示す適例である。
4)『女郎花』は夢幻能でありながら、一方で日常的な言葉を使っていたり、主な登場人物が高貴な人物でなかったりという現在能の特徴もあわせ持っているので、それぞれのタイプにおけるその他の能を視野に入れて詳細に研究することが、この能の鑑賞には不可欠である。
5) 他の能と同じく、『女郎花』から、それが普及していた当時の社会的・政治的勢力を探ることができる。
6) この能のその筋書きに関しては、往々にして、男性の明らかな女性蔑視、女の自殺、男の自殺、そして地獄での男にたいする制裁といった要素がある、と言われてきた。そして、そのような考え方のもとでは、『女郎花』を解釈するには能の内外から女性の役割を問う必要がある、とされてきた。この種の問題はこれまでに、ニューヒストリシズム・ジェンダー研究の双方の立場から論じられている。
7) この能は石清水八幡を舞台とし、宗教性が強く、最終段には「地獄」の場面があり、また放生会にかんする言及もある。こうしたことから、能にとり入れられた神道および仏教それぞれの信仰や制度という側面からの分析ができる。
8)『女郎花』は作者不詳であるので、この能を研究する上で、作者特定のため、さまざまな作者による複数の能作品を視野に入れることができる。
9) オミナエシを主題にした他の能が、この『女郎花』の解釈にとって貴重な題材となり得る。

10）『女郎花』は、今日定期的に上演される演目であり、東京・千駄ヶ谷の国立能楽堂図書館閲覧室ではビデオ鑑賞することもできる。したがって、演技や音楽的要素を批判的に調査できる。こうした調査は重要である。というのも、各流派によって衣装（面を含む）や主人公の舞の趣向が異なっているからである。この能にふさわしい衣装あるいは舞はどのようなものか、そういったことを理解するには、この能じたいの解釈にくわえ、他の能にたいする知識も必要とされる。

以上のような理由から、研究者が一同に会し、まずはワークショップをひらき、それをふまえた上で学会で議論する、という方式が採用されることになった。

同年、夏の暑い週末、アメリカ人８人の能研究者がニューヨークはイサカのコーネル大学に集まり、『女郎花』について意見を交わし、且つ、この能が一学会の主題として成り立つのかどうか話し合った。各研究者はこの能――現在おみなえしとよばれる花にちなんでそう名づけられている――に関して、それぞれの視点から意見を述べた。グループ発表においては次のような視点から報告がなされた。

・何通りもある衣装・面、舞台での動きについて。またその選択可能性について。
・他文献からの詩歌の引用、音楽的パターン、この能を解釈する上での中世古注釈の有用性。
・最終段に関する議論。
・この能と、他の能、特に『女郎花』が引用されている能との対比。
・能／謡曲全体における狂言の役割と、この能が人気を博した江戸時代の観客にとっての狂言の影響。
・ワキの重要性。

さらに、参加者の２人が能の一部をそれぞれ観世流、喜多流で演じ、その相違が示された。このワークショップをふまえ、学者６名と日本から参加の能楽師、それにアメリカ人２名を含む、『女郎花』を主題とする学会の開催が決定した。

学会は秋の七草の１つ、おみなえしが日本で開花する１０月、ピッツバーグ大学で開催された。参加者による論文発表はなく、その代わり、各研究者が担当箇所を割り当てられ、それぞれの箇所が朗読され、そしてビデオで上映された。その後、参加者全員によるディィスカッションが行われた。参加者は各々の視点から能を研究してきており、議論は表面的なものにとどまらず活発に続いた。座談会にくわえ、鵜沢久氏がピッツバーグシアターのリチャード・エマート氏、鵜沢光両氏の協力で『女郎花』の後半部を演じられた。また脇田晴子氏による「井筒」が披露された。エマート氏は能で使用されるさまざまな楽器を紹介された。

後日、学会参加者の多くが、個々の観点に基づき論文を執筆した。その論文を集めた本書は、『女郎花』をめぐる問題を数多くとりあげ、と同時に、そうした問題は多様な面から考察され得るということを例証するものである。編集者として、各論文に対しわずかながらの提案はさせてもらったが、論文の構成や術語等についての規格化・統一化をすることはしなかった。論文の形態は各人によってさまざまで、脚注やイラストの有無は各執筆者によって異なるし、能の要約とその翻訳を載せた論文もあれば、関連する古書をふんだんに用いているものもある。こうした編集方針をとった所以は、日本および北米の学者——いずれの学者も皆、能研究に有効な多種多様の専門領域を持つ——のいろいろな視点やアプローチを変えることなく読者に伝えたい、という希望があったからである。論文の視点が多岐にわたっているため、論文中の引用文にたいしてその参考文献は脚注にて示すようにした。本書を通じ、能「女郎花」の読み、解釈、鑑賞にたいする新たな議論に触れていただき、さらに、能の研究一般を取りまく問題、そして能研究の面白さを、あらためて認識していただければ幸いである。

Acknowledgments
謝 辞

This volume and the conference from which it arose were both funded by the generous help of the Toshiba International Foundation, the Japan Iron and Steel/Mitsubishi endowments and a grant from the United States Department of Education to the Asian Studies Program at the University of Pittsburgh. In addition, the Japan Foundation made a sizeable contribution to the conference, as did the Richard D. and Mary Jane Edwards Endowed Publication Fund to the publication of this volume. The inclusion of illustrations in color could not have been realized without a gift from the Haro Foundation.

The thoughtful contributions of Karen Brazell, Richard Emmert, and Gerry Yokota-Murakami greatly enhanced the discussions at the conference. The efforts of the staff at the University of Pittsburgh's Asian Studies Program, including Dianne Dakis, Jonathan Wolff, and Elizabeth Greene, on behalf of the conference, those of the staff at Cornell University's East Asia Program, in particular Karen Brazell, on behalf of the workshop held at Cornell, and Karen Smith's coordination of the volume's publication for the Cornell East Asia Series, deserve special notes of gratitude. Murayama Atsuko assisted with translations, which Yamanaka Reiko kindly read through. Takabatake Sachiko and Jana Adamitis both helped with proofreading. Marilyn Scott carried out a vital two readings of the manuscript near the end of the process and Tamaki Norio helped in the preparation of the index. The dedicated effort and patience of Komiyama Kiyoshi were key to the long process and successful preparation of the camera-ready copy of this book. Richard Smethurst's assistance before, during, and after the conference was crucial to the completion of this volume.

今回の学会開催と本書の出版は、東芝国際交流財団の多大な援助により可能となった。さらに当学会の開催にあたっては、国際交流基金をはじめ、日本鉄鋼連、三菱財団、そしてナショナルリソースセンターであるピッツバーグ大学アジア研究所への米国教育省からの基金より、多くの寄付をいただいた。また、挿し絵入りの完全版下と色刷りのカバーはハロ財団の多大なる協力なしには実現し得ないものであった。本書への寄稿者にくわえ、カレン・ブラゼル氏とジェリー・ヨコタ村上氏には、貴重なご意見・ご見解をいただいた。カレン・ブラゼル氏はコーネル大学でのワークショップ実現への計画と準備に尽力された。

ピッツバーグ大学アジア研究所のスタッフ、特にダイアン・デーキス、ジョナサン・ウルフ、エリザベス・グリーン各氏による学会へのご協力、コーネル大学東アジア学部のスタッフ、なかでもコーネル大学でのワークショップにご協力いただいたカレン・ブラゼル氏にはあらためて賛辞を呈したい。高畠幸子氏とジャナ・アダミティス両氏には校正の面で、村山敦子氏と山中玲子氏には翻訳の面でそれぞれ助力いただいた。マラリン・スコット氏には出版前の最終段階に原稿を二度通しで確認いただき、玉置紀夫氏は索引の準備において助力いただいた。また、小宮山清氏の献身的な協力及び忍耐が、長期間にわたる工程を経た完全版下制作成功への原動力となった。

最後に、本書の完成にあたり、学会の準備段階から学会当日、そして学会終了後に至るまで、リチャード・スメサースト氏の援助があったことを付言しておきたい。

Introduction

Mae J. Smethurst

The dramatic action of *Ominameshi* follows a pattern found in many two-part *mugen* noh. An *ai-kyōgen* section divides the first half, in which an old man (*shite*) and a priest (*waki*) talk together and exchange poems, and the second half, in which the same priest waits until the ghosts of a man (*nochijite*) and a woman (*nochizure*) appear. The ghosts sing of their past; the *nochijite* dances, relates his sufferings in hell, and asks the priest to pray on his behalf.

More specifically, in the first half of *Ominameshi*, the priest (*waki*) is traveling from Kyushu to Kyoto, but en route stops at Yawata between Osaka and Kyoto to visit the Iwashimizu Hachiman Shrine. On his way to the shrine he pauses and admires some *ominaeshi*, (maiden flowers) which he is about to pick, when the old man (*shite*) appears and says, "Don't pluck that flower." The two men exchange poems on the subject of *ominaeshi* and the fact that a priest especially should not pluck such a flower. Then the old man says: "Oh, well, go ahead and pick a flower." But now the priest does not want to do so and instead says he meant to see the shrine and forgot all about his purpose in coming to Yawata. The old man says he will guide the priest up the mountain to the shrine. In a song sung by the chorus, as the two actors walk about the stage slowly, they exclaim over the beauty of the shrine and its surroundings. But then the priest asks what the relationship is between the *ominaeshi* and the mountain, Otokoyama, where the shrine is located. The old man says that there are graves of a man and a woman at the foot of Otokoyama. The man's name was Ono no Yorikaze. He does not give the woman's name. At this point in the action the old man disappears and a villager from Yawata (*kyōgen*) enters the center of the stage to narrate a story about the man and the woman buried there, a story that helps immeasurably in filling out the background to the story of the couple: Yorikaze and his wife/woman.

In the second half of the noh, the priest sings a waiting song and then the ghost of Ono no Yorikaze (*nochijite*) appears, followed by the ghost of his wife/woman (*nochizure*). They both speak and sing about the graves and repeat part of the villager's story—the woman says she made a pledge of love with the man. He says he buried her when he found her body lying by the river. Her kimono was dripping with dew and a flower grew up on the spot, which bent away from him when he approached it. So he drowned himself in the same river and now suffers the tortures of hell, including swords that pierce his body as he climbs up the mountain overgrown with blades growing from trees. He asks the priest to pray for his deliverance.

This noh follows the structure and the action of other noh in some respects, but also is unique in a number of others. For example, the *nochijite* is not the spirit of the flower, as one expects in plays named after flowers, such as in *Kakitsubata* and *Yūgao*—he is instead the spirit of Ono no Yorikaze. The *waki* is a very important dramatic character in the first half of this *mugen* noh. There are more poems quoted or alluded to than in most noh. In addition, the play raises many questions of interpretation, as mentioned in the Preface to this volume, ranging from authorship to its historical, religious, ritual, and cultural contexts, to its structure, to its relationship to other noh, including others on the subject of *ominaeshi*, as well as to its provenance within the tradition of medieval commentaries, to its performance and costuming, and to the function of the *ai-kyōgen* within the play. Most of these questions have been broached within this volume, sometimes by more than one contributor and sometimes with different answers.

It is a given that the play celebrates the importance of the Iwashimizu Hachiman, a shrine that replaced the parent in Kyushu, the Usa Hachiman Shrine. In addition, we know that travel for merchants and tradesmen between Kyushu and Kyoto of necessity brought them through Yawata, the location of the shrine on Otokoyama. Politically the displacement of the shrine from Kyushu to Otokoyama in the ninth century may have made a statement about the political power then. In the Muromachi period when the play was written, the shoguns Ashikaga Yoshimitsu and Yoshimochi are on record as having visited the shrine at least 20 and 30 times respectively, and the next shogun Yoshinori was selected as such by a lottery drawn at the Iwashimizu Hachiman Shrine in 1428. (See articles by Brown and Thornhill.) These suggest an important political role on the part of the shrine for the shogunate. In fact, Hachiman was the tutelary protector of the shogun. And thus one might assume that he and his entourage would have garnered pleasure from the play by virtue of its setting.

The following lines of the Iwashimizu song appearing toward the end of the first half of the play describe the shrine and enhance the setting and by implication the power of the shogun:

The everlasting moon of the katsura trees on Otokoyama
The man in the moon of the katsura trees on Otokoyama
Shines cloudless clear all because viewed from such a holy place where
Fall colors add their radiance, while
The fading sun too shimmers on Iwashimizu
Its moss robe divinely exquisite.
On the three sleeves of the three robes the radiance is reflected
The robes are stored in the chest treasured
At this temple/shrine of the Holy Law. A most sacred and auspicious place, indeed![1]

It is a shrine that, as the words of the noh confirm, brings prosperity to the people living around it. Because the shrine belongs to the god Hachiman, it is also connected with warriors. As a warrior god who justifies killing, Hachiman is especially useful to the shogunate. However, the shrine also celebrates an appeasement for killing with the Hōjōe festival held at the shrine every year, even today. The two—Hachiman and the festival—can work hand in hand to portray the shogunate as makers of both peace and war.

From a religious point of view the play is highly textured. Thornhill is one of the contributors who examines the Iwashimizu song, along with the surrounding passages, in the light of the religious history of Otokoyama and Hachiman's transformation from Shinto divinity to Buddhist avatar. The shrine is that of Hachiman, a Shinto warrior god, but it is also a temple. The priest of the play is a Buddhist priest. The hell, which Yorikaze suffers at the end of the play, is Buddhist. Is there a problem in having suicide and suffering the tortures of hell juxtaposed with the Hōjōe, which is one of liberation, that is, the freeing of animals and fish as a symbol of the saving grace of

[1] The Smethurst translation is used here and elsewhere in the Introduction.

Hachiman? It seems that the dramatic action of the play takes place on the day of the festival, although not necessarily, according to Takemoto. As the priest and the old man begin to climb the mountain the chorus sings:

> In the middle of August one bows down and worships at this place where the god's procession stops.

Actually, the line allows us to reconcile the two religions at this shrine. Thornhill argues that the observance atones for wartime killing on the part of the semihistorical ruler of the fourth century, Emperor Ōjin, whose mother, Empress Jingū, had led an invasion on the Korean peninsula. Ōjin, in turn, was the transformed figure of a local *kami* who was the Hachiman of Otokoyama. According to Wakita, the god's procession during the festival enshrines the god temporarily away from the top of the mountain where Yorikaze confronts his hell. That means the hell and the god need not meet. Hachiman and sacred places like the Iwashimizu Hachiman Shrine are deeply connected to the bakufu and the state authority, but ghost gods are part of the everyday belief of the common people. Thus the two components of the noh are accommodated for more than one audience.

Near the end of the play, in the *kuse* there is a vivid description of the hell that Yorikaze faces:

> The fiend too amorous inflicts torture on the body.
> In ardent desire as he climbs along the steep way up the mountain overgrown with blades of swords,
> On the summit the form of the one he loves appears.
> With joy in the heart he continues his way up, but
> The swords pierce through his body and
> Rocks roll down and crush his bones.
> Oh, what does he see there?
> Oh, how terrible!
> The branches of swords bend down, so great is their weight.
> Indeed the results of what kinds of sins bear fruit like this?

The man of the play suffers this hell on the Man Mountain, Otokoyama, where the warrior god is enshrined, but for the course of the festival is temporarily absent. This means the Buddhist god is not contaminated by the warrior's sin and the Buddhist god can serve as a vehicle of liberation.

The play's title is *Ominameshi*, not a man's name; it is the name of a woman flower, not of the man, Yorikaze. What is the connection between the man, the mountain, and the *ominameshi*? First of all, in the play the old man points to a man's and a woman's graves. There still exist the graves of the woman, left nameless, who committed suicide when her husband did not return home from the capital and she thought he was not going to return to her, and of Ono no Yorikaze, who committed suicide in the river when he learned that his wife had done so because of him. These graves stood and still stand at the bottom of Otokoyama; however, even before there was any record of the story of this husband and wife there were two *kofun* (grave mounds), a man's and a woman's standing there. What we have today are traces of these near Yawata-shi, as Wakita points out in her article. What seems to have happened is that an aetiological explanation was needed for the existence of a man's and a woman's tomb. A story arose, first recorded in the Preface to the *Kokinwakashū*, about a man and a woman, which existed in the early Heian period. Otokoyama arose as the name of the mountain because of Yorikaze's burial there, but before that from the *Nihonshoki* and the time when the location of the shrine was transferred to the location near Kyoto the name was *Ozan*, i.e. Male Mountain, as Amano explains in his article. The *kofun* date from the end of the fourth and beginning of the fifth century; the name of the mountain dates from after that; and the story about the man and woman first appears later in the early Heian period. People in the audience, if they knew about the shrine, the mountain, or the existence of the two graves/*kofun*, as well as the story, would derive especial pleasure from a performance of *Ominameshi*.

Second of all, in *Ominameshi*, the title of the play refers to a flower, today called *ominaeshi*, of which the three *kanji* in the name taken separately have the meanings *jo* "woman," *rō* "man," and *ka*, i.e. *hana* "flower," and together mean a kind of flower, what is sometimes translated as a "maiden or damsel flower." In addition, the first two characters together, at least in the Edo period (see Wakita's article) came to refer to a courtesan of low rank, the meaning with which the noh play begins. Looking at it from one direction we could say that the play is an empowerment of the potential in the various meanings of the title and the place at which the noh is set, namely, Otokoyama, "Man Mountain," as Klein argues (see also LaFleur's article). At first the audience's attention is directed to the *omina*, a form of the woman who is a flirt and attracts men. For example, after the priest (*waki*), enters, he is attracted to the flowers "at the height of their season and in profusion." The verb *midareru* suggests sexual license. He also mentions the "color" (*iro*) of the abundant flowers. In the context of a man, that is, the *otoko* of Otokoyama, this color has erotic connotations. The priest adds in the first *sashi* of the noh that the flowers are bedecked with dew (*tsuyu*), sometimes erotic in meaning, here a euphemism for moisture that may suggest the flowers await their lover. The beauty of the flowers is intense enough to attract the insects, the priest adds, and the field grasses don flowers that are like bright Chinese robes (*shokukin*), such as a young woman might wear.

The characterization of the sexually attractive woman is established for the *ominameshi*. (Some of the contributors speak to the erotic connotations of the words in this first *sashi*; Nishino examines the *sashi* in the light of the music and a parallel elsewhere in the noh repertory.) Next, attention is directed to the woman who is more vulnerable, fragile, and ephemeral and third to a woman who has a man (*rō*), both the mountain and a husband. However, because she feels betrayed by the latter, she kills herself and then becomes resentful. She becomes so resentful that in the form of a flower, (*ominameshi*, all three *kanji* in the name) she turns into an instrument of vengeance against him. And finally, there is a hint in the play that again as a flower she herself might have reached salvation, although women usually cannot.

Not only do these meanings emerge during the course of the play, but also the author, whoever he was, points metapoetically, that is, self-consciously, to his awareness of the rhetorical device (see Klein article). For example, there are explicit references made to the name, as in the first *mondō* "on asking the name even playfully," and in the old man's quotation of Bishop Henjō's poem: "because the name entranced me," and again in the *ageuta* "with that flower, because its name was written 'woman.'" These and other ways of acknowledging the rhetorical devices, including etymologizing and paronomasia, and the self-conscious quotation of and allusion to other poetry enhance the text of this noh with a richness of verbal texture.

Ominameshi, like many noh plays that end with the punishment of a main character in hell, depicts torture verbally and kinetically in a dance (illustrated by Bethe in her article)—the man becomes a fiend too amorous, inflicting his own torture as in ardent desire he climbs the mountain, the same mountain it seems that the priest and the old man had climbed before, luxuriant in trees, now overgrown with trees whose branches are swords, this Tsurugi no Yama (Sword Mountain) is one of the Eight Great Hells (*samghata*), to which those guilty of murder, theft, and adultery are condemned. And yet, although Yorikaze's body is pierced by the swords and rocks crush his bones, he continues to climb the mountain where he sees the form of the one he loves appearing at the top. She attracts him ever onward up through his hell. She/the plant has become the instrument of revenge, as LaFleur argues. The playwright makes the revenge poignant by quoting for the last poem in the noh, one from the *Kin'yōshū*, often ascribed to Izumi Shikibu, and the first poem written by a woman in this work: "The branches of swords bend down, so great is their weight (that is, from heads of the dead). Indeed, the results of what kinds of sins bear fruit like this?" We see how sweet the revenge can be for the *ominameshi* woman.

In our play, it can be argued that the limitations on women are transformed into salvation, when in the last lines we hear from the chorus, singing for Yorikaze, the following words:

> It was all for naught, for but a brief moment the flower swayed in the wind,
> Dreamlike, *ominameshi*. Onto the dewy calyx because of his kinship with the flower.
> Deliver him, he prays to you, deliver him from his earthly sins, he prays to you.

Yorikaze renounces the past and prays for deliverance onto the calyx of Buddha's lotus, which is dewy (*tsuyu*), but dewy with a jewel drop, not pollution. The precious gem saved the Dragon Girl in a story found in the Lotus Sutra; according to a poem written by Jien, the *ominaeshi* could be saved;[2] and now in the play it seems that Yorikaze,

[2] See Edward Kamens, "Dragon-Girl, Maidenflower, Buddha: The Transformation of a Waka Topos, 'The Five Obstructions,'" *Harvard Journal of Asiatic Studies* 52:3 (1993): 389-442, for a discussion of this and other points made in the Introduction.

who has repented his sins, hopes for deliverance by virtue of a kinship with a flower, that is, the *ominaeshi*, which he associates with the calyx of Buddha's lotus.

At the very least, we know that in later plays about *ominameshi*, the spirit of the flower is saved. If these plays took our play as an example, as Matisoff argues, the playwrights assumed that the *ominameshi* could serve as a model for women and provide them hope. In the play *Henjō ominameshi*, for example, the Bishop Henjō, whose poetry is quoted and alluded to in our play, comes to Otokoyama to pluck a flower. The *shite*, a woman, tells him not to do so and quotes poetry about the *ominameshi*. In the second half of the play the *shite* is the spirit of that flower for whose soul the priest prays. She is saved, as she is in *Saga ominameshi* and *Funaoka*.

Inasmuch as there actually existed and still exist the two grave mounds of the man and the woman at Otokoyama, it may be that our play provides an *engi*, an aetiological explanation for their presence there, and dramatizes the fact that Otokoyama and the *ominaeshi* have a special relationship, a relationship that does not pollute a most holy sanctuary connected with the imperial family and the capital city. The one grave mound belongs to a man, *ipso facto* his grave can stand at the mountain. The other belongs to a woman, and it too can stand at the mountain inasmuch as after death she turned into a flower whose name by means of the progression of the noh and the poetry is cleared of the worst aspects of femininity, *jorō*, indeed of all femininity (*jo*). One way of interpreting the noh is that she *qua* flower becomes an offering to the Buddhas of the three ages, that is, the past, present, and future, mentioned when the old man quotes Henjō's poem early on and Sugawara Michizane's words about making an offering to the Buddhas of the three ages without plucking a stem of the flower. The priest does not pluck the flower, a surrogate for the woman, and does leave it pure.

Even if one is not convinced that the *ominameshi* woman is saved at the end, the playwright created a richly textured and thought-provoking play, one that was very popular in its day, named after the *ominaeshi*—the flower, the woman, her name, and the subject of poetry.

The Articles in this Volume

In the beginning of this volume there are included translations of *Ominameshi* by Steven Brown and Mae Smethurst. The two translations of the noh are different not only because they are based on different texts, those of Itō Masayoshi and Sanari Kentarō respectively that appear in the Appendix at the end, but also because the Smethurst translation, accomplished with the helpful suggestions of Shimazaki Chifumi, is more literal.

After the translations and Japanese texts, there follow articles written by the Japanese participants in Japanese and by the American participants in English. Because most of the pieces in this volume do not lend themselves well to a translation without undergoing major changes in style and because it is safe to assume that most scholars of noh can read Japanese and that Japanese scholars and students of noh can read some English, these articles have not been translated. However, for the readers who do not read both English and Japanese, at the end of each article there appear the authors' short summaries of their own articles in the other language.

The arrangement of the articles runs from my introductory essay to the final two pieces on the subject of performance at the end. These two are an article written by Monica Bethe on elements of performance—the costumes, masks, and dance—which include illustrations and sketches, and the noh actor Uzawa Hisa's reflections on her experience of performing *Ominameshi* in Pittsburgh. Each article in this volume can stand on its own and need not be read in the light of another. However, the articles are arranged, for the sake of providing some structure, as follows. The first two articles include background material and facilitate a reading of the poetry and an appreciation of the relationship of the two halves of the play to each other: Susan Klein's examination of the play in the light of medieval commentaries that preceded the writing of the noh, and the importance of the narration by the *kyōgen* in Carolyn Morley's discussion of the *ai-kyōgen* section, which dates from the Edo period. The historical, political, and social issues surrounding the play are treated in detail by both Steven Brown and Wakita Haruko. The articles of LaFleur and Matisoff both address the fate of the two main characters at the end, the former from a religious point of view, the latter from the viewpoint of other noh about the *ominameshi* figure. It would be a mistake to read any of the articles as only a part of a small subgroup. The themes treated overlap. However, for the sake of this volume I have placed the articles by Arthur Thornhill and Nishino Haruo, as well as those by both Amano Fumio and Takemoto Mikio, together. They make an interesting quartet of differing approaches to the question of authorship. Only the Nishino article is focussed on the subject of authorship; however, the other three also deal with this subject within their articles.

Some of the pleasure of hearing different approaches to and different interpretations of *Ominameshi* during the conference can be gleaned from a reading of the articles in this volume, which are interrelated to an amazing extent, given that the participants did not read each other's articles. They only knew what was of interest to the others from their presentations at the Cornell workshop and from the discussions at the conference in Pittsburgh. To be sure, there is as a consequence a certain amount of repetition in the articles; however, a variety of viewpoints is also very much in evidence and the "Flower," *Ominameshi*, is indeed viewed from many directions. For example, in the process of trying to identify the author of the play, which like the date is unknown, the different interpretations are exceptionally numerous. In his article Nishino sets out fully not only a background to various aspects of the study of *Ominameshi*, but also the dangers inherent in the various approaches to determining authorship. He makes a tentative suggestion, based on the style of music in the first *sashi* sung by the *waki* and a musical parallel in the noh *Tamakazura*, that the author might be Komparu Zenchiku. This is a possibility that Thornhill, offering other supporting arguments, such as the play's sophisticated exploration of a Shinto-Buddhist dialectic, and Morley, in her discussion of the *kyōgen* section, entertain. On the other hand, Takemoto believes that the author remains unknown, that the Iwashimizu song in the second half of the noh, which describes the mountain on which the Iwashimizu Hachiman Shrine was located, and the noh itself were written by different people. The author of the noh, if it was one person, in Takemoto's opinion, was someone who did not grasp the principles of composition fully and fell into the *dengaku* lineage for the music of this noh, that is, some time in or after the second half of the fifteenth century. Amano posits the view that our play may be the *Yorikaze* of Komparu Daiyu Motoyasu, an ascription with which Brown agrees, because the title suggests that the main character is a man, like the *shite* Yorikaze in our play, not a woman, as they think was the case in the lost *Ominameshi* written by Kiami and mentioned by Zeami.

Another area in which there was a variety of opinions lay with the Iwashimizu song, quoted in translation above, which Amano and others thought was structurally awkward. Amano at first thought that it would be easier if the Iwashimizu song and that section were left out completely. However, he thinks that the noh assumes structural coherency with the song included if it is read as a portrayal of the solemnity of the top of Otokoyama where the Iwashimizu Hachiman Shrine is located and thus a hint at the salvation of Yorikaze. The Komparu text makes a clear connection between the two graves—Yorikaze's Otokoyama, "Man Mountain," corresponds to *otokozuka*, the grave of the man Yorikaze after he committed suicide in the wake of the woman's suicide, and the *ominameshi* to *onnazuka*, the grave of the woman. Amano's conclusion is that the noh should not be read as centering around the woman but rather on Yorikaze. Thornhill examines the song in detail as a part of his argument that the play exhibits a sequence bearing a striking resemblance to Komparu Zenchiku's "six circles, one dewdrop" typology found in numerous performance treatises.

On the matter of the mountain's name, Amano says that thanks to the Preface to the *Kokinwakashū*, we can determine that there existed before its time a legend about the man and the woman/husband and wife, which serves as the background to the noh. In addition, it was thought that Otokoyama arose as the name of the mountain because of that man Yorikaze's burial there. However, Amano writes, as mentioned above in my introductory essay, that the name of the mountain actually comes from the *Nihonshoki*, and "Male Mountain"(*Ozan*) from an earlier time when the location of the Iwashimizu Hachiman Shrine was transferred to its location near Kyoto from the Usa Hachiman Shrine in Kyushu. Therefore, he writes, the connection of the origin of the mountain's name to the *ominameshi* tragedy is historically incorrect.

Klein's article, "Turning Damsel Flowers to Lotus Blossoms: *Ominameshi* and Medieval Commentaries," examines the secret thirteenth-century commentary *Kokinwakashūjo kikigaki*, probably written by Fujiwara Tameaki and explores, as she says, how some of the medieval problematics that helped to generate the system of secret transmission continued to play themselves out, even if in an attenuated form, via the incorporated material from Tameaki's secret commentaries. Klein treats the obvious thematic issues of the play, but also examines how certain religious subtexts would have framed the medieval audience's understanding of the play, in particular, she says, whether the path of poetry could be a path to enlightenment, Shinto-Buddhist syncreticism, and the esoteric non-dualism summed up in the phrase *bonnō soku bodai*, passion as ultimately identical with enlightenment. She shows how some of the surface contradictions and gaps that have caused problems in an analysis of the play can be resolved.

Morley points out in her article, "A Woman's Journey Through Hell: *Ominameshi* Seen from the Perspective of the *Kyōgen* Interlude," that because of the *ai-kyōgen* section, which she places into its historical context, the woman of the story becomes important as she does not without this section. She is variously depicted, for example, as a waitress in an inn on Yorikaze's way to Kyoto to see to lawsuits. Her serving *sake* creates an image of her that brings her down to earth, making her, and Yorikaze as well, more human and thus more accessible and sympathetic to the popular audiences of the Edo period. Morley's use of other materials, such as the *etoki* (picture narrators) and mandala, help to suggest that both the lawsuit and the affair add interest for the audiences and may explain the man's suicide in the wake of the woman's killing herself and the hope for salvation. Morley and Wakita both think that an appreciation of the noh in its historical contexts depends in large part on an appreciation of the changes that took place in the relationship between women and men and the status of women.

Wakita, in her article, "The Foundations of the *Ominameshi* Legend and the Noh *Ominameshi,*" agrees with the other contributors that the *Preface* brings the mountain and the flower's name together. She thinks that the story of the man and the woman arose as an aetiological explanation of two burial mounds that existed there. She also thinks, as I said above, that these were the two *kofun* of which we have traces today, one the male and one the female. The *kofun* date from the end of the fourth or beginning of the fifth century; the story first appears later in the early Heian period. Wakita also traces the meaning of the word *ominameshi* and its relationship to the position of women and how this pertains to our play. In the Edo period in patriarchal families the woman was the organizer and responsible for an heir. Outside lovers were sexual objects and their roles determined by men. Within the noh *Ominameshi* a division exists in the image of *ominameshi* between her being a primary wife and a woman outside the home. There is also the meaning: a fickle, pitiable woman. Earlier, as in the *Man'yōshū*, *omina* refers to women of a noble class, writes Wakita, but in the Edo period it means courtesan.

Brown, writing in the article "*Ominameshi* and the Politics of Subjection," from a different historical perspective, concludes that this play offers "a performative analogue between the Hachiman-inflected religio-politics of subjection and the gender politics of subjection" and that the woman is not allowed to tell her own story. The woman signified by the *ominameshi* is displaced by Yorikaze, and reduced to a mere botanical trope. However, in "Vegetation from Hell: Blossoms, Sex, Leaves, and Blades in *Ominameshi*," LaFleur, examining the changes in the image of the flower within the play itself and drawing on earlier religious and literary texts for evidence, hypothesizes that these changes constitute the main action of the play—the *ominaeshi* as flower is at first alluring but becomes a physical threat. Indeed, it metes out painful retribution to those enticed to come near it by virtue of a linguistic projection (one plant with another) that fuses the *ominaeshi/ominameshi* with the branches of the sword-tree which lacerate the ghost of Yorikaze suffering in hell. This reading of the play establishes the *ominameshi*, the flower figure, as a main actor in the noh named after her and one who in effect experiences a "personality change." Medieval audiences of the play would have appreciated the fact that sentience for humans and plants involves pathos, both suffering and inflicting pain.

Matisoff, considering other noh in the context of *Ominameshi*, in her article, "Flowering in Wild Profusion: *Ominameshi* in the Context of Other Plays," looks at the flower image from another point of view—*ominameshi* is linked to the lotus calyx in paradise. This could suggest that the prayers of Yorikaze for salvation might be for both him and her as well. In some plays that antedate ours and contain the name of the flower, as Matisoff points out, the flower appears in human form and reflects the possibility of rebirth for grasses and trees. Matisoff examines several noh, some on the subject of *ominameshi* and others, like *Motomezuka*, that bear similarities to or contain lines that are identical to those in our noh. On the basis of her reading of *Henjō ominameshi*, which postdates our *Ominameshi*, she suggests that a priest's proper behavior is at issue in the noh. On the other hand, she also suggests the possibility that *Motomezuka*, which predates our noh and in which the ghost of a woman tells of her terrible suffering because of the deaths of men who loved her, might have inspired our noh, in which the spirit of a man suffers because of the death of the woman who loved him. *Motomezuka* figures prominently in the articles of others also as a precedent for theme, words, and focus on a grave and the *shite*'s suffering in hell.

Thornhill, in his article, "The Tempered Light of Hachiman: *Wakō Dōjin* in *Ominameshi*," like Brown, treats still another noh, *Yumi Yawata* and, in addition, *Hōjōgawa*, for comparison with *Ominameshi*. He illustrates a religiously imbued connection between these and our noh. Brown suggests that *Yumi Yawata*, which with our noh contains more references to Otokoyama than any other play in the repertory and which was often performed with it, was performed at the inaugural celebration of the shogun Yoshinori, one of the Ashikaga, who regarded Hachiman as the tutelary deity of their lineage. He writes that the play is not one simply in praise of the emperor, but one that blurs the boundaries between the figure of the emperor and that of the shogun and even serves as a performative appropriation of imperial prerogatives and symbolic capital for the shogun. These connotations associated with *Yumi Yawata* are likely to resonate "intertextually" with the mountain in our play.

Thornhill discusses the image/motif of *wakō dōjin* (softening the light, merging with the dust) and how it enriches the spiritual dynamics of the play. He concludes that the darkness of the lower realms in *Ominameshi*, that is, the river and the suffering of Yorikaze's ghost, is merely the tempered light of the Hachiman deity who is engaged in salvation for all. The question of how one reads the Buddhist and Shinto elements of the play vis-à-vis each other received much attention from many of the other participants of the conference as well. Some see the juxtaposition of a suicide and suffering the tortures of hell and the Buddhist Hōjōe, a festival of liberation, as a problem.

Matisoff and Thornhill think that the festival suggested a promise of universal salvation; Takemoto suggests that the Hōjōe has nothing to do with the noh, unless it is just a reference to the festival and not the actual day. Wakita says that timing the action of the noh on the festival day is important, as I mentioned above. It allows the god to be carried from the top of the mountain in a portable shrine to the *otabisho* on the special festival occasion.

The absence of the god from the mountaintop shrine makes room for two views of the god—the folk/popular and the state. Hachiman is the rightful god of union between Buddhism and Shinto; but the ghost gods in the everyday belief of common people are in sharp contrast to sacred places like the Iwashimizu Hachiman Shrine with their deep connections to the bakufu and state authority. Thus to move the god away for the interim of the last scene in which Yorikaze is suffering the tortures of hell places a distance between the two, as Wakita argues. Brown suggests that the woman's suicide is connected with Hōjōe, the festival, which he claims ideologically justifies killing for religio-political purposes. Hachiman does good but also kills; the rite legitimates the violence of dominant authority, writes Brown; it atones for wartime killing in the noh *Hōjōgawa*, according to Thornhill.

These and other subjects that arise in a reading of the play also pertain to elements of performance. Bethe, in her discussion of costume and mask and dance, demonstrates how the choices of actors and schools change the degree to which the scene of the tortures of hell is the primary focus of interest, as it seems to be in a variety of interpretations on stage. For example, the costume of Yorikaze betrays his lower aristocratic status, mentioned also by Wakita and Amano, and the use of the *chūjō* mask, used for courtiers and warrior courtiers, is likely to make the actor more restrained than is normal in a *shūshinmono*, to which category *Ominameshi* is usually assigned. On the other hand, if one uses the *yase-otoko* mask, more appropriate because it is that of a suffering ghost, it would be out of character with the portrayal of an indecisive Yorikaze. Bethe describes the effect of choosing other mask types, including the *ayakashi*, which might place too much emphasis on the brief hell scene. The variants between schools and between actors occur in the dance patterns as well: during the final scene there is calmness at the end, Bethe illustrates, in the Kita version, and a smoothness in the movements of the Kanze version. Both of these versions release the great intensity of Yorikaze's suffering, as we could observe in the performance of the Kanze version by Uzawa in Pittsburgh during the conference.

Damsel Flower (*Ominameshi*)

Translation by Steven T. Brown

Dramatis Personae
Maejite (*Shite* in Part I): Old Man
Nochijite (*Shite* in Part II): Ghost of Ono no Yorikaze
Nochizure (*Tsure* in Part II): Ghost of Yorikaze's Wife
Waki: Itinerant Priest from Matsura
Ai: Local Person

PART I

NANORIBUE
NANORI (*spoken*)

PRIEST

Here before you is a monk who has come from Matsura in Kyushu. Since I still have not seen the capital, I plan to make a trip there this fall.

AGEUTA (*congruent, yowagin*)

PRIEST

I left the village of Matsura,
I left the village of Matsura,
where I lived for many years,
the future I know not, haunted by
the unknown fires at Tsukushi Lagoon
so quickly receding behind me,

Note: This translation is based upon the text of *Ominameshi* in Itō Masayoshi, ed., *Yōkyokushū* in vol. 57 of *Shinchō Nihon koten shūsei* (Tokyo: Shinchōsha, 1983), 246–55.

my journey's path stretches far off into the distance,
my journey's path stretches far off into the distance.

TSUKIZERIFU (*spoken*)

PRIEST

Having hastened, I have already arrived here at Yamazaki in Tsu province. I believe the hallowed shrine on the opposite shore, to which people pray, is called Iwashimizu Hachiman Shrine. Since it is identified with Usa Hachiman Shrine in my province, I wish to go there. Oh, how the *ominameshi* of this field now bloom in profusion and begin to scatter! I intend to stop and gaze at them.

SASHI (*noncongruent, yowagin*)

PRIEST

And when one approaches the field at the foot of Man Mountain,
seeing the flowers of a thousand grasses
adorned in multifarious colors, holding droplets of dew,
even the sound of insects creates the impression of true elegance.
The field grasses bear flowers, as if displaying the finest Chinese brocades side by side;
the *katsura* grove brushes away the rain, as if keeping rhythm with the music of the wind through the pines.

UNSPECIFIED (*spoken*)

PRIEST

The *ominameshi* on this Man Mountain are well-known plants celebrated in ancient poetry. Since it would make a fine souvenir to bring home, I would like to pick just one. So saying, upon approaching the *ominameshi* . . .

MONDŌ

OLD MAN (*spoken*)

Excuse me, please do not pick those flowers! The flower's color is like steamed millet. It is commonly called "damsel," so that even when one hears the name in flirtation, they say it is a pledge to live together as husband and wife until one's hair turns gray.

OLD MAN (*noncongruent, yowagin*)

Especially here, with the name of Man Mountain
in mind, the blooming *ominameshi*
are distinguished from numerous other flowers by their special relation to this place,
so why do you cruelly pluck them?
Oh, what a truly insensitive sightseer you are!

PRIEST (*spoken*)

Well, what sort of person are you that you feel such pity even for the *ominameshi* that bloom and scatter?!?

OLD MAN

Expressing pity for the flowers is perfectly natural, as I am the flower guardian of this field.

PRIEST

Even if you are the flower guardian, please be so kind as to take a good look at me. As I myself am a priest, certainly you may grant me a single flower: consider it an offering to the Buddha.

OLD MAN

Indeed, since you yourself are a priest, one would expect you to want to make an offering to the Buddha, but please do so without plucking a flower from the sacred plum tree, as Sugawara no Michizane wrote. So, too, in the following ancient poem:

(*noncongruent, yowagin*)

"If one picks a flower,
the hand becomes stained
just standing there . . ."

(*spoken*)

When offering flowers and other such things to the Buddhas in the three worlds of past, present, and future—especially for a priest such as yourself—it is only right to feel even more compassion.

PRIEST

Citing another ancient poem in that connection, is that why the revered Archbishop Henjō composed poems such as the following?

"Only because I have fallen in love with your name
did I pluck you,
ominameshi."

OLD MAN

No, it is for that very reason that he deeply concealed the poem's final lines:

"Do not tell others
that I have altogether fallen away from my vows."

Concealed in a patterned robe from Shinobu, he must have made a vow with an *ominameshi*, since there is no doubt that he arranged his traveler's pillow of grass side by side with one. If you, good sir, cite that revered figure of speech, your own understanding as a priest must be in error.

PRIEST (*noncongruent, yowagin*)

When I hear you speak in this manner,
making fun of my inconstant heart
in love with flowery colors and fragrances and
female charms,

(*spoken*)

no matter what I say, it will not change your mind, so I will just bid farewell and be on my way.

(*noncongruent, yowagin*)

I will continue on the road that brought me here.

OLD MAN (*spoken*)

Oh, how elegant it is here! Surely, sir, you know the ancient poem associated with this site.

UTA (*congruent, yowagin*)

CHORUS

What a refined traveler!
This flower, the *ominameshi* with a husband,
since I admire the name of him who understands the
connection,
I humbly give you permission:
please pick one flower.

AGEUTA (*congruent, yowagin*)

CHORUS

Ominameshi stand there showing off their charms,
ominameshi stand there showing off their charms

—does the attention make them feel uneasy?
Who might it have been who made the pledge to live together as husband and wife until their hair turned gray
because the name of the flower was written as "damsel"?
Surely it is true,
surely it is true:
the case of the dream lived for fifty years in a world of refinement
on that ephemeral pillow in Kantan.

MONDŌ (*spoken*)

PRIEST

Because I have been gazing earnestly at the *ominameshi* of this field, I still have not gone to Hachiman Shrine.

OLD MAN

What? Why have you still not proceeded to Hachiman Shrine? I myself am climbing up the mountain. I will guide you to Yawata. Please come.

SASHI (*noncongruent, yowagin*)

PRIEST

What an exceedingly august and blessed sacred place it is, beyond what I had heard!

OLD MAN

At the foot of the mountain, people's houses lie side by side.

OLD MAN & PRIEST

Even as the dust mingles with the divine light of Buddhas and Bodhisattvas,

in the flow of the muddied inlet, fish float to the surface of the water—certainly, to liberate living beings such as these
shows that the profound vow of Buddhas and Kami has become miraculously manifest.
Such benevolence!
Flourishing as I climb up luxuriant Man Mountain—how blessed!

UTA (*congruent, yowagin*)

CHORUS

Around the middle of the eighth month,
we bow our heads and worship at the traveler's place,
where the gods progress and are temporarily enshrined.

AGEUTA (*congruent, yowagin*)

CHORUS

In the clear light of the celestial orb,
lunar *katsura* trees and the Man in the Moon shine brightly over Man Mountain,
lunar *katsura* trees and the Man in the Moon shine brightly over Man Mountain,
this clean, manly image is the spirit of the place,
along with the colors of autumn shining in the moon's light,
Iwashimizu Shrine, where pure water shimmers in the sunlight,
where the priest's fine robe of moss
has hallowed images traced onto its three sleeves,
where the sacred box containing the imperial seal is stored,
where Kami and Buddhas, shrines and temples, coexist according to the Buddhist dharma,
how blessed is this sacred place!

UTA (*congruent, yowagin*)

CHORUS

Pines rise high above the cliff,
mountains tower over, valleys surround below
with multifarious tree boughs,
when the dove crosses the summit in this direction and looks down,
even the three thousand worlds do not appear far away,
even the thousand villages are gathered together in the brightness of the same moonlit evening,
at dawn gazing at the scarlet-jewelled fence and brocade curtains of state,
I bow down and pray in awe at such a blessed scene.

MONDŌ (*spoken*)

OLD MAN

Here before you is Iwashimizu Hachiman Shrine. Please pray with reverence. Since the day quickly draws to a close, I must humbly bid farewell.

PRIEST

Excuse me, what is the history of the association between the *ominameshi* and this Man Mountain?

OLD MAN

What?!? Earlier when I cited the ancient poem about the *ominameshi*, I spoke in jest: it was to no avail. That it is called Man Mountain is surely because of its history with the *ominameshi*. Moreover, at the foot of the mountain, I would like to show you the tombs of a man and a woman. Please come this way.

MONDŌ (*spoken*)

OLD MAN

This is the man's tomb, and that is the woman's tomb. The history of the *ominameshi* is also connected to these two tombs, the man's and the woman's. The two buried in the earth were husband and wife.

PRIEST

Well, from what province did this married couple harken? What was their family name?

OLD MAN

The woman was from the capital; and as for the man, here on Mount Yawata,

(*noncongruent, yowagin*)

he was called Ono no Yorikaze.

UTA (*congruent, yowagin*)

CHORUS

How abashed I am! I do not know whether I should
tell the story of these past events or not.
Since I do not speak of such matters, to whom will it occur to pray even occasionally for the repose of their dead spirits?
As the wind blows, Yorikaze approaches under the late-night moon,
concealed in the shadows of the trees,
like a dream he disappears, like a dream he disappears.

MONDŌ/KATARI (*spoken*)

A local man tells the priest the story of Yorikaze and the ominameshi, *and recommends that he hold a service to mourn their departed spirits.*

PART II

AGEUTA (*congruent, yowagin*)

PRIEST

I will lie down here for the night
on a sheaf of grass near a tomb marked by stag's antlers,
on a sheaf of grass near a tomb marked by stag's antlers,
chanting sutra passages to pray
for the restless spirits who have appeared out of the shadows.

SUTRA CHANT (*noncongruent, yowagin*)

PRIEST

Homage to the restless spirits! May you attain release from the karmic cycle of life and death and enter Nirvana.

DEHA ENTRANCE MUSIC

SASHI (*noncongruent, tsuyogin*)

YORIKAZE

How uncommon it is to see people pass through this vast plain! What else is there besides my old tomb?!?

YORIKAZE'S WIFE

Impossible to stop the beasts of prey from attacking and greedily devouring the corpses.

ISSEI (*noncongruent, tsuyogin*)

YORIKAZE

How nostalgic I feel when I hear the autumn winds of old!

CHORUS

Is it lavender—the color of resentment—on the back side of the arrowroot leaf?

YORIKAZE

If you turn it over, let us go together as husband and wife,
if we return, let it be together as coupled waves breaking upon the shore.

NORIJI (*congruent, tsuyogin, ōnori* rhythm)

CHORUS

The bejewelled cord of life,
the spirit of the *ominameshi*,
which had vanished,
has now reappeared
together with her husband.
How blessed is the Law of the Buddha!

KAKEAI

PRIEST (*noncongruent, tsuyogin*)

Like shadows, the restless spirits appear. How strange!

YORIKAZE'S WIFE (*noncongruent, yowagin*)

I am someone who used to live in the capital.
I made a vow of marriage to that Yorikaze.

YORIKAZE (*spoken*)

Because of a brief period when I could not visit you, did you really think that I had broken off relations altogether?

YORIKAZE'S WIFE (*noncongruent, yowagin*)

The fragility of a woman's heart:
it is because I left the capital yearning for one man alone
that my resentful thoughts are even more profound
as I hurl myself into the depths of the Life-Releasing River.

YORIKAZE (*spoken*)

I, Yorikaze, heard this and was terribly frightened; when I went to see what had happened,

(*noncongruent, yowagin*)

there was only her corpse, so fragile and transient, too late to save.

YORIKAZE'S WIFE (*noncongruent, yowagin*)

Crying he took away my corpse, and buried it in the earth at the foot of this mountain.

YORIKAZE (*spoken*)

From her burial mound, as if thinking in her heart of Yorikaze, a single *ominameshi* sprouted forth. Yorikaze thought to himself:

(*noncongruent, yowagin*)

Now that my wife has turned into an *ominameshi*,
I am even more nostalgic for her flowery colors and charms;
both her sleeves of grass and my own sleeves
begin to moisten with the dew of tears when I draw near.
But this flower keeps giving me a look of resentment:
whenever I, her husband, approach,
she flutters and moves away;
and then as soon as I withdraw,
she returns to her earlier state.

UTA (*congruent, yowagin, yowagin*)

CHORUS

In view of this place, Ki no Tsurayuki, too,
wrote in beautiful calligraphic style of
"recalling past days on Man Mountain,
or lamenting the brief life of the *ominameshi*."
A passage cherished by future generations!

KUSE (*congruent, yowagin*)

CHORUS

At that time, Yorikaze
understood her sadness:
"It was because of my own cruelty
that she disappeared like insignificant foam on the water.
She who died in vain
has me to blame most of all!
Not wishing to outlive her in this floating world of pain and sorrow,
I shall follow the same path to the world of the dead."

YORIKAZE

Following her, I throw myself into this river . . .

CHORUS

Since the time they buried me in the earth together with her,
my grave facing hers,
it has been called Man Mountain.
The tombs I speak of are these here, and I am the husband
who has come as a ghostly apparition.
Please, sir, be so kind as to pray for the repose of my spirit.
Please, sir, be so kind as to pray for the repose of my
spirit.

ISSEI (*noncongruent, yowagin*)

CHORUS

Oh, how I long for the land of the living!

KAKERI

NORIJI

CHORUS (*congruent, tsuyogin, ōnori* rhythm)

Cursed devils of sexual infidelity
incite me, then reproach me, torturing my body,
cursed devils of sexual infidelity
incite me, then reproach me, torturing my body,
blind willpower
impelled by desire along the path of peril,
on top of Sword Mountain
my beloved has appeared.

How gratifying!
But as I climb,
double-edged swords penetrate my body,
enormous rocks crush my bones.
How terrifying it all is!
Sword-branches
bend down under the weight of my sin.

(*congruent, yowagin, ōnori* rhythm)

What sin engendered this end?!?
An utterly foolish one.

UTA (*congruent, yowagin*)

CHORUS

Even lamenting
the brevity of the flower's life is but a dream!
Ominameshi,
upon your dewy calyx tied to the lotus flower pedestal,
I beseech you: let me float up to Pure Land paradise,
send my sins to the surface and deliver me from them!

Ominameshi

A literal translation by Mae J. Smethurst

SECTION 1

With the Nanori-bue, *the* waki, *a priest of Matsuragata, enters and stops at the naming place (stage back right).*

Waki (Traveling monk)

Nanori

This is a monk from the coast of Matsuragata in Kyushu. Having not yet visited the Capital, I decided this fall to make a trip there.

Michiyuki

The place that was home for a long time,
The village of Matsura, I leave behind.
(repeat)
Ahead the unknown fires of Tsukushi Bay
Recede before one knows it into a distance.
The way to be traversed is still long and far,
The way to be traversed is still long and far.

[*Tsukizerifu*][1]

This one has hurried and is already at a place named Yamazaki in Tsu Province. Over there one can see Iwashimizu Hachiman Shrine,

Note: This translation is based upon the text and commentary of *Ominameshi* in Sanari Kentarō, ed., *Yōkyoku taikan*, vol. 5 (Tokyo: Meiji Shoin, 1983), 246–55. The sections into which the translation is divided, the names of types of song, speech, chant or music, the ascription of roles, and the stage directions are all taken from Sanari's text.

[1] Brackets indicate additions to the Sanari text.

dedicated to the same deity as Usa Hachiman Shrine in my native country. So I think that I will visit that shrine.

Goes to the stage center front.

Now in this field ominameshi[2] are at the height of their season and in profusion. I think I will go there for a while and look at the flowers.

[*Sashi*]

Now I am come to the fields at the base of Otokoyama and
See a vast number of flowers in bloom, displaying their color and bedecked with dew.
Even the voices of the insects sound sensitive to the beauty.
The field grasses donning flowers spread out a rich brocade.
Brushing away the rain from the katsura trees
The wind in the pines makes music.

Spoken

As for the ominameshi of this Otokoyama, according to songs of old it is a famous plant. Saying, "So that it become a memento to take home, let me pluck one stem of this flower," he approaches the ominameshi. . . .

SECTION 2

Shite (Old man)

Yobikake [*Mondō*]

No, don't pluck that flower.
"The color of the flower is like prepared millet.
Commonly it is called a woman.
'On asking the name even playfully
One would make a life-long pledge of love,'" it is said.

[2] The present-day spelling is *ominaeshi*. I use that of Sanari's text and do not italicize this frequently appearing word.

kakaru

And even more [because] this is Otokoyama,
The[se] blooming ominameshi are famous.
From among other flowers blooming in abundance,
Why do you heartlessly pluck this [flower in particular]?
Oh, what an inconsiderate traveler you are!

Waki

I wonder who you are to begrudge me the ominameshi blooming in such profusion.

Shite

There is a reason for begrudging. I am the guardian of the flowers in this field.

Waki

Given that you are the guardian of the flowers, look. As you can see I am a monk. Considering it an offering to Buddha, permit him to pluck just one stem.

Shite – *He enters the main stage and stands at the jō-za.*

Since you are a monk, I think it is for an offering to Buddha that you pluck the flower. However, with regard to Sugawara's sacred tree, something is said to the effect of "without plucking make an offering." There is also an old poem:

"If I should pluck it, it will be contaminated by my hands.
Leaving it standing, I am offering the flower to the Buddhas
of the three ages."

Especially since you are a monk, more than others you should refrain from plucking it.

Waki

Since you quote an old poem, let me ask about Sōjō Henjō's poem:

"Because the name entranced me
Was the sole reason I plucked you, oh,
Ominameshi."

Why did he compose it like that?

Shite

But then in the same poem he says:

"Do not tell the others
That I have fallen [so] low."

Hiding deep beneath the robe with a fern-leaf-pressed (design), love was pledged with the woman flower on the pillows of grass placed side-by-side. There is no doubt about that. By quoting the poem as an example, you, a monk, make a mistake.

Waki

kakaru

According to what you say, even if you are being playful, It [all] stems from a flowering heart that loves colors and perfumes.

So all this is idle talk. Let me say farewell and return. On saying this,

kakaru

I move on and go the way I came from.

Shite

Oh how refined [you are]! You know an old poem about this place.

kakaru

"Ominameshi
Gazing upon it with regret,
I go on my way because I think
'Tis on Otokoyama
That the flower is blooming."

Ji

Sageuta

An admirable traveler you are!
A flower with a man is ominameshi.
And yet, since you are so knowledgeable, out of
Admiration I grant permission.
Now go ahead and pluck one stem.

Ageuta

Charming and beautiful stands the ominameshi,
Charming and beautiful stands the ominameshi,
Perhaps feeling uncomfortable (about all the attention).
With that flower, because its name was (written) "woman,"
Who made a pledge of love lasting a lifetime?
On the pillow of Kantan for but a brief sleep (it was),
Fifty years of dreaming (but only as long as it took for the) millet to be cooked.
Thus most truly indeed we see the sadness of life (as in a short-lived flower),
Thus most truly indeed we see the sadness of life (as in a short-lived flower).

SECTION 3

Waki [*Mondō*]

I have been looking at the ominameshi in this field for so long (and was so fascinated) I have not yet visited Hachiman Shrine.

Shite – *They stand center stage.*

It so happens that this old man is right now on his way up the mountain. I will be your guide to Hachiman.[3] Come this way.

Waki

kakaru

This surpasses what I have heard about it.
Most blessed and auspicious are the holy precincts!

Shite

At the foot of the mountain houses standing eave by eave . . .

Shite & Waki

Soft radiance divine mingles with the dust on the muddy river.
In the river's water swim scaly creatures.
Indeed, it seems as if they were released alive.
Marvelous indeed is the divine pledge profound.
In God's mercy trees grow thick on Otokoyama,
Whose sloped paths, how blessed, we now climb.

[3] Pronounced Yawata here.

Ji

Sageuta

In the middle of August
One bows down and worships at this place where the god's procession stops.

Ageuta

The everlasting moon of the katsura trees on Otokoyama
The man in the moon of the katsura trees on Otokoyama
Shines cloudless clear all because viewed from such a holy place where
Fall colors add their radiance, while
The fading sun too shimmers on Iwashimizu
Its moss robe divinely exquisite.
On the three sleeves of the three [priestly] robes the radiance is reflected.
The robes are stored in the chest treasured
At this temple/shrine of the Holy Law,
A most sacred and auspicious place, indeed!

Uta

Pines are growing high on the rocks.
The mountain peaks tower with valleys around them.
Many trees grow with their branches linked closely together.
When crossing the Hato no Mine one sees
3000 worlds in a glance.
1000 miles under one moon's light, on such a night,
Bright within the vermilion fence, a holy curtain of Brocade hangs, filling one with awe beyond words [i.e. too inspiring for words],
We kneel down and pray.

SECTION 4

Shite

This is none other than Iwashimizu Hachiman Shrine. Take a good look at it. Since the day has grown dark, I will leave you.

Waki

Now, as for ominameshi, is there a relationship between it and this Otokoyama?

Shite

You disappoint me. [That is, I already told you, don't you remember?] Before I referred to an ominameshi poem playfully. It was all a waste of time. As for ominameshi, it is especially connected to this very place, Otokoyama. And at the foot of this mountain there are a man's and a woman's burial mounds. I will show them to you. Come this way.

This one here is the man's burial mound. And this one is the woman's burial mound. As for the man's and the woman's burial mounds, there is a story related to ominameshi [something they talk about]. A man and his wife are buried under these mounds.

Waki

Where are the couple from? What are their names?

Shite

The woman was a person from the capital, the man this Yawatayama.

His name was Ono no Yorikaze.

Ji

Ageuta

How embarrassing! The past long gone
One hesitates to reveal.
But if not told, then for the departed soul
Even on a rare occasion who would come to pray?
Who would think of Yorikaze?
Among the wind-swept
  Trees, the form, lit by the late night's moon, is now hidden,
Like a dream the form has disappeared,
Like a dream the form has disappeared.

Nakairi

Ai-kyōgen tells the *waki* the story of Ono no Yorikaze and his wife and how ominameshi grew on the woman's grave. He thinks the old man is the ghost of Yorikaze and suggests that the *waki* pray for the departed souls.[4]

SECTION 5

Waki

Machiutai

Here for just one night,
Short like the new growth of a deer's antler,
By the grave, on the grass of the burial mound,
Short like the new growth of a deer's antler,
By the grave, on the grass of the burial mound, (I rest).
For the soul seen to appear from the shade
I offer prayers, chanting aloud the holy words.

[4] See the translation of the *ai-kyōgen* by Carolyn Morley, pages 98–99.

Awazu

Hail Buddha. I pray to Buddha. May the departed souls be freed from the vicissitudes of life and death and swiftly attain Buddhahood.

SECTION 6

To the accompaniment of the music, the nochijite *(the ghost of Yorikaze) and the* nochizure *(the ghost of Yorikaze's woman) come out together. The* tsure *enters the stage and stands at the pillar closest to the* hashigakari; *the* shite *stops at the first pine of the* hashigakari.

Nochijite (Ghost of Ono no Yorikaze)

[*Sashi*]

Oh, the desolate field where almost no human form is seen.
But for our grave mounds, what is there?

Tsure

The fierce animals that fight for corpses
Are not to be fended off.

Shite

[*Issei*]

Ah, the memory!
Listen, the sound of the autumn wind of the past long gone
Tsure

[Wailing as if] with resentment. To the reverse side purple arrowroot leaves

Shite

Turn [and turn back]. [If you turn back, return], let me follow you.
[Like] twin waves, a man and his woman—

Ji

[*Noriji*]

Their souls faded away—their (life's) cord cut (short).
Ominameshi
The flower couple have appeared.
Oh blessed
Are the divine prayers.

Waki

Kakeai

Like shadows the ghosts of the departed souls
Appear. Oh, how strange!

Tsure

I, a woman, used to live in the Capital.
With that Yorikaze over there I pledged love; however,

Shite

When I had to be away from her for a while, perhaps thinking the brief separation permanent—

Tsure

kakaru

So fragile is a woman's heart,

Alone I wandered out of the Capital.
The bitter feeling within me still deep [heavy]
Into the Hōjō River I threw myself.

Tsure kneels center front, then goes and sits left of the Waki.

Shite

Yorikaze, hearing of this, in consternation hurriedly went only to see a lifeless body lying there.

Tsure

kakaru

In tears, in tears, taking up the body,
He buried it here at the foot of the mountain.

Shite

spoken

From the grave mound one ominameshi sprang up. So Yorikaze at heart thought

Now he knows, "my woman
Has turned into an ominameshi."
Oh, how the color of the flower recalls memories so dear!
The sleeves of the flower and the sleeves of my robe are dripping
With dew. When I went near her,
The flower, as if with an air of resentment,
At my approach, bent away, and,
When I drew away, it stood up as before.

Ji

[*Sageuta*]

It is because of this that Tsurayuki wrote,
Thinking of Otokoyama of long ago,
"Ominameshi only for a moment
Sways." The traces of his brush strokes
Fill one's heart with fond thoughts even into the next life.

SECTION 7

Kuse – Shite dances.

Yorikaze at that moment
Thought about the sorrow of the dead (woman).
How pitiful! All because of this one,
Like the vain foam on water, there for no reason, she vanished,
And ceased to exist. For that
Nobody but this one is to blame.
It is best to cease living in this sad world.
And to go the same way she went. Thinking thus,

Shite

Following her, into this river he threw himself.

Ji

Like her he was buried under the ground, so that,
While her grave is called the Woman's Grave Mound,
The site of his grave is called Otokoyama.
The grave you see there, I am the resident of it.

Now in a vision he has appeared to you.
For the repose of his departed soul please say a prayer.
For the repose of his departed soul please say a prayer.

Issei

Oh, how I long for the earthly world!

Kakeri by Shite

Kiri

The fiend too amorous inflicts torture on the body.
The fiend too amorous inflicts torture on the body.
In ardent desire
As he climbs along the steep way up the mountain overgrown with blades of swords,
On the summit the form of the one he loves appears.
With joy in the heart he continues his way up, but
The swords pierce through his body and
Rocks roll down and crush his bones.
Oh, what does he see there? Oh, how terrible!
The branches of swords bend down, so great is their weight.
Indeed the results of what kinds of sins bear fruit like this?
It was all for naught, for but a brief moment the flower
Swayed in the wind, dream-like, ominameshi,
Onto the dewy calyx because of kinship with the flower
Deliver him, he prays to you,
Deliver him from his earthly sins, he prays to you.

Turning Damsel Flowers to Lotus Blossoms: *Ominameshi* and Medieval Commentaries

Susan Blakeley Klein

At first glance the thematic issues of *Ominameshi* (The Damsel Flower) may seem obvious: the damsel flower as female surrogate serves as a symbol of female exclusion from Buddhist and Shinto institutions, as a symbol of the negative power of obsessive love and guilt, and, paradoxically, the damsel flower also signifies the possibility for redemption from the hell of passionate desires. Like other readings in this volume, my analysis will address these important issues, but I will also explore a few of the more hidden religious and linguistic conflicts that are nevertheless crucial to our understanding of how the play would have been understood by a medieval audience. In particular I have chosen to concentrate on the hidden source for the basic story (*honzetsu*) underlying *Ominameshi*: a secret thirteenth-century commentary, *Kokinwakashūjo kikigaki* (Lecture Notes on the *Kokinshū* Preface). The following preliminary discussion of the development of *Kokinwakashūjo kikigaki* and other secret allegorical commentaries, which were widely used as sources for noh plays, will lay the groundwork for my analysis of how some of the issues that helped to generate the secret commentaries continued to play themselves out, albeit in an attenuated form, in *Ominameshi*.

Kokinwakashūjo kikigaki appears to have been written in the 1280's by the Shingon priest-poet Fujiwara Tameaki (c. 1230's–1290's), a lesser-known son of Fujiwara Tameie (1198-1275) and grandson of Fujiwara Teika (1162–1241).[1] Tameaki's *Kokinwakashūjo kikigaki* was just one of a number of secret commentaries Tameaki developed that used "etymological" interpretation of imagery, puns, and graphs in Heian classical texts such as *Ise monogatari* (Tales of

[1] For a more extensive biography of Fujiwara Tameaki, see Susan Blakeley Klein, "Fujiwara no Tameaki," in *Medieval Japanese Writers*, ed. Steven D. Carter (Detroit, 1999), 26–34.

Ise) and the first imperial anthology, *Kokinwakashū*, thereby transforming them into complex religious and historical allegories. Tameaki used these commentaries as the basis for a pedagogical system of secret poetic initiations modeled on the ordination and transmission system (*kanjō*) within Shingon esoteric Buddhism.

The genesis of the commentaries can be explained on one level as an attempt to address the economic and social crisis facing court families who had been pushed out of power by the Kamakura Shogunate. By claiming access to "secret" knowledge of court poetry, a younger son such as Fujiwara Tameaki could parlay his family connections to Fujiwara Tameie and Fujiwara Teika into social prestige and monetary support from *nouveau riche* samurai who wanted to acquire some cultural polish.

However, one can also argue that the *waka* initiation system and secret commentaries developed at least in part in response to a complex of religious issues involving the attempt to mediate and syncretize felt contradictions between Shinto and Buddhism, poetic and religious vocation. The theoretical linchpin of the attempt to syncretize native *kami* with Buddhist deities was the *honji suijaku* 本地垂迹 theory of hypostasis, which claimed that *kami* were "manifest traces" (*suijaku*) of Buddhist deities who formed their "original ground" (*honji*). According to *honji suijaku* theory, the Buddhist deities took the form of *kami* to prepare the Japanese so that they would be ready when the more advanced teachings of Buddhism entered Japan. The commentaries, which were strongly influenced by Shinto-Buddhist syncretism, employed *honji suijaku* theory to argue that *kami* such as Sumiyoshi Daimyōjin and Tamatsushima Myōjin, who in the medieval period were worshipped as guardian deities of *waka* poetry, were *suijaku* manifestations whose true purpose was to transmit Buddhist enlightenment through poetry. They also argue that certain important human poets (most often Ariwara Narihira and Kakinomoto Hitomaro) were incarnations of both *kami* and Buddhist deities who manifested themselves in human form to further the Path of Poetry as a path to enlightenment.

A related concern of medieval poets was the conservative Buddhist argument that the literary arts were nothing but sins of language, *kyōgen kigo* 狂言綺語 (wild words and ornate phrases), that would lead the unwary poet to reincarnation in one of the lower, more hellish, of the Six Realms.[2] The phrase *kyōgen kigo* was first used by the Tang poet Po Chü-i to designate his worldly writings, which he had come to reject in favor of Buddhist truths.[3] However, in Japan the term came to mean that even apparently frivolous texts could become an "expedient means" (*hōben* 方便) to enlightenment. One of the most basic assumptions of commentaries such as *Kokinwakashūjo kikigaki* is that although the *Kokinshū* and *Ise monogatari* may appear superficially to be secular literature, once readers are lured by the frivolous pleasure of reading they will be open to initiation into the true esoteric meaning of the texts. In this way the commentaries transformed *Kokinshū* and *Ise monogatari* into expedient means enticing people onto the path of enlightenment. Whereas for ordinary people sexual indulgence might lead to reincarnation in one of the lower realms of hell, for the initiated who understand that there is no ultimate difference between passion and enlightenment (*bonnō soku bodai* 煩悩即菩提), sex can become a means to enlightenment.

Tameaki developed two main kinds of commentaries that addressed these ideological issues: esoteric and anecdotal. Since *Kokinwakashūjo kikigaki* is mainly an anecdotal commentary, I will only briefly describe the form and content of the esoteric commentaries. Meant for higher-level initiates, they used a form of etymological allegoresis (the explication of puns and graphs to show hidden meaning) that appears to have originated within Esoteric Buddhist-

[2] William LaFleur discusses the problem of *kyōgen kigo* in detail in the first chapter of *The Karma of Words: Buddhism and the Literary Arts of Medieval Japan* (Berkeley, 1983), 1–25. H.E. Plutschow also addresses the problem of *kyōgen kigo* in his article, "Is Poetry a Sin? *Honjisuijaku* and Buddhism versus Poetry," *Oriens Extremus* 25 (1978): 206–18.

[3] Towards the end of his life, Po Chü-i presented an anthology of his poetry to a Buddhist library. In the preface to this set of poems he wrote:

> My devout prayer is that the karma of writing worldly literature in this life, the error of wild words and ornate phrases, be transformed in lives to come into an instrument of praise for the Vehicle of Buddha, a link that turns the Wheel of Law.

Although known previously, the phrase was widely disseminated in Japan after Fujiwara Kintō anthologized it under "Buddhist Matters" (588) in his *Wakan rōeishū* (A Collection of Japanese and Chinese Verses for Chanting, ca. 1013). Kawaguchi Hisao, *Wakan rōeishū zenshakuchū* (Tokyo: Kōdansha Gakujutsu Bunko, 1982), 440.

Shinto syncretism as a method to reinforce *honji suijaku* identifications. The main focus of these higher-level commentaries was to demonstrate profound esoteric religious meaning in what at first would appear to be non-religious poetry. By using etymological allegoresis to reveal the hidden esoteric content of apparently secular love poetry, these commentaries were able to demonstrate, for example, that the patron deity of *waka* poetry, Sumiyoshi Daimyōjin, was a *suijaku* incarnation of Dainichi Nyorai; that the celebrated ninth-century poet and lover Ariwara Narihira was actually a Bodhisattva; and that ultimately the paths of poetic and religious vocation were "one not two."[4]

The anecdotal commentaries, on the other hand, appear to have been meant primarily for lower-level initiates, introducing them to a supposedly secret "history" of court poetry. *Waka* poetry's five lines of a mere 31 syllables can be frustratingly abstract and cryptic. When a poem is cut off from the circumstances of its initial composition, its enigmatic brevity practically demands some kind of explanatory context, a lacuna that the anecdotal commentaries attempted to fill. Fujiwara Tameaki did not invent the anecdotal commentary. We can see examples at least as far back as the twelfth century with *Fukurozōshi* (Commonplace Book, ca. 1157-60) and *Ōgishō* (Poetic Profundities, ca. 1130's) by Fujiwara (Rokujō) Kiyosuke (1104–1177). But Tameaki went much further in his willingness to invent "historical" contexts for *Kokinshū* and *Ise monogatari* poems with no identifiable author (*yomibito shirazu* 読み人知らず) or topic (*dai shirazu* 題知らず). Tameaki's anecdotal commentaries were aimed at provincial warriors and poet-priests who were willing to pay for knowledge of the inner circle of court poetics. The commentaries played to this desire by providing the names of the "hidden" authors of *yomibito shirazu* poems and the "secret" historical context—when, where, why—of *dai shirazu* poems in the *Kokinshū*. They also produced stories describing the "historical" origins for names of places, flora, and fauna, imagery that by the medieval period had become highly conventionalized. These etymological origin stories worked to

[4] For a more detailed analysis of the interpretive allegoresis used by medieval esoteric commentaries, see Susan Blakeley Klein, "Allegories of Desire: Poetry and Eroticism in *Ise monogatari zuinō*," *Monumenta Nipponica* 52:4 (Winter 1997): 441–65.

nativize and revitalize dead metaphors. Last but not least, the anecdotal commentaries provided plausible definitions of terms that had become obscure with time.

Although the esoteric content of some of Tameaki's commentaries limited their appeal, his idea of an ordination and transmission system for poetry (*waka kanjō* 和歌灌頂) rapidly spread to the other poetic houses, who understood its usefulness in encouraging support from important patrons who were willing to pay for such initiations. Its most visible legacy was the Nijō school's *Kokin denju*, a body of secret transmissions on the *Kokinshū*, which the Nijō and their poetic descendants continued to use as poetic capital throughout the medieval period. In the Muromachi period, Tameaki-affiliated commentaries began to seep into popular culture, where they had an inordinate amount of influence.

Among Tameaki's commentaries, the anecdotal works were generally treated as introductory texts, so they were disseminated more widely than the esoteric texts, and were accepted as legitimate commentaries much longer. *Kokinwakashūjo kikigaki* (Lecture Notes on the *Kokinshū* Preface, hereafter *Kikigaki*) was one of the most influential of these commentaries. As the name implies, it is a commentary on the *Kokinshū* preface; that is, it goes through the preface line by line identifying allusions to poems, providing the supposedly historical stories behind them. Another important commentary in this context is the Bishamondō *Kokinshū chū* (Bishamon Hall Commentary on the *Kokinshū*), which incorporates a good deal of material from *Kikigaki* on the *Kokinshū* preface, and then goes on to enumerate various stories behind other *Kokinshū* poems. *Kikigaki* and Bishamondō *Kokinshū chū* appear to have been disseminated quite broadly in the late thirteenth to early fourteenth century, since their stories appear in a wide variety of *otogizōshi* and noh plays. For the noh, one of the most important sources of *honzetsu* was *Kikigaki*'s explication of the section of the *Kokinshū* preface that listed appropriate occasions for poetry via a series of toponyms (*makura kotoba*) and personified metaphor/metonymies culled from poems selected for the anthology.[5] *Kikigaki*'s explication of phrases from this section was used as the

[5] Saeki Umetomo, ed. *Kokinwakashū* in vol. 8 of *Nihon koten bungaku taisei* (Tokyo: Iwanami Shoten, 1958), 97–8.

basis for a number of noh plays.[6] The non-*bangai* plays include *Takasago* ("the twin pines of Takasago and Suminoe growing old together"), *Matsumushi* ("yearning for a friend at the sound of the pining cricket"), *Fujisan* ("comparing one's smoldering passion to Mt. Fuji's rising smoke"), and *Ominameshi* ("recalling the past of Man Mountain, reflecting on the brief life of the damsel flower").[7] Important allusions appear in *Hakurakuten, Kinsatsu, Naniwa, Ukai, Asagao*, and *Sotoba Komachi* among others. Tameaki-affiliated commentaries on *Ise monogatari* provided the plot and poetic content for *Izutsu, Kakitsubata, Oshio, Ukon,* and *Unrin'in*. His commentaries also provided material for Zeami and Zenchiku's treatises on noh (particularly Zeami's *Rikugi* and Zenchiku's *Meishukushū*). And allusions to their material appeared in popular tales such as *Soga monogatari* and *Arokassen monogatari*, as well as in a wide variety of *otogizōshi*.

Commentaries such as *Kikigaki* revealed the supposedly secret etymological origins for many of the personified nature images conventionalized in Japanese *waka*. In other words, they revealed the "persons" behind the personifications, providing the "historical" circumstances under which the image was first used: who, where, and why. By the late thirteenth century the severe restrictions placed on poetic diction meant that metaphors and metonymies had become highly conventionalized—perhaps this search for anecdotal etymologies was an attempt to revitalize poetic diction, bring back some kind of sense of personalized experience. But another factor was clearly the secret nature of the commentaries and the initiations in which they were transmitted. Anyone who studied the classic texts, particularly the *Kokinshū*, should have been able to get a general sense of the conventionalized meanings of an image. Materials transmitted in secret initiations, however, were playing to the provincial samurai's desire to know the secrets of classical court culture, and therefore had to go

[6] Katagiri Yōichi, ed. *Kokinwakashūjo kikigaki: sanryū shō* in vol. 2 of *Chūsei Kokinshū chūshakusho kaidai* (Kyoto: Akao Shobundō, 1973), 259–68.

[7] For an analysis of the use of medieval *Kokinshū* commentaries in some of these noh, see the following articles by Itō Masayoshi: "Kokinchū no sekai—sono han'ei toshite no chūsei bungaku to yōkyoku," *Kanze* 6 (June 1970): 3–9; "Yōkyoku to chūsei bungaku," *Chūsei bungaku* 33 (1988): 34–44; and "Yōkyoku *Takasago* zakkō," *Bunrin* 6 (1968): 111-25. See also Kumazawa Reiko, "*Kokinshū* to yōkyoku—chūsei *Kokin* chū to no kanren in oite," *Kokugo kokubun* (October 1970): 1-20.

beyond (or behind) those relatively easily discernible conventionalized meanings. The fact that these new readings were secret almost demanded that they be counterintuitive, and this led to readings of images that were not always congruent with previously established denotations and associations.

What is interesting about a play like *Ominameshi* is that it attempts to incorporate both the older conventionalized meanings of the *ominaeshi* "damsel flower," which has antecedents in poetry written in both Japanese and Chinese dating back to the *Man'yōshū* period, and the more newly nativized origin of the damsel flower as presented in *Kikigaki*. The movement back and forth between these two interpretive readings of the damsel flower creates a metaphoric dissonance, a gap that the noh play must attempt to bridge. To understand how this dissonance works itself out in the play, we need to begin by briefly reviewing the pertinent conventionalized meanings of the damsel flower as developed within court poetry from the eighth through thirteenth centuries.[8]

The Development of the Damsel Flower Image in Poetry and Commentaries

In the *Man'yōshū*, Yamanoe Okura (660–733?) first lists the damsel flower as one of the seven flowering plants of autumn appropriate for verse.[9] In *Man'yōshū* 2279 it appears as part of a group of poems in which autumnal flowers are used as metaphorical substitutes (*hana ni yosu* 花によす) for love objects:

[8] Here I will restrict my review to denotations that are pertinent to my argument. For a more thorough review see Edward Kamens' article, "Dragon-Girl, Maidenflower, Buddha: The Transformation of a Waka Topos, 'The Five Obstructions,'" *Harvard Journal of Asiatic Studies* 53:2 (1993): 389–442. Kamens discusses the *ominaeshi* metaphor (which he translates "maidenflower") on pages 416–30.

[9] The seven flowering plants (*nanagusa no hana*) of autumn are listed by Yamanoe in *Man'yōshū* 1537 and 1538: *aki no ni / sakitaru hana o/ oyobi ori / kaki kazoureba / nanagusa no hana* ("When one counts the blossoming flowers one picks in the autumn fields, there are seven"); *hagi no hana / obana kuzuhana / nadeshiko no hana / ominaeshi / mata fujibakama / asagao no hana* ("bush clover, eulalia, kudzu, wild pink, damsel flower, wisteria-trousers [eupatorium], and morning glory").

I cannot keep my heart from yearning for her,
that damsel flower blooming even now in my home.

waga sato ni ima saku hana no ominaeshi
taenu kokoro ni nao koinikeri

In this poem the damsel flower already figures as both flower (*patrinia scabiosaefolia*) and as an attractive young woman (*omina*).[10] By the Heian period the damsel flower has been well established in poetry written in both Japanese and Chinese as a flower-woman endowed with a beauty nearly irresistible to men. For example, the following poem, originally written in Chinese by Minamoto Shitagō (911–983) and collected in *Wakan rōeishū* (A Collection of Japanese and Chinese Verses for Chanting, ca. 1013), explicitly plays on the name and its power to elicit passion even in old men:

The hue of its blossoms is like steamed millet.
Popularly called "damsel,"
just hearing the name tempts me to pledge life-long love,
but she'll probably dislike the frost on this old man's head.[11]

Hana no iro wa museru awa no gotoshi,
shoku yobōte jorō to nasu.
Na o kikite tawabure ni kairō o chigiramu to sureba
osoraku wa suiō no kōbe no shimo ni nitaru o nikumamu koto o

And in a famous poem by Archbishop Henjō quoted in the *Kokinshū* preface, the damsel flower takes on the nuance of a sensual and seductive charm that can cause men to break their vows of chastity:

Damsel flower, I only plucked you because I was entranced by your name.

[10] As Edward Kamens points out, the word "*omina*" (*womina*) as a term for young girl is easily attested, but the meaning of the final syllables "*eshi*" (*heshi*) have not been explained. Kamens, "Dragon-Girl, Maidenflower, Buddha," 416. In the *Man'yōshū* a variety of *kanji* were used for *ominaeshi*, but by the Heian period the *kanji* had been standardized as 女郎花, an orthography that reinforced its use as a feminine personification. See Katagiri Yōichi, *Uta makura, uta kotoba jiten* (Tokyo: Kadokawa Shoten, 1983), 459–60.

[11] *Wakan rōeishū* 279.

Don't tell anyone that I fell![12]

na ni medete oreru bakari zo ominaeshi
waga ochiniki to hito ni kataru na

Henjō plays wittily on the meanings of "*oreru*" (literally to pluck, but here implying sexual relations) and "*ochiniki*" (literally to fall, metaphorically to break vows of chastity).

In this poem and others the damsel flower was used as a metaphor by male poets, standing in for an unnamed, irresistibly charming woman. For male priests, the flower represented women in general as seductive lures from the straight and narrow Buddhist path. But by the medieval period this personifying function had been appropriated by female poets to rather different ends. In poem tales such as the following about Izumi Shikibu, the damsel flower was used as a surrogate, thereby allowing women at least to nominally participate in rituals at Buddhist temple-shrine complexes such as Mount Hie that practiced the exclusion of women (*nyonin kinsei* 女人禁制).

When a monk passed [Izumi Shikibu's] house carrying a damsel flower, she asked him where he was going, and when he said, "I am taking this flower as an offering for the *nembutsu* rite on Mount Hie," she wrote this and attached it to the flower:

If this truly is its name, it faces the Five Obstructions,
And yet how enviable, this flower that mounts the heights![13]

Ie no mae o hōshi no ominaeshi o mochite tōrikeru o izuku e yuku zo to towasekereba, Hie no yama no nembutsu no tatebana ni namu motomakaru to iikereba, musubitsukekeru:

na ni shi owaba itsutsu no sawari aru mono o
urayamashiku mo noboru hana ka na

[12] *Kokinshū* 226, Archbishop Henjō, topic unknown. According to the interlinear notes in the *Kokinshū* preface, this poem was composed by Henjō when he fell off his horse; Bishamondō *Kokinshū chū* adds the information that it was a white horse, and that it happened at Sagano. This supplies the secondary meaning: "don't tell anyone I fell off my horse." Saeki, ed. *Kokinwakashū*, 100; Yoshisawa Yoshinori, ed., [Bishamondōbon] *Kokinshū chū* in vol. 4 of *Mikan kokubun kochū taisei* (Tokyo: Teikoku Kyōikukai Shuppanbu, 1936), 73–4.

[13] *Shinsenzaishū* 894, attributed to Izumi Shikibu. Translation, slightly modified, from Kamens, "Dragon-Girl, Maidenflower, Buddha," 425.

The poem and story are most likely apocryphal, since their first appearance in *Shinsenzaishū* (dated 1359) occurs over three hundred years after Izumi Shikibu's death, but, as Edward Kamens has pointed out, an earlier poem by Fujiwara Mototoshi (1060-1142) indicates that the practice of sending damsel flowers as female surrogates to Mt. Hie's *fudan nembutsu* 不断念仏 (continuous Amida meditation) was already in place by the eleventh century:

> A certain woman, wanting to send damsel flowers as an offering for the "non-stop *nembutsu*" in the eighth month, asked him to write a poem for her to send with them:
>
> Like me, these flowers face the Five Obstructions;
> How can they be made into lotus blossoms?[14]
>
> *Aru onna, hachigatsu futai no nembutsu ni ominaeshi o tatematsuru tote, uta kohaberishikaba, kawarite iitsukawashikeru:*
>
> *waga gotoko itsutsu no sawari*
> *aru hana o ikaga hachisu no mi to wa nasubeki*

According to Kamens, the *fudan nembutsu* was a "continuous moving meditation" (*jōgyō zanmai* 常行三昧), a meditative form that involved a "continuous circumambulation of an image of Amida Buddha while chanting his name and mentally contemplating his Pure Land or his thirty Buddha marks."[15] It seems that by the Muromachi period the practice of sending damsel flowers as altar flowers for this ritual was well established, their surrogacy allowing women vicarious access to the power of Amida Buddha's vow to save all beings. The conventional associations of the damsel flower in the medieval period thus reprised the situation of women in Japanese Buddhism: from a male perspective, the damsel flower represented the female body as a seductive lure; but from a female perspective its surrogacy functioned

[14] *Mototoshishū* 115, Fujiwara Mototoshi. Edward Kamens translates the poem, "Is there some way for this flower, which like me, faces the Five Obstructions, to be made into a being who can be born anew upon the lotus?" Kamens, "Dragon-Girl, Maidenflower, Buddha," 429.

[15] Edward Kamens, *The Three Jewels: A Study and Translation of Minamoto Tamenori's* Sanbōe (Ann Arbor, 1988), 343 n.2.

as a possible aid in overcoming the Five Obstructions hindering women from achieving enlightenment and Buddhahood through its link to Amida Buddha and affinity with the lotus, a fellow flower. As we shall see, both of these meanings are crucial to our understanding of the noh play *Ominameshi* as well.

Turning now to the commentary sources, the *Kikigaki* and the Bishamondō *Kokinshū chū* focus their analysis on the line from the *Kokinshū* preface: "*otokoyama no mukashi o omoiidete, ominaeshi no hitotoki o kuneru nimo*" (recalling the past of Man-mountain, reflecting on the brief life/season of the damsel flower).[16] In the *Kikigaki* the origin story is given as follows:

> With regard to the line, "*otokoyama no mukashi o omoiidete, ominaeshi no hitotoki o kuneru*," both the *Nihongi* and *Genji monogatari* commentaries say that in the era of Emperor Heizei [r. 806–809], there was a man named Ono no Yorikaze. He lived in Yawata but loved a woman from the capital; so both of them traveled back and forth to visit. One time, when he visited the woman, he promised before leaving that he would definitely come on a certain day at a certain time. The woman waited for him, but he did not come, so she went to his house in Yawata to find out what happened to him. A servant in the house told her that just recently he had started seeing another woman and was visiting her. The woman, bitterly angry, went to the Yawata river; taking off her robe decorated with yellow mountain roses (*yamabuki*), she threw herself into the river and died. When the man returned to his house, the servant told him that the woman from the capital had visited and then left. He chased after her, and found the robe with the mountain rose decorations on the riverbank. He realized this was the robe she wore everyday. Then to his dismay, he saw her lifeless body floating in the river. He gathered up her body and the robe, and returned home, where he performed a memorial service. Because he spent some time in the capital in service at the palace, he thought he might like to have the robe with him as a memento (*katami* 形見), so he sent

[16] Saeki, op. cit., 97–8.

for it, but it had decayed into the ground and become damsel flowers. When the messenger told him of this, Yorikaze went to see, and found a riot of damsel flowers blooming. When he drew near, the flowers appeared to feel bitter anger and bent away (*kuneru*) from him. When he moved away, they returned to normal. The line "*ominaeshi no hitotoki o kuneru*" refers to this incident. It was from this that the flower got the name "damsel flower." The man felt as though the woman had come back to life and expressed her bitter resentment. Thinking that she had thrown her life away for him, he decided he would do the same for her, in the hope that they might be reborn together. He threw himself into the same river and drowned. Because the man had lived in the Yawata mountains, that place became known as Man Mountain (Otokoyama). The site where the woman was buried is the Woman's Grave Mound. The river at Yawata is called the River of Tears (Namidagawa).[17] In a poem:

How great is the bitterness between man and wife?
The scandal spreads as a river of tears.

ika bakari imose no naka o uramiken
yukina nagaruru Namidagawa kana

The poem tells of the bitterness between this man and woman. From this poem the river became known as the River of Tears.[18]

The Bishamondō *Kokinshū chū* gives a somewhat abbreviated version:

As for the phrase, "*otokoyama no mukashi o omohiidete, ominaeshi no hitotoki o kuneru*," *ominaeshi* is written with the characters 女郎花 and is said to mean "woman." One tradition holds that the word "*kuneru*" indicates irony about the behavior of a damsel flower shamelessly growing on Man Mountain.[19] The

[17] In the following analysis I will use the translation "Man Mountain" for "Otokoyama" when the usage is primarily metaphorical and "Otokoyama" when the usage is primarily to indicate geographical location.
[18] Katagiri, ed. *Kokinwakashūjo kikigaki*, 262–3.

> true story is given in the *Nihongi*: there was a man named Ono no Yorikaze who lived in Yawata, but he was courting a woman who lived in the capital at Nara. One time the woman came to visit him, but he had become involved with another woman and was visiting her. In her grief, the woman killed herself. When the man heard this he killed himself as well. They were buried side-by-side. Damsel flowers grew from the woman's grave, but they refused to bend (*kuneru*) towards the man's grave, even when the winds blew. The word "*hitotoki*" means "one [brief] season" (一季 *hitotoki*). In the anthology *Monzen* [Ch. *Wen Xuan*] the character for "season" (季) is read "*toki*."[20]

The Bishamondō version is less detailed, and since the *ai-kyōgen* section in *Ominameshi* includes details that appear to be from the *Kikigaki*, it seems likely that a version related to the *Kikigaki* was used as the foundation for the play.

The *Kikigaki* and the Bishamondō *Kokinshū chū* appear to ignore the accumulated conventional associations of damsel flowers and Man Mountain to provide a "historical" basis for the metaphors. There is nothing here about the seductive power of beautiful women, or the use of damsel flowers by women as ritual surrogates. Nevertheless one can see traces of the three poems from the *Kokinshū* that are usually cited as the poetic sources for Ki no Tsurayuki's line. *Kokinshū* 889, anonymous, uses Man Mountain as a metaphor of regret for lost youth:

> I've fallen to this, but long ago, in my prime, I too ascended Man Mountain
>
> *ima koso are ware mo mukashi wa Otokoyama sakayuku toki mo arikoshi mono o*

Kokinshū 1016, by Archibishop Henjō, comments on the brief but showy lives of damsel flowers:

[19] Based on an identification of the line with *Kokinshū* 227 by Furu no Imamichi that criticizes the damsel flowers for growing on Man Mountain.

[20] Yoshisawa, ed. [Bishamondōbon] *Kokinshū chū* 18.

> Damsel flowers swaying flirtatiously in the autumn fields, what bold blossoms!
> And yet how brief their season.
>
> *aki no no ni namameki tateru ominaeshi ana kashigamashi*
> *hana mo hitotoki*

Kokinshū 227, by Furu no Imamichi, combines the damsel flower and Man Mountain in one poem:

> On seeing damsel flowers at Otokoyama when he went to Nara to visit Archibishop Henjō.
>
> > As I travel on my way I cast reproachful glances at the damsel flowers.
> > What made them decide to grow on a mountain named for a man?
>
> *Henjō Sōjō ga moto ni Nara e makarikeru toki ni Otokoyama nite ominaeshi o mite yomeru.*
>
> > *ominaeshi ushi to mitsutsu zo yukisuguru*
> > *Otokoyama ni shi tateri to omoeba*

Given that the *Kikigaki* version of events is dated to the reign of Emperor Heizei it makes sense that the story does not directly allude to the poems in the *Kokinshū*, which dates to the early tenth century. Nevertheless, the anecdote manages to prepare the way for their themes of male regret (889), the brevity of a young woman's life (1016), and the problematic placement of damsel flowers on a mountain named "Man" (227). It thereby sets up a historical ground for the poems most closely associated with Ki no Tsurayuki's line in the *Kokinshū* preface, while ignoring other thematic associations.

There are four main etymological points to the story in the *Kikigaki*: 1) why the *kanji* for female is used in the name of the flower; 2) how Man Mountain got its name; 3) how the River of Tears (Namidagawa) got its name; and 4) why Tsurayuki used the word "*kuneru*" in the line about the damsel flower. The play incorporates 1, 2, and 4, but substitutes a different river, Hōjōgawa (Life-Releasing

River), for Namidagawa.[21] In the case of the first and second points, the commentary produces a secret "historical" origin for the names, placed firmly in Japan with no reference to China. This is in keeping with the commentaries' general principle of resisting *ateji* from the Chinese.

As for the fourth point, the focus on a word such as *kuneru* is quite common for the commentaries; for obvious reasons they tended to pick out obscure or difficult words to explicate. It seems likely that already by the medieval period, readers found the usage of *kuneru* difficult to understand. This is not surprising; usually *kuneru* means "to twist, bend, or be curved;" in addition it seems to have had a feminine, sexual connotation. In the *Kokinshū* Preface, however, it is hard to see how "bend" or "be curved" could work, and the interpretation of "*kuneru*" in this context would seem to be problematic to this day. The Iwanami *Kokinshū* text supplies "*guchi o iu*" (complain) for the meaning, whereas the Iwanami *Kogo jiten* cites this line in support of its definition of "*hiniku o toraeru*" (to take ironically, or sarcastically).[22] Bishamondō *Kokinshū chū* does cite the interpretation of *kuneru* as "irony" via a reading of *Kokinshū* 227: "One tradition holds that the word *kuneru* indicates irony about the behaviour of a damsel flower shamelessly growing on Man Mountain." However, the commentary immediately negates the reading of *kuneru* as "irony." Instead, the more usual meaning of the word *kuneru* is understood in the story about a damsel flower that "bends away" (*kuneru*) from her former lover (*hito*) because of her bitter resentment. And this extremely feminine movement of twisting away and hiding her face from the man in anger and resentment helps explain why the characters for "woman" should be in the name. From our point of view today the pivotal moment in the commentary story—the bending away of the damsel flower from Ono no Yorikaze—was generated by anxiety about a problematic usage in the preface. But if we believed, as the medieval reader would have, that the story came first, then it would be natural to think Tsurayuki purposefully placed the unusual

[21] Susan Matisoff and Stephen Brown both discuss the metaphorical implications of Hōjōgawa in their articles.

[22] Saeki, op. cit., 98 n. 1; Ōno Susumu et al, eds., *Kogo jiten* (Tokyo: Iwanami Shoten, 1990), 421.

usage of *kuneru* in the preface as a hint for the initiated that there is a secret commentary that reveals the true history. As usual for these commentaries, hidden puns can be pointed to as (tautological) corroboration of the commentary's truth.

The distinctive coloration of the flower is also explained. The standard description of the damsel flower's color is in Shitagō's poem in the *Wakan rōeishū*, which compares the color of the damsel flower to steamed millet. This simile for yellow appears to have been a misreading of a simile in the popular anthology of Chinese poetry and prose, *Monzen* (Ch. *Wen Xuan*), which compares the color of yellow jade to steamed chestnuts (the *kanji* for chestnut and millet are very similar).[23] *Kikigaki* provides the damsel flower's color with a nativized origin: the woman's robe. It is not clear whether the robe was simply the same yellow color as mountain roses (*yamabuki*) or was decorated with mountain roses, but the yellow color seems to have stained the damsel flower that emerged from the woman's grave.[24]

Ominameshi (The Play)

When we turn to the play we find a sometimes confusing combination of five main elements, two from the poetic tradition and three from the noh: 1) the traditional associations of the damsel flower and Man Mountain in poetry, including the temptations of charming

[23] *Wakan rōeishū* 279. The source for Shitagō's simile is taken to be a letter to Zhong Yao (the Chamberlain for Law Enforcement) from Emperor Wen of the Wei dynasty (r. 220–226) which praises four colors of fine jade, comparing white to a slab of fat, black to fine lacquer, red to a coxcomb, and yellow to steamed chestnuts. Kaneko Motoomi and Emi Seifū, eds., *Wakan rōeishū* (Tokyo: Meiji Shoin, 1942), 175-6. Kawaguchi Hisao notes that although Shitagō might easily have misread millet (*awa* 粟) for chestnut (*kuri* 栗), at least one version of *Wakan rōeishū* has chestnut, which may indicate a transcription error. Kawaguchi Hisao, *Wakan rōeishū zenshakuchū* (Tokyo: Kōdansha Gakujutsu Bunko, 1982), 216–7. On the other hand, Kaneko and Emi suggest that since damsel flowers are more like the color of steamed millet than steamed chestnuts, the substitution may have been intentional.

[24] It is also not very clear what happened to the robe. The *Kikigaki* seems to imply that it was left on top of the grave where it decayed and was transformed into the flowers. In the noh play the *ai-kyōgen* says that the woman was buried in the robe and the flowers then grew up from the grave.

flower-women for priests; 2) the commentary version of the two images' "historical" origin; 3) an introduction to a famous pilgrimage site or temple-shrine complex (here the Iwashimizu Hachiman Shrine on Otokoyama) and its founding history (*engi*), 4) a typical noh plot in which the ghosts of embittered lovers appear, reenact their tragic deaths, and ask for prayers to achieve release from their passionate attachment; and 5) the common noh theme in which a non-sentient plant, as surrogate for a human being (usually female), achieves enlightenment.

The *waki*, a priest from the Usa Hachiman Shrine in Kyushu, begins his journey to the capital. Along the way he passes Tsukushi Lagoon, known for its mysterious flickering lights (*shiranuhi*, literally, "unknown fires"):

> Destination unknown, the mysterious fires of Tsukushi Lagoon
> lie far behind me;
> like the road to the extinction of passions
> a distant journey stretches out before me.[25]

> *sue shiranuhi no tsukushigata*
> *itsushika ato ni tōzakaru*
> *tabi no michi koso haruka nare*

Within *shiranuhi no tsukushigata* (the mysterious fires of Tsukushi lagoon) one can find *hi no tsukushi*, "the extinction (*tsukusu*) of passion (*hi*)," a pun that foreshadows one of the themes of the play, the problem of passionate attachment.

The *waki* arrives at the foot of Otokoyama, and noting that the Iwashimizu Hachiman Shrine is related (*ittai* 一体) to his home shrine

[25] This translation is based on the annotated version of the play in Itō Masayoshi, ed., *Yōkyokushū* in vol. 57 of *Shinchō Nihon koten shūsei* (Tokyo: Shinchōsha, 1983), 246–55. *Sue shiranu*: my destiny/destination is unknown. *Shiranuhi no Tsukushigata*: in Tsukushigata there are mysterious flickering lights on the ocean horizon called "*shiranuhi*" (literally, "unknown fires"). *Hi no tsukushi*: the extinction (*tsukushi*) of passion (*hi*). *Shiranuhi no tsukushigata itsushika ato ni toizakaru tabi no michi haruka nare*: I've exhausted (*tsukushi*) an unknown (*shiranu*) number of days (*hi*) [traveling], how many left to go on this distant journey, whose path leads off into the distance? Itō, op. cit., 247.

in Kyushu he decides to visit. Before he can do so, however, he is distracted by the damsel flowers at their height:

> My, the damsel flowers are blooming in such wild profusion here in this field, I'll just go a little closer to look at them.
>
> Venturing out to look at the fields at the foot of Man Mountain,
> flowers of a thousand grasses are blooming,
> garlanded with color, dripping with dew.[26]
>
> *mata kore naru nobe ni ominameshi no ima o sakari to sakimidarete sōrō*
> *tachiyori nagamebaya to omoisōrō*
>
> *sate mo Otokoyama fumoto no nobe ni kite mireba*
> *chigusa no hana sakan ni shite*
> *iro o kazari tsuyu o fukumite*

Given that "*midare*" is often linked with the chaotic emotions (and tangled hair) involved in sexual relationships, "*sakimidare*" (to bloom wildly) has a strong nuance of promiscuity. The flowers are garlanded with *iro* (literally color, but also passion/sex appeal), suffused with *tsuyu* (literally dew, but clearly also a more sexual kind of moisture). Garlanded with passion, drenched with dew, blooming in promiscuous profusion—it would seem the damsel flowers are being set up as highly sexualized. Such a sexualization follows the traditional meanings attributed to the flower in *waka* poetry.

The *waki* cannot resist the flower's charms and noting that the damsel flowers of Man Mountain are famous for their association with an old poem (left unnamed, but probably *Kokinshū* 227), decides to pluck one as a "souvenir." The *shite*, an old man from the area, enters and attempts to stop the *waki* from picking the flowers. He claims that the damsel flowers on Man Mountain are especially famous, but again does not directly quote *Kokinshū* 227, the obvious choice. Instead the *shite* quotes a slight variation on the first four lines of the poem by Minamoto Shitagō collected in *Wakan rōeishū*:

[26] Itō, op. cit., 247–8.

> The hue of its blossoms is like steamed millet. Popularly called 'damsel,' just hearing the name stirs me to playfully pledge lifelong love.[27]
>
> *hana no iro wa museru awa no gotoshi*
> *shoku yobatte jorō tosu*
> *tawamure ni na o kiite dani kairō o chigiru to ieri*

Why did the playwright use this poem, originally in Chinese, rather than a *waka* poem? Some possible answers: first, Shitagō's poem clearly uses the damsel flower as a personification for an unnamed woman, the central premise of the play.[28] Second, it argues that via a flirtatious play on words (*tawamure ni*) the name "damsel flower" alone is enough to stir the passions, at least of poets. And finally, it implies that such supposedly frivolous play may lead the poet to make a pledge to grow old together with the flower-woman. By leaving off the last line of the original poem, "*osoraku wa suiō no kōbe no shimo ni nitaru o nikumamu koto o*" (but she'll probably dislike the frost on this old man's head), the play eliminates the poem's suggestion that the young woman personified by the damsel flower is not likely to take the poet-persona seriously. Instead, the play will show that such a pledge may have tragic consequences if taken seriously by the woman but not by the man.

The *shite* then accuses the *waki* of being "*nasake nashi*" 情けなし (without compassion) and "*kokoro nashi*" 心無し (literally, to be heartless) for wanting to pick a flower. Here *kokoro* has both a metaphysical and metaphorical aspect. In the Buddhist sense, to be *kokoro naku* is to be non-sentient. In the metaphoric sense, to be *kokoro naku* is to lack aesthetic sensitivity. However, as in other plays which focus on the passionate attachment and search for enlightenment of suppos-

27 Itō, op. cit., 248. *Wakan rōeishū* 279, Minamoto Shitagō.

28 One obvious question that comes up when reading both the play and the commentary on which it is based is why the man is given a name (Ono no Yorikaze) but the woman is left nameless. One explanation may be that in virtually every poem that employs the damsel flower image, the surrogate function of the damsel flower either makes the flower representative of women generally, or is meant to preserve the anonymity of the woman involved.

edly non-sentient flora and fauna, the fact that the *shite* accuses the *waki* of being *kokoro naku* has a certain amount of irony.[29]

When the *shite* tells the *waki* that he is the flower's guardian, the *waki* switches gears and states that he is only plucking the damsel flower as an offering to the Buddha. In this he appears to be taking on the female position vis-à-vis the damsel flower, one more suitable for a man of the cloth. But the *shite* responds with an allusion to a *Shinkokinshū* poem recited in a dream by Sugawara Michizane as the deity Tenman Tenjin, accusing someone who broke off a branch of his favorite flowering plum of being *nasake nashi*.[30] He follows up with a quotation from a poem by Archibishop Henjō:

> If you break off a branch, it will wither in your hand,
> but if you leave it growing it will serve the Buddhas of past, present and future.[31]
>
> *oritoraba tabusa ni kegaru tatenagara*
> *miyo no hotoke ni hana tatematsuru*

The *waki* responds with the first three lines of *Kokinshū* 226 by Henjō that indicates he himself plucked a flower on at least one occasion:

> Damsel flower, I only plucked you because I was entranced by your name.

[29] As Donald Shively has pointed out in his article, "Buddhahood for the Nonsentient," the search for release from passionate attachment is a privilege extended not only to great warriors and court ladies but even unto supposedly nonsentient plants and grasses. See Donald Shively, "Buddhahood for the Nonsentient: A Theme in Nō Plays," *Harvard Journal of Asiatic Studies* 20 (1957): 135–61. William LaFleur also addresses these issues in his essay in this volume.

[30] *Shinkokinshū* 1853, anonymous: "This poem was composed in the spring of the second year of Kenkyū 建久 (1191). Someone was making the rounds of temples in Tsukushi and he broke off a branch of flowering plum at the Anraku temple. That night the deity [Sugawara Michizane as Tenman Tenjin] appeared in a dream and recited the following: *nasake naku oru hito tsurashi waga yado no aruji wasurenu ume no tachie o* (The plum standing by my old house has not forgotten its master; it is the person who breaks off a branch who lacks feeling)." The headnote refers to the famous plum tree that flew to be with Sugawara no Michizane in exile at Daizaifu in Kyushu because he wrote a poem yearning for it. Anraku temple was built on Michizane's supposed burial site.

[31] Itō, op. cit., 249. *Gosenshū* 123, Archbishop Henjō. *Kegaru*, translated as "to wither," literally means "to be defiled."

na ni medete oreru bakari zo ominaeshi

However, the *shite* counters with the last two lines of the poem, "Don't tell anyone that I fell!" (*ware ochiniki to hito kataru na*).[32] The *shite* argues for a "historical" reading of the poem, claiming that there is no doubt that Henjō was a "fallen" priest, who "in secret trysts shared a pillow of grass, pledging his love faithfully beneath moss fern-rubbed robes."[33] The use of the images "grassy pillow" and "moss fern" echo and reinforce the image of having sex with a flower/woman, and the *waki* immediately realizes that he has strayed into the ambiguous area of *kyōgen kigo* (wild words and ornate phrases). The example of Henjō wakes the *waki* up to the fact that his playful desire for the damsel flower may be inappropriate:

> Now that you mention it, to say, even in jest,
> that one is entranced by the color and fragrance of a flower's heart,
> is really without merit.
> I should take my leave,
> and returning to my former path, "travel on my way."[34]

> *kayō ni kikeba tawamure nagara*
> *iroka ni mezuru hana gokoro*
> *to kaku mōsu ni yoshi zo naki*
> *itoma mōshite kaeru tote*
> *moto kishi michi ni yukisuguru*

The *waki* uses the term *tawamure* (in jest) from Shitagō's poem, reiterating the dangers of flirtatious wordplay for unwary Buddhists who might, like Henjō, become "entranced" (*mezuru*) with the "color/sex

[32] Itō, op. cit., 249.
[33] *To fukaku shinobu suri koromo*: multiple puns on *shinobu*. *To fukaku shinobu* implies that the poem has a secret meaning: the pun on *ochiru* that conceals Henjō's illicit relationship with a young woman. *Fukaku shinobu* can mean both "deeply secret tryst" and "deeply yearning for." Shinobu is also a place name whose literal meaning is "faithful spouse." And finally, *shinobu suri koromo*: *shinobu* is a moss fern used to rub a random pattern into a robe.
[34] Itō, op. cit., 249.

appeal" (*iro*) of the damsel flower and fall from their vows. The *waki* characterizes such flirtatious play as "*yoshi nashi*": literally "meaningless," in Buddhist terms, "lacking merit." The *waki* seems to have learned his lesson about being seduced by *kyōgen kigo* from the straight and narrow path, and now proclaims his intention of returning to his original goal of visiting the capital.

As he makes his departure, however, the *waki* almost inadvertently uses the phrase "*yukisuguru*" (to travel along, pass by). The *shite* jumps to the conclusion that the *waki* has finally alluded to *Kokinshū* 227, the poem that most closely associates damsel flowers and Man Mountain:

> As I travel on my way I cast reproachful glances at the damsel flowers.
> What made them decide to grow on a mountain named for a man?
>
> *ominaeshi ushi to mitsutsu zo yukisuguru*
> *Otokoyama ni shi tateri to omoeba*

Apparently the allusion to this poem is what the *shite* has been waiting for all along; as soon as the *shite* believes the *waki* has demonstrated knowledge of it, his attitude changes completely:

> What a refined traveler!
> You who understand the essence
> of this flower, a damsel with a husband,
> have my permission to be "entranced by her name"
> and pluck one stalk.[35]
>
> *yasashi no tabibito ya*
> *hana wa nushi aru ominameshi*
> *yoshi shiru hito no na ni medete*
> *yurushi mōsu nari*
> *hitomoto orase tamae ya*

It appears in retrospect that the entire exchange has been a test, and now that the *waki* has proven that he is a "*ominameshi yoshi shiru*

[35] Itō, op. cit., 249–50.

hito" (someone who understands and appreciates the poetic essence of the damsel flower), he has permission (like Henjō) to be "entranced with her name" despite the apparent dangers of *kyōgen kigo*. Why would such a sudden reversal occur?

One possible explanation has to do with the understanding of the term *kyōgen kigo* within medieval Japanese poetics. As discussed above, for many within the Buddhist establishment, indulgence in the literary arts could only be a distraction from the Way of the Buddha. The following remonstration by the Zen patriarch Dōgen (1200-1253) makes this point quite clearly:

> If in the short space of this existence you would cultivate some art or pursue some line of learning, then let it be the Way of the Buddha that you practice, the Law of the Buddha that you study. Literature, poetry, and the like are useless pursuits. I need hardly say they are best abandoned.[36]

The counterargument was that even apparently frivolous texts could become an "expedient means" (*hōben*) to enlightenment, and following the path of poetry as *kyōgen kigo* was thereby transformed into a path to enlightenment. Fujiwara Tameaki's esoteric commentaries played on this reversal, arguing that whereas for ordinary people writing love poetry might lead to reincarnation in one of the lower realms of hell, for the initiated who understand that there is no ultimate difference between passion and enlightenment (*bonnō soku bodai*), writing about sex, and even sex itself, can become a means to enlightenment.

I would argue that the plot of *Ominameshi* replicates the medieval *kyōgen kigo* debate by reproducing the process of a *waka* initiation. The *shite* as gate keeper (flower guardian) tests the *waki* on his knowledge of the poetic canon to make sure he is worthy of initiation: if he wants to pluck a damsel flower he has to be able to produce the proper poetic authority for his action, including the all-important al-

[36] Dōgen, *Shōbō genzō zuimonki* in vol. 81 of *Nihon koten bungaku taikei*, ed. Nishio Minoru et al. (Tokyo: Iwanami Shoten, 1965), 341–2. Translation from Thomas Harper, *Motoori Norinaga's Criticism of the "Genji Monogatari": A Study of the Background and Critical Content of his "Genji Monogatari Tama no Ogushi"* (Ann Arbor, 1971), 49.

lusion to *Kokinshū* 227 that places the damsel flowers on Man Mountain. In the course of this testing the *waki* argues that he simply wants the flowers as a Buddhist offering, but the *shite* reminds the *waki* of the dangers of becoming too entranced in wordplay with names (*na ni medete*); that just as for Archbishop Henjō, the line drawn between plucking a damsel flower and having sexual relations is all too easily crossed. Up to this point, the *waki* appears to be taking a very conservative position vis-à-vis *kyōgen kigo*. However, having convinced the *waki* that he should avoid the sin of *kyōgen kigo*, the *shite* abruptly reverses position. As a *shiru hito*, someone who has demonstrated proper aesthetic sensitivity and understanding, the *waki* is now encouraged to be enamored of the wordplay of names, to even "pluck" a flower if he wishes. One possible way to look at this sudden reversal is that the conflict between two conventional images of the damsel flower—one as chaste female substitute in Buddhist rituals, the other as enticer of priests to break their vows of chastity—has been resolved through the understanding conveyed in the medieval commentaries of *bonnō soku bodai*, that ultimately there is no difference between passion and enlightenment. Once the *waki* has proven his poetic and religious credentials, he is initiated into a different level of understanding that would allow him "free play."

The phrase "*nushi aru ominameshi*" (the damsel flower has a husband/owner) plays a key role in this reversal of position. On one level, the term *nushi* simply foreshadows the *shite*'s revelation that he is the "husband" of the damsel flower, Ono no Yorikaze.[37] On another level, given that the damsel flower is a metaphor, the *waki*'s "permission" can be read in more literary terms. To begin with, the term *nushi* could refer to the poetic idea put forward by Fujiwara Tameie in *Eiga no ittei* (The Single Style of Composition, 1275) that certain phrases are so distinctive that they might be thought of as having "owners" (*nushi aru kotoba*), and so should not be used for allusive variation (*honkadori* 本歌取り). Given that in the next line we find the phrase "*na ni medete*" (entranced with the name) from *Kokinshū* 226 by Henjō, the underlying *nushi* may also be Henjō as the poet most

[37] Itō Masayoshi suggests that the *nushi* could be the mountain itself as the metaphorical male counterpart to the female flower. Itō, op. cit., 249 n. 21.

strongly identified with the use of the damsel flower in the *Kokinshū* and in this play. Henjō might be thought of as an alternate persona of the *shite*, a subtextual presence that works to reinforce the *kyōgen kigo* problematic. And the term *yoshi*, which the *waki* used to indicate that flirtatious wordplay was without merit (*yoshi naki*), here takes on another, more literary meaning, that of a topic's poetic "essence." The combination of the terms *nushi, yoshi* and *shiru hito* indicates a literary subtext: the *waki* has demonstrated sufficient poetic knowledge and aesthetic refinement to use properly the poetic metaphor of the damsel flower and so has permission to appropriate it. He can now be "initiated" into the origins of the Iwashimizu Hachiman Shrine and the secret commentary version of the origins of the relationship between the damsel flower and Man Mountain.

The section immediately following the *shite*'s granting of permission, an *ageuta* chanted by the chorus, might be thought of as transitional. It appears to return us to the conventional meaning of the damsel flower while dropping hints of the tragedy to come. The *ageuta* combines allusions to three poems (*Kokinshū* 1016, *Kokinshū* 237, and *Wakan rōeishū* 279) with a reference to the noh play *Kantan*:

Flirtatious damsel flowers swaying,
might make us feel guilty.
The flower named for a damsel—
who was it vowed to grow old with her?
On his pillow Kantan
dreamt of 50 years wedded bliss;
how dream-like this pledge as well.[38]

namameki tateru ominameshi
ushirometaku ya omōran
jorō to kakeru hana no na ni
tare kairō o chigiriken
kano Kantan no karimakura
yume wa isoji no aware yo no
tameshi mo makoto narubeshi ya

[38] Itō, op. cit., 250.

The first line, *namameki tateru ominameshi* (damsel flowers that sway seductively/flirtatiously) is taken from *Kokinshū* 1016:

> Damsel flowers swaying flirtatiously in the autumn fields, what bold blossoms!
> And yet how brief their season.
>
> *aki no no ni namameki tateru ominaeshi ana kashigamashi hana mo hitotoki*

Here the seductive swaying (*namameki tateru*) of the damsel flowers may be an ironic presentiment of their resentful bending (*kuneru*) to come. And although the last line of Henjō's poem, *hana mo hitotoki* (the brief season/life of the flowers), is not quoted in the play, it is worth remembering that the line is usually cited as the source for Ki no Tsurayuki's phrase "*ominaeshi no hitotoki*" (the brief season/life of the damsel flower) in the *Kokinshū* preface. Although not fully quoted, for knowledgeable audience members the allusion may be hinting at the tragedy to come.

In the next line, the phrase *ushirometaku* (to feel guilty about) is taken from *Kokinshū* 237 by Prince Kanemi:

> Composed when he saw damsel flowers planted in a garden of a house he visited.
>
> Damsel flower, how guilty I feel about your fate,
> left standing all alone at that rundown dwelling.
>
> *Mono e makarikeru ni, hito no ie ni ominaeshi uetarikeru o mite yomeru.*
>
> *ominaeshi ushirometaku mo miyuru kana*
> *aretaru yado ni hitori tatereba*

The combination of *namameki* (seductive, voluptuous) and *ushirometaku* (feel guilty, sad about) brings us back to the idea that these flowers are highly sexed, and that we might feel both guilty about our attraction to them and sad about their fate.

The following phrase, *jorō to kakeru hana no na ni tare kairō o chigiriken* (who was it who made a lifelong pledge to the flower named "damsel"?), alludes once again to *Wakan rōeishū* 279 by

Minamoto Shitagō. Framing the allusion as a question hints at the coming revelation that the *shite* is actually the ghost of Ono no Yorikaze. But the allusion may have a more ironic twist: Shitagō's poet-persona playfully pledged to grow old together with the damsel flower. Ono no Yorikaze may have also made such a pledge, but perhaps because he did not take her seriously enough he failed to keep his promise to the woman he loved, a failure with tragic consequences.

The *ageuta* ends with an allusion to *Kantan*, the story of a Chinese man who wishes to devote his life to Buddhism, but is distracted by his desire for worldly fame and success. He stops for the night in the village of Kantan and the innkeeper, hearing of his difficulty, lends him a miraculous pillow that has the power to endow enlightenment to those who sleep upon it. While his meal is being prepared, the young man has a dream in which he is made emperor and lives a life of luxury and pleasure for fifty years. When he wakes from the dream, he is enlightened as to the transience of material success and is able to decide to devote himself completely to Buddhism. Placed in juxtaposition with the *Wakan rōeishū* poem's promise of a love that will last into old age, the allusion to *Kantan*'s dream of fifty years foreshadows that Yorikaze's pledge of love to the damsel flower will turn out to be just as ephemeral, and perhaps, just as problematic for their mutual enlightenment.

With the conclusion of the transitional *ageuta*, there is a distinct shift in mood and place. The *waki* realizes that he has been so wrapped up in the damsel flowers that he has neglected to go to the shrine. The *shite* offers to be his guide up the mountain. As they climb, the text describes the benefits accruing both to the surrounding villages and to visiting pilgrims. These benefits flow from Hachiman as a *suijaku* incarnation of Amida Buddha and the ritual performed for the releasing of life (Hōjōe 放生会) at the shrine complex:

Shite:
At the mountain's foot, eaves of houses vie in prosperity.

Waki and Shite:
From above, Buddha's tranquil light, descending
to mix with dust, muddies the stream

in which swim countless fish,
set free to live by profound vows renewed.
This flourishing growth, a blessing,
along the way up verdant Man Mountain's slope.[39]

Shite:
sange no jinka noki o nobe

Waki and Shite:
wakō no chiri mo nigori e no
kasui ni ukamu urokuzu wa
geni mo ikeru o hanatsu ka to fukaku chikai mo arata nite
megumi zo shigeki Otokoyama
sakayuku michi no arigatasa yo

We can see an implied subtextual parallel in this passage: just as Amida Buddha has chosen to incarnate as Hachiman, mixing his tranquil light (*wakō* 和光) in the dirt and grime of this world in order to fulfill his Bodhisattva vow of saving all beings, so human beings can save other lower forms of life (here fish) through the Hōjō ritual. The material benefit (*megumi*) accruing to these acts is conveyed by the term used to describe the climb up the mountain, *sakayuku*, which means both "flourishing fortune" and "to climb the slope" (as a pilgrim). The village houses at the foot of the mountain are prosperous (their eaves vie for prominence) and the vegetation growing on the slope of the mountain is luxuriant because of Hachiman-Amida's beneficence; the Hōjō ritual renews profound vows that promote the people's flourishing fortune. In addition, the use of *sakayuku* alludes to *Kokinshū* 889, anonymous:

> I've fallen to this, but long ago, in my prime, I too ascended Man Mountain.
>
> *ima koso are ware mo mukashi wa Otokoyama sakayuku toki mo arikoshi mono o*

[39] Ibid.

In the context of the noh the term *sakayuku* primarily reinforces the present prosperity of the shrine and its surrounding villages, but the allusion to *Kokinshū* 889 echoes an overall yearning for the vigor and prosperity of one's lost youth, represented metaphorically as Man Mountain.

It just happens to be the fifteenth day of the eighth month, the day when the Hōjō ritual is performed, and the *waki* and *shite* stop to perform a prayer. The chorus continues with the origin story of the shrine, albeit somewhat veiled by the poetic language used:

Chorus:
The distant
moon above the katsura trees of Man Mountain
shines brightly;[40]
autumn leaves glow
in its dappled light at Iwashimizu, Shrine of Stone Pure Water,
where robes of moss,[41]
sleeves traced with three hallowed images,
are sealed in a box and stored
in this Dharma Temple-Shrine.
How blessed is this sacred ground![42]

Chorus:
hisakata no
tsuki no katsura no Otokoyama

[40] A nearly complete quotation of a poem in the *Shokukokinshū* (700): *hisakata no tsuki no katsura no Otokoyama sayekeki kage wa tokoro kara [kamo]* (The distant moon shines so brightly here on the katsura trees. Perhaps that's why this place is called the Man in the Moon's Katsura Mountain). The poem alludes to a story about a Chinese Taoist adept gone bad who was punished by having to cut down all the katsura trees on the moon (each one thousands of feet high). Every branch he cut off would grow back almost immediately, so it was a never-ending task. The implication is that the katsura trees on Otokoyama grow so large and luxuriantly that they could be those that grow on the moon.

[41] *Koke no koromo* (mossy robe) is a metaphor for a priest's robe. *Mitsu no tamoto* (three pockets) refers to *sanne*, the three robes allowed a priest; it is *engo* for *koke no koromo. Mitsu* (three) also refers to the number of images imprinted on the robes.

[42] Itō, op. cit., 251.

sayakeki kage wa tokorokara
kōyō mo terisoite
hi mo kagerō no Iwashimizu
koke no koromo mo taenare ya
mitsu no tamoto ni kage utsuru
shirushi no hako o osamunaru
nori no jingūji
arigatakarishi reichi kana

In order to understand this passage, one must know the origin story of the Iwashimizu Hachiman Shrine.[43] According to *Iwashimizu Hachimangū Gokokuji ryakki* (An Abbreviated History of the Founding of Iwashimizu Hachiman Shrine, dated 863), Gyōkyō Oshō, head priest of the Daianji Temple in Nara, spent the summer of 859 performing devotions at the Usa Hachiman Shrine in Kyushu. On the fifteenth day of the seventh month he received an oracle from Hachiman, asking Gyōkyō to make arrangements to move him closer to the capital in Kyoto so he could offer his protection there. On the twenty-fifth day of the eighth month, Hachiman appeared again, this time indicating a shrine complex should be established for him on Otokoyama, and Gyōkyō followed his instructions. According to *Zoku kojidan* (ca. 1219), at the time of Hachiman's first appearance, images of the Amida trinity (Amida Buddha and his attendant Bodhisattvas Kannon and Seishi) shone mysteriously on Gyōkyō's robes. The images, imprinted on the robes, were transferred to the Iwashimizu Hachiman Shrine at Otokoyama and placed in a sealed box in the wall at the back of the main temple building.

[43] For a more detailed discussion in English of the political ramifications of the origin story of Iwashimizu Hachiman Shrine, see Stephen Brown's contribution to this volume; see also Keller Kimbrough's discussion in his dissertation, *Imagining Izumi Shikibu: Representations of a Heian Woman Poet in the Literature of Medieval Japan* (New Haven, 1999), 141–2 and Christine Guth Kanda, *Shinzō: Hachiman Imagery and Its Development* (Cambridge, Mass., 1985), 41–3. *Iwashimizu Hachimangū Gokokuji ryakki* is published in Shimamura Kunihiro, et al., eds., *Hachiman jinja kenkyū* (Tokyo: Sōbunsha, 1989), 202–4; *Zoku kojidan* is published in Hanawa Hokiichi, ed. *Gunsho ruijū*, vol. 17 (Tokyo: Keizai Zasshisha, 1898–1902), 679. See also Yamada Yoshio et al., eds., *Konjaku monogatari shū*, vol. 33 (Tokyo: Iwanami Shoten, 1961), 142–3.

The use of *kage* as both light (影) and shade (陰) is striking in the passage from the noh play: the moon, symbol of enlightenment, shines brightly (*sayakeki kage* さやけき影) on Man Mountain, yet its light is shaded (*hi mo kagerō* 日も陰ろふ) at Iwashimizu where the three robes are imprinted with the glowing images (*kage utsuru* 影うつる) of the Amida trinity. One way this seeming contradiction might be understood is in terms of Amida Buddha's tranquil light being hidden in his incarnation as Hachiman, the miraculous evidence for their *honji suijaku* identification a glowing image hidden away in a sealed box in the innermost sanctuary.

When the *shite* and *waki* finally reach the shrine, since the day is drawing to a close, the *shite* starts to take his leave. The *waki* stops him and asks about the story of the damsel flower and Man Mountain. The *shite* replies that it was indeed frivolous (*itazura*) to have quoted poems about the damsel flower in jest (*tawamure ni*). Although only shortly before the *shite* was encouraging the *waki* to become enamored of the flower's name and even to pluck her, now he appears to have reverted to the conservative Buddhist position that such activities are problematic, if not downright harmful to one's soteriological status.

According to the *shite* the tombs of the woman and man of the story are at the foot of the mountain, and he offers to guide the *waki* back down the mountain and show him the tombs. When they arrive, the *shite* explains that the woman was from the capital and the man, Ono no Yorikaze, lived here on the mountain. The *shite* hints that he is the ghost of Ono no Yorikaze through a wordplay on his name. Expressing the embarrassment and shame typical of noh ghosts, who know that it is a Buddhist sin to be caught in this world by a passionate attachment, he then vanishes.

Other than the minimal allusion to *Kokinshū* 889, this section of the play seems quite distinct from what precedes and what comes after. We are guided to the main site of the shrine plus the tombs of the woman and Ono no Yorikaze, and presented with the shrine's founding story, which serves as an advertisement for the benefits of the Hōjōe ritual and Hachiman as the *suijaku* embodiment of Amida Buddha. Such travelogues are common in noh plays, since their performances were often subsidized by temples and shrines. If we assume that the play reflects the reality of the Iwashimizu Hachiman

Shrine when it was first composed, it would appear that within a hundred years or so of Fujiwara Tameaki inventing the story about the damsel flower and Ono no Yorikaze, their tombs had already been created at Iwashimizu Hachiman shrine and were part of the pilgrimage route through the shrine. The creation of tombs for fictional and semi-fictionalized characters such as Genji, Murasaki Shikibu, Ariwara Narihira, and Ono no Komachi was common in the medieval period; more research, such as that by Wakita Haruko, needs to be done on the process by which it occurred.

During the interlude (*nakairi*) a local villager (the *ai-kyōgen*) fills the *waki* (and by extension, the audience) in on the basic details of the story of Yorikaze and the damsel flower/woman. This is a useful intervention because when the ghosts of Ono no Yorikaze and the woman from the capital return, they concentrate more on their feelings than on facts. Once the local villager departs the *waki* begins to perform ritual prayers, beginning with a *dharani* spell specific to pacifying ghosts. The prayer incites the dead spirits' appearance and their first words are complaints about the desolate location of their tombs and the rarity of visitors. As they warm to their theme, the introductory *issei* includes this exchange between the woman from the capital and Yorikaze:[44]

Tsure (woman from the capital):
  Bitterness, a clinging purple vine

Shite (Ono no Yorikaze):
  that turns and turns, like the waves on Husband and Wife River
  take me with you when you return to this shore.[45]

Tsure:
  ura murasaki ka kuzu no ha no

[44] The version edited by Itō Masayoshi substitutes the chorus for the *tsure*, but most other editions assign the "*ura murasaki*" line to the *tsure*. Since these lines are part of a series of exchanges between the husband and wife, assigning it to the *tsure* is more logical.

[45] Itō, op. cit., 253.

Shite:
kaeraba tsure yo Imose no kawa

These lines are especially impacted with wordplay foreshadowing the story to come. *Ura murasaki* includes *murasaki* (purple, the color of passionate attachment); *ura* (underside); and *uramu* (bitter resentment). *Kuzu no ha* is a kudzu or arrowroot vine; the underside of its heart-shaped leaf is purple. Here the damsel flower-woman, trapped by her passionate anger, compares herself to another plant whose tenacity of clinging has made it a metaphor for clinging to passion and resentment.[46] In Yorikaze's response, *kaeraba* puns on turning (leaves/waves): *kuzu no ha no kaeraba* (if you turn the kudzu leaf over [you find its purple underside]). The kudzu leaves turning with passionate resentment here may hint at the turning (*kuneru*) of the damsel flowers in the commentary, a turning that directly led to Yorikaze's suicide. Finally, *kaeraba* can mean "if you return." Yorikaze, who committed suicide in the hope that he could be with his love in the afterlife, begs her to take her with him: *kaeraba tsure yo Imose no kawa* (If you return [to the shore/to this world] take me with you, [together like the] waves of Imose [Husband and Wife] River).

The ghosts of the damsel flower and her husband acknowledge that although long dead, they appear now because they are joined by a karmic jeweled thread (*tama no o*) via the damsel flower, a link reinforced by the *kakekotoba* pivot on *o* (thread) and *ominameshi* (damsel flower).[47] The jeweled thread represents the passionate tie between husband and wife that keeps them caught in the cycle of reincarnation. But they are also linked to the *waki* by his prayers, and they express their thanks for his intercession on their behalf. They then turn to an explanation of their current situation and how they came to be trapped as ghosts. In so doing, however, they skip over the specific incident that prompted the woman's suicide. Since the *Kikigaki* and the Bishamondō *Kokinshū chū* provide slightly differing versions of

[46] Compare the noh play *Teika*, in which the spirit of the poet Fujiwara Teika becomes a *kudzu* vine that clings to the tomb of his dead love.
[47] *Kienishi tama no ominameshi*: the pun on *tama* (spirit, jewel) and the *o* (thread) in *ominameshi* yields *kienishi tama* (vanished spirits) and *tama no o* (jeweled thread, fate).

that incident, it may be that the playwright was simply avoiding any contradiction. But he may also have been deliberately leaving the proximate cause ambiguous, so that neither party would seem completely innocent or completely guilty.

The woman introduces herself as a woman living in the capital who put all her trust in Yorikaze's vows (*kano Yorikaze no chigiri o komeshi ni*). Yorikaze defends himself, saying that she should not have been so upset by what he terms a "small impediment" (*sukoshi chigiri no sawari*), implying that it was she who failed to trust him enough. The woman points out that a woman's feelings are fragile, implying that he was still to blame for her suicide drowning in the ironically named Life-Releasing River (Hōjōgawa 放生川). There follows a description of Yorikaze's despair when faced with the damsel flower's resentment, apparent from her bending (*nabikinoki*) away from him when he draws near. Dragged down by guilt and sorrow, and hoping to be reunited with her in the afterlife, Yorikaze also throws himself into the river.[48]

The scene then shifts abruptly to Yorikaze's torment in the Hell of Sword Trees, a hell reserved for those obsessed with passion.[49] In this hell, each person is stationed by a tree. Seeing a vision of their beloved at the top of the tree, they are overcome with passion and attempt to climb up to their love. Unfortunately for them, the tree's leaves have razor-sharp under-edges that slash the lover as they climb. When they reach the top, they find the vision of their beloved has vanished, only to reappear on the ground, beckoning them seductively. Caught in the obsessive grip of desire, they climb back down, only to find that the leaves bend and turn so that the razor edge is now on top. By the time they reach the ground they have been cut to shreds, but finding once again that their beloved is calling to them from above, they are unable to resist the siren call of passion and turn to climb again. Caught in blind desire, they hurt themselves over and over again.

This hell has a clear soteriological moral: the torture that occurs is not imposed from without, by horrific demons for example, but from

[48] Itō, op. cit., 253–54.
[49] See William LaFleur's more detailed description of the Hell of Sword Trees in his contribution to this volume.

within. If the lovers were just able to see that it is their desire alone that causes their pain and give up that desire, the torture would end at once. In this sense, the Buddhist hell is not some specialized sphere; it is in fact no different from ordinary life where we torture ourselves with useless attachments. This point is subtly reinforced by the play's reference to Yorikaze's personal hell being sited on "Sword Mountain" (*tsurugi no yama*).[50] Yorikaze, obsessed with his lost love, is deluded into believing that Man Mountain has become Sword Mountain, the location of his torture in hell. The site of tragic events in his life is ultimately no different from the site of his torture in the afterlife.

The hell found in noh plays tends most often to be of this self-inflicted kind; but in noh we also find that by a paradoxical twist a displaced object of passionate attachment can be both torturer and liberator. For example, in *Kinuta*, a woman who is angry at her husband's neglect takes out her grief and resentment by beating kimono on a fulling block. Succumbing to her grief, she falls ill and dies. In the second half of the play, when her husband returns home for her funeral service she appears before him as a ghost and explains that she has been condemned to hell for her passionate attachment. She then goes on to describe vividly how the fulling block, which in life had been the displaced object of her furious resentment over her husband's neglect, has now in death become the instrument of her torture in hell. And yet in the end when the sounds of the fulling block are equated with the sounds of the chanting of the *Lotus Sutra*, it becomes the paradoxical instrument of her salvation (*gyakuen*).[51]

In *Ominameshi* we can see a similar pattern at work, but it is complicated by the ambiguous persona of the woman from the capital as damsel flower. In *Kinuta* the wife is clearly the victim of her husband's neglect and it is her passionate anger and grief about that neglect that keeps her in hell. The woman in *Ominameshi* also believes herself to be the innocent victim of Yorikaze's false

[50] Itō, op. cit., 255.

[51] I have made a similar argument for the function of the bell in *Dōjōji*; see Susan Blakeley Klein, "Woman as Serpent: The Demonic Feminine in the Noh Play *Dōjōji*" in *Religious Reflections on the Human Body*, ed. Jane Marie Law (Indiana, 1995), 119–21.

promises: his apparent cheating proved that his vows to grow old with her were only so much frivolous play (*tawamure*) and in despair over his lack of seriousness, she commits suicide. She is thus very much in need of the *waki*'s prayers. However, in her identification as the damsel flower she is not so innocent. This is the view presented in the opening section of the play, where we are guided through a series of poems on damsel flowers that circumnavigate the problem of charming damsel flowers seducing priests from the straight and narrow path. And when she is reborn as a damsel flower, the woman tortures Yorikaze by refusing to bend toward him, plunging Yorikaze into a morbid regret that causes him to commit suicide in turn.

In his contribution to this volume, William LaFleur suggests a further identification: that of the damsel flower with the sword tree. I would argue that this identification is supported by a series of associated terms. The damsel flower who turned away from Yorikaze becomes a sword tree whose razor-edged leaves turn (*tawamu*) to slash at him. A secondary meaning of *tawamu* is to be weighed down, bent over (as with fruit). Thus, in the penultimate passage of the play, we find that Yorikaze's thoughtless wordplay (*tawamure*) has borne sinful fruit (*tsumi no nareru hate*): sword branches that turn on him (*tawamu*) and a guilt that weighs him down (*tawamu*), keeping him bound in hell:

How horrifying it all is!
Sword branches
weighed down with sin,
how came they to bear
such meritless fruit?[52]

osoroshi ya
tsurugi no eda no
tawamu made
ikanaru tsumi no

[52] Itō, op. cit., 255. An allusion to *Kin'yōshū* 644 by Izumi Shikibu. "Upon looking at a hell screen in which people were being pierced by sword branches." *Asamashi ya tsurugi no eda no tawamu made ko wa nani no mi nareru naruran* (How frightening! With what fruit/bodies are these sword branches weighed down?). There is a pivot on *mi* meaning both "fruit" and "bodies." In the noh play, *hate* pivots to mean both "fruit" and "fate."

nareru hate zo ya
yoshi nakarikeru

At this point in the play we seem to have returned to a very conservative Buddhist view of horrific retribution in hell for the meritless (*yoshi nakarikeru*) sin of *kyōgen kigo* and the passion that words can inspire. However, in the final *uta* there appears to be a sudden reversal, somewhat ambiguous but nevertheless holding out the possibility of a more hopeful resolution:

"Reflecting on the brief life of the flower,"
its bending too, but a dream; on the damsel flower's
dewy calyx, via our link to the flower of enlightenment
may we float free
of sin, may we float free.[53]

hana no hitotoki o
kuneru mo yume zo ominameshi
tsuyu no utena ya hana no en ni
ukamete tabitamae
tsumi o ukamete tabitamae

The key phrase in this passage is "link to the flower" (*hana no en*) which points simultaneously to the damsel and lotus flowers. *En* can mean "conjugal or marital relationship," a binding tie equivalent to the karmic jeweled thread (*tama no o*) that was earlier said to link Yorikaze to his love, binding them to this world as ghosts. In this sense *hana no en* refers to Yorikaze's sexual relationship with the damsel flower. However, *en* can also mean "a karmic relationship with a Buddhist deity that leads to enlightenment," and in this sense *hana no en* points to the lotus flower, the preeminent flower of enlightenment through its association with the *Lotus Sutra*. Because the lotus grows in dank, muddy waters, and yet is known for the purity and beauty of its flowers, it signifies that enlightenment is possible for everyone, no matter how sinful.

Through this alternate identification with the lotus the imagery surrounding the damsel flower is suddenly transformed. Whereas before

[53] Itō, op. cit., 255.

the bending (*kuneru*) of the damsel flower was the means of Yorikaze's unending torture in both life and death, now it is said to be ephemeral as a dream. The dew, which previously signified sexual moisture, is now the enriching moisture of enlightenment associated with the Buddha in "The Parable of Medicinal Herbs" section of the *Lotus Sutra*.[54] The damsel flower's calyx becomes the lotus pedestal upon which believers are reborn in the Pure Land. And whereas Yorikaze threw himself into the river because he was weighed down by grief and guilt over the death of his lover, and continued to be crushed with the burden of his guilt and passion (fruits of his sin) in hell, now he is able to float free of his attachments, like a lotus flower in a pond, and achieve enlightenment.

Conclusion

One difficulty for the contemporary reader of *Ominameshi* is that at first glance the play does not seem to contain the kind of rich exfoliation of imagistic wordplay (what Karen Brazell has referred to as noh's "unity of image"[55]) that plays such as *Izutsu* or *Matsukaze* exhibit. Instead the play strikes the reader as composed of four fairly disconnected segments: 1) an introduction to the conventional poetic associations of the damsel flower and Man Mountain; 2) a description of the origin of the Iwashimizu Hachiman Shrine and efficacy of the Hōjō ritual performed there; 3) a retelling/re-enactment of the commentary story about Ono no Yorikaze and the damsel flower; and 4) a description of Yorikaze's torture in hell and release. Although I have tried to show some development of imagery, primarily via the wordplays on *tawamure* and *tawamu*, the connective tissue of thematic punning imagery that distinguishes the best of noh is disappointingly absent, and this absence may explain scholars' relative lack of interest in the play up until now.

Instead of imagistic unity the play appears to be held together thematically by medieval religious issues addressed in secret literary

[54] See Burton Watson, trans. *The Lotus Sutra* (Columbia, 1993), 98, 101.
[55] See Karen Brazell, "Unity of Image: An Aspect of the Art of Noh," in *Japanese Tradition: Search and Research*, ed. Judith Mitoma Susilo (Los Angeles, 1981), 25–43.

commentaries (such as *Kokinwakashūjo kikigaki*) that were used as the basis for the play. Structurally the framework of the play as a whole appears to have been taken from the *waka* initiation process itself, in which apparent oppositions on the exoteric level are revealed ultimately to be non-dual on the esoteric level. In each half of the play, the conservative Buddhist view of *kyōgen kigo* is presented: any metaphorical play with damsel flowers is at best without merit, and at worst may be positively dangerous if it leads via passionate attachment to reincarnation in hell. However, at the end of the first half, when the *shite* invites the *waki* to pluck a flower, and at the end of the second half, when the woman and Yorikaze are released from hell, a sudden reversal of attitude occurs. In both cases the underlying theoretical mechanism appears to be *bonnō soku bodai* (passion is ultimately identical with enlightenment), a fundamental concept underlying Fujiwara Tameaki's commentaries and the initiation system within which they were transmitted. When the damsel flower, strongly associated with passion, is understood to be identical with the lotus flower, symbol of enlightenment, the damsel flower becomes a *gyakuen* 逆縁, a paradoxical link to enlightenment. The damsel flower-woman is transformed from an avenging torturer to liberator. With this shift in understanding, both the woman and Yorikaze are released from their sins of passion and achieve enlightenment.

This leaves us, however, with the question of the proximate cause of this sudden shift in understanding. It is nowhere to be found in the text; yet the shift that occurs enables the very transformation of damsel flower to lotus so earnestly prayed for by the woman in Fujiwara Mototoshi's poem:

> A certain woman, wanting to send damsel flowers as an offering for the "non-stop *nembutsu*" in the eighth month, asked him to write a poem for her to send with them:
>
> Like me, these flowers face the Five Obstructions;
> How can they be made into lotus blossoms?[56]

I believe the answer can be found in the introduction to Mototoshi's poem as well as in the apocryphal anecdote about Izumi Shikibu men-

[56] *Mototoshishū* 115, Fujiwara Mototoshi.

tioned earlier. Both stories indicate that the damsel flower was used as a surrogate for women excluded by *nyonin kinsei* from seeing the continuous *nembutsu* ritual performed on Mt. Hiei in the eighth month. According to Minamoto Tamenori's description of the continuous *nembutsu* in *Sanbōe* (Illustrations of the Three Jewels, 984) this ritual was performed annually at Enrakuji on Mt. Hiei, beginning at dawn of the eleventh day of the eighth month and continuing without interruption until the seventeenth. As it happens, this same ritual was introduced to the Iwashimizu Hachiman Shrine by the eleventh century.[57] Since we are explicitly told in *Ominameshi* that this is the fifteenth day of the eighth month, the medieval audience viewing the play would have known that in the background of the events occurring on stage, the *nembutsu,* whose primary purpose was to call on Amida Buddha's vow for the salvation of all beings, was being continuously performed. Although the tombs of the woman and Ono no Yorikaze are at the foot of the mountain, the efficacy of this ritual is such that the enlightenment bestowed on pilgrims by Hachiman as Amida Buddha would extend down to their uneasy spirits as well. And it makes perfect sense that the damsel flower, which in the medieval period was used as a surrogate to enable women's participation in the salvation afforded by the performance of the continuous *nembutsu*, would in the noh play function as the means for salvation of both the woman and Ono no Yorikaze. In this way the seemingly unconnected story of the founding of Iwashimizu Hachiman Shrine presented at the end of the first half turns out to be central to our understanding of the final moments of the play.

As this example proves, when we remove noh plays from the aestheticized vacuum of literary analysis and re-embed them in the contemporaneous beliefs and practices of the medieval period, a number of the surface level contradictions and fragmentary gaps that cause plays like *Ominameshi* to resist our scholarly analysis and translation may be resolved. Although anyone in the medieval audience of *Ominameshi* would have known that the continuous *nembutsu* was being performed at Iwashimizu Hachiman Shrine on the fifteenth day of the eighth month and that knowledge would have facilitated their understanding of the conclusion of the play, it is not mentioned in any

[57] See Edward Kamens, *The Three Jewels*, 342–43.

of the contemporary scholarly annotations of the play. As the essays in this volume demonstrate, however, when scholars move beyond the identification of literary allusions to the even more difficult task of historicizing noh's complex religious and political pretexts (as well as its performative aspects), neglected plays such as *Ominameshi* will begin to recover at least some of their original intellectual richness and thus, perhaps, their scholarly allure.

女郎花から蓮花への転化
－『女郎花』と中世の秘伝註釈－

スーザン・ブレイクリー・クライン

『女郎花』に纏わる本説の出所としては、13 世紀における秘伝的古註釈と云われる『古今和歌集序聞書』が相当すると云えるのではないだろうか。この『古今和歌集序聞書』は、1280 年代に、真言宗僧・藤原為顕(1230 年頃から 1290 年頃まで)によって作成されたと思われる。この藤原為顕とは、藤原為家(1198–1275)の児子の中ではさほど有名ではないが、藤原定家(1162–1241)の孫息子にも当たるという人物である。さて、この『古今和歌集序聞書』は、為顕が展開した数多くの秘伝的古註の中では単なる一作品に過ぎないが、それには『伊勢物語』や『古今和歌集』のような平安時代の古典文献における形象や掛詞、また文字に関する語源学上の解釈が用いられており、しかもその解釈を複雑な宗教的、且つ歴史的アレゴリーへと変容させたものである。為顕は、これらの註釈を真言密教上の伝法灌頂をもとにした秘伝の和歌伝授における教授法の基準として用いた。この論説では、秘伝伝授法の生成を助長する結果となった中世における問題点が、希薄な表現形態ではあるが、為顕の秘伝的註釈に織り込まれた資料を通して、いかに延々とその問題点が作用し続けたかを探究してみることにする。また、『女郎花』に関するその他の解釈と同様に、当書における私の分析は、明白な主題の論点を扱うことになる。(例えば、女人禁制、妄想的恋愛、自責と救済という象徴としての女郎花)。しかし、私の解釈は、宗教的なサブテキストが、謡曲に対する中世の観衆の理解をいかに確実に体制化しているかを考察することにもなる。特に、狂言綺語に関する論争(和歌の道と悟りの道との同一性に関する論点)や本地垂迹説(神仏習合説)、また煩悩即菩提説に概説されるような密教的な不二一体などの点である。『女郎花』という謡曲を中世の同時代の信仰や儀式の作法に再構築させることにより、『女郎花』のような謡曲の学術的分析や翻訳に問題を生じさせるような表面化された矛盾や断片的な相違が、少なくとも解明可能であることを論述してみたいと思う。

A Woman's Journey Through Hell: *Ominameshi* Seen from the Perspective of the *Kyōgen* Interlude

Carolyn A. Morley

Preface

The *katari-ai* (interlude *kyōgen* role) in *Ominameshi* is deceptive, seeming to occur quite independently of the dramatic unfolding of the noh. And yet, a reading of the play that privileges the *katari-ai* provides a unique insight into the story of the noh as well as into the audience at the time in which the *katari-ai* was recorded. An assumption of veracity is associated with the *ai*, in part due to his position outside the dramatic action on stage. In addition, the *igatari-ai* texts are presumed to provide the audience with the accepted "factual account" of the drama occurring on stage. Dating back to the preliterate times, *katari* have long been associated with the telling of history.[1]

The original audience for whom the *katari-ai* were recorded and performed, dating from the late sixteenth and early seventeenth centuries, at least a century after *Ominameshi* was first produced, was a newly expanded audience. Until this time the only records available for *katari-ai* consist of notes in the *utaibon* which do little more than record the presence of the *ai* role. The elaborate written texts available today are the property of the *kyōgen* schools which first began to record the *ai* in the late sixteenth century.

Just how prominent the *ai* becomes in performances depends to a large extent on what the audience needs, or wants, to hear. In fact, the first question we must ask is what this new audience needed in order to make sense of the *Ominameshi* story. Secondly, is there evidence of similar detail in other popular arts of the period? And, finally, how

[1] See Robert Brower and Earl Miner, *Japanese Court Poetry* (Stanford, 1961), 53.

does a careful reading of the *katari-ai* change our understanding of the play?

Significantly for *Ominameshi*, a reading and viewing of the play that highlights the *katari-ai* helps to resolve the odd thematic disjunction experienced by many in the audience when the *katari-ai* is ignored. That is to say, what is missing in this play, ironically considering the title, is the woman herself. Although she appears as a flower image in the poetic exchange in the *maeba*, and in the *nochiba* as a shadowy presence (*tsure*) behind the man (*shite*), the only time we hear the story from her perspective is in the *katari-ai*. The dilemma for the audience is how to resolve the seeming discontinuity between the poetic opening in the first half and the unconvincing hell scene in the second. Presumably, the man (*nochijite*) faces the tortures of hell because he has committed suicide after learning that a former lover, whom he had forgotten, has thrown herself into a river over his apparent betrayal of their love. Only when the play shifts in focus to the affair, as presented in the *katari-ai*, is the contemporary audience supplied with the details necessary to make the leap from the poetry of the temptations of love to suffering in a Buddhist hell.

History of the *Katari-ai* Role

If, as seems to be the case, many of the recorded *katari-ai* in their extended form postdate the noh texts by some years, then we must ask just how attentive the authors of the noh texts were to the content of the *katari-ai*. The possibilities for exploiting the interlude role were explored as early as Zeami Motokiyo in his critical works, the *Shudōsho* and the *Sarugaku dangi*. Prior to Zeami, in the plays generally acknowledged to be those of Zeami's father, Kan'ami Kiyotsugu, the *ai* role is ill-defined and frequently interchangeable with the *waki* role. (For examples, see *Sotoba Komachi* and *Jinen koji*). In fact, according to Koyama Hiroshi and Omote Akira, the term *igatari,* which specifies the type of seated narration seen in *Ominameshi*, was not used until the writing of Komparu Zenpō, several generations after

[2] Koyama Hiroshi, Taguchi Kazuo, and Hashimoto Asao, *Kyōgen no sekai: Nō kyōgen* (Tokyo: Iwanami Shoten, 1987), 358–9.

Zeami. Zeami himself refers to the *okashi* or *kyōgen* role in the plays without categorizing the interlude further.[2]

Under Zeami the interlude role seems to have become more strictly defined, that is to say, no longer interchangeable with the *waki*, but to have been limited to two or three lines, sometimes offered in an exchange with the *waki* (*oshie-ai*). The role of the interlude is limited in Zeami; however, there is also evidence of Zeami's active intervention in the creation of the *ai* speech to foreshadow the events in the second act of the play.[3] In his record of *Matsuura* he suggests the following: "Sayohime boarded the boat, and set out for sea, clutching the mirror to her breast, she flung herself into the offing." In view of the fact that a number of Sayohime stories were in circulation at the time, Zeami appears to have selected this particular version in order to emphasize the theme of the play. His interlude announces the action which follows in the second act of the play. While there is no way of knowing whether the *kyōgen* actor incorporated this simple speech into a longer improvised delivery, the general consensus of scholars is that the interludes were brief. In view of the length of a day's program during this period, there seems to be little possibility of an extended narrative. In fact the noh itself is thought to have been performed in about half the time that it takes today.

The use of the interlude to foreshadow the second act of a play is seen again in Zeami's holograph of *Eguchi*. Here Zeami has combined several stories in the interlude to create a new version of the tale which identifies the inn maiden, a prostitute, specifically with the Bodhisattva of song and dance, Fugen. As in the *Matsuura* play the *ai* foreshadows the events to come in the second act, as well as offering a selective retelling of the legend.[4] The fact that Zeami inserts the speech for the *ai* indicates his effort to control the *ai* role. However, changes in the *ai* in later texts for these and other plays show that he was not entirely successful in limiting the freedom of the *kyōgen* actors.

Very few records exist of the *katari-ai* after Zeami until the late Muromachi period. According to Omote Akira, Zenchiku, the pre-

[3] Koyama and Omote Akira discuss the early *ai* role in both Kan'ami and Zeami. The *Matsuura* and *Eguchi* examples are both from this work.

[4] Koyama, et al., op. cit., 348-9.

sumed author of *Ominameshi*, does not mention the interlude at all in his texts. The term *ai* is used for the first time in the work of Komparu Zenpō but with very few passages that do more than indicate that an *ai* interlude appears. This does not mean that the *katari-ai* was removed from the plays during this time only to reappear in a more complete form a century later. An innovation of such proportions would be difficult to imagine without some kind of substantiating documentation. Rather, scholars believe that, because the *katari-ai* were the property of the *kyōgen* families, they were rarely included within the *utaibon* texts. Moreover, the clear division of the noh plays into two acts, necessitating a clearly marked *katari-ai*, is in itself a late development. In contrast, the second major category of *ai*, the *ashirai-ai* (interactive *ai* roles, integral to the noh play) were included in *utaibon* texts as far back as the plays of Kan'ami and continued to be so without interruption. Obviously, the interaction of the *ai* with the *waki* and *shite* roles required that they be recorded in these cases.

From evidence gleaned in Zeami's works, scholars have concluded that the formal seated interlude (*igatari*), such as we see today in *Ominameshi*, was a late development. In its place scholars speculate that a brief standing exchange between the *waki* and *kyōgen* actor was used (*oshie-ai*). The likelihood is that the change to an *igatari* style of seated *katari-ai* came about in the late sixteenth century with the expansion in the length and complexity of the narrations. Omote Akira posits several reasons for this change to the formal *igatari-ai*.[5] First of all, during this period of intense internal warfare, the shogun and daimyo who had been the main patrons of the *sarugaku* noh troupes were no longer able to continue their support and the troupes were forced to seek larger, more varied audiences outside the capital. The support of local unofficial noh troupes (*tesarugaku*) by the rising local daimyo as well as the expansion of the audience for the established noh troupes is well documented.[6] This new, uninformed audience required longer and more detailed explanations of the stories be-

[5] Omote Akira in Koyama, et al., op. cit., 362–4. See also Omote Akira, "Aikyōgen no henbō: igatari no seiritsu wo chūshin ni," in vol. 22 of *Kanshō nihon koten bungaku yōkyoku kyōgen* (Tokyo: Kadokawa Shoten, 1977).

[6] For an interesting book on the patronage of noh actors in this period, see Amano Fumio, *Nō ni tsukareta kenryokusha* (Tokyo, Kodansha, 1997). Amano's particular interest is in Toyotomi Hideyoshi's craze for noh.

hind the plays. Second, the noh actors were using more and more elaborate costumes because they received more and more robes as payment for their performances, necessitating a longer interlude for the *shite* actor's costume change between acts. The *kyōgen* actors were thus asked to expand the narrations. Finally, as the new audience became educated in the noh, they seemed to have developed an appreciation for the recited narrative as an art form. This resulted in efforts to refine the *katari-ai* in terms of the speed and manner of delivery, as well as the content.

While the early collections of *ai* from the Edo period indicate that the conventions of the *igatari* were set by this time, there is also evidence of a transitional period in late Muromachi when the longer *igatari* speeches were first being developed for the plays.

The movement to systematize the *ai* in this period is a reflection of parallel trends: to distribute the *utaibon* for the popular use of an expanded audience, and to record and systematize the independent comic *kyōgen* plays. Concurrently, the *kyōgen* actors began forming their own schools in order to vie for the patronage of the newly formed Tokugawa government. In the earliest written records of *katari-ai,* the *kyōgen* actor Okura Toraakira, both records some sixty-six *ai* (of various types) and comments on the methods for performing the *katari-ai.* He takes pains to instruct his followers to observe the story of the noh without deviation: "you speak to the *waki*, the *waki* speaks to the *ai*, most of the speech is set. Whatever the *ai*, the speech is based on the noh; what is not in the noh, is not appropriate."[7] In this he is in agreement with Zeami. The fact that he found it necessary to specify in detail suggests that the *kyōgen* actors had been improvising more freely than was then deemed appropriate. On the other hand, contrary to Zeami, Toraakira explicitly warns that the *ai* must not foreshadow the second act of the noh: "Technique for creating the *ai*: when there is no *utai* (in the first act), the *ai* is an exchange (with the *waki*); when there is *utai*, the *ai* is a narration . . . take care to follow the theme of the *utai*. For the most part, the *ai* must not speak of the events to occur in the second act. In any case, say nothing inappropriate."[8] Many of Toraakira's *ai* are no longer extant and

[7] Ōkura Toraakira, *Waranbegusa* section 4, in Koyama, et al., op. cit., 365.
[8] Ibid., 365–6.

others have been relegated to *kae-ai* or alternate *ai* because they consist of entirely independent plays within the noh. (*Taue-ai,* for example, is a rice-planting scene with song and dance which is performed on rare occasions in *Kamo.*)

Records of interaction with the noh troupes in the creation and performance of the *ai* in Toraakira's writings document an ongoing dialogue on the role of the interlude in the noh. Toraakira notes, for example, changes made at the request of the noh actors in the entry music for the *ai* in *Shakkyō*. Traditionally both the *nochijite* and the *ai* entered to the same *ranjō* music of the *ōtsuzumi*. Toraakira agreed to change the entrance for the *ai* to *hayatsuzumi* with a *kotsuzumi* drum (a messenger entering to rapid drum). At least, according to Toraakira, this was done so as not to undermine the *shite* actor. This change was not institutionalized apparently, as later texts do not recognize it.[9] In any case, examples like this suggest that, at least in Toraakira's time, the interludes were expected to complement the noh performance and that efforts were being made to ensure that this was the case.

The Source (*Honsetsu*)

Like all noh plays the story of *Ominameshi* is said to be based on a designated source (*honzetsu*) for the play. If we allow that the noh play follows the theme initiated by the *honzetsu* then a comparison of the *honzetsu* for the noh with the story as it appears in the *katari-ai* should help to illuminate the changes inserted into the play later through the extended *katari-ai*. When we do so for *Ominameshi,* we find that the *honzetsu* has been used selectively in the *katari-ai* and then embellished. The details selected and the themes emphasized in the *katari-ai* are not those which are brought out in the text of the noh, although they are complementary. The *katari-ai* seems to flesh out the story in the noh and to redirect the attention of the audience to the woman character. This new focus on the woman in the play, as I shall demonstrate later, can be seen as a response to the audience of the late sixteenth century in which the more complex *katari* was inserted.

[9] Omote Akira, *Nōgaku shi shinkō*, vol. 2 (Tokyo: Wanya Shoten, 1986), 233–49.

First, however, we need to look carefully at the *honzetsu* for the play.

There are two acknowledged sources for the *Ominameshi* play and therefore for the *ai-katari* as well.[10] Both are commentaries on poems from the *Kokinwakashū*: *Kokinwakashūjo kikigaki* (Fujiwara Tameaki, 1230-1290)[11] and *Bishamondōbon Kokinshū chū* (1300).[12] The commentaries purport to offer the stories behind the poems in the *Kokinshū*, although in many instances the poems probably predate the stories. In the case of *Ominameshi,* the play is said to be based on a poem quoted by Ki no Tsurayuki in the preface to the *Kokinshū*. The poem seizes upon the image of *Otokoyama*, located in the Yawata mountains, and the woman flowers (*ominaeshi*) growing there. (We see evidence of the gendering of mountains in other plays as well. For example, in the play *Mitsuyama*, two mountains are said to be female rivals for the third, male mountain.) In the preface to the *Kokinshū*, Ki no Tsurayuki writes of taking solace in the following poem fragment: "Recalling the past of Man Mountain, and the woman flower who turned away for a moment, offended (*kuneru*) . . ." The line is referred to three times in the second half of the *Ominameshi* play to describe the actions of the woman flower and by inference, the woman, upon being approached by the man who betrayed her. In many ways the play is the embodiment of *kuneru*, meaning variously "to turn or twist away" and "to withdraw in a feminine pique" (affronted). The woman's absence and her replacement by the flower, which then withdraws in turn, suggest the elusiveness and illusory quality of the love affair. And yet, while the story of the flower's withdrawal (*kuneru*) forms an important part of the commentary, the *katari-ai* omits it altogether. The transformation of the woman into the yellow, wild flower is the product of the man's illusion for which he suffers in hell, and not relevant to the woman's story at all. The most detailed record of the legend in the *Kokinwakashūjo kikigaki* is as follows:

> "Recalling the past of Otokoyama, and the Ominaeshi that turns away for a moment, offended . . ." is recorded in the

[10] See essay in this volume by Susan Klein.

[11] Nishino Haruo, ed., *Yōkyoku hyakuban* in *Shin nihon koten bungaku taikei* (Tokyo: Iwanami Shoten, 1998), 518. Nishino quotes from the poem fragment and the legend of Yorikaze in the *Kokinwakashūjo kikigaki.* My translation.

[12] Yoshisawa Yoshinori, ed., *Mikan kokubun kochūshaku taikei*, vol. 4 (Tokyo: Teikoku Kyōikukai Shuppanbu, 1935), 18. My translation.

Nihongi (also in the commentary on the *Tale of Genji*). During the reign of the Emperor Heizei, there lived a man named Ono no Yorikaze. He lived in Yawata, but fell in love with a girl from the capital and they visited one another. At some point, he took leave of her, and promising that he would be back one day, he left for home. The girl waited but since he did not come, she went to his home in Yawata and asked for him there. A servant came to the door and said, "He's just taken a wife and is off visiting her." When she heard this, the girl felt betrayed and headed for Yawata river where she removed her robe of yellow mountain roses, hurled herself into the river and died. When the man returned, his servant informed him, " A girl from the capital was here but I sent her away." In a panic, the man set out after her. By the bank of the river there was a robe of yellow mountain roses. When he drew near, he recognized it as the robe she always wore. Though it hardly seemed possible, there was her body in the river. He lifted her out, had sutras read over her, and returned home with her robes as a keepsake. When he was sent by the shrine to the capital for a time, he longed for this keepsake of her, the robe, and he sent a servant after it. His servant reported that when he lifted up the robe, it crumbled into earth. From the rotted pieces grew an *ominaeshi*. Hearing this, Yorikaze went to see for himself, and discovered *ominaeshi* blooming everywhere. He tried to draw near to one of the flowers but when he did so, it fluttered away as if offended. When he backed away, it fluttered back again. From this incident comes the line, "The *ominaeshi* turns away for a moment, offended." It is from here that the flower was given the name, *ominaeshi*. The man felt that she had returned to life as a flower to spite him. She had died because of him and now, wishing to die and be reborn with her, he flung himself into the same river and died. Because they carried his body up into the Yawata mountains, this mountain is called Otokoyama. The woman's tomb at the foot is where the girl is buried. The reason that Yawata River is called Namidagawa is because of this tale.

How deep the bitterness between man and wife
spreading its tale in a river of tears.

> This poem refers to the bitter enmity between these two, man and wife. From this comes the name, Namidagawa.[13]

The *honzetsu* provides an explanation for the name of the mountain which seems to predate the noh play. The details concerning the man having taken a wife are not referred to in the noh text. Neither the *honzetsu* nor the noh text provides an adequate or credible context for the man's suicide, which seems unconnected to the woman's. A casual flirtation would seem to have had an extraordinary outcome. However, if we compare this story with different versions of the *katari-ai* for the play we receive a more comprehensive explanation for what is happening in the play on a human level.

The *Katari-ai* for *Ominameshi*

In each of the variant texts the *katari-ai* follows the story of the *honzetsu* in general outline, but with significant additions of realistic detail and color. For example, we learn how and why Yorikaze meets the girl, what her position is in the capital, and why she feels she cannot return to the capital when she is spurned at his door. On the other hand, the entire section about Yorikaze's taking the robe as a keepsake and the flower's rebuff, while central to the second act of the noh text, is missing from the *katari-ai*. Perhaps affording a poetic reason for Yorikaze's suicide, these sections do nothing to explain the anxiety of the woman, which is the central aim of the *katari-ai*.

Although the *katari* were improvised to an extent even after they were formally recorded in the seventeenth century, the early *ai* texts for *Ominameshi* suggest a general agreement in the content. The most important texts for our purposes are the late sixteenth-century *Okura Matsuibon* text, the early seventeenth-century Sagi text found in the *Shōwaban* (Kanze school *utaibon* which contains the Sagi school *ai* from the Edo period) and the Izumi school text in the *Kyōgen shūsei* collection from the late Edo period. The Okura school (the oldest *kyōgen* school with the most viable history of texts) performed with

[13] Katagiri Yoichi, ed., *Chūsei Kokinshū chūshakusho*, vol. 2 (Kyoto: Akao Shōbundō, 1971-1987), 262-3. My translation.

the Komparu noh troupes. The Izumi *kyōgen* actors performed in Nagoya as well as for the imperial court in Kyoto. The Sagi school performed almost exclusively with the Kanze noh school, receiving the patronage of the Edo government. What the three texts share in common, and what is clearly missing from the *honzetsu,* is the detail concerning the woman's anxiety and her feelings upon being driven from the man's door. On the other hand, while mention is made of the *ominaeshi* growing from the woman's grave in the *ai* texts, there is no mention of the flower's rebuff of Yorikaze, such as we find in the *Kokinwakashū* source poem. Since the rebuff by the flower (*kuneru*) is central to the noh text, the absence of this scene in the *katari-ai* significantly alters the focus of the play.

The following is a translation of the text as it appears in the *Jōkyō Matsuibon*:[14]

> I am a man who lives at the foot of the Yawata mountains. The *ominaeshi* is truly famous here, but I've been too busy lately to go and see it. They say that it is just now at its peak so I'll just go take a look. What! There's a priest stopping there. Where are you from? I never expected such a question! I do live around here but that all happened long ago. I don't know anything about it, but I'll tell you what I've heard. Now then, long ago there lived a man called Ono no Yorikaze around here. He was away in the Capital for a long time because of a lawsuit. He stayed in the capital so long that I suppose he got lonely. He met a woman there. At first it seemed nothing but a casual affair but later they fell deeply in love. They pledged their love forever. Then, Yorikaze made her promise to visit him in Yawata, since Yawata was not far from the capital, after he won his law suit; however, once he got home, he was so busy that I suppose he forgot what he'd pledged. There was no word from him and so, at some point, the woman from the capital decided she would go to find him in Yawata, and she set off after him. Since there had been no word from him, she grew anxious. She was told that he was out and was turned away roughly from the door when she explained

[14] *Jōkyō Matsuibon*, Taguchi Kazuo, ed., *Okuraryū ai-kyōgenbon nishū* in *Nōgaku shiryō shūsei*, Hōsei Daigaku Nōgaku Kenkyūjo (Tokyo: Wanya Shoten, 1983), 30–2.

why she had come. She lost all hope. She had not imagined even in her dreams that she would be turned away. Then everything he had said to her in the capital had been a lie! She knew now the weakness of a woman's heart. To have come this far was bitter indeed. What was the point in living? She flung herself into Hōjō River over there. Everyone around was shocked and upset and they dragged her from the river. But it was already too late. She was dead. Just then, Yorikaze came down the mountain. He wondered why so many people had gathered at the river and went to see. He was told that it was a woman from the capital who had drowned herself in sorrow when she was unable to meet the man she'd come to see. He was worried and when he approached, it was, as he expected, the woman with whom he'd had an affair in the capital. The absurdity of it! She had felt deceived but it wasn't so. It should never have happened. He buried her here in the fields. Not long after, Yorikaze drowned himself and he too was dragged out of the river. He was buried in a tomb near hers. That is called the tomb of the man and the other, the tomb of the woman. When the woman threw herself into the river, she was wearing a yellow robe decorated with mountain roses and this was buried with her. The color became the wild flower that grew from her grave and they say that that is why the *ominaeshi* is the famous wild flower of these parts. However, it all happened so long ago that I don't know if it's true. Anyway, that is what I've been told. Why do you ask? . . . What you say is amazing. There isn't usually anyone like that at the foot of the mountain. And I certainly don't know of anyone who recites old poems about the *ominaeshi*. If he disappeared around the tomb, then he's the ghost of Yorikaze, without a doubt. This happened because your reverence is so holy. I expect he'll show himself again. So, stay here for a while. You should pray for the souls of Yorikaze and his wife . . . you stay the night here, he will come to you. . . . Yes, sir.

The *Matsuibon* version of the *ai* lacks some of the more colorful details added later. For example, the Sagi version describes the woman in the capital as "a beauty who served him sake" (*mayume yoki onna ni shaku nado torasetamahi*).[15] In the Izumi version she is described as a serving girl (*onshakutori no josei no mashimashikeruga*).[16] In each of the texts Yorikaze is said to have asked the girl to visit him, but in the Sagi and Izumi texts his words are referred to as empty lover's talk (*soragoto*) on the one hand, and a story (*monogatari*) on the other. When she calls on him at Yawata, she is turned away by his wife in the Sagi text (*uchiyori nyobo no onrusu to kotaeshi wo kiki*), and questioned in the Izumi text (*namameitaru onna no Yorikaze wo tazunetekitaruwa ikanaru mono zo*). Although the *Matsuibon* merely tells us that Yorikaze is out, both the Sagi and the Izumi texts say that he is visiting Hachiman Shrine on Otokoyama. Presumably, he was affiliated in some way with the shrine and performed some kind of function there. Finally, in the Sagi text, the woman's feelings of shame at having believed in the man are what motivate her suicide (*hitono omowaku menbokuno ya omowareken*). These details are missing from both the *Kokinwakushū kikigaki* and the first and second acts of the play in the noh text. They add significantly to our sympathy for the woman and, ironically, for Yorikaze as well. The play is given a context with which a popular audience could easily relate. How then does this reading of the play from the perspective of the *katari-ai* change our understanding of what is happening in performance?

The Play

On one level the play is a light, *haikai*-like story of a man's dalliance with a woman, wine, and song. When the woman takes in earnest what was meant in pleasure, the story assumes a darker cast. We are given a hint at the close of the first act of what is to come in the abrupt revelation by the *shite* (an old man, guardian of the flowers) of the presence of two graves on Otokoyama, the tomb of a man, Ono no Yorikaze, and the tomb of a woman. In the second act, the *shite* reenters as the spirit of Ono no Yorikaze accompanied by the

[15] *Kanzeryū Shōwaban*, "Ominameshi," (Tokyo: Hinoki Shoten, 1930).
[16] Andō Tsunejirō and Nonomura Kaizō, eds., *Kyōgen shūsei* (Tokyo: Nōgaku Shorin, 1974), 771.

woman (*tsure*). In a few shared lines, the *shite* and *tsure* tell how they pledged themselves to one another when Yorikaze was visiting the capital. When Yorikaze did not come back, she fell victim to her "weak, woman's heart" (*onnagokoro no hakanasa*) and made her way alone to Otokoyama. Finding herself betrayed, she then hurled herself into Hōjō River. Yorikaze buried her and from her grave grew an *ominaeshi*. When Yorikaze approached the flower, it pulled back as if offended by him (*kuneru*). Unable to bear the burden of his guilt towards her, now manifested in the natural world as well, he threw himself into the same river to die. The story is told by the *shite* and *tsure* in the second act as follows:

> Tsure: (*facing the* waki) I was from the capital. I pledged myself to him, Yorikaze, but . . .
>
> Shite: (*facing forward*) for a time we were unable to meet. Did she believe this momentary parting would last forever?
>
> Tsure: (*approaches the front of the stage and looks down as if to fling herself into the river, then passes before the* waki *and stops behind him*) Weak is a woman's heart. All alone, she had made her way from the capital, and so her bitterness was deep. She flung herself into the depths of Hōjō River.
>
> Shite: (*goes to stage front and looks around. Weeps and returns to* waki za *and sits*). When Yorikaze heard of this, he headed there amidst cries and confusion but, when he looked, there was only a body no longer of this world.
>
> Tsure: (*seated at the* waki za) Lifting her in his arms, he wept and wept over the body and buried her here at the foot of this mountain.
>
> Shite: From that grave, a single *ominaeshi* grew. Yorikaze longing for her said, "My wife has become this *ominaeshi*. The very color of the flower is dear to me. The sleeves of grass and my own sleeves too, drenched in dew." He approached to touch it with his sleeve but the flower showed its resentment and flut-

tered away. And, again, when he withdrew, it fluttered back again.

Chorus: When he stopped here, Tsurayuki too, thinking of the past of Otokoyama, left behind a poem he had jotted down, "The *ominaeshi* withdraws for a moment, offended." Oh how I long for the past.

Chorus: (*Yorikaze stands at center stage, facing front*) Then Yorikaze finally felt the depths of her despair. I am so ashamed. It is because of me that she has disappeared, pointlessly, with the foam on the water. My fault alone that she has come to this. No longer could he remain in this floating world; he would follow in her wake.

Shite: (*approaches the front of the stage*) He hurled himself into this river after her.

Chorus: Since they are both buried here, this is called Otokoyama and that, the woman's tomb. His tomb is here, and I, his phantom, am come to you. Please pray for me. Please pray for me.[17]

The *shite* then describes, through the chorus, his fall into hell and the torment he suffers for his lust. He is punished by a mountain of sword trees which he must climb, pierced to the bone at every turn, a seductress perched at the top, beckoning him on. On one level then, this is a play about the obsession of a man with his own guilt and the hell which he creates to atone for his lust. The audience sees Otokoyama of the first act, the mountain of the Gods and Buddhas, the seat of Iwashimizu Hachiman Shrine, transformed by Yorikaze's obsession into a mountain of sword trees in the second act. He begs the priest (*waki*) to raise him up to the lotus, a flower after all, like the woman flower. This reading of the play finds its basis in the Tendai Buddhist doctrine that three thousand worlds are contained in one

[17] Itō Masayoshi, ed., *Yōkyokushū* in vol. 1 of *Shinchō Nihon koten shūsei* (Tokyo: Shinchōsha, 1983), 253–4. My translation.

mind (*ichinen sanzen*) and, therefore, the man's hell is contained within his own mind, as is his release from that hell. He can both dwell in the Buddhist paradise pictured on Otokoyama in the first act, and suffer the tortures of hell on the same mountain in the second act.[18] Read in this way, the play would seem to belong to the man alone. The woman remains in a perpetual state of withdrawal (*kuneru*), and out of reach.

What the *katari-ai* does is to open up another possible reading for the play. Instead of a play about a man's obsession, the focus shifts to the woman, inviting us to read the play as one about a couple, a man and a woman, each of whom falls prey to the weaknesses of his/her gender. Unable to disentangle themselves from their obsessions, hers with her bitterness over his betrayal of her love, and his with his guilt at having precipitated her death, they fall into their respective hells. The detail provided in the *katari-ai* moves the play from the realm of poetic abstraction to realism, which complements the graphic depiction of hell in the final scene. The tension created by the seeming absence of the woman from the play is resolved by the replacement of the woman in the *katari-ai*. In other words Yorikaze suffers his fate not because of a flower but because of the very real suffering of a very real woman. He, whose job presumably had been to perform the Shinto rituals which kept the natural and human worlds aligned, had thrown them out of kilter.

Popular Culture and the Noh

It is fair to ask whether this reading of the play for the period under discussion, the late sixteenth century, is legitimate. Unfortunately the mindset of a popular audience in any historical period is not immediately available to us and we are left to reconstruct it as best we can from the limited sources available on popular culture. With regard to *Ominameshi,* in particular, some useful sources are to be found in

[18] Thornhill, Arthur H., III, *Six Circles, One Dewdrop: The Religio-aesthetic World of Komparu Zenchiku* (Princeton, 1993), 113–7. Thornhill discusses Tendai thought in the critical discourse of Komparu Zenchiku; he does not mention *Ominameshi*, however.

kanazōshi, *kyōgen* plays, and the popular picture-telling genre, *etoki*.

That there would have been an interest in the role of the woman at the time of the insertion of the expanded *katari-ai* seems likely from a new focus on women in a variety of popular entertainments. Among the numerous *kanazōshi* story books for women, for example, we have a book of good conduct for women entitled *Ominameshi monogatari,* probably compiled by Kitamura Kigin (1642-1705), which warns women against behaving flirtatiously, like the *ominaeshi* flower.[19] The work draws parallels between the *Ominameshi* flower and the daughter of the dragon king who rose from the sea to attain buddhahood. The author further points to the apocryphal story of Izumi Shikibu in which she asks that a priest carry the *ominaeshi* flower up Mt. Hie in her stead for the *nembutsu* rite because the mountain is forbidden to women. We are told that the flower "becomes the seed for equal achievement of buddhahood by such non-sentient entities as grasses and trees, nations and lands."[20] The moral of the work is that women must guard against the dangers of their sex to themselves and to the men with whom they associate. Hope is offered in the form of the experience of the dragon king's daughter. The tone is notably didactic and negative reflecting the Buddhist climate of the period. Works like this supply us with popular images associated with women and the *ominaeshi* in the late medieval period and suggest a new popular interest in the roles women might play. This interest in women is reflected in at least two other popular genres, *kyōgen* and *etoki*.

Given the large and diverse audiences attracted to *kyōgen* performances in this period, we can safely assume a familiarity with *kyōgen* among the viewers of *Ominameshi*. Since the actors for the comic plays and those for the *katari-ai* in the noh were the same, some cross-over would seem to be inevitable. Indeed, we find a number of plays on the theme of a man returning from the capital after pursuing a lawsuit, usually over land reclamation (*Onigawara, Suminuri*, to name a few). Such lawsuits were of great interest to medieval man as

[19] Kamens, Edward, "Dragon-Girl, Maidenflower, Buddha: The Transformation of a Waka Topos, 'The Five Obstructions,'" *Harvard Journal of Asiatic Studies* 53:2 (1993): 426–7.
[20] Ibid., 428.

they provided a means for transforming one's economic and social status. Although the man in *Ominameshi* is said in the *honzetsu* to be working at the Hachiman Shrine and visiting the capital on shrine business, in the *katari-ai* he is only said to be bringing a lawsuit. (His business in the capital is not mentioned at all in the noh text itself.) The *katari-ai* thus offered the popular audience a social context to which they could easily relate. If we compare, for example, the *ai* for *Ominameshi* with the play *Suminuri* (Ink Smears),[21] we see the relationship of the man and his lover in the capital depicted in reverse. A country bumpkin-landowner is ready to return home after a successful land suit and must now take leave of the woman with whom he has been having an affair. Worried over her reaction to his leaving, he pleads with his one servant, Tarō Kaja, to relay the information for him. Tarō Kaja refuses. When the master does manage finally to tell her they both dissolve into tears. However, Tarō Kaja notices that the woman's tears are being helped along by a bowl of water which she assiduously applies to her cheeks. Since his master refuses to listen to his revelation about the woman, he surreptitiously adds a dollop of ink to the bowl. Soon the woman's face is covered with black ink. When the master realizes that he has been duped, he tricks the woman into gazing into the water as if it were a mirror and there she sees Tarō Kaja's ruse played out on her face. She is so angry that she chases the master off the stage.

Here we have all of the gossipy details of a man's dalliance with a woman, but in an inverted comic vein. Instead of a deceived woman hurling herself into a river to die, we have a woman dipping her hand into a bowl of water to deceive a man. Although no direct link can be established between the *katari-ai* for *Ominameshi* and the *kyōgen* play *Suminuri*, we can assume that the *kyōgen* actor and popular audiences brought the same interest in the social phenomena and contexts of their period to the noh plays. This would certainly account for the insertion of details on the lawsuit and the affair provided in the *katari-ai*.

Changes in at least one other related popular entertainment genre, *etoki* (picture telling), are persuasive in arguing for an audience attuned not only to popular social phenomena, but to the role of

[21] *Kyōgen shūsei*, 233–5.

women in particular. This is especially significant for *Ominameshi* and the category of *etoki* known as the hell mandalas. In purely physical terms, the entertainers of *etoki* and noh could conceivably have performed in the same place at the same time. Entertainment, after all, took place during festivals at the local shrine or temple. The entertainers, whether *etoki* (picture narrators), or *sarugaku* noh performers, were closely affiliated with the shrines and temples. The narrators of the pictures were quasi-priests and later nuns (*bikuni*) who used the pictures to teach religious truths. As Hattori Yukio[22] points out, the medieval commoner read pictures much as we follow a play today. That is to say, they expected the picture to have a story (*katari*) to tell.

Throughout the Muromachi period the pictures to which commoners were exposed were religious: primarily *engi* (histories of holy spots of worship), pilgrimage pictures, mandalas of heaven and hell, and portraits of the Bodhisattva Kannon and Jizō. The line between religion and entertainment was hazy to the point of non-existence. By the late Muromachi period, *etoki* gathered both at religious festivals and at markets, performing for the same audience as the *sarugaku* noh troupes. According to Hattori, the early relationship between pictures and performance meant that performers continued to be perceived as part of a religious realm well into the Edo period. He notes the equation of the Fugen Bodhisattva of song and dance with women entertainers in general. The pictures performed by the *etoki* endowed the commoners in the audience with a wealth of images, images they brought with them to the noh.[23]

For the first time in late Muromachi, we see in the hell mandalas the introduction of specific hells for women juxtaposed to those for men. Above all, women were headed, by sole virtue of being female, for the burning blood bath situated next to the sword tree of lust for men.[24] From the pool emerge women with snake-like heads, transformed by their jealousy. Above the pool is a Kannon to whom the women may pray. The possibility of rescue is evident from a woman

[22] See Introduction, Hattori Yukio, *Edo no shibai-e wo yomu* (Tokyo: Kodansha, 1993).

[23] Ibid.

[24] Yashima Shin, "Chūsei no jigokue ni egakareta kyūsai," *Chūsei shomin shinkyō no ega* (Tokyo: Tatematsu Bijutsukan, 1993), 9–12.

in white, seated upon a lotus which rises up from the pool.[25] Hell screens of this type were particularly popular in the late sixteenth and early seventeenth centuries, the same period during which the expanded *katari-ai* was inserted into the play and the same period during which the noh actors began performing for a wider, more varied audience. It is not difficult to imagine this audience supplying from their imagination the images of hell for the woman character of *Ominameshi,* just as they had seen them in the hell mandalas. The refocus of the *katari-ai* narrative on the woman character in *Ominameshi* would seem to parallel this new interest in the fate of women in the period as revealed in the attention given to women in the hell mandalas.

Having suggested that the audience may have made such a connection and brought therefore a second reading to the play we should perhaps look a little closer at the story of hell being recited by the *bikuni* at the time, and the audience toward which it was directed. According to Kuroda Hideo,[26] the *Kumano kanjin jikkai mandara* (Kumano Mandala of the Ten Worlds) is the most representative of the hell mandalas of the late sixteenth and early seventeenth centuries with close to thirty versions extant today. Kuroda argues that the rough brushwork is proof that it was directed at a general population for teaching purposes. Probably in response to the decline in the pilgrimage craze of the fifteenth and early sixteenth centuries, itinerant nuns began to make their appearance in the Kyoto environs, bringing the pilgrimage to the people by means of various pilgrimage mandalas from which they instructed. Kumano *bikuni* are first seen represented in a screen from the sixteenth and early seventeenth centuries, entitled "Sumiyoshi sha satsurei zu byōbu."[27] The *bikuni* pictured here is instructing her audience, composed mostly of women and children, in the *Kumano kanjin jikkai mandara.* According to Kuroda, this type of itinerant nun was seen commonly in the cities, seaports, and at shrine festivals of the period.

[25] Ibid., plate 28, *Kanjin jikkaizu rokudōshinoji* sixteenth century, page 56 and plate 29, *Kanjin jikkaizu daienji* seventeenth century, page 57.

[26] Kuroda Hideo, "Kaiga shiryō ni miru chūseijin no ikizama," Nichibunken symposium, Kyoto, June 1998.

[27] Screen of a map of the Sumiyoshi Shrine Festival, Freer Gallery.

In the *Kumano kanjin jikkai mandara*, the iconography of the passage through the ten worlds is based on earlier pilgrimage mandalas illustrating the routes to various shrines and temples. At the center of the Kumano mandala is the Chinese character for heart (*kokoro*) and from this extend strings to each of the ten worlds of Buddhist thought. Accordingly, one can be rescued from even the depths of hell by appeal to the Buddha, reflecting the Tendai principle of three thousand worlds contained in one thought. The Bodhisattva Jizō and Kannon are represented in the various levels of hell. A Kannon is placed above the woman's burning, blood bath and to the right of both the sword tree of lust and a stone woman hell (*umazume jigoku*) in which childless women are condemned to pull up bamboo shoots. In the center of the picture above the character for heart, we see the region of enlightenment pictured with Amida Buddha. Below the character, we see the hell of the hungry ghosts and beneath this Jizō and the innocent children whom he seeks to rescue from hell. A man and a woman are pictured in the upper half of the picture on the right in a wealthy mansion with their baby. Kuroda suggests that we can follow them as they begin their climb in an arc across the uppermost part of the mandala, through their lives, to their graves on the left side. Four gates lead to the four realms of hell and we can pick up images of the man and woman throughout the various hells. In the lower half of the mandala on the left, we see them led out of hell by Jizō. In other words, the cycle of birth and rebirth is created through circular iconography framing the picture, with an escape provided by Jizō on the left. The use of parallel imagery of life/death, day/night, spring/fall, male/female is similar to that in the earlier pilgrimage mandalas.

Kuroda argues that this type of mandala was aimed at women and therefore the focus is on the images of women, children and couples in hell. There is no possibility of rebirth in the upper realms for a woman, the only possibility of escape being through appeal to the Bodhisattva Kannon. While hell iconography and hell screens date back to early periods, the images of the woman's hell, as mentioned earlier, are new to these screens. The *bikuni* directed the women's attention to these hells as well as to the images of women praying for men suffering for lust on the sword tree and on the demon's pitchfork. Women are depicted as being responsible by their very nature for the suffering of men but they are also offered a means to make amends through prayer. In Kan'ami's play *Motomezuka,* the hapless woman, surely an apt victim for the woman's blood bath, suffers instead on the mountain of swords and in the burning cart. Hells targeted specifically for women had not been invented at the time of the writing of her hell scene in the second act.

Reading the Play from the Perspective of the *Katari-Ai*

When we reread the play from the perspective of the *katari-ai* with the hell-screen imagery close at hand we gain a context for the tragedy which occurs, a context conspicuously missing from the noh alone.[28] The play opens with the priest's journey from distant Kyushu up to the capital and his arrival at Otokoyama. He stops at Yawata with the intention of visiting Iwashimizu Hachiman Shrine on Otokoyama. The priest is delighted by the masses of *ominaeshi*, small yellow wild flowers blooming along graceful stems. He starts to pick one to take home with him when the Guardian of the Flowers (*shite*) enters and stops him. Far from sounding menacing, the *shite* stops him with a melancholic, almost hypnotic tone. They have an elegant contest, exchanging old poems, establishing themselves as kindred spirits of the poet priest Bishop Henjō of old. The poems, many by Henjō, refer to the *ominaeshi*, variously imagined as a wanton seductress, a lonely maiden, and an offering to the Buddha. Out of this exchange of verses the Guardian of the Flowers recognizes the priest as one worthy of the flower, one sensitive to poetry and love, and allows him to pick one. The priest does not pick the flower but he does follow the old man on a pilgrimage up Otokoyama to witness the glories of the Gods and Buddhas revealed in the natural beauty of the mountain, and the scene of Hōjō River below. This passage turns out to be ironic when we discover that the couple killed themselves in this very river, whose name means "life-saving" since it was the site of annual Buddhist rites sanctifying life through the catch and return

[28] Comments regarding performance are with reference to the Kanze school (see video recording of *Ominameshi* in the Kokuritsu Nōgakudō archives, Tokyo).

of fish. For an informed audience this is meant as a foreshadowing of events to come. Before the first act closes the priest asks the old man whether there is some story connecting the *ominaeshi* and Otokoyama. The old man is chagrined; the priest did not understand the import of the earlier poetic exchange. He then points out two graves, the tomb of the Man and the tomb of the Woman, and, revealing that he is that man, disappears.

The *katari-ai* is brought into the play at this point as an interlude between the acts. Up until this point, no mention has been made of the actual woman beyond the mention of her tomb. We know only that Yorikaze, here manifested as the Guardian of the Flowers, has some intimate connection with a woman manifested as the *ominaeshi*. The *katari-ai* as recorded above, brings the story into a more realistic realm, and through the introduction of a social context, invites our sympathy for the couple.

The second act of the play ushers in the spirits of Yorikaze and the woman. The woman presents a few lines describing her journey from the capital and then retires to the *waki* seat. The remainder of the play, the climax, is devoted to the *shite*'s story of the flower's revenge, and of his hell in the *kiri* scene. The *kiri* dance is more usual in warrior plays and the vigor of the movements here seems to reflect Yorikaze's frustration with the woman who has thrown her life away so needlessly and thus condemned him to his hell. On the other hand, the hell scene is in no way as dark and depressing as that in *Motomezuka* with which it is often compared.

What is of particular interest is Yorikaze's depiction of hell on the mountain of sword trees with the seductress beckoning him from the top, and his plea to the *waki* to pray for him and deliver him up to the lotus. His lines are sung by the chorus as he dances the *kiri*:

> Demons of lust torment me.
> Demons of lust torment me
> on that path of obsession up precipitous sword mountain
> to the top where I can see the one I love.
> Oh, the ecstasy!
> But as I climb the swords pierce through me
> boulders crush my bones.
> Oh the terror!

What sin brought me to this?
Until the sword branches yield
hopeless . . .[29]

If we return to the hell mandala for a moment, we can visualize the woman in the blood bath of jealousy juxtaposed to Yorikaze's hell as described above. Within that blood bath is an image of a lotus with a woman in white (saved) seated upon the flower. The woman has been saved by the Kannon, pictured near the blood bath. However, next to the sword tree we see another woman seated in prayer. She would seem to be praying for the man condemned to the sword tree of lust. With this scene in mind, it is not impossible to hear Yorikaze's final plea for salvation, made as he turns on stage toward the *waki* seat, as a plea both to the *waki* and to the *tsure* (the woman seated beside the *waki* on stage),

> The flower's turning away for a moment in offense, this too was no more than a dream, *Ominameshi*, rise up to the lotus, a flower too. Raise up my sins and wash them away.[30]

The final scene would thus seem to echo the iconography of the hell screen and bring closure to the *katari-ai* story of the woman. She is given a final role to fulfill in the prayer of the shite. Her position on stage, seated beside the *waki*, is a convention, but like all conventions of the noh, it can be put to a specific purpose.

Conclusion

Noh allows for multivalent readings. The layers of meaning in both textual imagery and performance encourage limitless interpretations of the plays. This is surely one reason for the endurance of this form of theater. On the other hand, there would seem to be two dom-

[29] Itō, op. cit., 255. My translation.
[30] Ibid., 255. My translation.

inant chords being sounded throughout the *mugen* noh repertoire. The plays operate on a metaphorical level, incorporating images endowed with a Buddhist world view towards attachment and release from attachment. In *Ominameshi* Yorikaze's story, as told in the two acts of the noh, seems to take place within his own tormented mind. The worlds of enlightenment and hell co-exist in his endless battle to free himself of his obsession with his self-generated guilt. As far as we know, he continues this relentless seesawing at the conclusion of the play. A more realistic level of meaning is revealed in the *katari-ai*. The figures of Ono no Yorikaze and the nameless woman take shape and reality for the audience. The hell of the second act is both the hell of Yorikaze's mind and an actual, physical hell shared with the woman, as represented so graphically in the hell mandalas.

Naturally, the type of *katari-ai*, its function, and the repercussions for how we view the noh differ with each play. Nevertheless, we can comfortably say that in most cases the *kyōgen* narratives bring a certain earthy context to the stories portrayed. Since the narratives have always been the property of the *kyōgen* families, and were created by the *kyōgen* actors, we should not be surprised if they reflect the art of *kyōgen* as much as they reflect that of the noh. Like the characters in a *kyōgen* play, the *katari-ai* narrator is usually a local common man, someone with whom the audience can easily identify. In the early versions of the *ai* we have ample evidence of humor and colorful descriptions in the *katari*. While these have been mostly deleted over the years in deference to the noh actors, the *katari-ai* still supplies a level of reality missing from the noh. In *Ominameshi*, the missing reality is that of the woman. Interestingly, both Yorikaze and the woman's graves are marked to this day in Yawata near Otokoyama. The monument to the woman has been carefully tended. Yorikaze's grave, on the other hand, as observed in 1997, was overgrown with weeds, hidden in an alley behind a store.

女の地獄旅
―間狂言からみた『女郎花』―

キャロル・モーリ

この論文は、語り間を通して16－17世紀の観客の心理を読み、「女郎花」を分析する試みである。現存する『女郎花』の語り間テキストは、狂言役者が流派を組み語り間を詳しく記録しはじめた16世紀のものであり、この論文では現存する三版、すなわち、「大蔵流間狂言」(善竹家)、「観世流昭和版謡本」(鷺流)、「狂言集成」(和泉流)、を利用した。

16世紀は、民族芸能が新たに発達し、能と狂言の観客が増加し変化した時期である。当時の狂言劇（例えば、「墨塗」)、御伽草子、地獄絵などから、女性の語り、観客としての女性への興味が新たにわいたことがわかる。それ故、語り間が『女郎花』の女の語りに注目し、それを詳しく華やかにしたことは驚くべきことではない。語り間から『女郎花』を読むことは、女の立場から読むことであり、また前場と後場の不合も消失することを意味する。つまり頼風の不可解な自殺が可解になり、『女郎花』はある男の奇妙な心理についてではなく、女と男の語りになることになる。換言すれば、『女郎花』に一般の観客が観たい次元が生まれたことを意味する。

Ominameshi and the Politics of Subjection

Steven T. Brown

Most noh plays dealing with the topic of female suicide involve the modus operandi of death by drowning, but differ according to the motives attributed to such acts of self-destruction. Using motive as a criterion, extant female suicide plays can be divided roughly into two groups. The first group consists of plays, such as *Motomezuka* and *Ukifune*, which deal with women who commit (or, in the case of *Ukifune*, attempt to commit) suicide because they are faced with the dilemma of having to choose between two competing suitors. The second group is comprised of plays, such as *Mitsuyama* and *Uneme*, which depict women who commit suicide out of despair over the neglect or abandonment inflicted upon them by their husbands or lovers. Although examples of male suicide by drowning also exist (e.g., in *Koi no omoni* and *Aya no tsuzumi*), that particular mode of death is more often than not gender-marked as feminine.

Among the dozen or so plays in the noh repertoire dealing with female suicide, *Ominameshi* stands out from the rest not only because extant performance records indicate that it was more popular than any other play of that genre performed during the Muromachi (1338-1573) and Azuchi-Momoyama (1568-1600) periods,[1] but also because it is the only female suicide play in the current repertoire in which the primary role of *shite* is given not to the suicide herself, but rather to her widowed husband.[2]

Note: This essay is an abridged chapter that originally appeared in my study published by Stanford University Press. From *Theatricalities of Power: The Cultural Politics of Noh* © 2001, by the Board of Trustees of the Leland Stanford Jr. University. Reprinted by permission of the publisher.

[1] Twenty-four performance records exist for *Ominameshi* between the years 1429 and 1602. This makes it as popular as *Izutsu*, one of the most frequently performed plays in the noh repertoire during the premodern period. See Nose Asaji, *Nōgaku genryūkō* (Tokyo: Iwanami Shoten, 1938), 1301–2.

[2] I use the term "husband" here loosely. Whether the couple was actually married or not seems impossible to confirm on the basis of available evidence that is ambiguous

Yet another striking aspect of *Ominameshi* is the peculiar way in which its narrative of female suicide is both inscribed and displaced by politically charged tropes linked to Iwashimizu Hachiman Shrine on Otokoyama.[3] In what follows, with a glance toward Judith Butler's work, I explore the multiple forms of "subjection" intimated in the interstices of *Ominameshi*, namely: (1) religio-political subjection, or the domination of individuals, groups, and/or territories within a network of religiously marked class and power relations; (2) narratival subjection, or the regulation of modes of articulation, naming, and inscription; and (3) psychic-corporeal subjection, or the production and domestication of gender-and class-marked subjectivities.[4]

In this essay, I analyze three Hachiman intertexts enframing the performance of *Ominameshi*—each one exemplifying a politics of subjection. The first intertext alludes to the institutional genealogy of Iwashimizu Hachiman Shrine. The second intertext reinscribes the Otokoyama of the god play *Yumi Yawata* with its appropriation of imperial symbolic capital[5] in the service of shogunal politics. Finally, the third intertext juxtaposes the woman's suicide with the Hōjōe 放

---

at best. But since Yorikaze's torture in the hell of adulterers (discussed below) seems more plausible and dramatic if it is assumed that they were married, I have done so throughout.

[3] Here I am not interested in determining the "causes" of the discourse of "Otokoyama" so much as I am in describing its complex correlations and collocations with other discourses. As Foucault has argued, the discourse of causality drastically oversimplifies the multifarious relations of dependence and dominance—whether intradiscursive, interdiscursive, or extradiscursive—emerging from a given discourse network. See Michel Foucault, "Politics and the Study of Discourse" in *The Foucault Effect: Studies in Governmentality*, ed. Graham Burchell, Colin Gordon, and Peter Miller. (Chicago, 1991), 58–9.

[4] These differentiations are my own. I am indebted to Judith Butler's incisive engagement with philosophical aspects of subjection vis-à-vis Hegel, Nietzsche, Freud, Foucault, and Althusser in *The Psychic Life of Power: Theories in Subjection* (Stanford, 1997).

[5] Here I follow the usage of Pierre Bourdieu, who employs the term "symbolic capital" to refer to the idea, historically inflected by the specific socio-cultural field in which it operates, that

> struggles for recognition are a fundamental dimension of social life and that what is at stake in them is the accumulation of a particular form of capital, honour in the sense of reputation and prestige, and that there is, therefore, a specific logic behind the accumulation of symbolic capital, as capital founded on cognition [*connaissance*] and recognition [*reconnaissance*].

生会, or Life-Releasing Ritual, performed at both Usa and Iwashimizu Hachiman shrines. I argue that what *Ominameshi* offers through such intertextual juxtapositions is a performative analogue between the Hachiman-inflected religio-politics of subjection and the gender politics of subjection dramatized by the narrative of female suicide.

Genealogies of Otokoyama

In an *ageuta shōdan* sung by the chorus just before the *shite* discloses the site of the tombs belonging to Ono no Yorikaze and his wife and their link to the history of the *ominaeshi* flower, the foundation myth of Iwashimizu Hachiman Shrine is intimated in the following gender-specific terms:

> In the clear light of the celestial orb,
> lunar *katsura* trees and the Man in the Moon shine brightly over Man Mountain,
> lunar *katsura* trees and the Man in the Moon shine brightly over Man Mountain,
> this clean, manly image is the spirit of the place,
> along with the colors of autumn shining in the moon's light,
> Iwashimizu Shrine, where pure water shimmers in the sunlight,
> where the priest's fine robe of moss
> has hallowed images traced onto its three sleeves,
> where the sacred box containing the imperial seal is stored,
> where Kami and Buddhas, shrines and temples, co-exist according to the Buddhist dharma,
> how blessed is this sacred place![6]

Symbolic capital, as Bourdieu conceives it, is relatively unstable, difficult to transmit, objectify, or quantify, and not easily convertible. Moreover, the specific efficacy of symbolic capital works only when "it is *misrecognized* in its arbitrary [and contingent] truth as capital and *recognized* as legitimate." See Pierre Bourdieu, *In Other Words: Essays Towards a Reflexive Sociology*, trans. Matthew Adamson (Stanford, 1990), 22, 93, 111–2. Also see Bourdieu, *The Logic of Practice*, trans. Richard Nice (Stanford, 1990), 112–21.

[6] Itō Masayoshi, ed., *Yōkyokushū* in vol. 57 of *Shinchō Nihon koten shūsei* (Tokyo: Shinchōsha, 1983), 251. All translations of *Ominameshi* are my own.

久方の、
月の桂の男山、
月の桂の男山、
さやけき影は所から、
紅葉も照り添ひて、
日もかげろふの石清水、
苔の衣も妙なれや、
三つの袂に影うつる、
璽の箱を納むなる、
法の神宮寺、
ありがたかりし霊地かな。

As is made abundantly evident here and elsewhere in *Ominameshi*, Iwashimizu Hachiman Shrine is gender-marked as masculine. The "clean, manly image [which] is the spirit of the place" (*sayakeki kage wa tokorokara* さやけき影は所から) juxtaposes the terrestrial masculinity of Otokoyama with the celestial masculinity of Katsura no Otoko 桂の男. To complicate matters further, this terrestrial-celestial gender politics is intertwined with the religious politics associated with Iwashimizu Hachiman Shrine's foundation myth.

The entire song, especially the description of the "the priest's fine robe of moss" with "hallowed images traced onto its three sleeves" (*mitsu no tamoto ni kage utsuru* 三つの袂に影うつる), invokes the narrative of the founding of Iwashimizu Hachiman Shrine on Otokoyama in the year 859 (Jōgan 貞観 1) by Gyōkyō Oshō, head priest of Daianji Temple in Nara. After receiving special oracular instructions during a pilgrimage to Usa Hachiman Shrine in Kyushu, Gyōkyō returned to the capital to establish a new shrine-temple complex for Hachiman on Otokoyama.[7] The legitimacy of this mandate was reportedly demonstrated by the fact that Hachiman Daibosatsu became manifest and traced the images of the "three revered ones" (*sanzon* 三尊)—namely, Amida Buddha, and his two attendant Bodhisattvas, Kannon and Seishi—onto the sleeves of Gyōkyō. Given such an illustrious genealogy, it is no surprise that, upon seeing Iwashimizu Hachiman Shrine for the very first time, the *waki* feels

[7] See Yamada Yoshio, et al., eds., *Konjaku monogatarishū* in vol. 24 of *Nihon koten bungaku taikei* (Tokyo: Iwanami Shoten, 1961), 142–3.

compelled to remark upon the foundational connection between this shrine complex and Usa Hachiman Shrine back in Kyushu, with which it is identified.[8] But concealed behind such an identification is the fact that Iwashimizu eventually attained administrative power over Usa.[9]

An even more significant political subtext to the founding of Iwashimizu Hachiman Shrine is the fact that its construction was authorized by the powerful *sekkan* politician Fujiwara no Yoshifusa 藤原良房 (804-872) soon after the accession of his grandson, Emperor Seiwa 清和天皇 (850-880), in 858 (Ten'an 天安 2). The first child-emperor in Japanese history, Seiwa's reign was administered by his maternal grandfather Yoshifusa in the role of *sesshō*, or regent. Later, during the reign of Emperor Kōkō 光孝天皇 (830-887), Yoshifusa introduced a differentiation between the regent, who advised an emperor before coming of age, and the chancellor (or *kanpaku*), who advised him as an adult. This subjection of imperial power by the northern branch (*hokke* 北家) of the Fujiwara clan after the enthronement of Seiwa thus marked the birth of *sekkan* (regent-chancellor) politics.

Viewed against the backdrop of this dispossession of imperial power by the Fujiwara clan, the founding of Iwashimizu Hachiman Shrine as a *gokoku* 護国,[10] or "state-protecting," institution suggests that it not only served as "the special guardian of imperial legitimacy," as Christine Guth Kanda has noted,[11] but also as a silent monument to Fujiwara politics and the *sekkan* reterritorialization of Heian power relations.

[8] Itō, op. cit., 247.

[9] Allan G. Grapard, "Religious Practices," in vol. 2 of *The Cambridge History of Japan*, ed. Donald H. Shively and W. H. McCullough (Cambridge 1999), 569.

[10] See Takeda Yūkichi and Satō Kenzō, trans. *Sandai jitsuroku* (Tokyo: Rinsen Shoten, 1986), 696 (see entry under Jōgan 18/5/28).

[11] Christine Guth Kanda, *Shinzō: Hachiman Imagery and Its Development* (Cambridge, Mass., 1985), 41. This is not to say that Fujiwara regents "owned" imperial power; rather, they exercised the imperial power they had displaced without usurping official "ownership" *per se* from the imperial line. For further discussion of the "ownership/possession dichotomy" in the Heian period, see Peter Nickerson, "The Meaning of Matrilocality: Kinship, Property, and Politics in Mid-Heian," *Monumenta Nipponica* 48:4 (1993): 449–52.

Almost six hundred years later, under the protective eye of Hachiman, another subjection of imperial prerogatives and symbolic capital—this time for shogunal purposes—was undertaken by the distant descendants of Emperor Seiwa via the Seiwa branch of the Minamoto lineage: the Ashikaga rulers Yoshimitsu and Yoshinori. This genealogical tie brings us to the second intertext linking *Ominameshi* to Iwashimizu Hachiman Shrine, this one viewed through the performative lens of the *waki* noh *Yumi Yawata*.

Shogunal Politics in *Yumi Yawata*

The only other play in the noh repertoire that comes close to invoking the topograph "Otokoyama" as often as *Ominameshi* is the god play *Yumi Yawata*, considered by Zeami to be a model play of its genre.[12] These two plays contain more inscriptions of Otokoyama (and its synonym Yawatayama) than any other plays in the repertoire, with *Ominameshi* containing eleven references total and *Yumi Yawata* seven.[13] Given the complementarity of their settings, it comes as no surprise that the two plays were often performed together on the same program. According to extant performance records covering the years 1429 to 1602, *Yumi Yawata* was performed on the same program as *Ominameshi* approximately 21 percent of the time.[14] Taking into consideration both the significant statistical and tropological associations between the two plays, it seems highly likely that the ideological connotations associated with the topograph Otokoyama in *Yumi Yawata* would have resonated intertextually with the Otokoyama of *Ominameshi*.

[12] See Omote Akira and Katō Shūichi, eds., *Zeami, Zenchiku* in vol. 24 of *Nihon shisō taikei* (Tokyo: Iwanami Shoten, 1974), 286. Although *Yumi Yawata* was not quite as popular a *waki* noh as *Takasago*, performance records indicate that it was one of the ten most popular plays performed during the Muromachi and Azuchi-Momoyama periods. See Nose, 1308, 1314.

[13] Otokoyama and Yawatayama are alternate names for the same place, each implying the other in the context of their usage in noh. The distribution of Otokoyama/Yawatayama inscriptions is most concentrated in three plays from the current repertoire: (1) *Ominameshi*: 10 (Otokoyama) + 1 (Yawatayama) = 11; (2) *Yumi Yawata*: 3 + 4 = 7; and (3) *Hōjōgawa*: 3 + 2 = 5. See Nonomura Kaizō, ed., *Yōkyoku nihyakugojūbanshū sakuin* (Tokyo: Akaoshōbundō, 1978), 237, 1318.

[14] See Nose, 1302, 1314.

Although *Yumi Yawata* has often been read as a straightforward "paean to imperial rule and to the peace that it has brought to the land,"[15] its politics are greatly complicated by the circumstances surrounding its production. In the context of his discussion of the "straightforward style" (*sugu narutei* 直成体) of congratulatory noh plays (*shūgen nō* 祝言能), Zeami singles out *Yumi Yawata* for praise in *Sarugaku dangi* 申楽談儀 and adds a tantalizing note regarding its inception: "Since it is a noh play that I wrote in honor of the inaugural celebration for the reign of the present shogun, there are no special secrets to performing it" (*tōgodai no hajime no tame ni kakitaru nō nareba, hiji mo nashi* 当御代の初めのために書きたる能なれば、秘事もなし).[16] The exact date of the play and the shogun for whom it was intended remain uncertain; however, circumstantial evidence seems to favor Ashikaga Yoshinori. Insofar as Yoshinori was the shogun at the time *Sarugaku dangi* was written—that is, in the eleventh month of 1430 (Eikyō 永享 2)—it seems highly likely that "the reign of the present shogun" (*tōgodai* 当御代) refers to Yoshinori. Moreover, the fact that Yoshinori was selected as shogun by a lottery drawn at Iwashimizu Hachiman Shrine in 1428 (*Shōchō* 正長 1) lends further credence to the view that *Yumi Yawata* was written in honor of Yoshinori's accession.[17]

Following the practice of their ancestors the Seiwa Genji, the Ashikaga clan regarded Hachiman as the *ujigami*, or "tutelary deity," of their lineage.[18] Thus, it is not surprising that the Ashikaga rulers made countless visits to Iwashimizu Hachiman Shrine, both to pay respects and to pray for continued protection. Yoshimitsu is on record as having visited the shrine twenty times and Yoshimochi thirty times.[19] But in light of the unique role played by Hachiman in select-

[15] Thomas Blenman Hare, *Zeami's Style: The Noh Plays of Zeami Motokiyo* (Stanford, 1986), 104.

[16] Omote op. cit., 286 (trans. mine).

[17] See Imaizumi Atsuo, ed., *Kinsei no taidō* in vol. 3 of *Kyoto no rekishi* (Tokyo: Gakugei Shorin, 1972), 169. See Omote and Katō, 286, 498 n. 167.

[18] See the following poem by the founder of the Ashikaga shogunate, Ashikaga Takauji, included in the *Shingoshūishū*:

More upright than he	身を祈る
who prays for himself	人よりも猶
is he who asks for the protection	をとこ山

ing Ashikaga Yoshinori as the next shogun following the death of his brother Yoshimochi—effectively legitimizing the reign of Yoshinori by means of divine favor in the context of a lottery drawing—it must be said that Yoshinori's regime had a special association with Hachiman.

In view of the special nature of Yoshinori's association with Hachiman and the context of shogunal investiture enframing the production and inaugural performance of *Yumi Yawata*, one might expect shogunal ideology to enter the play in some fashion, but scholars have traditionally insisted upon reading *Yumi Yawata* as pro-imperial and anti-shogunal in its rhetoric. Take, for example, the following *sashi shōdan*[20] sung by the *shite*, the god of Kawara disguised as an old man:

> May the emperor's reign [*kimi ga yo* 君が代] endure
> For a thousand years,
> For thousands of years,
> Till small pebbles become a large boulder
> Covered with moss.
> May it endure forever
> Like the color of the pine needles
> On Eternity Mountain.
> The azure sky is calm,
> The emperor secure [*kimi ansen ni* 君安全に],
> The people are kind-hearted,
> Passes have not been closed.

---

of his uprightness	すなほなるをぞ
at Man Mountain.	まもりとは聞く (no. 1507)

That a poem by the founder of the Ashikaga *bakufu*, praying at Otokoyama for protection, would be included in an imperial collection of *waka* suggests the importance of the Hachiman deity and shrines to the descendants of the Seiwa Genji.

[19] Itō Masayoshi, ed., *Yōkyokushū* in vol. 79 of *Shinchō Nihon koten shūsei* (Tokyo: Shinchōsha, 1988), 480; Imaizumi, op. cit., 167.

[20] Sung with minimal inflection in the higher register and without strong underlying rhythm, *sashi shōdan* are typically used to highlight important passages by rendering the text as accessible as possible. For further analysis of the *sashi* of *Ominameshi*, see the essay by Nishino Haruo included in this volume.

From the beginning, ours has been a land
Where the gods protect the emperor [*kimi wo mamori no shinkoku ni* 君を守りの神国に].
The vow of this god in particular
Illumines the night
Like the light of the moon.
The waters of Iwashimizu flow ceaselessly,
And as long as the stream runs on
Living beings are released.
How glorious is the god's compassion!
Truly this is an auspicious time.[21]

With an eye towards passages such as this (and others in which the reign of legendary Emperor Ōjin is glorified), Ross Bender writes: "Although the play was written in Muromachi times . . . its view of Hachiman denies the contemporary association of the god with the ruling military house. It rather dramatizes an earlier conception of the deity, portraying a Hachiman who is intimately linked with the imperial institution."[22] And Bender is not alone in this view: the philosopher Watsuji Tetsurō states even more strongly his view that "it must be said that it is quite evident that, within the setting of this play, the rule of the military houses, the shogun, and the daimyos are completely non-existent."[23] Such comments are typical in their underestimation of *Yumi Yawata*'s ideological equivocality. Neither Bender nor Watsuji considers the circumstances surrounding the play's production, such as the fact that it was expressly written, according to Zeami, "in honor of the inaugural celebration for the reign of the present shogun."[24] *Yumi Yawata* may not be the most dramatic play in

[21] Ross Bender, "Metamorphosis of a Deity: The Image of Hachiman in *Yumi Yawata*," *Monumenta Nipponica* 33:2 (1978): 171–2 (trans. altered). Japanese text from Sanari Kentarō, ed., *Yōkyoku taikan*, vol. 5 (Tokyo: Meiji Shoin, 1985), 3224–25.

[22] Bender, 169. Gerry Yokota-Murakami follows Bender's interpretation: see Yokota-Murakami, *The Formation of the Canon of Nō: The Literary Tradition of Divine Authority* (Osaka: Osaka University Press, 1997), 43.

[23] Watsuji Tetsurō, "Yōkyoku ni arawareta rinri shisō: Japanese Ethical Thought in the Noh Plays of the Muromachi Period," *Monumenta Nipponica* 24:4 (1969): 473. Also see Sanari, 3222.

[24] Omote and Katō, 286 (trans. mine).

the repertoire, but I would contend that it is more complex than many commentators have allowed.

The crux of the matter is how to translate and interpret the ideologically charged terms *kimi ga yo* 君が代 (or *miyo* 御代) and *kimi* 君, which are repeated throughout the play and translated above as "emperor's reign" and "emperor," respectively. There is no denying that this is the most common interpretation of these terms, but as Wakita Haruko has argued, the Muromachi usage of such designations was far from unambiguous. More specifically, Wakita suggests that the usage of *kimi* in *waki* noh was not limited to the emperor, but was also used to refer to the shogun.[25] Moreover, as Zeami's own usage in *Sarugaku dangi* of *godai* 御代 (an alternative reading of the same characters composing *miyo*) attests, a similar ambiguity applied to honorific designations referring to the reigns of both emperors and shogun.

Another argument put forward in defense of the pro-imperial interpretation of *Yumi Yawata* is that the play's reference to the *seki no to* 関の戸,[26] or "toll barrier gates," in the line "passes have not been closed," symbolizes "a time before military rule was established."[27]But the opening of the toll barrier gates does not in itself imply either imperial or shogunal rule so much as it suggests a country that is not at war. Since the authority to establish and administer toll barriers had been transferred from the emperor to the shogun around the turn of the fifteenth century,[28] such a trope could just as easily be construed as describing peace during the new shogun's reign. Indeed, when one takes into consideration the shogunal context of its production, as well as the undecidability of its most crucial ideological signifiers, it seems just as plausible to read *Yumi Yawata* as a celebration of shogunal rule and a prayer for continued peace as it

[25] Wakita Haruko, "Nōgaku to tennō shintō" in *Tennōsei: rekishi oken daijōsai*, ed. Irokawa Daikichi (Tokyo: Kawade Shobō Shinsha, 1990), 132.

[26] An alternative way of referring to *sekisho no kado* 関所の門.

[27] Bender, op. cit, 172 n. 19; also see Watsuji, op. cit., 471.

[28] Kenneth Alan Grossberg, *Japan's Renaissance: The Politics of the Muromachi Bakufu* (Cambridge, Mass., 1981), 94. Also see Kobayashi Yasuo, "Nanbokuchō-Muromachiki no kasho hakkyū ni tsuite—Muromachi bakufu shikiseishi no kisoteki kōsatsu" in vol. 1 of *Nagoya Daigaku Nihonshi ronshū*, ed. Nagoya Daigaku Bungakubu Kōkōshigaku Kenkyūshitsu (Tokyo: Yoshikawa Kōbunkan, 1975), 391-2.

does to read it as "a paean to imperial rule and to the peace that it has brought to the land."[29]

What *Yumi Yawata* stages is not merely a blurring of boundaries between the figure of the emperor and that of the shogun, but a performative appropriation of imperial prerogatives and symbolic capital on the stage of the inaugural celebration for the new shogun. Just as the northern branch of the Fujiwara clan had subjected imperial power to non-imperial purposes, so too, Ashikaga rulers, such as Yoshimitsu and Yoshinori, subjected imperial prerogatives and symbolic capital to shogunal purposes. This is not to reduce *Yumi Yawata* to a passive reflection or transparent representation of the historical context out of which it emerged, but rather to explore the complex interchange between the historicity of a noh performance text and the textuality of its history. Rather than simply mirroring the sociopolitical context in which it was produced, *Yumi Yawata* performatively contributed to the subjection of imperial symbolic capital aspired to by Yoshinori.[30] To ignore this constitutive reciprocity by reducing the performance text to a mere product of historical influence or the ideological reflection of economic infrastructure would be to efface the text's active, productive force in the theater of the Ashikaga shogunal imaginary.

Taking Ashikaga Yoshimitsu as precedent, the shogun became resubjectivized yet again under Yoshinori's regime in the figure of the *Nihon kokuō* 日本国王, or "king of Japan."[31] By officially legitimizing the shogun with this title, the Tally Trade Agreement with the Ming dynasty both usurped the emperor's control over foreign affairs and repositioned the shogun as monarch. As John Whitney Hall has remarked: "Whether or not Yoshimitsu intended to displace the

[29] Hare, op. cit., 104.

[30] This is not to say that such ideological expediency necessarily ensured long-term patronage for Zeami's troupe. Despite the success of *Yumi Yawata*, Zeami's troupe quickly fell out of Yoshinori's favor. A successful performance was obviously no guarantee of continued patronage.

[31] In sharp contrast, Yoshimochi rejected this title and discontinued trade with China. On the politics of *Nihon kokuō*, see Sasaki Gin'ya, *Muromachi bakufu* in vol. 13 of *Nihon no rekishi* (Tokyo: Shōgakkan, 1975), 51–53. Also see Grossberg, 34, 36, 49; and John W. Hall, "The Muromachi Bakufu," in vol. 3 of *The Cambridge History of Japan*, ed. Yamamura, Kozo (Cambridge, 1990), 192–3.

emperor, he and his successors as shogun did preside over the demise of the tradition of imperial rule as it had been up to that point."[32]

Hōjōe and the Subjection of the Hayato

The third and last Hachiman intertext I shall consider juxtaposes the woman's suicide in *Ominameshi* with the Hōjōe, or Life-Releasing Ritual, performed at both the Usa and the Iwashimizu Hachiman shrines. The first inscription of the Hōjōe appears in Part 1, where the *shite* and *waki* celebrate the auspicious syncretism associated with that ceremony of liberation:

> Even as the dust mingles with the divine light of Buddhas and Bodhisattvas,
> in the flow of the muddied inlet, fish float to the surface of the water—certainly, to liberate living beings such as these
> shows that the profound vow of Buddhas and Kami has become miraculously manifest.
> Such benevolence!
> Flourishing as I climb up luxuriant Man Mountain—how blessed!

> 和光の塵も濁り江、
> 河水に浮かむ鱗類は、
> げにも生けるを放つかと深き誓ひもあらたにて、
> 恵みぞ茂き男山、
> さかゆく道のありがたさよ。

Another inscription appears in the second part of the play in one of the very few passages actually sung by the *tsure* herself:

> The fragility of a woman's heart:
> it is because I left the capital yearning for one man alone
> that my resentful thoughts are even more profound
> as I hurl myself into the depths of the Life-Releasing River.

> 女心のはかなさは、

[32] See Hall, "The Muromachi Bakufu," 192.

都を独りあくがれ出でて、
なほも恨みの思ひ深き、
放生川に身を投ぐる。

For the wife of Yorikaze to commit suicide by throwing herself into the Hōjōgawa, the river into which one released life, is not only ironic, it may also have been subversive. Such an act of suicide would have polluted the Hōjōgawa's pure waters of liberation, suggesting a darker subtext haunting the Hōjōe ritual with connotations of subjection and death as opposed to emancipation and life. Moreover, as various *engi* 縁起 (foundation narratives) dealing with the genealogy of the Hōjōe attest, the ritual appeasement of victims of political subjection was central to its performative function.

According to accounts in *Hachiman Usagū Hōjōe engi* 八幡宇佐宮放生会縁起 and *Rokugō kaizan Nimmon daibosatsu hongi* 六郷開山仁聞大菩薩本紀,[33] the establishment of the Hōjōe derives from political incidents that occurred in southern Kyushu in the early eighth century. In the year 719 (Yōrō 養老 3),[34] the Hayato people of Ōsumi and Hyūga provinces launched an organized rebellion against the hegemony of the centralized Yamato government. Acts of rebellion by the Hayato had occurred previously, but 719 marked the first time that an all-out assault was waged with the intent of conquering Japan.

Fighting escalated in 720 when the governor of Ōsumi province was assassinated. In response to these events, the Yamato court issued an imperial petition requesting assistance from the Hachiman cult at Usa Hachiman Shrine. Hachiman responded with an oracle that ordered the subjugation of the Hayato and offered to lead the government's army in that endeavor. After two years of fighting, the Hayato rebels were finally suppressed.

[33] On *Hachiman Usagū Hōjōe engi*, see Jane Marie Law, "Violence, Ritual Reenactment, and Ideology: The *Hōjō-e* (Rite for Release of Sentient Beings) of the Usa Hachiman Shrine in Japan," *History of Religions* 33:4 (1994): 325–57. On *Rokugō kaizan Nimmon daibosatsu hongi*, see Allan G. Grapard, "Lotus in Mountain, Mountain in Lotus: *Rokugō Kaizan Nimmon Daibosatsu Hongi*," *Monumenta Nipponica* 41:1 (1986): 21–50. The present discussion of the ideological implications of the Hōjōe is largely indebted to these studies.

[34] Other accounts record the year as Yōrō 4 (720): see Edward Kamens, trans. *The Three Jewels: A Study and Translation of Minamoto Tamenori's Sanboe* (Ann Arbor, 1988), 345–8.

Although the *Rokugō kaizan Nimmon daibosatsu hongi* states that "following the subjugation of the Hayato rebels, peace and tranquillity were restored to the people and to the empire,"[35] other sources indicate that a plague broke out in the region, which was attributed to the malevolent spirits of fallen Hayato.[36] In order to appease the Hayato and provide ideological closure to the violence authorized by the Bodhisattva Hachiman, the following oracular command was issued in the year 724 (Jinki 神亀 1)[37] to establish the Hōjōe: "I, the god, as the retribution for killing many of the Hayato, decree that on separate years we will do a *Hōjō-e*."[38] Greatly complicating the performative force of that appeasement is a statement included in *Hachiman Usagū Hōjōe engi*, in which the subjugation of the Hayato is legitimized by means of Buddhist rhetorical sophistry:

> The rite began with the Great Bodhisattva Hachiman. Even though he kills, because he has an enlightened status and does good there is a lot of merit in his killing. The internal proof is that there is no hiding the bright light, and the rays cross each other. As a result of this rite at Usa, they began to perform the Hōjō-e in all the provinces.[39]

One notices that in the metaphorics of Hachiman's meritorious killing, which shines forth with the bright light of his divinity, the trope of the "*wakō no chiri*" 和光の塵, or dust which mingles with the divine light of Buddhas and Bodhisattvas, is translated into murder ideologically justified for religio-political purposes. Such a politically charged subtext for the Hōjōe casts into a radically different light the ritual release of birds and fish performed on the fifteenth day of the

[35] Grapard, op. cit., 43.

[36] Law, op. cit., 335.

[37] The earliest recorded performance of the Hōjōe at Usa Hachiman Shrine is 745 (Tenpyō 天平 17). At Iwashimizu Hachiman Shrine, the earliest record is for 939 (Tengyō 天慶 2), but it may have been performed as early as 863 (Jōgan 貞観 5).

[38] Law, op. cit., 345.

[39] Ibid. A similar ideological justification for religio-political violence is included in *Rokugō kaizan Nimmon daibosatsu hongi*: "Because I set my mind on governing the world from generation to generation by means of forced conversion and all-embracing compassion, I have taken many lives. In order to bring these spirits to salvation, a ceremony to return living beings to freedom shall be performed" (Grapard, op. cit., 45).

eighth month each year to celebrate Buddhist compassion for all sentient beings and honor the prohibition against taking life.

As Jane Marie Law has suggested in a provocative article on the ideological history of the Hōjōe:

> At the heart of this rite is a deep concern over the violence within the Hachiman cult and the need to make amends and appease the victims. It also demonstrates how a public rite and spectacle ultimately legitimates the violence of dominant authority, even when claiming to appease the victims of the original event itself.[40]

In sum, the ideological logic of the Hōjōe in its religio-political context of performance is twofold: the subjection of military enemies is both legitimized in the name of Hachiman and domesticated through the appeasement of Hachiman's victims. Even as living beings are saved in the ritual performance of the Hōjōe, such a liberation takes place on the basis of a previous subjection of living beings. In effect, the Hōjōe's ritual liberation appeases by means of substitution: metaphorically transforming the victims of military violence into the bodies of fish and birds that are then released into nearby rivers and fields.[41] In time, other victims of political subjection and military violence besides the Hayato—ranging from the victims of Empress Jingū's legendary subjugation of Korea to the defeated Mongol forces who invaded Japan in the late thirteenth century[42]—also came to be included among the appeased, but the Hayato remain the paramount political subtext.

[40] Law, op. cit., 327.

[41] Law, op. cit., 350: "A legend from the region of the Kohyō shrine adds another dimension to the story: at the time of the revolt, the Hayato from the two remaining castles fled into the sea rather than be captured. Each and every one of them drowned, the legend says. At about the same time, all along the coastline, there was a marked increase in snails. It was believed that these Hayato had become snails. Shortly after this, a plague broke out, and it was assumed these two problems were the curse (*tatari*) of the Hayato."

[42] Law, op. cit., 327.

Subjecting *Ominameshi*

Perhaps the most difficult question facing any micropolitical reading of *Ominameshi* is what the ideologically charged tropes of Iwashimizu Hachiman Shrine and its related intertexts have to do with the narrative of female suicide. All of the Hachiman intertexts considered—the genealogy of Iwashimizu Hachiman Shrine, the shogunal politics inscribing Otokoyama in *Yumi Yawata*, and the political subtexts of the Hōjōe—share a politics of subjection. I would contend that what *Ominameshi* offers through such juxtapositions is a performative analogue between the religio-politics of subjection and the gender politics of subjection.

The wife of Yorikaze, whose name is unknown to us, drowns herself because of her husband's infidelity. Wracked with guilt and grief, Yorikaze then takes his own life, hoping to join his wife in the next world, but instead is cast into the hell for adulterers. At first glance, it might seem as if the only one who is subjected in *Ominameshi* is Yorikaze. In the climactic scene of the play, sung in the heightened emotional style of the *noriji shōdan* ノリ地小段, the phallocratic implications of Otokoyama are disclosed in phantasmagoric detail as Yorikaze articulates through the mouthpiece of the chorus a nightmarish vision involving the violence of penetration:

Cursed devils of sexual infidelity	邪婬の悪鬼は、
incite me, then reproach me, torturing my body,	身を責めて、
cursed devils of sexual infidelity	邪婬の悪鬼は、
incite me, then reproach me, torturing my body,	身を責めて、
blind will power	その念力の、
impelled by desire along the path of peril,	道も嶮しき、
on top of Sword Mountain	剣の山の、
my beloved has appeared.	上に恋しき、
	人は見えたり、
How gratifying!	嬉しやとて、
But as I climb,	行き登れば、

double-edged swords penetrate my body,	剣は身を通し、
enormous rocks crush my bones.	磐石は骨を砕く、
	こはそもいかに、
How terrifying it all is!	恐ろしや、
Sword-branches	剣の枝の、
bend down under the weight of my sin.	撓むまで

According to the imaginary geography of the play, the stage of Otokoyama has now been transformed into its dark underside: Sword Mountain. As the poetics of Otokoyama is translated into the eroticized horrors of Sword Mountain, Yorikaze the philanderer experiences firsthand the pain of subjection. The fact that it is Yorikaze who is tortured on Sword Mountain rather than his self-destructive wife stands in sharp contrast to another play in the noh repertoire concerning female suicide: *Motomezuka.*

In *Motomezuka*, the young maiden from Unai, who commits suicide when faced with the competing claims of over-zealous suitors, suffers tortures similar to those of Yorikaze. For her indirect involvement in the deaths of her two suitors, she, too, suffers on Sword Mountain, in terms probably borrowed from Genshin's elaborate description in *Ōjōyōshū* of the numerous divisions and subdivisions of the Buddhist network of hells. That it is the man who is punished for the woman's suicide in *Ominameshi* rather than the other way around, as in *Motomezuka*, might strike some viewers and readers as a form of poetic justice. After all, compared to the philandering ways of a Genji, who pursues and abandons multiple lovers with only the occasional twinge of conscience, Yorikaze pays dearly for his sexual infidelity. But from another perspective, although Yorikaze is punished for precipitating the suicide of his beloved, the narrative of Yorikaze's suffering displaces the story of his wife, which all but disappears.

Much more than simply a play about a neglected wife who commits suicide and her adulterous husband who sees the error of his ways, the story of the *ominameshi* is displaced not by the other woman (as is the case in female-suicide plays such as *Mitsuyama*), but rather by her own husband. The fact that Yorikaze chose to commit suicide by drowning underscores the depth of his grief and the extent of his identification with his wife's suffering, and yet his suicide and subsequent torture in the hell for adulterers results in the upstaging of her story.

Just as the Hayato are not permitted to tell their own story, but function only as mute signifiers of political subjection and objects of appeasement in the performance of the Hōjōe, so too, the woman in *Ominameshi* is not allowed to tell her own story, since it has been displaced by the narrative constructed for her by her husband Yorikaze. In other words, the religio-political subjections implied by the Hachiman intertexts are paralleled by the narratival and psychic-corporeal subjection of Yorikaze's nameless wife. Even as Yorikaze, disguised as an old man in the first half, preached against plucking the *ominameshi*, against taking the life of any being, whether sentient or non-sentient, he has already taken the life out of the *ominameshi*'s story by appropriating her narratival voice for himself and subordinating her subjectivity to his own. The woman behind the *ominameshi* is quite literally reduced to a mere botanical trope.

Translating the plight of Yorikaze's wife into the botanical *ominameshi* is clearly a reinscription of the Buddhist doctrine of *sōmoku jōbutsu* 草木成仏 and the debate over whether or not non-sentient beings, such as plants and trees, are capable of attaining or have already attained Buddhahood.[43] But it is also symptomatic of Buddhist patriarchal discourse, which objectifies the female body—in this case, literally turning the female body into a botanical "thing," an *ominameshi*—as a rhetorical strategy in the service of Buddhist soteriology—in this case, the salvation of the *ominameshi*'s husband Yorikaze. At the end of the play, the gender politics of subjection come to the fore as the *ominameshi* is translated into yet another sort of flower—a lotus flower—the vehicle by which Yorikaze hopes to gain entrance into Pure Land paradise:

> *Ominameshi*,
> upon your dewy calyx tied to the lotus flower pedestal,
> I beseech you: let me float up to Pure Land paradise,
> send my sins to the surface and deliver me from them!

[43] For an excellent discussion of the *sōmoku jōbutsu* debate, see William R. LaFleur, "Saigyō and the Buddhist Value of Nature," *History of Religions* 13:2 (1973): 93–126.

女郎花、
露の台や花の縁に、
浮かめて賜び給へ、
罪を浮かめて賜び給へ。

It is no accident that the alternate title for the play is *Yorikaze*,[44] since it is the proper name of Yorikaze that provides the measure of subjectivity, just as Otokoyama provides the gender-marked, religio-political space in which both the woman's subjection and the man's subjectivity emerge. That it is the man's story as much as (if not more than) the woman's that is being told here is also suggested by the traditional classification of the play as a fourth-category "male attachment piece" (*shūshin otokomono* 執心男物).

Told from the perspective of the man whose infidelity precipitated the woman's tragic end, the staging of female suicide on Otokoyama is upstaged by the man's own suicide, thus making the subject of *Ominameshi* that of subjection itself. Although female suicide sometimes functioned in the medieval cultural imaginary as an act of resistance against the unchecked circulation of masculine desire and the patriarchal exchange of female bodies, in *Ominameshi* such an act of resistance is co-opted by the very fact that it is Yorikaze who tells the story of his wife's suicide, it is Yorikaze whose narrative of his wife's suicide ends up displacing her own. In the end, the woman's suicide becomes simply another emotionally charged moment in the karmic history of the man. This may very well be an allusion to the medieval commonplace that "worldly desires and enlightenment are one and the same" (*bonnō soku bodai* 煩悩即菩提), but to leave it at that would be to underestimate the politics of subjection infusing Yorikaze's exploitation of the female body in the service of his own enlightenment. That Hachiman discourse played a constitutive role in the theatrical framing of such exploitation sheds new light on the performativity of power and desire in the Muromachi period.

[44] Maruoka Katsura, *Koken yōkyoku kaidai*, ed. Nishino Haruo (Tokyo: Kokon Yōkyoku Kankōkai, 1984), 262.

『女郎花』と従属化の政治

スティーブン・ブラウン

女性の自殺を扱った数々の謡曲のなかでも『女郎花』の精読を基に、テキストが巧妙に含蓄しつつも隠蔽する三つの異なる従属化のプロセスを相互に関連づけながら分析する試みである。この論文は、シテの語りが孕む男性中心的なジェンダーの表象を分析する理論的試みであるとともに、テキストの意味内容を「女性の従属化」にのみ還元することなく、文化的意味の生産がつねに歴史的、宗教的政治的権力関係や階級的民族的な社会的実践の内部でのみ有効、可能である点を強調する。特に、石清水八幡宮の制度的起源をめぐる政治的宗教的な地勢学にも焦点を当てながら、『女郎花』の上演が生産するさまざまな意味と視点を、歴史的に遍在した個々の従属化との関係のなかで位置付け、再解釈するものである。つまり、こうした解釈作業が理論的前提として要求するのは、『女郎花』を取巻く石清水八幡宮がいかに詩的に審美化されようとも、その起源、変遷において刻まれた宗教的文化と暴力の位相は、八幡のイデオロギー的系譜の探究に欠かせないという事実である。ゆえに、石清水八幡宮の制度的歴史についてのテクスト群に関し、その政治性に注目した再読を促す。

八幡の背後にあるサブテクストには常に従属化のための宗教的または政治的実践が存在する。そして『女郎花』において男性であるシテがその妻の自殺を語りテクスト化する時、同様の従属化の実践が再演される。こうして女性の自殺をめぐる語りが、石清水八幡宮と関連づけられた、イデオロギー的な比喩の数々によって記されているいっぽう、そうした比喩が本来の語りの視点をずらす働きもしている。当論文では、自殺の語りと八幡のテクストを併置することによって、『女郎花』という謡曲は、宗教政治的な従属関係と自殺をめぐる語りが劇的に前景化した階層的なジェンダー関係が類似している事実を浮かび上がらせる。

女郎花説話の成立と能楽女郎花

脇　田　晴　子

は じ め に

本論は能楽「女郎花」を歴史的な過程における一つの作品と位置づけて、その歴史的な背景を問うことを目的とする。男山という地名の成立、それに照応する女郎花説話の成立が、二つの古墳の存在に負っているのではないかと言うことを、能楽にもある「求塚」を傍証として考えてみた。また、オミナの漢字を女郎としたこと、その女郎の意味の変遷などから、この作品が男女の性愛をどのように扱っているか、中世女性史において、また、女性史の長い歴史的な過程の中で、どのような位置を占めるかについて考えていきたい。

能楽研究においては、かかる視点からの考察は、今までには行われていないので、意義のあるのではないかと考えている。

1.　能楽「女郎花」と石清水八幡宮

この作品は、石清水八幡宮の所在地である男山を題材として、男山の対句となっている女郎花とに、題材を取っている。それは紀貫之の『古今和歌集』仮名序の「男山の昔を思ひ出で女郎花の一時をくねるにも、歌をいひてぞ慰めける」[1]を基調として、僧正遍昭の和歌[2]などをあしらって歌問答を行い、「男山と女郎花」[2]から連想される男女の関係をそのまま説話化したような心中の物語を能楽化したものである。おそらく能楽「女郎花」のすじに取り入れられている説話、すなわち男を不実であると誤解して、それを怨んだ女の自殺、

[1]『古今和歌集』日本古典文学大系、岩波書店、1958年、97~8頁
[2]同上、1016号、314頁

男の後追い心中という話は、貫之が『古今和歌集』仮名序に書いた時には人口に膾炙していたことと思われる。

能楽「女郎花」は、その話を前提として、その亡霊が出現するという筋立てである。しかし、その場所は、石清水八幡宮の鎮座している聖地である。したがって曲中には、石清水八幡宮の参拝、名所としての案内も入っており、当然、曲に石清水の由緒を説く目的も含まれている。石清水八幡宮は九州宇佐八幡宮から勧請した社であるので、ワキも九州松浦から出た僧にしている。いわば、男女の心中説話を題材にしつつ、石清水八幡宮に場を取ることによって、名所案内的な要素を十分に加えたものと見ることができよう。小野頼風という名を与えられている主人公の男も、その亡霊の装束は、狩衣または水干に白大口袴で神官のような装束である。いわば女郎花説話は石清水八幡宮と二重写しになっているようである。だから一見、心中物語は石清水八幡宮の鎮座以後のことであるような印象を受ける。

しかしながら、この能の前場のシテの尉が八幡宮を案内し、霊地のありがたさを説くことと、後場の地獄の責め苦とは、何も連関がなく結びついていない。それは霊験あらたかな神仏としての八幡神との矛盾を来すものであった。その矛盾は見事に能楽の中に解決が付けられている。すなわち、時は8月15日の石清水八幡宮の祭礼の日で、神の乗った神輿が御旅所に遷幸して、山上は留守中であるという設定にしてあることに注目すべきである[3]。すなわち、国家の尊崇を受けている正統な神の留守中に、この世に思いを残しつつ自殺した男女の亡霊という地獄に沈んでいる魑魅魍魎のような存在が現れて、往時を話し再現するという設定である。作者の用意周到さはなかなかのものというべきであろう。

そして亡霊の心中事件というのは、謡曲の詞章でいえば、「邪淫の悪鬼は身を責めて」という詞に表現されるように、刀葉林地獄の有り様を活写するという形になっている。男女の後追い心中は建前

[3] 女郎花研究会中、男山からお旅所を遙拝することに疑問を呈した私に対して、竹本幹夫氏は祭礼の日で神輿がお旅所に行って、神は男山に鎮座していないという設定に気づかれた。研究会の一つの成果として感謝したい。

ではあくまで邪淫であって、仏教に習合して放生会を行う清浄なる八幡神とは違うのである[4]。八幡神がお旅所への神幸の留守中に現われてくるように、建前としては否定さるべきものである。その前提に立ちつつ、心底では賛美して、男女の恋や死してのちの地獄の責め苦を謡いあげるという複雑な構成を持った能楽といえよう。

2. 古墳景観の投影による女郎花説話の成立

ところで、石清水が男山と、なぜ呼ばれたのであろうか。その起源は明らかではない。男山と女郎花が対になって語られる説話の形成は、『古今和歌集』序以前と見ることができるが、『古今和歌集』ができたのは、905年（延喜5）である。すでに796年（延暦15）に牡山（おとこやま）に蜂（のろし）を設けることが見え、行教筆と伝える「護国寺略記」には860年（貞観2）僧行教が八幡宮を男山に勸請したときに「石清水男山の峰」に神霊を移したことが見える[5]。この地名の男山と女郎花説話の男山が同一であるかどうかが問題であるが、古今集序では男山と女郎花はすでに対になって語られている。『万葉集』では、女郎花説話はうたわれていない。摂津（現神戸市）の処女塚古墳の後追い心中説話は後述するように歌われているのに対して、女郎花は花としてのみ作歌の対象となっているので、女郎花説話の成立は、平安時代初期と考えられる。『古今和歌集聞書　三流抄』[6]には、小野頼風の女郎花説話を載せて、平城天皇の時としている。大体のところとして時代は合っている。貞観の八幡宮鎮座直前か、それによって脚光を浴びた結果として、かかる説話も有名になったのかもしれない。

通常、男山というのは、常陸の筑波山のように二つの山が並んでいる場合に、高い山を男山、優しい形容の山を女山、あるいは女神

4 動物などを供犠される神道の神と、放生会を行われる神との違いは脇田晴子「中世被差別民の生活と社会」『部落の歴史と解放運動　前近代編』部落問題研究所、1985年、74～79頁

5『京都府の地名』日本歴史地名大系26、平凡社、1981年、156頁

6『中世古今集注釈書解題』赤尾照文堂、1981年

山と言う場合が多い。したがって、この男山の場合も、対になる女山があったはずであるが、それがどの山であるかは現在では明らかではない。

さて、本題の男山女郎花説話であるが、ここには東車塚（八幡市八幡町大字志水字女郎花塚）、と150メートル程北西の西車塚（八幡市八幡大芝）があった[7]。この二つの古墳は、南北に通る町道の両側にある[8]。私は平安初期ごろに、この古墳が男塚・女塚といわれ、それを人々が紡いでいった物語が、やがて男山にある女郎花説話となったものだと思う。

さて、東車塚は、北北西に面する前方後円墳で、後円部の西方に小円墳[9]を伴っている。この小円墳が女郎花塚といわれているものである。遺物などから、4世紀末から5世紀初頭とされている。西車塚古墳も4世紀末から5世紀初頭とされている。

この両車塚が男塚・女塚とよばれ、さらに陪塚が女郎花塚と呼ばれるに至ったと云うのは推測に過ぎないが、説話と何の関係もない古墳が、そのあり方から悲恋物語に発展してゆく例は、摂津国兎原郡（現神戸市）の処女塚と二つの求女塚に見いだされる。この説話は二人の男に恋され、二人の男を通わせていた一人の乙女が、板挟みになって海に身を投げて死に、二人の男も身を投げて死ぬというもので、その三人を葬ったのが、この三つの古墳であるという。

この説話は『万葉集』に収載された田邉福麿（タナベノフクマロ）の歌「葦屋處女（アシヤノオトメ　）の墓を過ぎる時に作る歌一首」高橋連蟲麿（タカハシノムラジムシマロ）の「菟原處女（ウバラノオトメ）の墓を見る歌一首」の一連の歌に見ることができる[10]。二人が同じ説話について歌を作っているのからみて、この説話は二人がこの里を通ったときには、すでに出来ていたことがわかる。古墳

[7]「龍谷大学文学部考古学資料室研究報告」1972年

[8]高橋美久二氏、竹中由里代氏の御教示に負うところが多い。記して感謝する。

[9] 小円墳・女郎花塚。説話や謡曲ができてのちの名所であり、頼風塚という塔を「山城名勝志」は女塚と見ている。（前略『京都府の地名』）164、165頁の写真を参照。

[10]『万葉集』巻9の1801、2、3号。1809、10、11号。日本古典文学大系，2の412~421頁、岩波書店、1979年

[11]「大和物語」146、『竹取物語　伊勢物語　大和物語』日本古典文学大系、岩波書店、1957年、310~316頁

築造から四百年を経た万葉の時代には、三つの古墳が並ぶ形状から、このような物語が里人たちによって紡がれていたのである。

この話はさらに発展して、平安中期の『大和物語』[11]ではそこに旅寝した旅人の夢に、二人の男が死後も争っていて、一人の男が旅人の太刀を借してくれといって、しばらくすると仇を殺したという夢を見るが、目覚めると夢に貸した太刀に血がついていたというのである。妄執の罪で、死後も修羅道を続けているという話である。

ところが、観阿弥作の能楽「求塚」[12]になると、逆に処女が地獄に堕ちる事になってしまう。二人の男に殺生戒を冒させたからか、妄執の故か、または二人の男を通わせたから多淫ということになるのか、その理由は書かれていない。地獄に堕ちて苦しむのは処女自身ということになる。時代によって話は変化するが、罪の主体が、男から女に変化し、双方の罪であっても、一方的に女の罪が拡大視されるところに中世の時代相がある。

ところでこの三基の古墳は、それぞれ時代が異なり、決して同時期のものではない。真ん中の処女塚は中心部を発掘していないので時期はわからないが、古い形状を持っていて、出雲との関係を示す土器を出土しているものだということである。西求塚は4世紀前半期の前方後方墳、東求塚は他の二つより新しく、4世紀後半期と考えられており、前方・後円部にそれぞれ埋葬施設がある可能性があるとのことである[13]。古墳は必ずしも一人一つの墳墓ではない。また、三人の若者が死んだからといって巨大な古墳を築くものではない。古墳築造より四百年近く経過した万葉時代ごろまでに作られた説話なのである。

したがって女郎花説話も、同じように両車塚古墳に基づいて作られた説話が、その前提としてあったのであろうと思われる。また、処女塚説話の高橋連蟲麿の反歌には、

墓の上の木の枝靡けり聞きし如、血沼壮士にし寄りにけらしも

とあり、処女の墓の上の木が好きだった男の方に靡いているという

[12] 能楽「求塚」『謡曲集』上、日本古典文学大系、岩波書店、1957年、66~74頁
[13] 神戸市立博物館、問屋真一氏の御教示による。

歌で、墓より生長した植物が魂の有り様を示していると云うのも、女郎花と同じ傾向である。

さらにその説話が能楽に作られるに及んで、人口に膾炙して、また小円墳が女郎花塚となるという展開を見せたものであろう。謡曲名所というものは、しばしば作られるものなのである。

さらに能楽「女郎花」の作者は、「求塚」を意識して作っている。「求塚」の後シテの出のサシのセリフ

シテ「おう曠野人稀なり、我が古墳ならでまた何ものぞ、屍を争ふ猛獣ハ、去ってまた来る」

が、「女郎花」ではシテとツレの台詞にわかれてツレの台詞が少し変わる。

シテ「おう曠野人稀なり、我が古墳ならでまた何ものぞ」
ツレ「屍を争ふ猛獣ハ禁ずる能はず

となっていて、「求塚」を流用したことは明らかである。

また、その構成は、「求塚」が前場は若い菜摘の女たちによる早春の叙景の謡ですがすがしさをだし、一転して後場で女の地獄の苦患を示すのに対し、「女郎花」は前場は尉をだし、後場では夫婦で男（後ジテ）は神主の装束で、趣向を変えようとしている。しかし、前がその場の風景と死者の話であり、後場が地獄のありさまという点は同じである。前者を意識して、後者が作られたのは明らかである。しかし、男の地獄を狙ったが、男の地獄は武人の修羅物としてはたくさんあるので、異色の公家風の神主の刀葉林地獄の様を描いたところにも特色がある。以上によって、能楽「女郎花」は能楽「求塚」を踏まえて、その異色化を狙ったものといえるであろう。

ところで「女郎花」の主人公たちは、古墳の霊であり、自殺した男女として、邪淫の悪鬼が身を責める地獄に堕ちた霊であった。それは神仏習合した正統な神としての八幡神と矛盾をきたすが、祭礼の日で、神はお旅所に旅行して、山上は留守であるという巧みな設定にしてあることは既にのべた。「女郎花」の男女は「神道集」[14]な

[14] 近藤喜博編『神道集東洋文庫本』角川書店、1959年

どの当時の説話の中では、いわば御霊神（= 荒人神）[15]とも云うべき存在であった。当時は石清水八幡宮のような朝廷・幕府の国家権力の尊崇厚い宮寺とは違って、一般庶民の信仰する神は御霊神的な神が多く、諏訪大社のような名神でも、甲賀三郎説話[16]のような説話が出来ていたから、「女郎花」の作能者は、石清水八幡宮の聖地としての名所と、民間信仰的な御霊神との双方を狙ったということができよう。

3. 「女郎」「郎女」「女郎花」の呼称の変遷—美人イメージ・性愛観の変化

本章においては少し目を転じて、「女郎花」のオミナについての呼称の意味するところの変遷から、女性のイメージ、さらには、性愛観の変遷について述べたい。

古代において「女郎」「郎女」はともに、女盛り・働き盛りの壮年女性の呼称であり、古風な呼称としてのイラツメに対して、『万葉集』編纂の頃には、ヲミナと呼ばれていたという。それは結婚適齢期の女性に郎子・嬢子・処女などを宛てて、ヲトメと読むのに対して、年齢階梯的な呼称で、氏の名 + 郎女・女郎 = 宿禰以上の貴族的女性人名表記であり、『万葉集』編者の大伴家持が意図的に採用した漢字表記だといわれている[17]。この「女郎」という字は、中国では「女子にして男子の才ある者」の謂であるという。ところで花の女郎花は、『万葉集』では「乎美奈敞之」である。

ところが、花のヲミナエシに「女郎花」を宛てるのは、おそくと

[15] 脇田晴子「「家」の成立と中世神話—神道集・能楽・縁起絵巻を中心に」脇田晴子・S.ハンレー編『ジェンダーの日本史』東京大学出版会、1994年、87–118頁。Wakita Haruko, “The Formation of the *Ie* and Medieval Myth: The *Shintōshū*, Nō Theater, and Picture Scrolls of Temple Origins,” Micah Auerback, trans. in vol. 1 of *Gender and Japanese History*, ed. Wakita Haruko, et al. (Osaka: Osaka University Press, 1999), 53–85.

[16] 前掲『神道集東洋文庫本』「諏訪縁起事」

[17] 関口裕子『処女墓伝説歌考・複数の夫をもった美女の悲劇』吉川弘文館、1996年

も9世紀末(898)の宇多天皇・皇后温子主催の「亭子院女郎花合」[18]が古く、10世紀には定着する。恐らくは女郎 = オミナの呼称から、「女郎花」があてられたのであろう。ちなみに『倭名類聚抄』では「女倍之」= ヲミナベシである。

ただし中国での「女郎花」は木蓮・こぶしの花であり、早春に凛と咲くイメージがある。それとは違って、日本では、「むせ返る粟のごとし」といわれ、「なまめきたてる女郎花」という色っぽい女のイメージになってしまう。「女郎花」は、「能因歌枕」[19]にも、「をみなへし、女にたとへてよむべし」とあって、平安時代、女性、女性の容姿等にたとえて詠んだ歌が多い。いわば「女郎花」は記号論的にいえば「女」であり、美しい女の記号であった。

『万葉集』では、花そのものの美しさが詠まれることが多い「ヲミナヘシ」が、だんだん、時代が下がるとともに、手折られる女のイメージになってくる。例えば『万葉集』[20]では、大目秦忌寸八千島の

ひぐらしの鳴きぬる時は女郎花咲きたる野辺を行きつつ見べし

や大伴家持の[21]の

をみなへし秋萩凌ぎさを鹿の露分け鳴かむ高圓の野ぞ

のごとくである。

しかし、平安時代の源順の漢詩[22]では、

花の色は蒸せる粟のごとし、俗呼ばって女郎となす、名を聞いて戯れに偕老を契らんと欲すれば、恐るらくは衰老の首の霜に似たるを悪まんことを

[18] 古典文庫「歌合巻上」・平安朝歌合大成一
[19] 「能因歌枕」『日本歌学大系』1、文明堂、1940年
[20] 前掲『万葉集』巻第17、3951号歌、日本古典文学大系、岩波書店
[21] 前掲『万葉集』巻第20、4297号歌、同上
[22] 源順「女郎花」『和漢朗詠集・梁塵秘抄』同上、118頁

とすでに、契りを結びたい美しい女のイメージとなっているが、「戯れに偕老を契らん」というのは、高貴な女性に例えているのではない。

これが『古今和歌集』では、能楽「女郎花」にも引かれている和歌を引用すれば、僧正遍昭の[23]

名に愛でて折れるばかりぞ女郎花、われ落ちにきと人に語るな

は、落馬とかけて、堕落をいい、出家の身で邪淫戒を犯すことに掛けている。また、布留今道の[24]

女郎花憂しと見つつぞ行き過ぐる、男山にし立てりと思へば

は、すでに主人が居る手折られた花を横目に見てゆくという意を、男山と女郎花に掛けている。

これらの平安時代初期の漢詩・和歌を踏まえて、能楽「女郎花」では、さらに現実的に妾・愛人の感じになっていく。現行の間狂言[25]は、いつごろできたかわからないが、江戸時代ではあろうが、訴訟で上京した頼風の止まった旅宿の「酌取の女性」で「なまめいた女」ということになる。そしてたづねてきた女を「内より」あらけなく答えて追い出したのは、はっきりいわないが、正妻ということを暗示させるようになっている。

江戸時代には、「女郎」は遊女のことをいうから、旅宿の「酌取の女性」というのは、「飯盛女」[26]の類だということになる。こういう時代になると、前掲の遍昭の歌も、狂歌の主題となっていく。『狂歌集』[27]では、

[23]『古今和歌集』226号、日本古典文学大系、岩波書店、1958年、145頁
[24]同上227号、146頁
[25]野々村戒三、安藤常次郎、編『狂言集成』能楽書林、1974年、771頁
[26]飯を給仕するという名目で売春をする女
[27]「蜀山百首」39号、『川柳　狂歌集』461頁、日本古典文学大系、岩波書店1958年

女郎花口もさが野にたった今、僧正さんが落ちなんした

嵯峨野と口さがないとを掛けて、落ちなんしたという廓言葉で表現して、女郎花で女郎（= 遊女）を表現している。「われ落ちにきと口どめも心もとなければ」という前書きがある。古代では豪族の女性を示した女郎という言葉は、遊女のことになっていく。

以上のような女郎 = オミナから女郎花、さらに女郎 = 遊女への変化は、男性に賞翫され、手折られる女、主有る女、堕落の対象としての女のイメージを示しているものである。しかし、この女郎という言葉の系譜は、必ずしも女性の地位の下降と同一過程と見ることはできない。それは短絡的である。遊女の地位の低下と家妻の地位の安定は、ある一定条件のもとでは、反比例するからである。以下に能楽「女郎花」にそって、その点を辿り、結びに代えたい。

結びに代えて

能楽「女郎花」では、男と愛人の話に、言外に家妻が絡んでいて、一夫一妻一妾的な構成を取っている。しかし一方で、女の自殺に対する男の後追い心中であり、その点では、『万葉集』はじめ古代説話によくあり、能楽「求塚」の処女塚説話と軌を一にする。ただし処女塚説話が複数の夫を通わせた、いわば多夫一妻的な女の悲劇であるところと、女郎花説話が一夫多妻的な点が違う。その意味で、古代の説話的な世界を伏線にして中世的な性格を持つものと考えられる。

平安時代初期の女郎花説話成立の時期では、別居婚である妻訪婚、同居婚である婿取婚が多く、何れにしても母所婚であった。別居婚である妻訪婚では正妻が複数存在する一夫多妻婚も多く、妻の地位は確定せず、婚姻関係は不安定であった。女郎花説話の都の女に対して、八幡にも女がいたとしても、どちらが正妻かはわからない。また、少し出会いの日数があくと、捨てられたと誤解する背景があった。

中世に入って、通常「嫁入婚」[28]といわれている夫妻の同居婚が各階層に成立すると、正妻は一人となり、妾が居たとしても、建前としての一夫一妻制は確立して、夫妻は「家」という同一組織体の経営者となるから、一応婚姻関係は安定する。そのなかで、妻妾の区別が明確化して、妻の地位が上がるにつれて、妾の位置は下がる。娼婦の地位も平安時代ごろから見て、だんだん差別視が強くなっていく。中世社会というのは、もちろん男女差はあるが、身分差が強く、同等身分のなかで、男女差が顕現化する社会であった[29]。

江戸時代に入ると、その「家」を基調としつつ、そのなかでの家父長制が強化されてくるから、そこでの女は、「家」内部の統括者であり、後継者の産育の責任者である正妻は、遵風美俗の権化であり、「家」外部の娼婦・愛人は性愛の対象であって、そのそれぞれの役割は男性によって分裂されてゆく。歌舞伎・文楽人形浄瑠璃などの心中物のパターンは、家職をとりしきり「家」の後継者を育てる妻と、心中の相手である愛人との対比である。その根は平安時代から、中世を通じて胚胎していたとはいえ、近世江戸時代にいたって強化されてきたものである。それは「家」の外部で進行していった男性中心の社会によって「家」の相対的な比重の低下によるものといえよう。

能楽「女郎花」にかえっていえば、女郎花の花のイメージは、家妻と「家」外部の愛人・娼婦に分裂する女の、後者のイメージを代表してきたものである。「女心のはかなさは」と謡われるが、儚くなよなよとして、純情、風に靡くという、男性の性愛のみの対象としての可憐な女のイメージにぴったりである。それは後の時代における男性から期待される女性像としてのさきがけたりうるものであった。

[28] 嫁取婚といっても江戸時代とは異なり、父系二世代は同居しないので、嫁姑関係が深刻ではない。夫婦と所生の子供のみ同居するから、嫁取婚と表現するのは適当ではない。

[29] 脇田晴子『日本中世女性史の研究・性別役割分担と母性・家政・性愛』東京大学出版会 1992 年、同『中世に生きる女たち』岩波新書、1995 年
Wakita Haruko, "The Medieval Household and Gender Roles within the Imperial Family, Nobility, Merchants,and Commoners," Gary P. Leupp, trans. in *Women and Class in Japanese History*, ed. Hitomi Tonomura, et al. (Ann Arbor, 1999), 81–97.

それにしても、「女郎」という言葉が、豪族クラスの女の身分呼称としての漢字表記として採用されたものが、なぜ江戸時代には娼婦の呼称となるのか、中国の「女郎花」が木蓮、こぶしの花を指すのに、なぜ日本ではオミナエシのイメージになるのであろうか。後日の課題としたい。

The Foundations of the *Ominameshi* Legend and the Noh *Ominameshi*

Wakita Haruko

This essay examines the historical background within which the play *Ominameshi* developed as a work from three points of view. First, the noh takes place at Otokoyama, the location of the Iwashimizu Hachiman Shrine, a site worshipped by warrior families and the bakufu in its capacity as representing the god of warfare. However, when the spirits of the deceased lovers appear in the *nochiba* and describe the ordeals of hell, the gratitude they express towards the shrine seems at odds with their description of the Hell of Sword-Leafed Trees, where, according to Buddhist thought, adulterous spirits suffer. And yet, since the spirits return to Otokoyama during the festival when the shrine god is transported to a separate location, the play may be interpreted as an attempt to accommodate both the nationally legitimized shrine god and the local spirits worshipped according to popular practices.

Second, the *Ominameshi* myth of a woman and a man who follows her into death dates back to the early Heian period and is based on a tale related to two pre-existing tombs. Supporting evidence is found in the Motomezuka myth, which appears as early as the *Man'yōshū*, and arises from the existence of three tombs, the basis of the story of the noh *Motomezuka*.

Third, in the *Man'yōshū*, the word *omina* (女郎), refers to women of powerful local clans. Over time it was associated with a woman delicate, coquettish and easily bent and plucked by a man. In the noh, this aspect is presented in opposition to that of Otokoyama, or Man Mountain. By the Edo period, the same Chinese characters (女郎) came to refer to lower-ranking courtesans (*jorō*). These developments seem to reflect an increasingly downward shift in women's status, but the case is not so simple, as this essay explains. The noh *Ominameshi* supplies rich material for considering the historical background to the changes in women's status.

Vegetation from Hell: Blossoms, Sex, Leaves, and Blades in *Ominameshi*

William R. LaFleur

Intertwined Moral Themes

There are, I wish to show, good reasons for taking exception to what seems a somewhat commonly held view of *Ominameshi* as being a noh play of fairly low value.[1] In order to give voice to a position with which I will here disagree, a beginning can be made by citing something in a "general comment" (*gaihyō*) introducing a modern edition of the text of this noh play but also making some comparisons that cast *Ominameshi* in an unfavorable light.

"This play, like *Kayoi Komachi, Teika, Funabashi*, and others, is one that depicts the obsessions that come from sexual infidelity between a man and woman, but this matter surfaces only briefly and in the very final lines of the play (*kiri*), so that we must say that, within the noh repertoire, *Ominameshi* expresses a twinge of conscience that is only very slight."[2]

Through this kind of comment we are led to expect, I surmise, that the play is somewhat less than a rousing success.

The assumption in this seems to be that *Ominameshi*'s theme can be stated simply as "obsessions due to sexual infidelity" and that, in addition, the theme does not really surface until the play's final lines. We need to ask: Is there little more than thematic and textual aimlessness up to that point? In the present essay I wish to suggest a reading which takes the moral and religious context of the play as considerably more sophisticated, unified, and interesting than comes forth in

[1] An example of this "low" opinion in English-language criticism can be found in Royall Tyler, "There is No Such Thing as Nō" in *Nichibunken Japan Review* (1998): 255–7.

[2] Sanari Kentarō, ed., *Yōkyoku taikan*, vol. 5 (Tokyo: Meiji Shoin, 1964), 3488.

this critic's reduction of its theme to "sexual infidelity" (*jain* 邪淫). I will attempt a reading which takes the play's final lines, rather than being the *first* disclosure of this theme, as the point at which a number of related themes, introduced far earlier in the play, are rather skillfully brought together. The claim here will be that this play needs to be interpreted using what can be known about medieval discussions in Japan about the "buddhahood of plants" and the moral implications—for both good and ill—that could be drawn, at least artistically, from this intellectual milieu.

Indications that sexual interactions and complications will be important in this play come early—in fact, when the traveling priest, the *waki*, arrives at Iwashimizu Hachiman Shrine to find that the condition of the yellow *ominameshi* (core meaning: *female* flower) is a "riot of color." In this phrase the term *sakimidarete* suggests not only blossoms in profusion but also, because the locution *midareru* connotes sexual license, a kind of *promiscuous* blooming.[3]

The message that this play is going to be about the possibilities of an erotic interaction between the sexes is reinforced when the priest goes across the fields to the foot of Otokoyama (core meaning: *male* mountain). This presents him as making his way between a female flower and a male mountain. And that the latter is understood to be in something of an "aroused" state is suggested when it is described as being covered with "flowering grasses" and "dews that are garlanded in color"—since the word for "color" (*iro* 色) here too performs its customary role of connoting eros.

The dynamic of this play derives from its capacity to work with things that are known about complexity, ambivalence, and the potential for physical aggressiveness and harm in the sexual interaction between males and females. Yet the genius of the presentation is communicated indirectly—that is, by setting up another context for discussing attraction leading to harm, one designed to parallel the first one in many details. This secondary but all-important parallel construct centers on the problem of how the interaction between humans and the botanical world can also involve attraction that progresses to physical violence. But in *Ominameshi*—and this is part of what makes the play so interesting—the harm envisioned is not only that done to

[3] Translation based on Sanari, op. cit., 3486.

plants by humans but also the reverse, namely humans being hurt by flowering plants. Passion can bring results that are not benign. Even vegetative forms can behave as if they came from hell.

The parallel construct arrives in the play but without being explicitly announced as such. It surfaces already when the *shite*, a ghost, comes on to the scene. Right off a question is posed concerning the *ominameshi* flower—whether or not it may be plucked. Here lies the motif of attraction leading to physical violation, temptation moving on to a "taking" by force.

Acts are not as simple and innocent as they may seem. Is the removal of a flower from its stem not the doing of some form of violence to life-form? To something that is sentient and, as such, has a capacity for feeling? By raising the question about the morality of plucking flowers, *Ominameshi* taps into what in Japanese history had been a long trajectory of debate about the status, both ontological and ethical, of vegetative life. The argument for doing so with impunity or without the pangs of conscience is put forward by way of two claims, both of which are, in the context of classical debates in Japan, problematic. The first comes through a reference to the flower as being, after all, insentient (*nasake nashi*) and the second is phrased as an insistence that a *single* flower will, in fact, hardly be missed when there exists such a vast multitude of blossoms. The "pro" plucking claim is made, in other words, first, by maintaining that a rigid, *qualitative* difference between humans and plants places such an act outside the realm of moral concerns and, second, that the obvious quantity of available items removes any need for real concern about the removal of only a single one of them.

Viewed somewhat superficially, a reference to a putative "insentience" in a plant or any part thereof would seem to draw the verbal *action* of the play away from its expressed concern with the relationship between the dead Yorikaze and his wife. In fact, however, it may be that this is a clever, perhaps even brilliant, circumlocution—one that will pay off much later in the play. That is, the author of *Ominameshi* here brings out just enough of a classic debate within the history of Japanese Buddhism—namely, the one centering on the sentience and "buddhahood" of plants and trees (*somoku jōbutsu* 草木成仏)—to suggest that the twisting off of a blossom would *on some level* be a form of life-taking. And this was because any categorical statement that a mere flower is clearly "without feeling" and, thus, something to be classified along with the "insentient" matter would be one smacking of precisely the position that had been largely rejected by those Buddhist philosophers who, already for some centuries in Japan, had taken up this topic in their debates. And we must assume that not a few people in medieval Japan, those who would have been the primary audience for this play, would have known this intellectual background much better than would their modern counterparts. One reason for assuming this is the very frequent references to "the buddhahood of plants and trees" within this theatrical tradition. Already four decades ago Donald Shively noted that this is a theme in noh.[4]

If, then, the positing of an *ethical* dilemma occurs already at this early point in the play, what follows is even of greater interest. Almost immediately *Ominameshi* begins to play with an interweaving of ethical issues: the hinted-at immorality of blossom-snatching and the one-sided tearing of a bond of fidelity, including its sexual dimension, of a human couple. To say this is not, however, to suggest that all the references to "picking a flower" are connected to the notion of "deflowering" a virgin—as would more likely have been the case if this image had appeared in European literature. In *Ominameshi* virginity and its loss are not the issue. Rather, what is assumed to be as fragile as a flower and in jeopardy is the still intact, unbroken vow of personal fidelity (*chigiri*).[5]

A widening and interweaving of motifs, however, at this juncture in the play permit a change of venue and of action. Once the question of the plucking of the *ominameshi* blossom has been posed as a kind of life-and-death matter, the life and death of the play's main human personae become involved. The death of the flower through its plucking gets connected to the death of the principal humans. The repeated references to Yorikaze and his wife as a "couple" turn suddenly[6] to a reference to "coupled *graves*," the *otokozuka onnazuka*. This theme is developed more directly and poignantly when, driven to desperation

[4] Discussion of this, the *sōmoku jōbutsu* issue, is in my "Saigyō and the Buddhist Value of Nature," in two parts, *History of Religions* 13:2 (November 1973): 93–126 and 13:3 (February 1974): 227–48. For the presence of this in noh see Donald H. Shively, "Buddhahood for the Nonsentient: a Theme in Nō Play," *Harvard Journal of Asiatic Studies* 20 (1957): 135–61.

[5] Sanari, op. cit., 3492.

[6] Ibid., 3495.

by her husband's infidelity, the wife of Yorikaze, we are told, killed herself and did so by "throwing herself"—with no little irony—"into the River of Rescued Lives" (Hōjōgawa).[7] The husband reveals that he followed suit by doing the same to himself.

The final section (*kiri*) of the play does provide the first *overt* mention of sexual infidelity by explicitly using the word *jain*, but, at least on the reading offered here, that theme had already by this point been thematically present during most of the play. Violation of vows had long been linked to the motif of physical transgression and violation. What had already been implicit now merely becomes explicit. Therefore, once this is recognized, at least one of the central reasons for charging *Ominameshi* with being an inferior play would seem to collapse.

Plants Getting into the Action

There is something, however, that *does* appear as new in the play's final section—although it is more in the nature of a supporting motif than that of a whole play's theme. What I have in mind is the introduction there of the powerful image of the sword-tree. I essay a translation of this portion of the play:

> The demon of sexual infidelity is always urging on the flesh. The demon of adultery tortures the body. One's willpower gets drawn along the steep road up the mountain of sword-blades. Up at the very top is spied a lover and one gets transported with rapture. But as one ascends, the swords slice one's flesh and the boulders break one's bones. It is an unspeakably terrorizing sight. The tree branches of the sword tree are weighty with their blades. All this comes as karmic retribution for unspeakable sins. But it can turn out for the best. We momentarily may have seen flowers foolishly or dreamily, but then on the calyx of an *ominameshi* / on the pedestal of the lotus: Please let this sinner rise to the surface . . . and let the sins float away![8]

[7] Ibid., 3599.

What may we say about this? I suggest we ought to see the *kiri* of *Ominameshi* as providing a rather common, Buddhist, double-optioned finale: the giving of statements about the inevitability of karmic retribution and a coupling of these with the prospect of another, an alternative future, namely through escape and salvation. This kind of laying out of two alternative paths into the future is not uncommon in noh.

In most plays, however, a plant with its flower will be put forward as the concrete frequent vehicle for salvation—especially when the plant in question is the lotus. It is much more rare to see plants presented as what will implement the opposite—that is, a dire—scenario for humans. Vegetative forms, especially flowering ones, tend in noh to appear most commonly as agents of redemption. We might even refer to them as the "lotus ex machina." *Tadanori* probably provides the classic case of a flower's calyx serving as the pedestal of a lotus and, thus, also that on which the welcoming, saving Buddha sits. In this way, a motif common in Buddhist sculpture gets inserted into the action of drama. In such cases, thus, for the desperate person to move in the direction of a plant would be to be embraced by what may rescue him or her from the karmic retribution for moral failure. It will not be a dangerous move.

Ominameshi, however, introduces a complexity that causes it to differ significantly and interestingly from the general trend in such presentations. What we are given in the final sections of this play is the image of a flower that has the potential for being anything but benign. And this is done by a linguistic projection that fuses the *ominameshi* with the "branches of the sword-tree" (*tsurugi no eda* 剣の枝). In a word this suggests that there is something about this plant that makes it dangerous—literally, possessing a capacity *to cut* or lacerate human flesh.

As discussed below, the identification at this point of the *ominameshi* with the "branches of the sword tree" clearly depends largely on a powerful allusion. But before noting the specificity of this as a trajectory in literature and art, it may be of value to pay attention to what might have been ordinary, empirical observations about the *botanical physiology* of this particular plant. These had, I conjecture,

[8] Ibid., 3501-2.

given this plant, at least within the medieval period, something of negative reputation. Certain things about this plant, we may assume, had been already keenly observed. That is, the *ominameshi* in its physical features had already given those who observed it closely at least the impression that it might be able to inflict some level of pain on the surfaces of human skin. That there was something "cutting" about this plant was not merely the product of a literary allusion. It may be that the author of *Ominameshi*, by virtue of being within a medieval rather than modern context, would not have thought it outrageous to expect his audience to know that this was a botanical species which either could cause pain to human flesh or, at the least, look like it *might* be capable of doing so.

What might have been the physical features of this plant that led people to assume there to be something not outrageous but appropriate and apt in conflating it with the literary motif of the "sword-tree"? The answer to this, I offer, can be seen in something provided in the study of plants in the *Man'yōshū* by Claude Péronny. In his *Les plantes du Man.yōshū* (sic), the item devoted to "*wominaheshi*" (and likely based on prior scholarship by Japanese researchers) Péronny makes a point of this plant's possession of juxtaposed leaves, strikingly identical on opposite sides of the stalk. The salient feature here is a pattern of "*feuilles opposées, profondément indentée.*"[9] We may assume, I suggest, that this rigid regularity within the plant connoted something of the structure of horizontally extended and long "blades" arranged in a vertical sequence.[10]

This visual or tactile perception of the *ominameshi* plant as dangerous was, of course, forcefully augmented by the allusive material it came to bear once it had been identified with the *tsurugi no eda* of earlier religious and literary texts. An exploration of what this concretely involved—both by way of written and visual texts—can prove helpful

[9] Claude Péronny, *Les plantes du Man.yō-shū* (Paris: Maisonneuve & Larose, 1993), 199.

[10] That this flower was not universally appreciated comes out in Sen Rikyū's prohibition in the *Nampōroku* (南方録) of it for use as *chabana* in the tea ceremony; he may have simply disliked the odor it emits when wilting, although it is not impossible that its association with the erotic was a reason as well. See Yamafuji Sōzan, *Chabana* (Kyoto: Tankōsha, 1966), 178–9. Rikyū's interdiction has not prevented its use. I am grateful to Mariko N. LaFleur for this reference.

in our grasp of what is happening at this point in the progression of the play.

We should probably not be surprised to find that it is the *Ōjōyōshū* of 985 that provides the details of the harrowing experience of coming into contact with the "tree of swords." Its author, Genshin, drawing upon continental Buddhist sources, described in vivid detail what it would be like for a human, having just died, to enter hell—not just in some generalized sense but as a complex comprised of localized regions and specific modes of bodily torture. The one to which *Ominameshi* makes allusion is that referred to as the "Hell of Bodily Clashes." My rendering of Genshin's depiction of this particular infernal realm is as follows:[11]

> Sometimes the wardens of hell seize those sent there and put them in the grove of trees whose leaves are really blades. If the men there look to the top of such trees what they see are seated women, former lovers, who are gorgeous and beautifully attired. This delights these men so much that they immediately try to climb such trees—only to discover that their leaves, like blades, cut into their skin and then pierce right to their muscles, lacerating their entire bodies. When at last these men reach the top of these trees they discover that the women they were after are now down on the ground level. But with coquettish looks these women turn their eyes up towards the sinful males at the top of the trees and say things such as they did in the past—phrases like: "It is my karmic destiny to be in love with you. That is why I have come here. Oh, you! Why don't you come down this minute to be close to me and embrace me?" At this point the deluded men get fired up with erotic passion once again and start to descend the trees. But when they do this the blade-leaves rotate so that, like razors, their edges now point upward—thus to sliver and slice completely the bodies of these males as they make their way groundward. And then when they reach that goal they discover the women are once again back on the treetops. So all over again the males begin their ascent of the trees. This process goes on for

[11] Genshin, *Ōjōyōshū* in vol. 6 of *Nihon shisōshi taikei*, ed. Ishida Mizumaro (Tokyo: Iwanami Shoten, 1970), 15–6.

more years than can be counted—at least ten trillion. This is what it is like to be deceived by the hallucinations that one manufactures in one's own mind. This is the infinite repetitions that are produced—the burnings that result from passions in the domain of sex and eros.

Why this text and its vivid images could serve as rich conceptual and imagistic bases for the *kiri* of *Ominameshi* can now be made clear. What early in the play had been hinted at as a nexus between this plant's flower and erotic allure has, via both this extended complex of allusion and a switch from conceiving of the *ominameshi* flower to the structure of the plant as a whole, brought the *menacing* dimension of things into play. That is, the play can now be read as structurally informed by its relationship to the allusive template set up behind it.

We may be able to suggest this structure by the following parallel:

Ōjōyōshū	*Ominameshi*
alluring women at top	attractive blossoms at top
swords extended horizontally from a vertical trunk	sharp, horizontally placed leaves along a vertical stalk
self-deceived, erotically-charged males in ascent, torn by leaf-blades	humans ready to tear off a flower/tear up a relationship of trust

That medieval persons would have had, at least compared to their modern counterparts, little difficulty seeing the nexus between these two may be conjectured from the fact that Genshin's text was portrayed in pictorial form during the medieval period. Two examples known to me are a hand copied facsimile of a Hell scroll in the collection of the Tokyo National Museum[12] and in the gold-engraved drawing on a mandala in possession of Ryūhonji.[13]

Poets in the medieval period who saw fit to write on hells also represented it. For instance, in his sequence of *waka* in the *Kikigaki-shū*

[12] See *Jigoku zōshi* image on page 166, courtesy Tokyo National Museum.

[13] See Lotus Sutra Mandala image on page 167, courtesy Ryūhonji and Mainichi Shimbun Publishers.

on the theme of "Having seen Hell Scrolls," Saigyō had written:[14]

konomi mishi
tsurugi no eda ni
nobore tote
shimoto no hishi o
mi ni tatsuru kana

This verse could be translated as follows:

Swords on which my eyes
once fastened with delight are
here branches of trees
ascended by bodies being flogged
by barb-studded whips.

The application of torture to naked bodies had gotten rather intense here. The spiny and blade-like branches of these trees have been augmented by demons bent on using spears, swords, and metal-studded whips.

Although Yamada Shōsen is certainly correct to have traced the allusion in Saigyō's poem to the portion of the *Ōjōyōshū* cited above,[15] we need also to recognize that it was set by Saigyō within a verse sequence suggesting personal anxiety concerning the karmic impact upon himself and his family of that family's own professional, deep involvement in warfare. That there were illustrious warriors in his *bushi* family did not seem to cancel out this Buddhist poet's sense that there was personal, karmic risk to himself in this inheritance from his family's past. This verse too is one in which the autobiographical matrix of a poem, far more common in Saigyō than in most poets of his time, *seems* fairly clear. Specifically, because it better fits the highly personalized context of the poems in this sequence, I see the attributive *konomi mishi* ("on which my eyes once fastened with delight") as qualifying *tsurugi* (sword) rather than *tzurugi no eda* (sword branches). Saigyō, whose fascination with weapons technol-

[14] Kubota Jun, ed. *Saigyō zenshū* (Tokyo: Nihon Koten Bungakkai, 1982), 335, no. 202.
[15] Yamada Shōzen, *Saigyō no waka to bukkyō* (Tokyo: Meiji Shoin, 1987), 126.

ogy clearly remained long after he had explicitly declared his profession as a north-facing-warrior (*hokumen no bushi*) to have been given up with his adoption of a Buddhist lifestyle, is in this poem giving expression to just such an ambivalence. He appears to be trying, as it were, to convince himself that his delight in looking at swords and relishing their own form of beauty are things of his past.[16]

What in this essay I have been most interested to show is that the author of *Ominameshi*, by virtue of being within his medieval context and able to depend on an audience's familiarity with his allusions, would not have thought it outrageous to expect that same audience to know about vegetation looking like it might easily cause physical pain—that is, laceration—to human bodies. In *Ominameshi* the transformation of an attractive flower into a coquette and from that point into one that metes out painful retribution to those enticed by her are core moves in the textual *action* of this play.

It is, then, not only for technical or histrionic reasons that within the action of this play it is the plant itself that takes on an active, that is an actor's, role. It could be argued that *Ominameshi* provides a striking example of the fact that in noh the roster of "actors" in a given drama is in no way limited to those who are explicitly named in the "dramatis personae." The categorical distinction between human players and non-human players breaks down in the course of things. In what to modern, Western critics of literature would be a flagrant instance of the putative "pathetic fallacy," a part of what happens in a play such as this one involves a kind of ontological epiphany—one very much in keeping with the Buddhism of the period and one which, through the medium of the play's very action, establishes the point that many things, in effect, are not what they might ordinarily seem to be. And this was, of course, the major thrust of the medieval discussions of the buddhahood of plants and trees. A play such as *Ominameshi*, built on that conceptual framework, played with it in a creative fashion, and reflexively reinforced it as the epistemic norm.

[16] The *Kikigakishū* is probably the most directly autobiographical portion in the corpus of Saigyō, a poet distinguished, according to Robert Brower and Earl Miner, by less "esthetic distance" than is to be found in the verse of his contemporaries. See their *Japanese Court Poetry* (Stanford, 1961), 300.

Botany and Risk

Finally, here I wish to draw out what was involved in the fact that in medieval Japan, as evidenced in this play, botanic forms could be seen as relating to humans in ways *other than* positive or simply benign. To have drawn, via the logical and text-based disputations within monasteries, vegetative forms within the ambit of "sentient" beings was also to have invested them not only with the positive but *also the negative* aspects of human behavior. To have claimed that plants and trees, by virtue of their "buddha nature," are "animated" or "sentient" (*yūjō* 有情) was simultaneously to have recognized within them the capacity for "sympathy" and "fellow feeling" (*nasake aru* 情け有る). That is, to have doctrinally upgraded botanical forms within the hierarchy of beings was at the same time to have "humanized" them to the extent that the range and vagaries of their own "emotional states" must include the negative, the aggressive, and the harm-producing possibility. That is, sentience—however much valued—was itself double-edged. The Buddhist philosophers of East Asia may have concluded that what we in the West have sometimes called "the pathetic fallacy" is itself a logical fallacy. However, there was a kind of "price" to be paid for so raising the status of botanical forms. Their capacity to be, like humans themselves, deceptive, nasty, vindictive, and physically hurtful to others would have to be recognized.

Genshin's treatise showed a rich and vivid imagination concerning botanical life and its possibilities. When it came to that point in his discussion when this Buddhist text depicted loci in this world where we might come face-to-face with that rather disgusting and loathed life-form known as the "hungry ghost" (*gaki* 餓鬼), Genshin included a sub-type as follows:

> There is still another kind of hungry ghost, of the type that is born and lives within plants and trees. Within these they are squeezed like worms in ferns. They are recipients of a terribly painful life-form. It derives from the fact that in earlier lives these hungry ghosts were persons who cut down the forests that provide cool shade and the groves both in monasteries and public places. All this is karmic retribution.[17]

[17] Genshin, op. cit., 31.

This too, significantly, came to be represented in medieval Japanese art—as, for instance, as hungry ghosts painfully squeezed within trees in the *Kitano engi emaki*. I have elsewhere argued that this trajectory of speculation in medieval Japan, one usually ignored, may serve to explain the reason for observed physical deformations in trees which we today would classify as "diseased" or anomalously developed.[18] That is, in their diurnal world real persons had seen real trees which looked shockingly like what in a text such as Genshin's had been defined as the tree that harbors the hungry ghost. This is where the "science" of the day interfaced with what we ordinarily think of as the "arts." One mode informed and supported the interpretative likelihood of the other.[19]

The point of importance here, then, is that within the mental ambience of medieval Japan the prospect that plants and trees were involved in the experience of pain and suffering was a given. Sentience necessarily involves pathos. And plants were on both ends of the karmic pain sequence: they both suffered and, because they are *not* unlike humans, they were also the agents of the suffering of others.

When tempted to assume that there may be something simple and straightforward about a putative "Japanese" respect for and appreciation of "nature," it can be instructive to see how deeply the medieval mentality reflected on the complexity—one involving moral give-and-take—in the relations between humans and the world of plants. A botanical nature that was, as some Buddhists argued, worthy of respect even up to the point of having ontological parity with humankind was also a nature which could and would show the potential for *retribution*. A nature offended could be a nature which, in response, would pose risks to humans.[20]

[18] See my "The Eccentric Tree: *Kami* and *Gaki* in the Botanical Imagination of the Medieval Japanese," in *Rethinking Japan: Literature, the Visual Arts, and Linguistics*, ed. Adriana Boscaro (Kent, England, 1991), 121-30.

[19] This nexus between "science" and "art" in medieval Japan is also explored in my "Hungry Ghosts and Hungry People: Somaticity and Rationality in Medieval Japan," in Part One of *Fragments for a History of the Human Body*, ed. Michel Feyer et. al. (New York: Zone Books, 1989), 270-303.

[20] Perhaps the poet of the period who most clearly articulated his own grasp of such a risk was Saigyō. In his poetry the role of the "blossom" (*hana* 花) is exceedingly—but also richly—complicated and clearly drawn up into the realm of moral and religious

Ominameshi may be an especially brilliant expression of an awareness of this risk-factor. What is initially presented as a flower with a basically benign and in some ways lovely aspect turns out, via the action and poetry of the play, to be anything but innocent. What makes this plant interesting is that during the play it goes through something roughly equivalent to a "personality change," and a very dramatic one at that. A blushing, yellow-flowered field plant turns into a kind of botanical *femme fatale*, armed to the teeth, and apparently taking delight in bodily mutilating the men she entices. Given these suppositions and perhaps especially for the intellectual and artistic vigor with which it pursues them, *Ominameshi* is, I here suggest, an unusually interesting play, one that deserves far more appreciation for its literary and intellectual feat than has been accorded it to date.

---

values. The early essay that most forcefully presented this dilemma in Saigyō was Ienaga Saburō, *Nihon shisōshi ni okeru shūkyōteki shizenkan no tenkai* (Tokyo: Sōkansha, 1941).

地獄からの植物
ー『女郎花』における花、セックス、剣、葉ー

ウィリアム・ラフレール

「女郎花」が、いかに巧みに構成され且つ非常に興味深い能であるかはこの花の持つイメージを変える事によって明らかになると思う。

以下は、私の仮説である。

1）この能は、冒頭から不実が主題であるが、結末には他のイメージと重なり合う。

2）花としての女郎花が“性格の変換”を遂げる。つまり、誘い込む様な比較的に寛大な優しいイメージを持つ花から、近寄る者には、肉体的に危害を与える様に身構える花となるのである。そしてその変換がこの能の主なる筋となっている。

3）この能は、仏教の教えである草木成仏を課題にしている能として類を見ない奥深さがある。草木が知覚力と感情を備えているという意味合いを含んでいるということである。しかしながら、草木と花は肯定的な側面があるものの、かつて人間と同様に分類された様に、他の者にも危害を与えることがあるという意味合いをも含んでいる。この論文は、源信の往生要集に描かれている姿と概念がこの能に具体化されているということを中心に述べた。

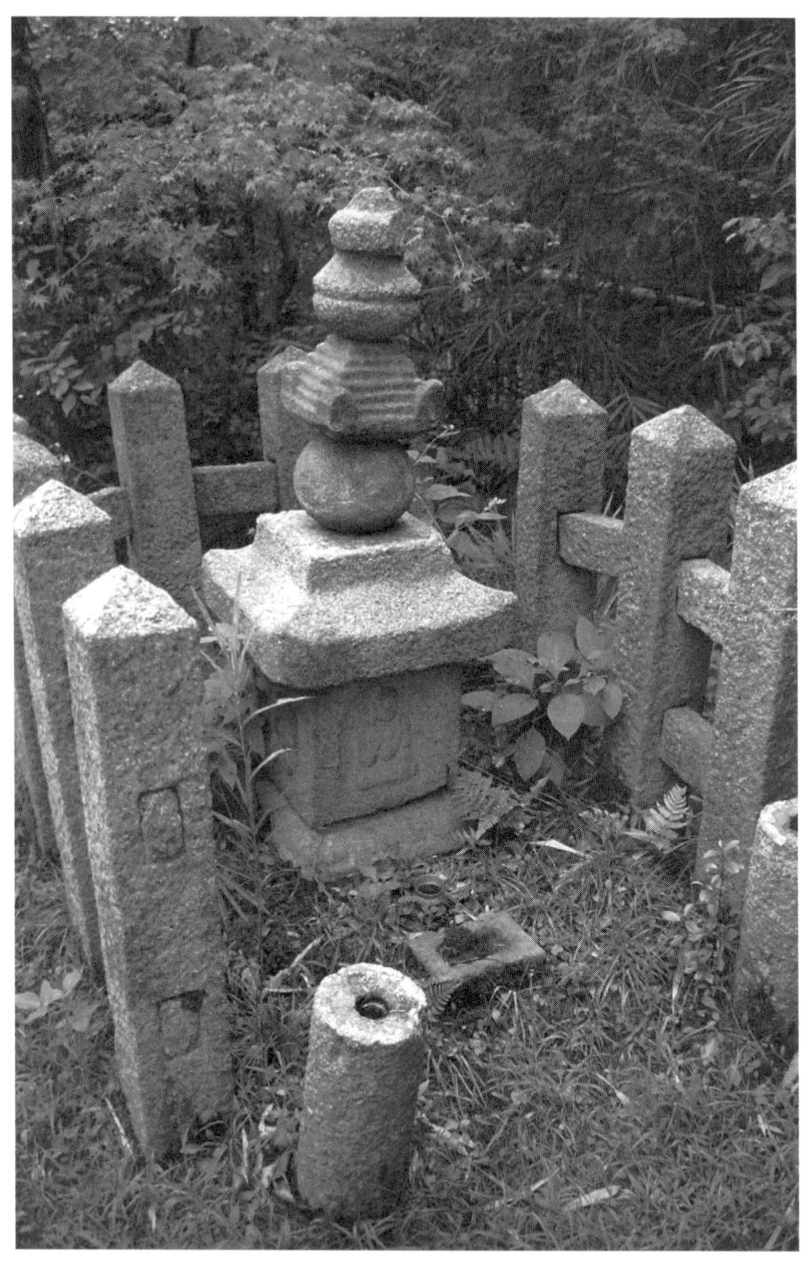

Woman's grave. Photo: Arthur H. Thornhill III.
女塚、写真、アーサー・ソーンヒル。

Man's grave. Photo: Arthur H. Thornhill III.
男塚、写真、アーサー・ソーンヒル。

Jigoku zōshi. Tokyo National Museum.
地獄草紙模本、東京国立博物館。

Lotus Sutra Mandala. Courtesy Ryūhonji and Mainichi Shimbun Publishers. Photo: Tokyo Historiographical Institute.
『法華経宝塔曼荼羅』立本寺、毎日新聞出版局、写真、東京大学史料編纂所。

Flowering in Wild Profusion: *Ominameshi* in the Context of Other Plays

Susan Matisoff

Ominameshi is a complex noh. Sacred space, sexual attraction, suicide, and access to salvation are all elements in this play which takes some surprising turns, such that its parts do not always seem to cohere entirely smoothly.[1] This article, mainly attending to matters of plot structure, approaches *Ominameshi* in comparison to other noh—several later plays inspired by *Ominameshi*, most of which reveal their indebtedness by including the name of the flower as part of their titles, and a few other plays thematically related to *Ominameshi*. Comparing *Ominameshi* to these works may help us grasp how *Ominameshi* was understood by earlier audiences and by playwrights inspired to write in reaction to it.

The time of *Ominameshi*'s first performance and the identity of its author are both uncertain and I leave speculation on these matters to others contributing to this volume.[2] And since similar uncertainties characterize most of the plays under discussion, this article does not attempt to prove influence on *Ominameshi* from earlier works so much as to suggest more broadly that an audience familiar with certain other plays might have drawn from them relevant resonances conditioning their reception of this piece. Moreover, later *Ominameshi*-related adaptations help pinpoint unusual, perhaps even uncomfortable, features of *Ominameshi*. What follows, then, is one possible interpretation of the play, drawn from an attempt to read both a little between and a little behind the lines.

The setting for *Ominameshi* is both the Iwashimizu Hachiman Shrine in Yamazaki and the hill, or small mountain, on which it

[1] This opinion is expressed by Konishi Jin'ichi in his article "Sakuhin kenkyū *Ominameshi*," *Kanze* (July 1966): 8–9.

[2] There is general agreement that the early playwright Kiami had a hand in creating a play called *Ominameshi*, but its exact relationship to the play known by that title today is uncertain. See Omote Akira, "*Ominameshi* no furuki utai kō," *Kanze* (July 1974): 4–11. See also the contribution to this volume by Takemoto Mikio.

stands. Two threads of meaning may be derived from the opening passage. The *waki* is not the anonymous wandering monk of many plays, but rather a monk whose origins, if not his name, are known. He is from Matsuragata in Kyushu. His familiarity with the Usa Hachiman Shrine in the area of his origins assures that when he comes upon the Iwashimizu Shrine by chance in the course of his wanderings near the capital his attention will be drawn to this site, a space of multivalent significance, sacred to the syncretic Shinto-Buddhist cult of Hachiman. Still, this monk seems less than fully diligent in his pilgrimage to Iwashimizu. Many noh begin with an itinerant monk's announcement of his interest in the important religious locales of every province, or of the area he is visiting, but in this case the monk has simply stated that he wants to see the capital. And when he does happen upon the Iwashimizu Hachiman Shrine, he is so easily distracted along the way that he nearly forgets to visit the shrine at all.

Indeed, *Ominameshi* takes an early turn toward a very different preoccupation on the part of the monk, triggered not by the shrine but by its physical setting. Around the base of the hill where the shrine is situated, plants at their peak of flowering attract the wandering monk's attention. They are called *ominameshi*, a name in which is embedded the word *omina*, modern *onna* (女) "woman."[3] These flowers are growing on Otokoyama "man mountain." Distracted by the flowers, the *waki* in *Ominameshi* does not proceed immediately to the shrine. Instead the play here unfolds around the amorous implications of the conjunction of names of the flower and the mountain.[4]

[3] *Omina*, implying a young woman, becomes *onna* the general term for "woman," in modern Japanese. The more usual pronunciation for the name of the flower is *ominaeshi*, which also preserves the embedded name of woman. For simplicity's sake I consistently refer to the flower as *ominameshi*, though the pronunciation in some poems, quoted in whole or in part within the various plays, is more commonly *ominaeshi*.

[4] The extensive deployment of an *ominameshi*/woman trope in Japanese poetry, from *Man'yōshū* onward is discussed at length in Edward Kamens, "Dragon-Girl, Maidenflower, Buddha: The Transformation of a Waka Topos, 'The Five Obstructions,'" *Harvard Journal of Asiatic Studies* 53:2 (1993): 389–442. The association of the trope with preoccupations about the difficulty of women's salvation, and with threats to priestly celibacy, long precedes its use for exploring such concerns in noh.

Some unknown Edo period playwright created an adaptation of *Ominameshi* entitled *Henjō ominameshi*.[5] Perhaps finding a dramatic flaw in the *Ominameshi waki*'s initial distraction from his journey to the shrine, the later playwright composed a different order of events. In *Henjō ominameshi*, the *waki*, an unnamed itinerant monk, visits the shrine immediately upon his arrival at Otokoyama. More than the title alone shows the debt *Henjō ominameshi* owes to *Ominameshi*. The lines describing the shrine are identical, word-for-word, between the two plays. Reading our *Ominameshi* in light of *Henjō ominameshi* raises the possibility that the *Ominameshi* monk from Kyushu was felt to have shown a certain dereliction in nearly forgetting the object of his pilgrimage. My reading of *Ominameshi* suggests that beneath the surface lie questions about proper practice, first signalled by the monk's easy distraction from his goal, the visit to the shrine.

Rather surprisingly for one who would be thought detached from close personal relationships, when the flowers in full bloom at the peak of their season catch his eye, the monk's first thought is to pick and take one of these *ominameshi* as a gift. The word for gift, *iezuto* (家づと), generally implies an item brought back by a traveler to present to one at home. The term is used in both *Ominameshi* and *Henjō ominameshi*. But plucking a flower for such a purpose seems an odd action for a religious itinerant, and, indeed, a woman whom the *waki* poetically calls the "guardian of the flowers," *hanamori* (花守), appears on scene to stay the traveler's hand. This causes the traveling monk to give a facile new explanation of his action: the flower, he now says, is to be an offering to Buddha.

One major difference between *Ominameshi* and its later adaptations is the identity of the *shite*. The *shite* in the first half of *Ominameshi* is an old man, the "guardian of the flowers," but in *Henjō ominameshi* the one who thwarts the monk's desire for the flower is a woman. She tells him that these are famous flowers and quotes two well-known poems concerning *ominameshi*, including one attributed to the Bishop Henjō. Immediately the woman reveals

[5] The text is included in Tanaka Makoto, ed., *Mikan yōkyokushū*, vol. 30 (Tokyo: Koten Bunko, 1978), 124–6. Tanaka suggests that the play is an Edo period composition. It includes several passages from *Ominameshi* verbatim. See Tanaka's introduction, 20.

her identity as the spirit of the *ominameshi* and then disappears into a grave at the foot of the hill. Her revealed spirit reappears, briefly alludes to her ill-fated love for one Ono no Yorikaze, and tells of her subsequent suicide. She expresses her happiness over attaining salvation through the priest's prayers and then vanishes again.

In yet another *Ominameshi*-derived play, *Saga ominameshi*,[6] the *shite* is also the spirit of the *ominameshi*, but the locale is Sagano, not Otokoyama, and the *waki* is Bishop Henjō himself. The play functions as an extended commentarial context for Henjō's poem inspired by falling from his horse (and by witty implication, falling from his vows as well) on seeing the blossoms:

> Entranced by its name, I would but pluck one,
> *Ominameshi*, do not tell others that I have fallen
>
> 名にめでゝ折れるばかりぞ女郎花, われおちにきと人に語るな

The presence of the bishop has brought her spirit forth, and the play ends vaguely but felicitously with her disappearance following a dance narrating beautiful and auspicious flower imagery.

These slim and obviously derivative plays exhibit a pattern unsurprising in noh though unlikely in other dramatic forms; that is to say, the spirit of a plant becomes manifest in human form. Though not a foregrounded issue in *Henjō ominameshi* or *Saga ominameshi*, in many such plays the plant-spirit attains Buddhahood through the prayers of a Buddhist practitioner.[7] *Bashō* and *Kakitsubata* are the best known comparable examples. Other plays on similar themes include *Asagao*, *Sumizomezakura*, and *Mutsura*. Typically taking as their core of inspiration one or more famous poems, and culminating

[6] The text is included in Haga Yaichi and Sasaki Nobutsuna, eds., *Yōkyoku sōsho*, vol. 2. (Tokyo: Hakubunkan, 1914), 37–9.

[7] In his commentary on *Ume*, a play composed in the 1760's, Sanari Kentarō notes that plays about the spirits of plants generally fall into two categories, those, like *Ume*, serving mainly to stage the context of a poem including the name of the plant, and those concerned with the salvation of plant-spirits. Sanari Kentarō, ed.,*Yōkyoku taikan*, vol. 1 (Tokyo: Meiji Shoin, 1930, rep. 1964), 424. One must note, however, that the categories are not neatly divided—in some plays the *kyōgen* interlude brings up the issue of Buddhahood for plants though it is not in the noh text itself. *Fuji*, mentioned below, is one such play.

in the release of the spirit of the plant through the power of prayer, such plays reflect medieval doctrinal debates favoring the possibility of rebirth for "grasses and trees" (*sōmoku jōbutsu* 草木成仏). Most, though not all, embodied plant spirits in noh are female. *Bashō* explicitly links plants and women, both problematic categories in the matter of attaining Buddhahood.[8]

By contrast, in *Ominameshi*, the problem will prove to be not salvation for plants, but rather the release of the soul of one particular woman. Though *ominameshi* are flowering in wild profusion (*saki midarete* 咲き乱れて), at issue is the picking of a single stem. And the single stalk of *ominameshi* will prove to be an apt symbol for an individual woman. But at least two later playwrights were somewhat disquieted by the fact that the *shite* of *Ominameshi* is manifest in male form, rather than as the female spirit of the plant. His identity is, of course, significant. Later in the play he will be revealed to be the ghost of the woman's lover and every bit as much in need as she of prayers for salvation.

But these developments will become clear only some time later in the play. In its opening sections the *ominameshi* blossoms remain abstract images of sexual attractiveness and—as they were understood to have been for Bishop Henjō—possible temptations for a monk, drawing him to stray from proper practice. Passively alluring, they lack even the hint of agency conveyed in plays where the *shite* is a woman understood to be the spirit of the plant.

Before proceeding with a reading of *Ominameshi* itself, two additional noh deserve at least brief mention. *Funaoka* is yet another play, thought to date from the Muromachi period, concerning salvation for the spirit of a plant.[9] As in *Henjō ominameshi* and *Saga ominameshi*,

[8] For background on such beliefs see William R. LaFleur, "Saigyō and the Buddhist Value of Nature, Part I," *History of Religions* 13:2. For a discussion of related noh, see Donald H. Shively, "Buddhahood for the Nonsentient: A Theme in Nō Plays," *Harvard Journal of Asiatic Studies* 20 (1957): 135–61.

The relevant passage in *Bashō*: "Ah, how happy I am. Hearing this (Lotus) Sutra the likes of women such as me, and even insentient grasses and trees, can thereupon rely." (*Ara arigataya kono onkyō o chōmon moseba warera gotoki no nyonin hijō sōmoku no tagui made mo tonomoshū koso sorae*), Sanari Kentarō, ed.,*Yōkyoku taikan*, vol. 4 (Tokyo: Meiji Shoin, 1931), 2534.

[9] The text is included in Tanaka Makoto, ed., *Bangai yōkyoku, zoku*, vol. 57, (Tokyo: Koten Bunko, 1952), 136–41. Tanaka's commentary on the play is on pages 24–5.

the plant is the *ominameshi*, but the locale is different. The *waki* is an itinerant monk making a general circuit of religious sites, now on his way to the Kamo Shrine in the capital. On arriving at Funaoka, a hill due north of Otokoyama, he sees *ominameshi* in bloom there and he quotes a poem containing the image of the flower:

> *Ominameshi*: I look on them reproachfully while passing by,
> to think that they are blooming even here on Otokoyama.

> 女郎花, うしと見つゝぞ行過る, 男山にし立りと思へば

The *shite* enters and chides the monk for the poem he has recited, giving two reasons for her reproach: as a monk he ought not to be speaking of "women." To do so is "a departure from the path of practice" (修行の道にははづれたり); moreover, the poem with its Otokoyama setting is, quite literally, out of place.

The *shite* further berates the *waki* for not knowing the *ominameshi* poem appropriate to this location, going so far as to inform him of the anthology containing the poem: the *Shūishū*. She then recites the poem:

> At Funaoka, growing on the plains, are *ominameshi*
> and every passerby will gaze on them I think

> 船岡の野中に立る女郎花, わたさぬ人はあらじとそ思ふ

The woman tells the monk that she wishes to make of the flowering *ominameshi*—perhaps one particular stalk—an offering to Buddha.[10] Revealing her identity as the spirit of the *ominameshi* she asks the priest to remain through the night offering prayers. And his prayers, holding out the possibility of "Buddhahood for grasses and

[10] Poem no. 894, in *Shinsenzaiwakashū* is attributed to Izumi Shikibu. Its headnote asserts that she sent an *ominameshi* as a flower offering for a ritual on Mount Hiei. The flower served as her stand-in, going where she, as a woman, was excluded. Kamens, op. cit., 425–9. As Kamens suggests, the attribution of the poem may be groundless. Izumi Shikibu's name does not figure in the text of *Funaoka*, but the *shite*'s desire to offer the flower reflects either this anecdote or a general practice of making such offerings.

trees and even the land of the realm" (草木国土悉皆成仏), draw her spirit forth again, in gratitude. Asserting that plants perfectly exemplify the ephemeral nature of life she chides: "Who calls them insentient?" (心なしとは誰か云). A poetic catalogue of flowers and their seasons follows, presumably along with a dance performed by the *shite*. Finally, thanks to the monk's prayers, the *ominameshi* attains Buddhahood, as do all the other flowering grasses on the plain.

The reference book *Kokon yōkyoku kaidai*[11] cites a noh title: *Kōya ominameshi*. It records that the *shite* is the spirit of the *ominameshi*. The *waki* is a traveling monk. The locale is Mount Kōya in Kii and the season autumn. There is only this much information about the plot: the spirit of the *ominameshi*, blossoming on sacred ground where women are forbidden, expresses her distress over poems that blame the flower because of its name and entreats the traveling monk to offer prayers.

Despite the brevity of the account, we can be certain that *Kōya Ominameshi* reflected the institutionalized exclusion of women from Mount Kōya. A powerful, though largely, invisible line of exclusion barred all women from ascending to the mountain-top monastery of Mount Kōya. Like Mount Hiei, Ōmine, and other sacred mountains, the entire area of the monastery was kept as a *nyonin kekkai* (女人結界), a restricted precinct, open only to males.[12] This practice is expressed in terms of fauna and flora in an early seventeenth century puppet play, *Sekkyō Karukaya* (説経かるかや), printed in 1631.[13]

[11] Maruoka Katsura, *Kokon yōkyoku kaidai*, ed. Nishino Haruo (Tokyo: Kokon Yōkyoku Kankōkai, 1984), 452.

[12] The term *shichiri kekkai*, "seven-li restricted precinct," was commonly used of Mount Kōya. It refers to a Shingon purification ritual thought to have been performed by the monastery's founder Kūkai 空海 (774–835) at the time of the establishment of the first temple on the mountain. The rite delimited an area protected from malevolent influences and extending seven li in all directions from its central point. Later *kekkai* became synonymous with *nyonin kekkai*, a restricted precinct excluding women, and with *shichiri kekkai*, a term which, along with some dialectal variants, passed into the common parlance as a general expression for a repellent person or thing to be kept at a distance. Matsuoka Shizuo, ed. *Nihon kokugo daijiten*, vol. 9 (Tokyo: Shogakkan, 1974), 621–2.

[13] Yokoyama Shigeru, ed., *Sekkyō shōhonshū*, vol. 2 (Tokyo: Kadokawa Shoten, 1968), 18. The same passage appears in Muroki Yatarō, ed., *Sekkyōshū* (Tokyo: Shinchōsha, 1977), 43.

> [Mount Kōya] is a restricted precinct, extending seven *ri*, a mountain where all alike strive toward salvation through their own efforts. For this reason, male trees grow on the peak and female trees grow in the distant valleys. Because male birds fly about the peak, female birds fly about the distant valleys. Since stags eat the grasses on the peak, does eat the grasses in the valley. Be they trees, reeds, grasses, birds or beasts, males may enter the mountain, but no females may enter. So all women are absolutely forbidden.

Perhaps *Kōya Ominameshi* involved a "female" flower who succeeded in transgressing the *kekkai* as an offering. This is, of course, mere speculation, yet it seems certain that the notion of a male zone at the top of the mountain and a female zone at the foot would have figured in this play.

With such distinctions in mind, we might look again at the topography of *Ominameshi*. When the monk from Kyushu quotes Bishop Henjō's witty poem about "falling" (or not) for the flower, his interlocutor questions the propriety of his monastic understanding. And it is he who, before long, guides the monk upwards to the shrine. Though the actual Iwashimizu Hachiman Shrine never excluded women it seems somehow fitting that the monk's guide to the shrine should be another male. In this play, too, the only level where we encounter a female, human or flower, is at the base. There, too, are "people's houses side by side." It is a zone of mixed meaning: secular, sexual *and* sacred.

The noh *Hōjōgawa* shares with *Ominameshi* its locale. Categorized as *waki* noh and thus overtly relating to gods and sacred rites, *Hōjōgawa* most likely is a Zeami composition, predating *Ominameshi*.[14] The *waki* is an attendant from the Kashima Shrine who, like the itinerant monk in *Ominameshi*, is visiting religious sites in the vicinity of the capital. His journey brings him to "the village of Yawata where the god is celebrated" (神祭る八幡の里に着きにけり),

[14] This assumption is based on the fact that a play entitled *Yawata* is mentioned in Zeami's *Nōsakusho* and cited as Zeami's in *Sarugaku dangi*, and on the assumption that *Yawata*, an alternate reading for the characters also read Hachiman, is the play now known as *Hōjōgawa*. The text of *Hōjōgawa* is included in Sanari Kentarō, ed., *Yōkyoku taikan*, vol. 4 (Tokyo: Meiji shoin, 1931), 2453–68.

there to visit the Iwashimizu Hachiman Shrine. As in *Ominameshi*, the time is the full moon of the eighth month, when a rite is conducted releasing living fish into the river running by the base of Otokoyama, the *Hōjōgawa*, "life-releasing river." An old man of the locale, later revealed as a minor deity, praises the shrine for its antiquity, beneficence, and deep associations with abundant life, the teeming fishes released in the Hōjōe (放生会).

Inversions abound here. The visitor, as yet unaware of the details of the rite, at first admonishes the old man, thinking he intends to kill, rather than free, the fish he is carrying. Inverting the symbolism of releasing living creatures, the old man explains the rite as guaranteeing the god's blessing that no being will slip out of the net of salvation.[15] The origin of the rite is also explained. It is performed in expiation for causing the deaths of many captives taken in warfare long ago, that their souls may attain salvation.[16] The muddy stream at the foot of the hill is protective, providing, through the effect of the gods, a pure habitat for fishes. "Even the muddy water, by virtue of the god's vow, is pure at Iwashimizu" (水の濁りも神徳の誓ひは清き岩清水). For an audience familiar with *Hōjōgawa*, the setting of *Ominameshi* calls to mind deeply fused Shinto-Buddhist religious practices, rites for the expiation of wrongful death, and the promise of universal salvation.

Despite the *waki*'s brief visit to the shrine, the area of most importance in *Ominameshi* is the space around the base of the shrine mound, near the Hōjōgawa. Sacred space (*reichi* 霊地) encompasses not only the shrine atop the hill but also the muddy river at the base.

> *Shite*: At the base of the mountain people's homes stand side by side.

> *Shite*: 山下の人家軒を並べ

[15] 魚は逃れわれはまた却つて誓ひの網に漏れぬ神の恵み
The image of the net is usually associated with Amida Buddha's vow of universal salvation, but Amida is not specified here.

[16] A passage in *Shoku Nihongi* is the earliest record of the origins of the rite, related to loss of life during campaigns in the Yōrō period, 717–24. Various engi of the shrine also mention the rite and its early origins. The *Shoku Nihongi* passage is quoted in Sanari, vol. 4, 2454.

Shite & Waki: Deities softening their luminescence mingle with the dust of mortal life. So, too, the waters are muddied and scaly creatures swimming in the stream attest to that deep vow of release for all living creatures.

Shite & Waki: 和光の塵も濁り江の河水に浮かむ鱗類はげにも生けるを放つかと深き誓ひもあらたにて

With these lines *Ominameshi* opens the possibility that the divine is accessible to all and everywhere, in the muddy rivers of the mundane world, not merely in elevated, visibly pristine, and purely male realms.

Led by the old man, the monk continues uphill to visit the Iwashimizu Shrine, and the chorus sings its praises. But as the old man who has guided him starts to take his leave, the monk's thoughts return to the matter of *ominameshi* and Otoyama. The old man shows his aggravation by asking whether they had not both been quoting and discussing poems related to these flowers and this mountain. Without specific textual mention of further movement, the two men apparently come down the slope to a place where, in a sudden revelation, the old man points out a pair of graves, Man Grave and Woman Grave (*otokozuka* 男塚, *onnazuka* 女塚). An *ominameshi* flower has some connection to the graves, as yet unclear. The graves' inhabitants are "a woman from the capital" and a man "called Ono no Yorikaze from here, from Mount Yawata."[17] Hinting that he is the spirit of that Yorikaze, in the deepening moonlight, the old man disappears "as in a dream."

The *kyōgen* interlude is crucial as it serves to introduce the history of the graves' occupants, Ono no Yorikaze and his wife. Following a very common *kyōgen* pattern, a man of no particular consequence explains this local lore and urges the monk to offer prayers on behalf of the dead.[18] When he does, the spirits of the deceased couple appear and recount their own deaths. The wife, a woman from the capital, drowned herself in the Hōjōgawa, believing that her husband had

[17] Since Yawata = Hachiman, this nomenclature, an alternate name for Otokoyama, amounts to calling it "Hachiman's mountain."

[18] See the article in this volume by Carolyn Morley concerning the *kyōgen* interlude.

abandoned her. The *ominameshi* growing from her grave revealed her resentment by shrinking at Yorikaze's approaches. Aware of her reproach and filled with guilt, Yorikaze buried her, then threw himself into the same river and joined her in death. Narrating his own suffering in hell, the ghost of Yorikaze implores the monk for prayers. The presence of the ghost of the *ominameshi* woman (she is the *tsure*) and the linking of flower images—*ominameshi* and lotus calyx in paradise—may suggest that his request is not for himself alone but for his wife as well. Nevertheless, the lack of subject pronouns sustains uncertainty, and with his entreaty *Ominameshi* reaches its open-ended conclusion.

The story of Ono no Yorikaze and his spouse is reminiscent of some other works in the noh repertoire. In *Motomezuka* we see the returned ghost of a woman who suffers in hell, having, however passively, caused the death of two men. Overwhelmed by their simultaneous courting, she threw herself into the Ikuta River and drowned, and after her death the two suitors killed each other.[19] Ikuta (生田), "field of life," is every bit as ironic a name for a place of death as Hōjōgawa "life-releasing river." Might Ikuta have suggested Hōjōgawa as another appropriate place to work out issues relating to wrongful death and guilty suffering? Might the earlier play—in which we see the ghost of a woman emerging from her grave to tell of suffering terribly because of the deaths of men who loved her—have suggested, by inversion, a play about the spirit of a man who suffers because of the death of the woman who loved him?[20] There is another tenuous connection to support this suggestion of resonances of *Motomezuka* in *Ominameshi*. The earlier title of *Motomezuka* was *Otomezuka* (処女塚) "Maiden's Grave."

Could some aspects of the legend of Ono no Yorikaze in fact have been inspired by the clearly earlier *Motomezuka* legend? Whereas the "seed" for *Motomezuka* goes back to the *Man'yōshū*, Ono no

[19] The latter half of *Ominameshi* as we know it today, the part which resembles *Motomezuka*, has the earmarks of early noh. See Omote, op. cit., 11. See also the contribution to this volume by Takemoto Mikio.

[20] Konishi suggests that Yorikaze is punished for licentiousness, op. cit., 9. But the immediate cause of the *ominameshi*-woman's death, and hence his guilt and suffering, would seem to be his failure to show continuing attraction, at least as much as the initial attraction itself.

Yorikaze seems to be a literary invention unrecorded earlier than the medieval poetry commentary that was evidently one source for *Ominameshi*.[21] Early in *Motomezuka* occurs the phrase "at the small fields of Ikuta in the morning wind." "Morning wind in the small fields" is *ono no asakaze* (小野の朝風) . Ono is a well established surname. How far a stretch is it to suggest that *asa*, "morning," suggested *yoru* (夜), "evening," and then transmuted into the form of the fictional name Ono no Yorikaze?[22]

The strongest evidence by far of the *Ominameshi* playwright's awareness of and indebtedness to *Motomezuka* is the borrowing of a full segment from the earlier play: the *waki-ageuta* passage immediately following the *kyōgen* interlude. Here the sound of the word for "grave" (*tsuka* 塚) suggests the homonym (*tsuka* 束) meaning "short space/hand-breadth," and the passage alludes obliquely to an old poem in which "the space between the antlers of a stag" (*oshika no tsuno no tsuka* 牡鹿の角のつか) pivots into the meaning "a brief moment" (*tsuka no ma* 束の間), here the "moment" the priest spends in prayer for the dead.[23] The allusion to the "space between the antlers of a stag" is arresting, yet rather gratuitous here. The borrowed passage, fitting uncomfortably, extends over several lines, continuing as the ghosts of the dead return saying, "To this wide and desolate plain few people come. Except for my grave, there is no one here. Only wild beasts roaming about and quarreling over my bones."[24]

Another play worth mentioning for its suggestive similarities to *Ominameshi* is *Aisomegawa*. *Aisomegawa* is an exceptionally long play with a notably large cast of characters. It includes little by way of poetic allusions and, as is relatively unusual for noh, the play at times progresses through the reading of letters written by the woman.

[21] Concerning the commentaries, see the article in this volume by Susan Klein.

[22] Sakakura Atsuyoshi, participating in a panel discussion on *Ominameshi* after a visit to its locale, confirms his belief in the fictionality of Ono no Yorikaze. See "*Ominameshi* no arekore," *Kanze* (July 1966): 15–6.

[23] Sanari cites the source poem as one attributed to Kakinomoto no Hitomaro, included in the *Shinkokinshū*. It is *Shinpen kokka taikan* no. 1374.

[24] I have here slightly adapted the translation of *Motomezuka* by Barry Jackman included in D. Keene, ed. *20 Plays of the Nō Theatre* (New York and London, 1970), 35–50. The translation of the passage under discussion is on pages 45–6. Konishi, op. cit., 10, points out the uncomfortable fit of these lines in *Ominameshi*.

おう曠野人稀なり。わが古墳ならで又何者ぞ。骸を争ふ猛獣は

In all respects this play is very similar to a narrative with the same title that survives in the form of an early seventeenth century woodbock printed edition.[25] The title *Aisomegawa*, means, depending on the character used for *ai* (藍/愛), both "indigo-dyed river and love-dyed river." Both the play and the tale are considered late Muromachi works.[26]

Nothing in *Aisomegawa* resembles the opening sections of *Ominameshi*; rather, the whole play unfolds as a story with resonances to the tale of Yorikaze and his woman. In *Aisomegawa* a woman commits suicide by drowning herself in a river, believing that her husband has deserted her. As in *Ominameshi*, she is a woman from the capital who comes inquiring after her spouse. He is a priest from Dazaifu in Kyushu, presumably an attendant of the Tenmangū Shrine there.[27] Their union had led to the birth of a son, and the young boy is traveling along with her. On her arrival in Dazaifu she has an intermediary deliver her letter to the priest's residence. There the priest's current wife reads the letter and in his absence composes a response she pretends is his. The "wife" from the capital is told to return home, and this rejection leads to her suicide.

In *Ominameshi* there is only this simple explanation of the searching woman's despair. Her returned ghost says, "I came from the capital, wandering alone, and with my resentment ever deepening, I threw myself into the depths of Hōjōgawa."[28] But when it first introduces the same event, the *kyōgen* interlude is somewhat more detailed. The man of the locale relates: "That woman came here and she told her story. It happened that at that time Yorikaze was up on the mountain. Since he was away from his home, someone there answered her roughly and so she thought that Yorikaze's feelings toward her had changed, and she left. Then she felt there was no rea-

[25] In Yokoyama Shigeru and Matsumoto Ryūshin, ed. *Muromachi jidai monogatari taisei*, vol. 1 (Tokyo: Kadokawa, 1973), 13–33.

[26] The play is included in Sanari, vol. 1, 225–46. Sanari's comments on dating the play may be found on page 225. Matsumoto Ryūshin's dating of the short story to the Muromachi period appears in *Muromachi jidai monogatari taisei*, vol. 13.

[27] This shrine venerated Tenman Tenjin, the postmortem transformation of an exiled culture-hero, the ninth century poet-scholar Sugawara no Michizane.

[28] 都を独りあくがれ出て, なほも恨みの思ひ深き放生川に身を投くる
Quoted in Itō Masayoshi, ed., *Yōkyokushū*, vol. 1 (Tokyo: Shinchōsha, 1983), 420–1.

son for her to return to the capital and she threw herself in the river and died."[29]

"Someone there answered her roughly" might mean many things. The version of Yorikaze's story in the medieval poetry commentary *Kokinwakashū jo kikigaki*[30] provides details which heighten the similarity to *Aisomegawa* around this point. It reveals the existence of another wife: "She went to the man's place at Yawata, and when she asked, someone there answered, 'He's not here just now, he's at his first wife's place.' So the woman, feeling resentful, went to the Yawata river, took off her yellow robe, tossed it aside, threw herself in the river and died."[31]

Following the suicide drowning of the disappointed woman from the capital, *Aisomegawa* unfolds very differently from *Ominameshi*. Having come to realize that the dead woman is his wife from the capital, the priest asks to view her body, even though in his role as a Shinto priest he "does not generally gaze upon the dead" (総じて死人を見る事はなけれども). The chorus describes in considerable and horrifying detail the disfigurement and decay of her corpse. Before the Tenman Shrine, the priest undertakes Shinto rituals on behalf of her spirit. Intoning norito prayers, he invokes the majestic force of Tenman Tenjin and the vow of universal salvation offered by this deity's original form (*honji* 本地), the Bodhisattva Kannon. The shrine reverberates with loud rumblings and Tenman Tenjin himself emerges. Though the miracle is not staged, the play concludes with the Tenjin's awe-inspiring narration of the dead woman's resurrection.

There is one last play to be considered. Its unknown playwright seems to have made a link between *Aisomegawa* and *Ominameshi*. This is *Genzai ominameshi*, "Present Time Ominameshi."[32] The title

[29] かの女尋ねて来り, その由申し候に, 折節頼風は山上に御座ありて, 御留守の事なれば, 内よりあらけなく返事を申す間, さては頼風の御心変わり行きたり, この上は都に帰りてもせんなしとて, 放生川へ身を投げ空しくなり給ひて候

[30] Ibid.

[31] 男ノ八幡ノ宿所ニ行テ問ケレバ, 家ナル者答テ云, 此程初メタル女房ノ座ズ間, 別ノ処 ニ座ズト云ケレバ, 女ウラメシト思テ八幡川ニ往テ, 山吹重ノ絹ヲヌギ捨テ, 身ヲ抛テ死ス

[32] The text is included in Tanaka Makoto, ed., *Bangai Yōkyoku*, vol. 33 (Tokyo: Koten Bunko, 1950), 70–5. In his commentary on the play, pages 33–6, Tanaka suggests that there were a considerable variety of *ominameshi* legends circulating in medieval

reflects the fact that the *shite*, the *ominameshi*-woman, is a living woman in the first half of the play.[33] As in *Aisomegawa*, her journey in search of her lover is enacted as the first half of the play, not merely through *kyōgen* narration or the retrospection of a returned ghost. In a remarkably telling detail, the woman identifies herself at the outset as "a woman who lives at Ichijō Imadegawa" (是は一条今出川に住女のて候), exactly the same words of self-identification spoken by the *shite* in *Aisomegawa*. When this woman from the capital finds Yorikaze's residence at Yawata and learns that he is "away," she quickly drowns herself in the Hōjō River.

Again as in *Aisomegawa*, the *waki*, her husband (in this case of course it is Yorikaze), returns home only to find her dead. There is a certain O. Henry-like quality here as he says he had been off looking for her in the capital. On the seventh day after her demise he goes to offer prayers and finds a single *ominameshi* blooming before her grave. He prays that she will "halve a lotus calyx and wait for me" (蓮台の半座を分て待ち給へ), expressing his wish to be reunited with her in paradise. Summoned by his prayers, she reappears; he has the chance to tell her of his unwavering love, and her spirit fades away. Compared to the stark ending of *Ominameshi*, we do not see Yorikaze suffering in the afterlife, and the implication seems to be that his prayers on her behalf will be to good effect. The contrast between *Ominameshi* and *Aisomegawa* could not be more striking. In *Genzai ominameshi* Yorikaze's prayers, not prayers offered by a passing priest, are the ones that matter and take effect. But in *Ominameshi*, Yorikaze's guilt causes him to join his wife in death and his suffering continues post mortem. By contrast, the priest of the Tenman Shrine, faced with the same dilemma, is able to summon so powerful a god that his wife will be returned to life. Considering these plays together

---

times. Moreover, performance lists and other noh reference works evince considerable confusion between this play and *Saga ominameshi*. And to confuse matters further, *Genzai ominameshi* seems also to have been known by the alternate title *Yorikaze*.

[33] It is worth noting that the *shite* in all *Ominameshi*-derived plays is a woman. Konishi observes that *Ominameshi*, too, would be a more coherent play if the *shite* were a woman. Konishi, op. cit., 10. At the Omimameshi conference, Professor Takemoto suggested that the author of this play evidently felt frustrated by the "standard" *Ominameshi*.

raises some provocative, though ultimately unanswerable, questions. Iwashimizu Hachiman Shrine and the Tenman Shrine were both syncretic religious centers. *Ominameshi* ends with souls still suffering in hell; the somewhat similar *Aisomegawa* concludes with a miracle. Even without imagining that everyone in the audiences for *Aisomegawa* truly believed Tenman Tenjin had the power to raise the dead, we can turn back to *Ominameshi* and wonder whether there is an implication hidden between the lines. Might the *waki*, so seemingly forgetful about his visit to Iwashimizu Shrine, also be seen as forgetting to call upon the power of its own syncretic deity Hachiman? Is Yorikaze to be understood as an attendant of the Iwashimizu Shrine, not just someone who happens to live nearby?

Another tension seems to lie behind these plays as well, the issue of monastic celibacy. The monk from Usa Hachiman, the *waki* in *Ominameshi*, seems rather like the many other itinerant Buddhist monks of noh. Like Bishop Henjō, he ought not be attracted to women. But the priest of the Tenman Shrine, the *waki* in *Aisomegawa*, is not just attracted to women, he is married, the father of a son, and able, through his faith, to save his wife. Easy generalizations about the syncretism of medieval Japanese religion may mask a touchy issue revealed by the constellation of noh considered in this article. There cannot have been an entirely seamless fusion between a native religious tradition readily accepting of sexuality and an imported tradition of *monastic renunciation*. Much negotiation must have been necessary to determine proper behavior for religious practitioners in service of combinatory cultic centers such as those devoted to Hachiman.[34] There is an undeniable disjunction between the celebration—through poetic *ominameshi* imagery—of female attraction in the earlier parts of *Ominameshi* and the grim suffering of ghosts in its second half. Rather than trying to explain away this uneasy fit, we may see in it the surfacing of unresolved tensions besetting the fusion of various strains of medieval Japanese religion.

[34] See Allan G. Grapard, "Institution, Ritual and Ideology: The Twenty-two Shrine-Temple Multiplexes of Heian Japan," *History of Religions* 27:3 (1988): 246–69.

咲き乱れて
—『女郎花』と関係のある能楽—

スーザン・マチソフ

この論文は、花の名前を題名の一部に組み入れることで『女郎花』から影響を受けたことが明らかな作品を含む他の能楽と比較して『女郎花』を扱う。話題となる最初の二つの能楽は『遍昭女郎花』(遍昭僧正による歌が中枢)と『嵯峨女郎花』(嵯峨を舞台に遍昭僧正が「ワキ」を演じる)両方の作品において,「シテ」は人間の形をとって女郎花の花の魂を現わす。表面に押し出されてはいないが、「草木成仏」の可能性を支持する中世における学説上の論争がここに反映されている。また寺院生活における禁欲主義という題材も間接に問題にあげられている。『舟岡』も同じ問題にふれる。

『放生川』はその舞台背景を『女郎花』と供している。それは『女郎花』に先行する世阿弥の構図かもしれない。『放生川』と『女郎花』の比較は、後者の能楽における空間感覚への洞察力をもたらす助けとなる。

次に『 求塚』について論じられる。ここでは不法死と受難という問題の核心が『生田』(生命の田)で演じられている。「生命を放つ川」という意味がある『放生川』の反語的題名は、この作品をそのような問題点を解かせるためのもう一つの適格な場面として持ち出しているのかもしれない。

『藍染川』では神社の従者の妻が夫の無関心に絶望したあまり弱死する。最期には天満天神への夫の祈りが妻の命をよみがえらせる。考慮される最後の能楽『現在女郎花』は女郎花の精である女が恋人を探し求めたあげく絶望して弱死するという点で『藍染川』と似ている。『藍染川』のように、その恋人は戻ってきて女の死に直面することになる。この恋人の祈りが重要でその効力を示すのである。

この論文はこれらの能楽が一組として、中世日本の宗教における融合された様々な精神的重圧を包囲する解決されない緊張感(特に禁欲主義の問題)を反映しているという提案で締めくくっている。

The Tempered Light of Hachiman: *Wakō Dōjin* in *Ominameshi*

Arthur H. Thornhill III

Noh drama has profound appeal to devotees of Japanese poetry not simply because of its lyrical language, but because many of its finest plays are poetic, rather than dramatic, in conception. Consider, for example, *Matsukaze*. The protagonists are personifications of natural phenomena—the wind in the pines and autumnal rain squalls—that have pre-existing emotional content within the world of *waka*. The entire play is synthesized from a *Kokinshū* legacy of Ariwara no Yukihira verses and an earlier song-and-dance piece that celebrates the beauty and pathos of life at Suma Bay. The one literary precedent for the Matsukaze protagonist is found in *setsuwa*—a *Senjūshō* account of a putative love affair between Yukihira and a local *ama*. In this sense *setsuwa* and noh both serve to "flesh out" pre-existing poetic landscapes with imagined narrative content.

Ominameshi fits this pattern quite closely. It is the result of the rhetorical juxtaposition of "Male Mountain" and "ladyflowers" in Ki no Tsurayuki's Kana Preface to the *Kokinshū*. Tsurayuki's original intent was to enumerate various poetic situations that engender strong emotion; he actually alludes to two separate, unrelated poems, *Kokinshū* 889 and 1016. However, later commentators merged the two motifs, and the Yorikaze legend was the eventual result, as recorded in medieval *Kokinshū* commentaries. In this process of dramatic embellishment, the locale is paramount. In the case of *Matsukaze*, Suma is replete with the poetic legacy of not only Yukihira's but also Genji's exile, enhancing both the loneliness and the latent nobility of the protagonists. In *Ominameshi*, the special nature of the setting is equally important, but in this case the site is renowned as a sacred locale. Therefore it is my intention to examine the religious identity of Otokoyama and its relation to the themes of the play.

The Iwashimizu Hachiman (or Yahata[1]) Shrine is considered a branch of the Usa Hachiman Shrine in Kyushu. Although originally the god of the Usa Shrine appears to have been a both a god of copper ore and a god of the sea, by the Nara period Hachiman came to be viewed as the deified form of Emperor Ōjin (r. 270-310), the son of Emperor Chūai (d. 201) and Empress Jingū (d. 269).[2] According to the traditional *Nihon shoki* account, Jingū served as regent after Chūai's death, launching an invasion of the Korean peninsula. This martial background contributes to Hachiman's frequent identification as a war god, invoked by the Minamoto forces during the Genpei War and again by militarists during the twentieth century. In 859 the divine presence of Hachiman was installed at Otokoyama by Gyōkyō, a Buddhist priest.

Gyōkyō was a member of the Ki family and priest at the Shingon temple Daian-ji in Nara.[3] In 807, on his return from a journey to China, he spent the summer in retreat at the Usa Hachiman, and subsequently enshrined Hachiman at Daian-ji as a protector deity. Much later, he was commanded by Grand Minister Fujiwara Yoshifusa to go to the Usa Shrine on the fifteenth day of the fourth month of 859. The original purpose of the pilgrimage was to pray for the accession of his nine-year-old grandson to the throne, but since the child had become Emperor Seiwa the previous winter, Gyōkyō spent the summer months praying for the emperor's continued rule, reciting the Mahayana canon during the day and performing esoteric Shingon rituals at night before the Hachiman divinity. It has been speculated that Yoshifusa's aim was to deflect criticism that three older princes had been passed over in the succession by arranging for an oracle from Hachiman to be publicized that endorsed his choice. As a result of

[1] "Yahata" is the original reading; it may be a phonetic transformation of "Yamatoyo (no kami)," a deity that was viewed as a kind of national spirit. See Nakano Hatayoshi, *Hachiman shinkōshi no kenkyū*, vol 1 (Tokyo: Yoshikawa Kōbunkan, 1976), 92–4. Later legend associates Yahata's literal meaning "eight banners" with a heavenly sign said to have appeared at Ōjin's birth.

[2] Ōga no Higi (or Namiyoshi), a shaman associated with the Miwa shrine, has been credited with identifying Ōjin's spirit with the deity at Usa in the late sixth century. See Murayama Shūichi, *Honji suijaku* (Tokyo: Yoshikawa Kōbunkan, 1974), 51.

[3] This account of Gyōkyō's life is based on Murayama, op. cit., 62–6 and Tsukamoto Zenryū, ed., *Mochizuki Bukkyō daijiten*, vol. 1 (Tokyo: Sekai Seiten Kikō Kyōkai, 1958), 573.

Gyōkyō's service, two of his disciples were given administrative positions at the shrine, and on the political front it was widely perceived that Hachiman was a supporter of the imperial line, and of the northern Fujiwara branch. In order to strengthen these ties, it was decided to install Hachiman at a location near Kyoto, and Gyōkyō was given the assignment. According to later accounts, in the summer of 859 both Gyōkyō and the emperor were instructed by Hachiman in dreams to build a temple at Otokoyama, and soon the task was completed. It is interesting to note the role of the Hachiman cult in cementing the powers of the Fujiwara; Yoshifusa was the first of the famous "Fujiwara regents," the first regent not of the imperial family.

Also significant is the Iwashimizu Shrine's connection with the Ki family. Before the founding of the Hachiman Shrine at Otokoyama, the mountain was the site of a Ki family temple, Iwashimizu-dera. This was transformed into the imperially-commissioned temple, Gokoku-ji, that eventually merged with the Hachiman Shrine. Even after Gyōkyō's time the shrine administrator (*bettō*) was chosen from the Ki family. This family connection might account for the prominence of Otokoyama in Ki no Tsurayuki's *Kokinshū*, both in the preface and in the poems included. Furthermore, from 929 onward, a hereditary father-to-son lineage for the *bettō* was established. This of course required that the official be openly non-celibate, and in fact this phenomenon predates the medieval practice of married priests in the Jōdo Shin sect. It is therefore possible that the tension in *Ominameshi* concerning the compromised celibacy of Buddhist priests on the mountain is a reflection of this historical pattern.

There are two first-category plays in the standard repertoire that feature the Iwashimizu Hachiman Shrine, *Yumi Yawata* and *Hōjōgawa*. The first of these does touch upon the martial theme associated with Empress Jingū, evident in the "bow" image found throughout, and in the following passage:

> (*sashi*)
> Thus due to Empress Jingū's
> subjugation of the three Korean kingdoms,
> and, similarly, Emperor Ōjin's sagely good fortune,
> the [current] Reign is long, the country prospers, and the people too

enjoy plenty in the peaceful realm under Heaven,
even now the generous tributes do not end.

然るに神功皇后。
三韓を鎮め給ひしりより
同じく応神天皇の御聖運
御在位も久し国富み民も。
豊かに治まる天が下。
今に絶えせぬ。調とかや[4]

The *kuse* presents a summary of the shrine's history:

From the moon laurel above the clouds
down to the masses below
the voices of delight are ceaseless,
so it is said, yet
because the blessings that protect our Lord are deep,
it was during Emperor Kinmei's reign that
in Buzen province,
in the district of Usa,
at the base of the Rendai temple
the Hachiman Shrine appeared;[5]
later, with eightfold flag-clouds beckoning,
in the capital region's
tall southern hills,
to protect the flawless Reign,
at Iwashimizu a pure,
sacred shrine appeared.

[4] Sanari Kentarō, ed., *Yōkyoku taikan*, vol. 6 (Tokyo: Meiji shoin, 1931), 3228.

[5] Kitabatake Chikafusa's *Jinnō shōtōki*, written in 1339, records, "Ōjin first revealed himself as a kami during the reign of Emperor Kinmei. Appearing at the Hishikata Pond in Higo province, Kyushu, he said: "I am Homuda-no-Yahatamaru of the sixteenth reign of human sovereigns." Homuda was Ōjin's original name and Yahata was his cognomen as an avatar (*suijaku*). Ōjin was later installed as the god Hachiman at the Usa shrine in Buzen province." Iwasa Masashi, et al., eds., *Jinnō shōtōki* in vol. 87 of *Nihon koten bungaku taikei* (Tokyo: Iwanami Shoten, 1965), 80; translation by H. Paul Varley, *A Chronicle of Gods and Sovereigns* (Columbia University, 1980), 105–6.

上の雲上の月卿より。
下万民に至るまで
楽しみの声尽きもせず。
然りとは申せども。
君を守りの御目ぐ恵み猶も深き故により
欽明天皇御宇かとよ。
豊前の国。
宇佐の郡。
蓮臺寺の麓に。
八幡宮と現れ。
八重旗雲をしるべにて。
洛陽の。
南の山高み。
雲らね御代を守らんとて。
石清水いさぎよき。
霊社と現じ給へり。[6]

The passage continues, linking celebrations at the shrine with Empress Jingū:

Just as Empress Jingū,
in order to subdue foreign lands,
prayed for seven days on the peak of Kyushu's Shiō Temple,
now we, in imitation of the bright
Heavenly rock-cave divine amusements,
gather and sing, with *sakaki* branches,
natural cloth streamers, and bleached white cloth streamers
in variety, the divine spirit
(*shite*)
transforms, following the traces of the Age of the Gods.

されば神功皇后も。
異国退治の御為に。
九州四王寺の峯に於いて七箇日の御神拝。
例も今は久方の。
天の岩戸の神遊び。

[6] Sanari, op. cit., 3228–9.

群れゐて謡ふや榊葉の。
青和幣白和幣とりどりなりし神霊を
シテ 移すや神代の跡すぐに[7]

Yumi Yawata establishes important motifs that recur in other plays. The historical sequence of Jingū—Ōjin—Usa Shrine—Iwashimizu Shrine is presented, as is a parallel centrifugal model of divine blessing, bestowed from the emperor above to the masses below. Significantly, the emperor is equated with the laurel tree said to grow on the moon.

This moon image also appears prominently in *Hōjōgawa.* According to the remarks of Itō Masayoshi,[8] this play, generally considered to be of later composition than *Yumi Yawata*, was written by Zeami and performed for the Ashikaga shoguns. Yoshimitsu and Yoshimochi were strong patrons of the Iwashimizu Shrine, in part due to its martial associations, making 24 and 36 pilgrimages, respectively. This play takes place during the Hōjōe, a major festival at the shrine celebrated on the day of the full moon during the eighth month. It features the Buddhist rite of "releasing living things" (*hōjō*), in this case thousands of fish and fowl into the river at the base of the mountain that has been dubbed "Hōjōgawa."[9]

The first song of the *shite* and *tsure* merges the divine lunar spirit of the beneficent god/emperor above with the liberated fish below:

On the waves that free the living fishes,
the moon, too, moves in the autumn waters.

〈一セイ〉 鱗類の生けるを放す川波に
月も動くや秋の水[10]

[7] Ibid., 3229.

[8] Itō Masayoshi, ed., *Yōkyokushū*, vol. 3 (Tokyo: Shinchōsha, 1988), 480.

[9] It has been speculated that originally fish were raised as shrine offerings; with the introduction of Buddhist ideology to Otokoyama, the practice was transformed to a release of the fish. See Murayama, op. cit., 70–1.

[10] Itō, vol. 3, 220. Similar imagery is found in *Hachiman gudōkun*, an important *engi* account probably written in the early fourteenth century by an Iwashimizu Hachiman priest: "At the foot [of Otokoyama] the river's water is clear, floating the light of the moon on the fifteenth day; this is the place where the release of living things is performed." *Zoku gunsho ruijū* 2, pt. 1, 58.

In *Sanbōe*, the *setsuwa* collection dated 984, it is recorded that the Hōjōe originated as an atonement for the subjugation of the Hayato, a rebellious ethnic group in southern Kyushu, in the early eighth century.[11] Accordingly, *Hōjōgawa* refers to the killing of "foreigners":

(*tsure*)
During the time of the subjugation of foreign lands
many of the enemy were destroyed;
as a virtuous action that returns us to the Buddha Nature,
the vow to free living things was made.
(*waki*)
Hearing this rationale, how thankful I feel!
Then where is the river where living things are released?
(*shite*)
Look, this stream's
clouded waters are due to the divine virtue's
pure promise, the clear waters emerging from the rocks
flow to one place, this river
whose bank I face . . .

ツレ 異国退治のおん時に
多くの敵を滅ぼし給ひし
帰性の善根のそのために
放生の御願を発し給ふ
ワキ 謂はれを聞けば有難や
さてさて生けるを放すなる川はいづくのほどやらん
シテ 御覧候へこの小川の
水の濁りも神徳の
誓ひは清き石清水の
ワキ 末はひとつぞこの川の
シテ 岸に臨みて[12]

[11] Mabuchi Kazuo, et al., eds., *Sanbōe, Chūkōsen* in vol. 31 of *Shin Nihon koten bungaku taikei* (Tokyo: Iwanami Shoten, 1997), 208. For translation and additional notes, see Edward Kamens, *The Three Jewels* (Ann Arbor, 1988), 345–8.
[12] Itō, vol. 3, 222.

Illustrated here is the Buddhist concept of *gyakuen*, or "backward connection." In contrast to *jun'en*, whereby one establishes a link to the Dharma by doing good deeds, *gyakuen* denotes a process by which evil deeds, or actions that violate the precepts, provide the connection. In this case, killing leads to atonement and the meritorious practice of *hōjō*. A similar "backward" logic is then presented through the sacred geography of the Otokoyama site: the cloudy waters in which the fish are released, seemingly impure, are in fact sacred because, flowing from the pure spring waters emerging from the rocks at Iwashimizu (literally, "pure water [from] boulders") Shrine, they are evidence of the deity's vow to descend to the lower realms. Next, the life-force of the fish is in turn seen as a blessing to the surrounding landscape:

As I release these fish
placed in this bucket
both skirt and sleeve get wet,
dipping into the water myself,
sinking to the water's bottom in the bucket,
the fish, delighted, wiggle their fins
and as they pierce the water,
by the shaded shore
the lotus leaves move.
At the sight of these frolicking fish,
indeed the vow to release life
is renewed.

[ワキ]水桶に
〈上ゲ歌〉[地]取り入れるる
このうろくづを放さんと
この鱗類を放さんと
裳裾も同じ袖ひぢて
掬ぶやみづから水桶を
水底に沈むれば
魚は喜び鰭ふるや
水を穿ちて岸陰の

潭荷葉動く
これ魚の遊ぶありさまの
げにも生けるを放すなる
おん誓ひあらたなりけり[13]

The play continues with a retelling of the shrine's founding:

(*kuri*)
Well then, the shrine in question,
counting from the past of Emperor Kinmei
over one hundred years had passed when
it was moved to this mountain.

(*sashi*)
Then as the deity of the royal monument,
guarding the realm, aiding the nation,
the two paths of literary and military arts spread widely;
the nine-fold palace leads to eight-flag Yahata,
in the deity's name too is the character "eight,"
showing that the emergence of the gods is Fundamentally Void,
indicating the path of the True Nature of Birthlessness,
denoting the Eightfold Path,
with a mind that the gods and Buddhas are not two,
the deity resides with a head of honesty.

(*kuse*)
Rather than other lands, to our country,
rather than other peoples, to our people
he pledged his blessing.
Indeed how thankful we are!
Such shallow people are we,
to shine on our blind wanderings,
his vow is before our eyes:
in Priest Gyōkyō's
Dharma water reflect the forms
of the flowery capital, to protect it

[13] Ibid., 222.

the southern-hill-dwelling clear moon's
light, full, in three-
fold sleeves is reflected.
Then, the imperial monument's
traces clearly Your Majesty's reign's
straight path express;
the land prospers, even to the people's hearths,
the lively tribute ships,
the waves of the four seas are calm.
The vow to benefit all the masses,
ease and pleasure in this world and the next,
this divine virtue ever prosperous on
Otokoyama where pines stand,
through both treetops and grasses the wind blows,
all echo True Form,
the mountain-wigs on the peak,
the village *kagura*,
the heart of repentance awakens from its dream,
the voices of the Realm
are indeed divine,
in moonlight lie the shadowing rocks of Iwashimizu's pure waters,
not shallow his vow,
indeed his vow is not shallow.

〈クリ〉そもそも当社と申すは
欽明天皇の昔より
一百余歳の世々を経て
この山に移りおはします

〈サシ〉しかるに宗廟の神として
御代を守り国家を助け
文武二つの道広く
九重つづく八幡山
神にも御名は八つの文字
それ諸仏出世の本来空

真性不生の道を示し
八正道を顕はし
人仏不二の御心にて
正直の頭に宿り給ふ

〈クセ〉人の国よりわが国
他の人よりもわが人と
誓はせ給ふおん恵み
げにあらがたや
われらごときの浅ましき
迷ひを照らし給はんの
その御誓願目のあたり
行教和尚の
御法の水に影うつる
花の都を守らんと
南の山にすむ月の
光もみつの
衣手にうつり給へり
さればにや宗廟の
跡明らかに君が代の
直なる道を顕はし
国富み民の竈まで
賑ふ鄙の御調船
四海の波も静かなり
利益諸衆生のおん誓ひ
二世安楽の
神徳はなほ栄行くや
男山にし松立てる
梢も草も吹く風の
みな実相の響きにて
峰の山かづら
そのほか里神楽
懺悔の心夢覚め
夜声も

いとど神さびて
月かげろふの石清水の
浅からぬ誓ひかな
げに浅からぬ誓ひかな[14]

This passage is the most important precedent for *Ominameshi*'s vision of Otokoyama; three central thematic conceptions stand out. First is the notion that the Shinto and Buddhist aspects of the site are fundamentally nondual, due to the recurrence of the number eight ("Ya" in Yawata, "Hachi" in Hachiman, and the Eightfold Path preached by the historical Buddha).[15] This amalgamation theme is also underscored by the god Hachiman's Buddhist title "Daibosatsu," and by the transference of Hachiman to Otokoyama through the agency of the Buddhist priest Gyōkyō. The second major conceit is the association of Buddhism with a robe: the flowers of the capital are seen in the "Dharma sleeves" of Gyōkyō, and the light of the clear moon reflects in his robe, resulting in an Amida trinity, according to legend.[16] And third, the natural elements of the landscape itself illustrate religious concepts: the depth of the pure spring waters flowing from the massive moonlit boulders at Iwashimizu is symbolic of the profound vow of Hachiman, and the sound of the wind blowing through the pines and grasses extols the law of impermanence, revealing True Form. The rest of the passage is sprinkled with various auspicious images appropriate for a celebratory play.

In *Ominameshi*, the religious history of Otokoyama is detailed after the extended initial dialogue between *waki* and *shite*. This passage presents many of the same images and motifs found in

[14] Ibid., 222–3.

[15] *Jinnō shōtōki* records: "The name Hachiman derives from an oracle that states: 'Upon acquiring the Way, he was endowed with an immutable Dharma nature. With the Eightfold Noble Path as his guide, he appeared as an avatar to assist all suffering people to attain salvation. This is why he is called Hachiman Daibosatsu.'" Iwasa, op. cit., 81; trans. in Varley, op. cit., 106.

[16] *Jinnō shōtōki* records: "There is the practice in Buddhism of placing eight-colored flags in eight directions. In the esoteric tradition, these flags represent Amida of the western region. Presumably this was why Hachiman revealed himself to the priest Gyōkyō in the form of an Amida trinity. Finding the image of this trinity glowing lustrously on his cape (*kesa*), Gyōkyō enshrined the cape at Otokoyama." Iwasa, ed., op. cit., 81; trans. in Varley, op. cit., 107.

Hōjōgawa, in a more concentrated form. It begins with the "clouded water" trope:

> The human dwellings beneath the mountain are lined up roof to roof,
> the dust of the softened light is the clouded water
> of the river where float fish—
> indeed renewed is the profound vow to release living things,
> how abundant the blessings at Otokoyama,
> how thankful the flourishing path to its summit.
>
> 山下の人家軒を並べ
> 和光の塵も濁り江の
> 河水に浮かむ鱗類は
> けにも生けるを放つかと深き誓ひもあらたにて
> 恵みぞ茂き乙子山
> さかゆく道のありがたさよ[17]

Here the clouded water is described in terms of *wakō dōjin* (softening the light, merging with the dust), an expression widely associated with Buddhist-Shinto amalgamation. This phrase actually originates in *Lao Tzu*, Chapter 4:

> Tao is empty (like a bowl),
> It may be used but its capacity is never exhausted.
> It is bottomless, perhaps the ancestor of all things.
> It blunts its sharpness,
> It unties its tangles.
> It softens its light.
> It becomes one with the dusty world.
> Deep and still, it appears to exist forever.
> I do not know whose son it is.
> It seems to have existed before the Lord.[18]

[17] Itō Masayoshi, ed., *Yōkyokushū*, vol. 1 (Tokyo: Shinchōsha, 1983), 250.
[18] Trans. Wing-tsit Chan, *A Source Book in Chinese Philosophy* (Princeton, 1963), 141.

This passage is often viewed as political advice for a ruler, who should diminish his charismatic wisdom and authority to effect change amidst the masses. As in *Hōjōgawa*, the *Ominameshi* playwright has skillfully equated darkness—a positive attribute of the Tao—with the clouded waters where the fish are released, thus further endowing the rite with spiritual benefit. The more immediate source for the concept of *wakō dōjin* in medieval religion, however, is the widely-circulated passage from the Tendai patriarch Chih-i's *Maka shikan* that gives the phrase its Buddhist significance: "Tempering the light and merging with the dust begins the connection to the Dharma, and attaining the Way through the Eight Phases determines completion."[19] These words indicate that the Buddha manifests in the world of dust to preach the Dharma and finish his mission of enlightening the masses. (Note that the full quotation contains the Eightfold Path motif that, through the number eight, is associated with Hachiman and Yahata, as noted above.) In its most common medieval usage, *wakō dōjin* is used to illustrate the *honji suijaku* theory: the "fundamental" cosmic Buddhas temper their light to appear in the world in the guise of native *kami*, their "trace manifestations." In my opinion, however, here the Buddhist/Shinto dialectic is not the focus; the thrust is simply that Hachiman's beneficence extends to the lower, darker reaches.

The passage continues:

> The time is the middle day of the eighth month,
> we bow down before the station
> of the Deity's august progress,
>
> The all-embracing
> moon's bright light at Otokoyama, recalling the laurel-man in the moon, by the nature of the place
> shines on the red leaves so brightly that
> even the sun is obscured,
> by the boulders of Iwashimizu with its pure waters,
> the moss robe is wondrous:

[19] Sekiguchi Shindai, ed. *Maka shikan*, vol. 2 (Tokyo: Iwanami Shoten, 1966), 7.

on the triptych sleeves the images have transferred,
now deposited in the treasured chest of signs
of this sacred shrine of the Law,
so grateful are we for this spiritual site!

ころは八月なかばの日
神の御幸なる
お旅所を伏し拝み

久方の
月の桂の男山
月の桂の男山
さやけき影は所から
紅葉も照り添ひて
日もかげろふの石清水
苔の衣も妙えなれや
三つの袂に影うつる
璽の箱を納むなる
法の神宮寺
ありがたかりし霊地かな[20]

This section can be viewed, first of all, as a microcosm of the shrine's religious history. The moon symbolizes the divinity of Hachiman that shines on the red leaves of the autumnal slopes of Otokoyama; blinding in its purity, even brighter than the sun, the divine spirit permeates the rocks and the pure waters. These waters in turn consecrate the Buddhist robe of the priest Gyōkyō, and an Amida trinity miraculously appears in its sleeves. In this progression of poetic imagery, the key transition from Shinto to Buddhist symbolism is accomplished through the phrase "Iwashimizu koke no koromo": the pure waters seep onto moss, which in turn is associated with the "moss robes" of Buddhist priests. The sacred treasure of this robe is now deposited as a permanent sign of the arrival of Buddhism on the mountain.

[20] Itō, op. cit., 250–1.

It is also possible to discern here a metaphorical pattern of procreation. In Japanese mythology, the male is often represented by the moon, the female by the sun, in contrast to most cultures. The most prominent examples are the sun goddess Amaterasu and her male counterpart at Ise, Toyouke-ōkami of the Outer Shrine, who is often associated with the moon in medieval Shinto. Furthermore, there is ample evidence that the moon is associated with semen, in contrast to the redness of menstrual blood. Therefore the light of the moon, explicitly male here (through the laurel man in the moon), is an impregnating force that shines on the red leaves, a symbol of the female (consider, for example, the *momoji* in *Momijigari*). The pillow word *kagerou no*, associated with words for rocks, alludes to Amaterasu's seclusion in the heavenly rock cave. This famous myth, widely interpreted as a solar eclipse, can also be seen as a pregnancy metaphor: the female secludes herself in the cave while the embryo develops, both finally emerging at birth. In this scenario, the waters would be the amniotic fluid.

At first glance this procreation line of interpretation might seem to be beside the point, but it is possible to combine it with the historical interpretation through the genealogy of the Hachiman deity. According to the *Nihon shoki* account, Emperor Chūai died shortly after Empress Jingū became pregnant with the future Ōjin. Serving as regent and vowing to invade Silla, she was said to insert a rock inside the birth canal to delay the delivery until her return to Japan.[21] Furthermore, after Ōjin lived out his life as an emperor and was enshrined as a Shinto divinity, he was said to take frequently the form of Hachiman in the guise of a Buddhist monk (*sōgyō Hachiman*), a popular icon in medieval religion. Thus the passage might be a symbolic account of Ōjin's birth and subsequent transition to a Buddhist deity,[22] just as the pure waters of the shrine transform into priestly moss-robes.

The text then shifts to a broad panoramic view, extolling the interconnectedness of the landscape:

[21] Sakamoto Tarō et al. eds., *Nihon shoki 1* in vol. 67 of *Nihon koten bungaku taikei* (Tokyo: Iwanami Shoten, 1965), 336. For translation, see W.G. Aston, trans. *Nihongi* (Rutland, Vt., 1972), 229.

[22] In the *Hachiman gudōkun* account, Ōjin's spirit first appeared in Buddhist form as "Ninmon Bosatsu;" see Murayama, op. cit., 328–9.

Craggy pines rise high,
mountains tower, encircling the valley,
the branches of all trees connected together.
Cutting through here to dove peak, we look:
all three thousand worlds are none other than this,
for a thousand leagues the same moon,
the moonlit night brightens as
the vermilion jewelled fence is visible, the inner sanctum's
brocade suspended, just to speak of it,
we bow down in awe.

巌松峙つて
山そびえ谷めぐりて
諸木枝を連らねたり
鳩の嶺超し来て見れば
三千世界も外ならず
千里も同じ月の夜の
あけの玉垣みとしろの
錦かけまくも
忝けなしと伏し拝む[23]

Once the Buddhist religion has been installed on the mountain, a specifically Buddhist vision of the sacred is celebrated; the natural landscape itself illustrates a teaching of interpenetration (this is similar to the "through both treetops and grasses the wind blows, / echoing True Form" concept in *Hōjōgawa*). The expression "three thousand worlds" (*sanzen sekai*) alludes to the doctrine of "three thousand worlds in a single thought" (*ichinen sanzen*), the Tendai notion that all realms of existence, from the highest Buddha lands to the lowest hells, are interpenetrating and mutually dependent. As a result, the moonlight of wisdom extends everywhere, consecrating the lacquered fence of the shrine compound and its inner treasure; once again, Buddhist and Shinto visions of the sacred are unified. Note how the previous section concludes with the temple that protects the

[23] Itō, op. cit., 251.

shrine, while here we return to the inner, seminal essence of the (lunar) Shinto divinity.

Looked at in tandem, the two sections discussed here exhibit a circularity, beginning and ending with the moon; within that cycle, there is a sense of macrocosmic creation, dispersion, and renewal. In my opinion, this sequence bears a striking resemblance to Komparu Zenchiku's "six circles, one dewdrop" typology as presented in numerous performance treatises.[24] It is not possible to go into great detail here, but to summarize, the first three circles can be described as a centrifugal sequence: 1) a unified, formless Absolute, a primal creative life force; 2) the generation of form and feeling; 3) the smooth ebb and flow of successive natural forms. The second set of three circles represents a centripetal sequence: 4) the composite diversity of the natural world; 5) the entropic dissolution of that seamless reality; 6) dissolution into a formless Absolute. The final One Dewdrop is the distilled essence of all six circles. While there are certainly Buddhist counterparts to the first three circles, the essential quest in traditional Buddhism—meditation upon, and deconstruction of, conventional reality to achieve a state of no mind—is found in circles 4-6. In contrast, Zenchiku himself assigned Shinto significance to only circles 1-3, as an analogue to the "division of heaven and earth" cosmogony as depicted in the Shinto classics.

The alignment with the *Ominameshi* passage is as follows:

1. Circle of Longevity (*jurin*) = all-embracing moon; potent divinity
2. Circle of Height (*shurin*) = moonlight shining outward, on red leaves
3. Circle of Abiding (*jūrin*) = seclusion beneath rocks, spirit stored in box; emergence of water, robes, Buddhism
4. Circle of Forms (*zōrin*) = Buddhist vision of interpenetrating mountain, valley, branches
5. Circle of Breaking (*harin*) = immediate reality shattered to embrace three thousand worlds
6. Circle of Emptiness (*kūrin*) = moonlight everywhere

[24] For translation and analysis of selected *rokurin ichiro* treatises, see Arthur Thornhill, *Six Circles, One Dewdrop* (Princeton, 1993).

7. One Dewdrop (*ichiro*) = hidden essence, the glimmering jeweled railing of the inner sanctum

Such an alignment could provide evidence to support a Zenchiku attribution for *Ominameshi*. The notion that Zenchiku might have incorporated *rokurin ichiro* patterns into his plays, just as Zeami implemented *jo-ha-kyū*, must be examined further before any firm conclusions can be drawn. But whoever the author might be, this pattern further clarifies the sacred geography of the Otokoyama site where the human story of *Ominameshi* unfolds. On the one hand, there is a clear dichotomy between the purity of the "male mountain" itself and the impure element of the ladyflowers. This bipolarity is reinforced by the pure vs. clouded water imagery discussed earlier, and by the corresponding upper slopes and lower liminal region, the river. But at the same time, when the perspective shifts from Shinto to Buddhist, a Buddhist vision of nonduality consecrates even the lower realms, providing a glimmer of hope that a rigidly dualistic world view denies. In particular, Buddhist ideology both clarifies the nature of sin and provides for its transcendence. An example is the Hōjōe, celebrated on the day the action of the play occurs: it both acknowledges the dark side of Jingū's beneficent rule and provides for its purification. It is perhaps significant that during the actual release of fishes, the shrine priests who descend to the river wear lively, bright colored robes, symbolizing the vitality of the liberated beings. However, as darkness falls they return to the mountain wearing white robes, emblematic of the world of death, according to the medieval account recorded in Musō Soseki's *Muchū mondō*.[25] Similarly, in the second act of the play darkness falls and the Buddhist afterlife is depicted, as Yorikaze's spirit suffers the consequences of a Buddhist-defined sin. The sacred mountain of the *maeba* becomes its spiritual inverse, a tortuous mound of swords in Buddhist hell. The *rokurin ichiro* parallel is particularly suggestive here, since in his critical writings Zenchiku often used the *sanzen ichinen* teaching to illustrate that even hell dwellers are non-dually unified with the Buddha. Furthermore, the potential of salvation appears at the end of the play, as the ladyflower is associated with the lotus through its "dewy calyx"; the dew image suggests the One Dewdrop.

[25] Quoted in Itō, vol. 3, 480–1.

The *wakō dōjin* motif further enriches the spiritual dynamics of the play. On the one hand, the brilliant white light of the male deity has his privileged preserve on the slopes of Otokoyama; it is a sacred site that preserves pre-Buddhist attitudes toward the polluting presence of death, and women, on its slopes. But when the light is softened, it descends to the lower realms (here, the river) and can engage licentious desire, killing in wartime, and animal suffering, all to complete the way of the Buddha and save sentient beings. At first glance, this configuration appears to give historical and ontological priority to the Shinto gods, who have provisionally appeared in Buddhist guise to spread compassion amidst the "dust" of the world. Such a pattern is functionally equivalent to the "reverse *honji suijaku*" doctrine, developed by Shinto scholars of the Yoshida family, that became increasingly popular in the fifteenth century. On the other hand, it is also possible to see here a standard *honji suijaku* pattern. Amida is the orthodox *honji* of Hachiman.[26] Often equated with the moon traveling westward, Amida might be symbolized by the moon at the beginning of the passage; Hachiman in any form is thus already a trace-manifestation of Amida. This would account for the images of the Amida trinity that manifested on the robe of Gyōkyō.

In conclusion, how does the Otokoyama site of *Ominameshi* measure up to Suma in *Matsukaze*? Consider the identities of the dramatis personae in the latter play. The *shite* and *tsure*, named Pining Wind (Matsukaze) and Fitful Rain (Murasame), represent deep, constant yearning and passionate, stormy love, respectively; Matsukaze is glorified as a model of eternal love. The Suma locale enhances the emotional depth of the play, providing a wealth of poetic detail. Furthermore, the outer facade of poverty and loneliness of Suma highlights the inner nobility and emotional profundity of the women who long for the elegance of the capital and their lover, the courtier Yukihira. *Yūgen*, defined as outer simplicity and darkness that implies inner depth and brilliance,[27] is thus enhanced by the literary heritage of Suma.

[26] See note 16 for the iconic connection between Amida and Hachiman. However, the first recorded *honji* for Hachiman is Shakyamuni; see Murayama, op. cit., 68.

[27] See Arthur Thornhill, "*Yūgen* After Zeami," in James R. Brandon, ed. *Nō and Kyōgen in the Contemporary World* (Honolulu, 1997), 39–41.

In *Ominameshi*, the *shite* Yorikaze is a personification of the glancing wind that causes the ladyflower, the *tsure*, to turn away in aversion. He is a less admirable figure than Matsukaze, his wandering (rather than constant) heart full of lustful desire. Furthermore, the willful suicides of the two principals seem to contradict the sacred stature of the mountain; they kill themselves in the very river where life is affirmed in the Hōjō rite. Nevertheless, I would argue that, no less than Suma, Otokoyama also generates a *yūgen* effect. Due to the phenomenon of *wakō dōjin*, the darkness of the lower realms—the river, the hellish suffering—is merely the tempered light of the Hachiman deity, engaged in salvation for all.[28] In fact, the deeper the darkness, the more profound the workings of *wakō dōjin* (in a logic reminiscent of Shinran's Amidist theology). In this way, the site provides the inner glow amidst external darkness of *yūgen* which, in Zenchiku's own words, is functionally equivalent to the Buddha Nature inherent in all things.[29] The result is a heightening of dramatic pathos and a deepened sympathy for the *shite*'s spiritual plight.

[28] The term *yūgen* actually appears in *Hachiman gudōkun*: "As for the actual body of [the deity's] trace-manifestation, its divinity is faint and dark (*shinryo yūgen ni shite*), so it is invisible to the impure eyes of the common person..." *Zoku gunsho ruijū* 2, pt. 1, 59. Elsewhere in the same work, Hachiman compares himself to a metallurgist, who refines away the dark impurities of sinners to reveal the inner gold of wisdom; furthermore, true believers benefit by basking in his tempered light (*wakō*). Ibid., 52.
[29] As discussed in his *Shidō yōshō*, a late performance treatise. See Thornhill, "*Yūgen* After Zeami," pages 50-5.

八幡菩薩の和光

アーサー・ソーンヒル

「女郎花」には男山という所在地が重要である。この地は根本的な詩的描写（男山、女郎花、吹き下ろす風）をもたらすだけではなく、石清水八幡宮の所在地でもある。この小論文は男山の霊地としての研究とこの地の「女郎花」の中でのテーマの重要性に関するものである。

当初、九州の宇佐に祭られていた八幡菩薩は、僧侶行教によって859年に男山に勧請された。それにより八幡は地方の神から国の神、つまり応神天皇の神体へと変化した。応神天皇は朝鮮半島の侵略を率いた神宮皇后を母にもつ4世紀の神話におびた天皇である。それ故に、八幡は能曲「弓八幡」や「放生川」に見られるように戦(いくさ)の神として知られている。「放生川」は戦時の殺生を償うため捕らえられた生類を放つ仏教の儀式、放生会に基づく。この儀式が行われる川は「女郎花」の心中の場でもある。

「女郎花」の前場の霊場の詳細な一節は、八幡が神道の神から仏教の権現へと変身する比喩的、小宇宙的な再説であり、なお、その懐妊と誕生の象徴的記述と読み取ることができる。また、この一節内の写象主義的進行と金春禅竹の「六輪一露」の象徴的類型とはよく似ている。これは禅竹の作品であるという証拠になり得る。

この能曲内における八幡菩薩の存在の重要な要素は、「和光同塵」、即ち光を和らげ、塵に混じる事で、菩薩は苦と闇の下界に入るために己の輝きを隠し、川の中の動物や苦しむ人間たち、特にシテである頼風に慈悲を施すということである。「和光同塵」という現象により、下界の闇は救済に励む八幡菩薩の和らいだ光と化す。実に、闇が深ければ深いほど、和光同塵の効果は凄まじいものである。このように、男山の地は幽玄の外面的な暗さに内面的な光を与えるもので、これは金春禅竹の言う仏性に機能的には相当する。

「女郎花」の作者は金春禅竹か

西　野　春　雄

1.　はじめに

私は、新日本古典文学大系『謡曲百番』「女郎花」[1]の各曲解題で素材・主題について、つぎのように記した。多少言葉を補い、仮に番号を付して再掲してみよう。

a. 古今集・仮名序の「男山の昔を思ひ出て、女郎花の一時をくねるにも、歌を言ひてぞ慰めける」に関する古今和歌集序聞書三流抄等の古注にみえる頼風説話に拠りつつ、男山に咲き乱れ秋風にくねる女郎花の風情を背景として、男の心変わりを疑い入水した女と、女の跡を追い身を投げた男の恋慕の妄執を描く。
b. 前ジテ花守の老人とワキ旅僧との女郎花をめぐる風雅で諧謔な詩歌問答は「雲林院」などと同趣向で、8月15日の放生会の夜の、さやけき月の桂の男山八幡の風光を愛でる名所教えとともに、前場は明るく長く、中入直前の男塚・女塚の話を転換点として、頼風夫婦の霊が地獄で「邪淫の悪鬼に身を責め」られる在様を描く後場は暗く短く、その対照は鮮烈である。
c. その後場は「求塚」に学んだらしいが、類曲「舟橋」に比べ優雅な趣が漂うのは、主人公小野の頼風の貴公子姿に拠るものであろう。
d. 世阿弥の五音や申楽談儀所引の「女郎花」（田楽喜阿弥作曲の古曲）とは別曲ながら、詞章の一部の借用や、女郎花の詠歌を多用した文飾など古曲の影響が看取される。
e. 文辞・作曲から作者は金春禅竹の可能性もある。
f. 死者の魂が草花に変じ墓から生じた話はギリシア神話や中国の虞美人草説話（「項羽」に脚色）など、洋の東西に共通する。

本論では、作者にかかわるｅについて、とくに節付ケの面から具体的な事例を分析し、作者として金春禅竹が古曲を基に新作した可能性を指摘してみたい。またｂも構想や人物描写の面から作者を考える手掛かりになる。さらにｄは成立過程を考察する上で注意したい点である。

2. 作者認定の方法

作者の認定は困難を伴うことが多い。横道萬里雄氏は『岩波講座能・狂言 III 能の作者と作品』[2]で、能本の作者の認定について次のように述べている。

> 能本は、その作者の認定が困難なものが多い。資料がすくなく、かつ不完全なためである。認定のための資料としては、数種の作者付があり、伝書類や上演記録などに散見する関係記事がある。またときには、写本の能本の奥書きが資料となることもある。
>
> 作者付は、ひとまとめに多くの能本の作者について知り得る点で便利だが、後に述べるように信頼度の低いばあいもある。成立事情から見て信頼度が高い作者付でも、演目によっては、まるのみこみに作者決定の材料とするわけにはいかないばあいがある。（略）
>
> 資料による作者の認定に不安があるときは、能本の内容に作者の特色を見るしか方法がない。素材のとらえかた、主題のおきかた、構想のたてかたをはじめとして、詞章の細部にいたるまで、意外に多方面に作者の特色は見出される。[1]

として、世阿弥作の「西行桜」と観世信光作の「遊行柳」を具体例に特色を指摘している。

ただ、こうした総合的な判断は、一歩踏み外すと独善的な方向

[1] 西野春雄、校注「女郎花」『謡曲百番』新日本古典文学大系、岩波書店、1998年
[2] 横道萬里雄、他、編『岩波講座能・狂言 III 能の作者と作品』岩波書店、1987年、102頁

> に走るおそれがあり、作者の認定を誤りかねない。だがそれをおそれるあまり、なんでもかでも否定的結論に結び付けるというのも、また正しい態度とは言えないであろう。そこのかねあいがむずかしいのだが、物事の研究には、常にある程度誤認の危険が伴うものなので、そこを乗り越えるのが研究者の識見と言うものであろう[3]

と結んでいる。

筆者は全面的に氏の見解に共感する。作者の確実な作品の分析を基礎にしながら、「素材のとらえかた、主題のおきかた、構想のたてかた」、作詞・作曲の進め方、古歌詩句の引用の仕方などを検討し、作品をして語らせ、その内なる声を聞くべきであろう。

3. 作曲者の作風

西洋音楽でも日本音楽でも、その作品には作曲者の作風がにじんでいる。アメリカの作曲家ジョージ・ガーシュインにはガーシュインの、イギリスの音楽グループのビートルズにはビートルズの音楽があり、あ、これは誰々の作曲だ、と感じることが多い。能でも、世阿弥が好む節付ケなり旋律があり、信光には「分離のトリ」を多用するいわゆる信光節が指摘できる。

世阿弥の作例をあげれば、『観世』1963年6月号掲載の諸家による「座談会『世阿弥の能』」の中の「世阿弥の能の典型」に見える横道萬里雄氏の発言が非常に示唆深く、作者の認定に生かしたい視点である。

> **横道**「井筒」は確かに世阿弥作だと思いますが、「融」も確実な世阿弥作だと思うんです。「井筒」の後と「融」の後とは節付の形式が非常によく似ています。ツヨ吟とヨワ吟の違いがありますが、他の曲には無い節付があるんですね。「われ筒井筒の」ってところで、現在の観世の節に翻訳すれば本バリが長く

[3] 同上、103頁

続く節になる。「融」の「融の大臣とは我が事なり。われ塩竈の浦に心を寄せ」ってところが同じ節ですね。それから「あの籬が島の松蔭に。明月に舟を浮かめ」ってところが「井筒」の「今は昔に業平の」ってところの形と同じです。あの節なんか他の人には無さそうな感じがするので、「井筒」と「融」が非常に近いことの証拠になると思いますけど…。節付の面で世阿弥独自の、世阿弥好みの傾向として比較的よくわかりますのは、今のような節とか、一セイを崩すのが好きだとか、さきほどの上ノ詠の使い方とか、そういう点ですね。まあ「井筒」「高砂」「融」あたりを、まず世阿弥と、構想の上からも節の上からも、文章の面からも、世阿弥作の典型とみていいんじゃないでしょうか。彼の書いた伝書の記事からも、そう言えそうです。[4]

筆者は1985年、学部4年生の時に、そのころは能楽研究を志すこともまだ決めていなかったし、謡の勉強など何もしていなかったが、横道氏の具体的な指摘にまさに「眼から鱗が落ちる」思いで読んだ。「井筒」「融」とも、世阿弥作たることは動かず、細かい節付ケのすみずみまで作者の好みが及んでいることが知られる。本稿は、上の発言にヒントを得て進めるものである。

4.　「女郎花」の作曲上の特異な点

1）〈サシ〉の「露を含みて」

「女郎花」は、九州松浦の僧が都へ上る途中、石清水八幡に参詣のため男山の野辺に到着するところから始まる。季節は秋、八月十五日、放生会の日。咲き乱れる千草のなかでも、今を盛りと咲き誇る女郎花に心ひかれる。ここは山頂に石清水八幡宮が鎮座する歌枕の「男山」。本曲は、その男（男山）と女（女郎花）とを対比させつつ、しだいに劇空間を作り上げていく手法がおもしろい。女郎花が叢生し、花影揺らめき、秋風に吹き乱れる光景がひろがるこの場

[4]『観世』1963年6月号掲載の諸家による「座談会『世阿弥の能』」の中の「世阿弥の能の典型」

面を、作者はつぎのように描写する。

〈サシ〉 ワキ（節）さても男山麓の野辺に来てみれば、千種の花盛んにして、色を飾り露を含みて、虫の音までも心あり顔なり、野草花を帯びて蜀錦を連ね、桂林雨を払つて松風を調む。

ここは現代語訳すれば、咲き乱れる野の草花は、まるで蜀の錦を連ねたように美しく、桂の林を吹きぬける風は雨の雫を払い、松風（琴の音）のような音を奏でる、といった趣きであろう。何か詩句の典拠があるらしいが見いだせない。「桂林」の語句は後出する「月の桂の男山」の縁で出したのかもしれない。

ところで、〈サシ〉の「露を含みて」の部分は古来節扱い上特に注意すべき箇所と認識されている。「露を」と浮かせ、「含み」は頭より中落トシ（ちゅうおとし）に落とし、「み」に浮キを持たせて、「て」を本バリ（ほんばり）の高さに張り上げ、その廻シ（まわし）の終わりを中落トシの扱いで落とす、という節扱いである。しだいに高く張りあげていくところなどは、聞いていてかなり耳だつ部分である。いま節の推移を図示し、五線譜で示してみよう。

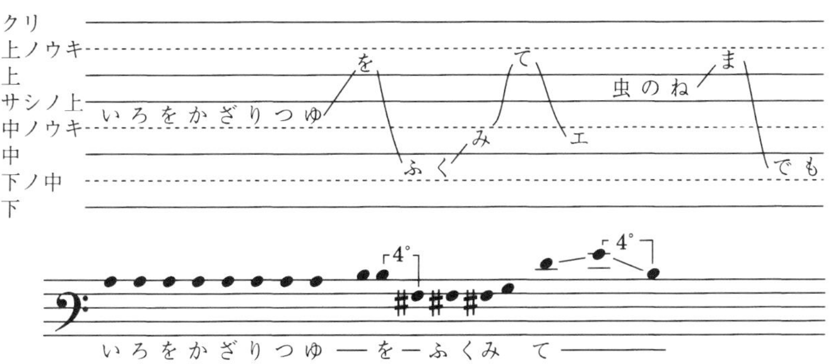

なお、《中落トシ》《本張リ（本バリ）》《本落トシ》について簡単に説明しておこう。

《中落トシ》

「中下ゲ(ちゅうさげ)」とも言う。弱吟（よわぎん）の〈サシ〉や「カヽル」と表記された小段において、出の上音（じょうおん）より初めての「下(げ)」に至った時、まづその前を浮かすのは当然であるが、その落とす程度は一般に、前からの上音とそれに準ずる中音（ちゅうおん）との中間、すなわち半降の音位にとどまるのを通則とするので、このように取るべき「下」に対し、この注記を添えてこれを表示する。そのため、ひとたび「中落トシ」に落ちたならば、以後はその音位を基調として、平常の音階規法に従い推移する。

《本張リ(本バリ)》

弱吟の〈サシ〉や「カヽル」と表記された小段において、出の上音よりいったん中落トシに落ち、そののちその音位を中の基調に取って、新たに高く上昇させる「ハリ」をいう。

《本落トシ》

弱吟の小段において、前来の上音より、真の中音まで落とすこと。すなわち、普通〈サシ〉や「カヽル」と表記された小段では、出の上音とそれに準ずる中音との中間位にとどめる落とし方をし、それを「中落トシ」というのに対して、真の中音まで落とすのでこのように称する。

ここが注意すべき節付ケであることは『縮刷参考謡本』[5]ほか諸書に見えるが、いま三宅紘一氏[6]の説明を借りると、つぎのごとくである。

—サシの本バリ(普通の上音)—

以上はサシ上音を中心としたサシ特有の変化であるが、サシでも一旦中音になった後に出てくるハルはもはやサシ上音ではなくて普通の上音であり、すべて一般の変化に還元することは総説で述べた。この普通の上音のことをサシ上音に対して「本バリ」という。本バリのあの下はむろん本落しであるから、両者を引っ括めて俗に「本バリ・本落し」と称する。(略)

5 『縮刷参考謡本』天・地・人の巻、観世流改訂本刊行会、1930年
6 三宅紘一『節の精解—新訂版—』檜書店、1967年

> たいていは右のような目安で見当がつくと思うが、ときにはサシ上音か本バリか疑わしいような形があったり、また当然サシ上音と思われるのが本バリであったりする。次にごく顕著な句を二三あげておく。[7]

として「女郎花」のほかに「玉鬘」ほかをあげている。問題の「女郎花」の当該部分についてはつぎのように説明している。

> 女郎花ワキの「色をかざり露を含みて」―これも８図（ロ）のように入廻シが本バリだが、廻シのあとが中落し（中浮音）になる。というのは、次句「虫の音までも」をやはり本バリに謡うからである。この句はサシ上音と誤認しやすいから注意されたい。[8]

とある。参考までに同書の譜図８の口を示す。

8（柔）サシの本バリ

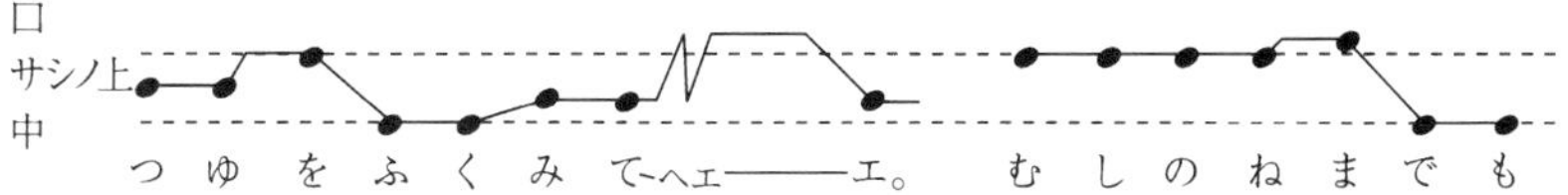

注意したいのは、三宅も指摘するように同様の例が「玉鬘」にあることである。すなわち、

〈サシ〉 シテ（節）あはれ思ひの玉蔓、かけてもいさや知らざりし 地（節）心づくしの木の間の月、雲居のよそにいつしかと、鄙の住居の憂きのみか、さてしも絶えてあるべき身を シテ（節）なほしをりつる人心の 地（節）あらき波風立ち隔て

ここは「木」より浮かせて「の」に移り、「の」の廻シの終わりを中落トシに落とし、「間」に浮キを持たせて、「の」を本バリに高く

[7] 同上、40頁
[8] 同上、42頁

張り上げ、その廻シの終わりを本落トシに落とす。したがって、「の」の本バリは常のハリ（上音）に比してさらに一段高く取るべきものとされている。ここも聞いていてかなり耳だつ部分である。以下に節の推移を図示し、五線譜で示してみると、まったく同一ではないものの、基本の音の推移はほぼ同じであることがわかる。

ふたつを重ね合わせると、多少の出入りはあれ、基本の推移はほぼ同じであり、これは注目していいと思う。こんにち「玉鬘」が金春禅竹作であることは確実視されている。たとえば、伊藤正義氏校注『謡曲集』[9]の各曲解題、あるいは味方健氏『能の理念と作品』[10]などに詳しいが、「玉鬘」と「女郎花」に同じ節付ケがみられることは、同人の作曲とみるのが自然であろう。

かりに「女郎花」が「玉鬘」をまねたということも想定されるが、「女郎花」には、以下に述べるように、そのほかにも金春禅竹作が確実な作品である「杜若」や「楊貴妃」と作曲上の共通点が指摘できるので、同一人物の作曲と考えられてよいと思う。

2)「あら心なの旅人やな」

僧が思わず女郎花に心ひかれ、ひともと手折ろうとした時、花守の老人が現れて、女郎花にまつわる古歌を引いて咎めるセリフに、作者認定に関連し注目したい言葉と節付ケがある。

[9] 伊藤正義氏校注『謡曲集』中、新潮日本古典集成、新潮社、1986年

[10]『能の理念と作品』和泉書院、1999年

〈問答〉 シテ なふなふその花な折り給ひそ、花の色は蒸せる粟のごとし、俗呼ばつて女郎とす、戯れに名を聞いてだに偕老を契るといへり、(節)ましてやこれは男山の、名を得て咲ける女郎花の、多かる花にとりわきて、など情なく手折り給ふ、あら心なの旅人やな。

下線部分「あら心なの旅人やな」が「杜若」のシテの謡にもあり、文句・節付ケともに同一なのである。すなわち、

〈問答〉 シテ なふなふおん僧、なにしにその沢には休らひ給ひ候ぞ
ワキ これは諸国一見の者にて候が、杜若の面白さに詠め居て候、さてここをばいづくと申し候ぞ
シテ これこそ三河の国八橋とて、杜若の名所にて候へ、さすがにこの杜若は、名に負ふ花の名所なれば、(節)色もひとしほ濃紫の、なべての花のゆかり共、思ひなぞらへ給はずして、とりわき詠め給へかし、あら心なの旅人やな。
ワキ（詞）げにげに三河の国八橋の杜若は、古歌にも詠まれけるとなり。

とある。もちろん、「杜若」の主人公は三番目物の女性で優美に、「女郎花」の場合は四番目物の老翁であるから、低めに、しかもしっかりと扱うべきであるが、文句・節付ケともに同一な点は同一作者の手法と見てよいのではあるまいか。

「あら心なの旅人やな」の部分の節扱いは《当タリ下ゲ》または《当タリ落トシ》ともいい、当たって下げる意で、「落チ節」に「当タリ」と「下」の符記号を付けた合成符章である。この《当タリ下ゲ》は強吟（つよぎん）・弱吟（よわぎん）いづれも、中音で出る謡句の首部、または途中にある節で、その直前に必ず「上ガリ節」（上ガリゴマとも）があり、しかも二字前は「小節」であるのを通例とする。

謡い方は強吟・弱吟により差異がある。まづ強吟句においては、直前にある上り節を少し突き上げるように、あたかも入リ節に近似の扱いをなし、そのままこの節に移って当たり、生ミ字以下を下ノ中に下げて歌う。弱吟句にあっては、直前にある上リ節をやや突っ

込むように扱い、そのままこの節に移って当たり、生ミ字よりいくぶん音調を変えて下げる。したがって、次句には常に浮キを控えているので、そこで元の中音に戻る。このように弱吟の《当タリ下ゲ》はいささか音調を変えて下げるため、別に《半クヅシ(はんくづし)》ともいわれている。

3)「鳩の－嶺越し来てみれば」ほか《分離のトリ》

花守の咎めに対し、僧も古歌を引いて応酬するうち、老人も心なごみ花を折ることを許す。やがて山上の石清水八幡宮へ案内し、これより八幡宮を中心とする場面へと展開していく。とくにワキ「聞きしに超えて貴くありがたかりける霊地かな」から、これまでの優美な景色とは一転し、山上の光景、神域の清高な風光をほめたたえる所であり、謡は爽やかにかつ健やかに敬虔な気分で進んでいく。

〈歌〉地 巌松そばだつて、山聳え谷めぐりて、諸木枝を連ねたり、鳩の－嶺越し来てみれば、三千－世界もよそならず、千里も同じ月の夜の、朱けの玉垣みとしろの、錦かけまくも、忝なしと伏し拝む。

眼前には、雄大な望景がひろがり、本曲前場ではもっとも大切な地謡の箇所であるが、ここで注意したいのは、「鳩の－嶺越し来てみれば、三千－世界もよそならず」のように拍律上の技法の一つである《分離のトリ》を用いていることである。ほかにもその前の〈上歌〉に「苔の－衣も妙なりや」、後場の〈クセ〉に「しかじ－憂き世に住まぬまでと」「ともに－土中に籠めしより」と、合計五箇所使われている。

《分離のトリ》は、韻律上、一句であるべきものの一部分を、曲節の変化のために、わざわざ引き離して別の句としたものである。たとえば、世阿弥作の「融」の後場にみえる「鳥は－池辺の樹に宿し」などであり、世阿弥は効果的に使用しているが、観世元雅も金春禅竹も、そして観世信光も金春禅鳳も多用している。したがって、《分離のトリ》の使用だけでは作者を一人には絞りきれないが、注意しておきたいところである。

4)「小野の頼風と申せし人」

石清水八幡宮へ案内し帰りかける老人に、僧は女郎花と男山の謂れを問うので、老人は先刻の問答も無駄だったかと失望しつつも、女郎花の謂れにつながる男塚・女塚に案内する。やがて自分はこの塚の主小野頼風と明かして、月影に消えうせ、中入りするが、ここでも注目したい節付ケが施されている。

〈問答〉 ワキ さてその夫婦の人の国はいづく名字はいかなる人やら
シテ 女は都の人、男はこの八幡山に、(節) 小野の頼風と申せし人。
〈歌〉 (節) 地 恥づかしやいにしへを、語るもさすがなり、申さねばまた亡き跡を、誰か稀にもとむらひの、便りを思ひより風の、更け行く月に木隠れて、夢のごとくに失せにけり、夢のごとくに失せにけり。

下線部「小野の頼風と」の「頼」である。音位の記号に「中」とあるものの、むしろ上音を抑えたような音でしっかりと出て、そのまま息を断たないようにして、さらに力をこめ、「頼風」のとハリを謡う。ここのハリを俗に《乙張り(メリバリ)》と称えていて、ハリの音をメラす。即ちハリを抑えて下に取り、十分にしっかりと張ルべきところである。

これとまったく同じ節付ケが金春禅竹作「楊貴妃」の〈問答〉「その初秋(はつあき)」の「初」の部分に施されている。すなわち、

〈問答〉 シテ げにげにこれも理りなり、思ひぞ出づる我もまた、(節) その初秋の七日の夜、二星に誓ひし言の葉にも。
〈歌〉 地 天にあらば願わくは、比翼の鳥とならむ、地にあらば願わくは、連理の枝とならむと、誓ひしことを、ひそかに伝へよや、私語(ささめごと)なれども、今洩れ初むる涙かな。

である。これら〈問答〉から〈歌〉に移る直前ないし少し前に施された特異な節扱いは、かなり微細な点に属するけれども、注意してよいと思われる。

この特異な節扱いは、ほかには「善知鳥」に見える。すなわち、越中の立山を尋ね地獄さながらの光景を眺め、下山した旅僧（ワキ）の前に現れた不思議な老人の霊（シテ）が、故郷の陸奥の外の浜の妻子へ弔いを頼み、証拠がなくては相手は納得しないだろうとの僧の言葉に、老人が衣の片袖をちぎって渡す次の場面である。

〈問答〉 シテ　や、思ひ出でたりありし世の、今はの時までこの尉が、
　　　(節) 木曽の麻衣(あさぎぬ)の袖を解きて。
〈上歌〉 地　これをしるしにと、涙を添へて旅衣、涙を添へて旅衣、
　　　たち別れ行くその跡は、雲や煙の立山の、木の芽萌ゆる
　　　遥々と、客僧は奥へ下れば、亡者は泣く泣く見送りて、
　　　行く方知らずなりにけり、行く方知らずなりにけり。

この下線を施した「木曽の麻衣」の節付ケである。節付ケには中とあるが上音をしっかり押さえたような調子で謡い出し、「木曽の」と「麻衣」との間を抜くように「ア」の音をこめ、ハリを内へ取り十分抑えて張るのである。細かい旋律ではあるが、案外「善知鳥」の作者の面影を忍ばせている部分として注目しておきたい。

5.　おわりに

これまで「女郎花」に見られる特異な節付ケを中心に、それと同一、あるいは類似、あるいは近似した作品例を示しながら、検討してきた。冒頭に列記した諸点のうち、e 文辞・作曲の面から禅竹の可能性もある、という点の、特に作曲面に絞って考察した。

従来、作者の認定にはほとんど注目されなかったこれらの特色は、いづれも小さな部分に過ぎないが、金春禅竹の作品であることが確実な「玉鬘」や「楊貴妃」に使われている特異な旋律の推移との共通性は、もっと注目してよいと考える。そして、それらを総合する時、「女郎花」の作者（特に作曲者）として金春禅竹の姿が浮かびあがってくるように思われる。筆者は、先行する古作「女郎花」（散佚曲。一部が謡物に伝存）を基にしつつ、金春禅竹があらたに創作した可能性が強いと考えているが、今後は「なほしも」など、

いわゆる《禅竹詞》をはじめとする文辞上の特色や、人物描写、あるいは構想面から検討して、より明確に提示したいと思う。

最後に、節付ケの解読にあたり、三線譜への記載、ならびに五線譜を用いての西洋音階による採譜などについて、この「女郎花研究集会」に参加された観世流シテ方の鵜澤久氏にご協力いただいた。記して御礼申し上げる次第である。

また、「女郎花」について、さまざまな視点から照射し、その多面性を浮き上がらせることに成功したアメリカ・ピッツバーグ大学での「女郎花研究集会」、およびそこに出席された諸氏、とりわけ中心となって研究集会の推進役を勤められたピッツバーグ大学メイ・スメサースト教授に対し、心から深甚の感謝を捧げたい。そして、研究集会の開会中、大きな支えとなってくださったご夫君リチャード・スメサースト教授にも、厚く御礼申し上げる。

Was the Author of *Ominameshi* Komparu Zenchiku?

Nishino Haruo

Based on an analysis of works whose authors are certain, we may determine the authorship for *Ominameshi*. By pointing out several specific musical characteristics, the aim of this essay is to suggest the high probability that the author of *Ominameshi* is Komparu Zenchiku.

In this essay, I analyze the musical aspect (*fushizuke*) of *Ominameshi*, comparing it to *Tamakazura* and *Yōkihi*, two works by Komparu Zenchiku. In *Ominameshi* we find specific melodies that are seen only in the works of Zenchiku. One is the "*tsuyu wo fukumite*" in the *sashi*. This is the song of a traveling monk of Kyūshū-Matsura, who was moved by the thousands of beautiful flowers blooming in the field at the foot of Otokoyama, on his way to Iwashimizu Hachiman Shrine. The other is the "*ara kokoro na no ryōjin ya na*" that forms part of the *mondō* between the monk (*waki*) and old man (*maejite*). As the monk is about to pick the *ominaeshi*, one of the most beautful and famous flowers on Otokoyama, the old man appears and reproaches him.

The structures of the melody lines in these pieces are surprisingly like those of *Tamakazura* and *Yōkihi*. Based on this similarity, we may assume the author of *Ominameshi* to be Komparu Zenchiku.

《女郎花》を読む
―その「作意」の把握をめざして―

天　野　文　雄

は　じ　め　に

能は現代の知識によっては容易に理解しがたい面を少なからず持っている、いささか「むずかしい」演劇です。その理由は、まずはなんといっても600年以上も昔というその制作時期の古さにありますが、それとともに、能を生み出した環境としての文化がやがて消滅してしまい、それが現代にはほとんど継承されていないことにある、といってよいでしょう。要するに、これは長い歴史的時間を時代をこえて生きてきた「古典」というものの宿命なのですが、現在も頻繁に上演されている能の場合は、そのような「むずかしさ」は古典劇としての能の行く末にもいろいろな影響をおよぼすように思われます。能楽研究の目的のひとつは、その「むずかしさ」をすこしでも解消することにあるのだと思うのですが、長年にわたって堆積している能作品における「むずかしさ」はなんと言っても膨大なものがありますから、この点は能楽研究の永遠の課題ということになります。

さて、古典劇としての能の「むずかしさ」は、程度の差はあれ、ほとんどの能作品に存在していると思いますが、ここで取り上げる《女郎花》もその例外ではありません。もっとも、《女郎花》は、たとえば《杜若》のように根本的なところで不可解なものをかかえているような作品ではなく―《杜若》はシテの杜若の精が二条の后でもあり業平でもあるような不可解な設定になっています―、その「むずかしさ」は「作意」の把握にやや苦労するというていどのものです。そのことは1997年10月のピッツバーグでのOminameshi Conferenceに参加して、アメリカの能楽研究者とともに《女郎花》を読んだときに強く受けた印象でもありました。その後は、とくに

《女郎花》をていねいに読みなおす機会もなかったので、筆者の《女郎花》についての理解は5年前のOminameshi Conferenceのときの印象のまま今日にいたりましたが、このたび、研究会の総括として《女郎花》についての論をまとめるにあたり、テーマとしてまず浮かんだのは、やはりその「作意」の把握ということでした。はたしてうまくゆくかどうか、かならずしも十分な目算があるわけではないのですが、以下は、この点についての筆者の現時点での答案です。

1. 妄執物としての《女郎花》

以上のように、この稿はその作意（作品としてのねらい）の把握を中心に《女郎花》を読んでみようというものですが、その問題に入る前に、《女郎花》が属している妄執物という曲柄のなかにおける《女郎花》の特色を確認しておきたいと思います。それは《女郎花》の「作意」を考える場合にも必要なことと思うからです。

《女郎花》が属している妄執物という曲柄は、能の曲柄としてはたいへん古いもので、14世紀（南北朝期）の後半には作られていた《通小町》《船橋》以来の系譜があります。『申楽談儀』によると、《通小町》は比叡山の唱導を得意とした僧の原作を観阿弥が改作したものであり、《船橋》は古作の田楽の能ということです。この2曲は現在知られているかぎりでは最古の能作品ですが、このように妄執物は能の歴史のごく初期から存在していた曲柄で、これは能という演劇の成立の経緯を考える場合に注意されることでもあります。妄執物の能は、その後、半世紀ほどのあいだに、妄執の因を恋愛や邪淫に求めた《玉水》《錦木》《求塚》《定家》《砧》、妄執の因を殺生などに求めた《阿漕》《善知鳥》《長柄橋》などが作られています。これらの作品はいずれも邪淫や殺生ゆえに成仏できないでいる人物が後場に登場して、不成仏の因となった生前の行いをワキ僧の前で再現するという形になっています。後場でおこなわれる生前の行いの再現は主人公の懺悔であり、その結果、主人公は救われるというものです。妄執物の能は、このように主人公の執心や救済を描いている—つまり主人公のそうした執心や救済を主題としている—という点で共通しています。もっとも、この《女郎花》もそうなのですが、妄執物で比較的成立がおそい作品のなかには「救済」を明示しないものがあります。この点は妄執物における微妙な変化としていささか注意されるところですが、ともあれ、このような内容の作品が能の歴史の初期から存在していて、それが強固な類型となって、その後も継続して同じ曲柄の作品を生み出してきたわけです。《女郎花》はこのうち、妄執の因を恋愛に求めたグループに属す能なのですが、このような一群の妄執物のなかにおいてみると、そこにはおのずから《女郎花》の妄執物としての特色がみえてきます。それを端的にうかがわせるのが、後ジテ頼風の扮装です。

妄執物の能の後ジテの扮装は、黒頭に面は痩男・阿波男・怪士というのが基本的なものです。また、《砧》《定家》などシテが女の妄執物の場合は面は泥眼です。つまり、いずれも亡者の姿なのです。これらから、妄執物の主人公は亡者姿が本来のものだったことが知られます。つまり、成仏できない亡霊が、その時点の姿である亡者の姿で登場するというのが妄執物の原形だったのですが、これにたいして、《女郎花》の後ジテである男山の小野頼風の亡霊は、現在は、邯鄲男か中将の面に、風折烏帽子・黒垂・狩衣・大口という扮装で登場します。古い演出資料をみると、面は平太・三ケ月などの場合があり、衣装は長絹・大口や法被・半切などでも演じられています。邯鄲男・三ケ月という面が使用されたりしていますから、やや神霊的な解釈もされているようですが、古い演出資料が伝える後シテの扮装は、基本的には、小野頼風の生前の貴人姿でほぼ一貫していると言ってよいでしょう。

このように、妄執物のなかでは、唯一、《女郎花》だけが、後ジテの姿が亡者ではなく、生前の姿—あるいはそれに近い姿—で登場するのです。この事実は、《女郎花》が妄執物の類型を破ろうと意図した作品で、妄執物としては比較的成立がおそいことを示すものですが、この《女郎花》のように、後ジテが生前の姿で登場するという設定は、妄執物以外に目を転じると、そう珍しいものではありません。というのは、《井筒》や《頼政》のような夢幻能の多くがこの設定になっているからで、《女郎花》が後ジテの頼風を生前の姿で登場させているのは、まず確実にそのような後ジテが生前の姿で登場する形の夢幻能の影響と考えてよいと思われます。この「生前型夢幻能」ともいうべき夢幻能は、《実盛》についての『満済准后日記』の記事から応永21年（1423年）以前には制作されていたことが知られますが、《女郎花》はこの「生前型夢幻能」の影響をうけていると考えてよいでしょう。これを要するに、《女郎花》は能の作品史のうえでは、古くから存在した曲柄である妄執物に、後ジテが生前の姿で登場するという新風の「生前型夢幻能」の特色を加味して作られた作品であり、妄執物の能としては、その点で類型から大きくはずれた作品ということになります。

なお、《女郎花》では、後ジテは自身の生前の悲劇的な事件を物語ったあとでカケリを舞います。生前の優美な貴人姿とカケリのとりあわせについては、これを「不調和」とする見方もありますが(『岩波講座能・狂言Ⅵ〔能楽鑑賞案内〕』)、「生前型夢幻能」である《頼政》《実盛》《八島》などの修羅能では、カケリなどのハタラキ事が演じられるのはごく普通のことですし、《女郎花》がそもそも妄執物の系譜につらなる作品であることを考えると、これはとくに「不調和」とみる必要はないでしょう。この点なども、妄執物として新境地を開いたものと評価してよいのではないかと思います。

2. 《女郎花》の展開についての一つの疑問

ここでようやく《女郎花》における「作意」の問題に入ることになります。さきにものべたように、筆者はピッツバーグでのOminameshi Conference以来、《女郎花》については、その「作意」をすっきりと把握できないという印象を持ち続けてきました。その理由をあらためて考えてみると、それは結局、前場において、頼風の化身である前ジテの老人と九州から上洛したワキ僧とのあいだで、男山山麓に咲き乱れる女郎花をめぐる長いやりとりのあとに、シテがワキを男山山上に案内するこれまた長い場面が置かれていることにあるのではないかと思うのです。この点についての疑問は、たしかOminameshi Conferenceのおりにも他の参加者から出されていたように記憶していますが、それはわれわれだけでなく、《女郎花》に接した人が等しく感じることのようです。たとえば、昭和6年に刊行された佐成謙太郎氏の『謡曲大観』の解説では、その能作品としての評価がつぎのように述べられています。

> 〔通小町〕〔定家〕〔船橋〕などと同様、男女邪淫の妄執を描いた曲であるが、この事はキリに少しばかり寧ろ唐突に述べてゐるだけで、類曲中、呵責の程度の最も軽いものといふべきであらう。第２節に古歌を多く引いてゐるのは、本曲創作の動機が那邊にあつたかを察せしめるだけで、別段わづらはしい感じを起さしめないが、第３節に男山八幡の縁起を説いてゐるのは、この曲柄には餘り似合はしい感を與へない。後段第６・７節は本曲の主想で、叙述も甚だ滑かに行つてゐる。[1]

『謡曲大観』は昭和初年という時期の刊行ですが、いまなお謡曲（能の詞章）の注釈書として有用な書で、上に引用したのはその《女郎花》の「概評」の部分です。この「概評」欄には、それが刊行された昭和初期だけでなく、近世末期〜近代という時代における能作品にたいする理解のしかたがよく集約されているように思われるのですが、ここで注目されるのは下線を施した部分です。つまり、ここで佐成氏は《女郎花》の構成にふれて、全体としてなめらかな展開ではあるが、唯一、前場で男山八幡の由来がのべられる場面－以下では「男山山上の段」と呼びます－が全体の流れからやや遊離している、と指摘しているのです。

たしかに、この部分はそういう印象を与えます。以下ではまずその点を確認しておくことにします。「男山山上の段」がある前場の段構成はつぎのとおりです。

1. ワキの登場＝九州松浦の僧が上洛の途次に石清水八幡に立ち寄る。
2. ワキの詠嘆＝僧は男山山麓に咲き乱れる千草の花に眺め入るうち、古歌にも読まれている女郎花を一本手折ろうとする。
3. シテとワキの応対＝花守の老人が現われて僧が花を手折ろうとするのをとがめるが、女郎花を詠んだ古歌をふまえたやりとりのあと、花守は僧が花を手折ることを許す。

[1] 『謡曲大観』第5巻、3488頁

4. シテとワキの応対＝僧がいまだ男山山上の八幡宮へ参詣していないというので、花守が山上の神前へ案内すると、僧はその荘厳なさまに感激する。
5. シテとワキの応対＝僧が男山という名称と山麓の女郎花とは関係があるのかと尋ねるので、花守は山麓の男塚と女塚に僧を案内する。
6. シテの中入＝花守は女塚の主は都の女、男塚の主は八幡の小野頼風という人物であると僧に教え、自分がその頼風であることをにおわせて消えてゆく。

この段構成は、現在広く読まれている新潮日本古典集成『謡曲集』や岩波新日本古典文学大系『謡曲百番』の段構成に基づいたもので、さきに用した『謡曲大観』の段構成とはすこし異なっています。しかし、それは新潮日本古典集成などのほうがすこし段を細かく区切っているためで、とくに両者の間に本質的な点で理解の相違があるというわけではありません。『謡曲大観』にいう第2節が右の第３段にあたり、第３節が右の第４段にあたるのですが、ともあれ、《女郎花》の展開のなかで、唯一落ち着きが悪い部分—解釈に苦しむ部分—は、上にかかげた段構成でいうと、第４段ということになります。

この「男山山上の段」は、第3段の前ジテとワキ僧の男山山麓の女郎花をめぐっての問答のあと、ワキ僧の「この野辺の女郎花にながめいりて、いまだ八幡宮に参らず候」という言葉をきっかけにはじまります。花守は、ちょうど私も山上するところだから、ご案内をしましょう、と言って、ともに山上の男山八幡神前に向かうことになります。以下、そこで描かれているのは、もっぱら男山八幡の神域としての荘厳なさまで、放生会で魚が放たれる放生川や、放生会のおりの御旅所などが登山途中の光景として叙されたあと、神々しい山上の神宮寺や八幡神前のようすがつぎのように描かれます。(引用は現行の観世流詞章。以下同断。)

〔上ゲ歌〕地 〽…月の桂の男山、さやけき影は所から、紅葉も照りそひて、日もかげろふの石清水、苔の衣も妙なりや、三つの袂に影映る、印の筥を納むなる、法の神宮寺、ありがたかりし霊地かな

〔歌〕地〽巌松峙つて、山そびえ谷めぐりて、諸木枝を連ねたり、鳩の峰越し来てみれば、三千世界もよそならず、千里も同じ月の夜の、朱の玉垣御戸代の、錦かけまくも、かたじけなしと伏し拝む

以上が問題の「男山山上の段」の内容です。このあと、この男山山上に小野頼風と女の亡霊が登場するのであれば、展開としてはまことに自然なのですが、この「男山山上の段」のあとは、花守はさらに頼風夫婦の墓である山麓の男塚・女塚を僧に案内することになって、舞台はふたたび山麓に移ってしまいます。そして、そのまま後場になって、ワキ僧の前に頼風と女の亡霊が現われて往時を再現する場所も、その男塚・女塚のある山麓なのです。このような展開をみると、「男山山上の段」が前場の展開のなかで、あるいは《女郎花》全体の展開のなかで、なんとなく落ち着きが悪いことがよく理解されるのではないでしょうか。

そもそも、通常、夢幻能の前場では、その地を訪れたワキの前に主人公の化身である前ジテが現われて、両者の問答になり、そのあとは、たとえば《井筒》でいえば業平夫婦の生前の物語のような主人公にかかわる話題へと移り、徐々にその作品の本題へと入ってゆきます。それが《女郎花》では、ワキと前ジテの問答（第３段）と、主人公にかかわる話題（第５段）のあいだに、花守による男山八幡の案内（第４段）が挿入されていて、この第４段がなんとなく前場全体の流れからはずれている感じで、落ち着きが悪いのです。この場合は、夢幻能一般のように、第３段の山麓の女郎花をめぐる問答から、第４段をとばして、男塚・女塚についての第５段へ続くほうが理解しやすいのですが、みてきたように《女郎花》の展開はそうなってはいないのです。このように第４段が加わった結果、《女郎花》の前場は、夢幻能の前場としてはかなり長いものになっています。最近の『謡曲百番』の解説でも、「さやけき月の桂の男山八幡の風光を愛でる名所教えと共に前場は明るく長く、中入直前の男塚・女塚の話を転換点として、地獄での責め苦を描く後場は暗く短く、その対照は鮮烈だ」などと評されていますが、前場が長くなっているのは、やはり第４段の存在ゆえと言ってよいでしょう。

いったい、花守が僧を男山八幡に案内するこの「男山山上の段」は、いかなる意図のもとにここに置かれているのでしょうか。この段がないほうが理解しやすいというのは、あくまでも通常の夢幻能を基準にした評価にすぎません。結局、われわれとしては、《女郎花》の前場にこの段があるという事実に立脚して、そのうえで、この段が《女郎花》のなかでどのような意味を持っているのかを考えてみる必要があると思うのです。

3. 「男山山上の段」の意味を考える

《女郎花》の作者はいかなる意図のもとにこの「男山山上の段」を置いたのでしょうか。ここでは、その手掛かりを、まず、これに続く場面（第５段）の花守と僧との問答に求めてみようと思います。その問答というのはつぎのようなものです。

> シテ「これこそ石清水八幡宮にて御座候へ、よくよくおん拝み候へ、はや日の暮れて候へば、おん暇申し候ふべし
> ワキ「なうなう女郎花と申すことは、この男山につきたる謂れにて候ふか
> シテ「あら何ともなや、さきに女郎花の古歌を引いて戯れを申し候ふも、いたづら事にて候、女郎花と申すこそ男山につきたる謂れにて候へ

ここでは、山上の石清水八幡への参拝をはたした僧が、「当地の女郎花はこの男山にまつわる由来があるのですか」と尋ねると、シテの花守が、「そのためにさきほど女郎花の古歌を引いて戯れを言ったのではありませんか。当地の女郎花はまさしくこの男山にまつわる由来があるのです」と答えています。つまり、ここではさきほど話題にしていた「女郎花」と、いま参拝を終えた「男山」とがふかいかかわりがある、とされているのです。そうであれば、ここでは「男山山上の段」が《女郎花》の主材である「女郎花」にまつわる物語とかかわりがあるらしいことが示唆されているわけで、この段が決して全体から遊離していないことをうかがわせもします。しかし、このあと、話題は「女郎花」と「男山」との関係ではなく、

さきに紹介したように、「女塚」「男塚」へと移り、せっかく一場面を設けてその荘厳なさまを描いた「男山」からは離れてしまいます。その結果、「男山山上の段」はいったいなんのための場面だったのか理解に苦しむことになるのですが、ここでは、もうしばらくこの問答にいう「女郎花」と「男山」の関係について考えてみたいと思います。

このシテとワキの問答は、上掛り（観世系）のテキストと下掛り（金春系）のテキストとのあいだにいささか異同がある箇所です。上にかかげたのは上掛りのテキストの文句ですが、この箇所は下掛りのテキストではつぎのようになっています。

シテ「これこそ天下に隠れもましまさぬ石清水八幡宮にて御座候へ、なんぼうありがたきおん事にて候ぞ
ワキ「承りおよびたるよりもいやましてありがたふ候
シテ「はや日の暮れて候ふほどに、この尉はおん暇申し候ふべし
ワキ「しばらく、さてさて男山と申すもこの女郎花につきたる謂れ候ふか
シテ「あら何ともなや、さきに女郎花の古歌を引いて、戯れを申し候ふは、さてはいたづら事にて候ふぞや、男山と申すことこそこの女郎花につきたる謂れ候ふよ

前半では、この下掛りの文句のほうが八幡宮への参拝をはたした僧の感激が強調されていますが、いま注目したいのは後半の下線を付した部分のちがいです。この部分は、一見すると、たんに「男山」と「女郎花」の順序が入れ替わっているだけのように思われるかもしれませんが、この異同はもっと大きな問題をはらんでいるように思われます。というのは、「男山と申すもこの女郎花につきたる謂れ候ふか」という僧の質問は、「ここを男山というのは女郎花にまつわる謂れによるのですか」という意味ですが、さらに明確に言うと、「ここが男山という地名になったのは女郎花にまつわる謂れによるのですか」という意味であり、「男山」という山名の由来を尋ねた形の質問になっているからです。これはワキの僧の質問ですが、これにたいするシテの花守の答えも、やはり「男山」という山名の由来を答えているわけです。

このように、下掛りのテキストによれば、この第５段の問答は、八幡神が鎮座する八幡山が「男山」と呼ばれるようになったのは「女郎花」にまつわる「謂れ」による、ということを説いているのです。その「謂れ」というのは、もちろん《女郎花》の典拠になった物語であり、後場で頼風夫婦によって再現的に語られる悲劇的な物語のことと考えてよいと思いますが、興味深いことに、これと同様の「男山」の山名の由来が、《女郎花》の典拠とされている『古今和歌集序聞書三流抄』にもみえているのです。以下にその説話をかかげてみます。「男山」という山名の由来に言及があるのは末尾の下線部です。

> 平城天皇ノ御時、小野頼風ト云人アリ。八幡ニ住ケルガ、京ナル女ヲ思テ互ニカチコチ行通フ。或時、女ノ許ニ行テ何時ノ日ハ必ズ来ント契テ帰リヌ。女待ケレドモ来ザリケレバ、男ノ八幡ノ宿所ニ行テ聞ケレバ、家ナル者、答テ云、「此程初メタル女房ノ座ス間、別ノ処ニ座ス」ト云ケレバ、女ウラメシト思テ八幡川ニ往テ、山吹重ノ絹ヲヌギ捨テ、身ヲ抛テ死ス。男、家ニ帰タリケルニ、家ノ者「京ノ女房ノ座ケルガ、帰リ玉ヒヌ」ト云。男、アハテヽ追付行ニ、川ノ端ニヤマブキ重ノ絹アリ。ヨリテ見レバ彼女房ノ常ニキタル衣也。アヤシミ思フ程ニ、川ノ中ニ彼女房死テアリ。女ヲバ取揚テ供養シテ彼絹ヲ取テ帰リ形見ニ是ヲナス。男依宮仕、京ニ久シク居タリケルニ、彼絹ヲバカレガ形見ニミント思フテ此衣ヲトリニツカハシケレバ、土ニ落テ朽テ女郎花トナレリ。使者、此由ヲ申ケレバ、頼風行テ見ルニ女郎花咲乱レタリ。花ノ本ヘ近クヨラントスレバ、此花恨ミタル気色ニテ異方ニ靡ク。男ノケバ又起直ル。此事ヲ引テ、爰ニ女郎花ノ一時ヲクネルト書也。是ヨリシテ女郎花ヲ女ノ郎ノ花ト名ク。男思ハク、彼女生ヲカヘテダニカク吾ヲ恨ル。サレバ、彼女、我故ニ身ヲスツ。我ハカレガ為ニ身ヲ捨テ一ツ処ニ生レ合ント思テ、同ク川ニ身ヲ抛テ死ス。<u>彼男ヲバ八幡山ノ中ニ送ル故ニ八幡山ノ中ニ男山ト云ハ彼所也。麓ニ女塚ト云ハ彼ノ女ヲ埋シ所也。</u>[2]

[2] 同上、1016号、314頁

これによると、八幡川（放生川）に身を投げた頼風の遺骸は「八幡山ノ中」に葬られ、以来、そこが「男山」と呼ばれるようになった、というのです。もっとも、この「男山」は頼風を葬った八幡山の一角をさしているようですから、八幡山全体をさしている下掛りテキストの「男山」とはすこしズレがあります。しかし、頼風女郎花説話と下掛りテキストの所説との類似は明らかであり、下掛りテキストで、「ここが男山と呼ばれるようになったのは女郎花にまつわる謂れのため」としているのは、明らかに頼風女郎花説話をふまえたものとみてよいと思います。もちろん、それは下掛りテキストの形が《女郎花》の原形であることを意味します。

こうしてみると、下掛りテキストで述べられている「男山」という山名の由来が、《女郎花》一曲のなかでいかなる意味を持っているかが明らかになってきます。つまり、「男山」というのは亡き妻のあとを追って死んだ頼風に由来する地名なのであって、それは頼風女郎花説話を本説とし、頼風を主人公とする《女郎花》にあっては、ぬきさしならない位置をしめていることになります。その頼風の化身である花守がワキ僧を「男山」に案内するのが問題の「男山山上の段」なのです。その「男山山上の段」をうけて、第５段で、「ここが男山と呼ばれるようになったのは女郎花にまつわる謂れのため」という説明があって、話題は本説である頼風女郎花説話の核心をなす「男塚」「女塚」へと移ってゆくのですが、こうしてみると、「男山山上の段」は全体の流れから遊離しているどころか、筋を徐々に一曲の核心へと進めるたくみな伏線として機能していることがわかります。[3]

これで、「男山山上の段」についての疑問はとりあえず解消したことになりますが、《女郎花》にはもう一カ所、以上のことと深くかかわる「男山」がみえます。それは後ジテ頼風の亡霊が生前のできごとを再現的に語ったあとの、頼風夫婦の墓である「女塚」「男塚」をさし示して僧に回向を頼む、つぎのような場面です（ここは上掛り・下掛りのあいだに異同はありません）。

〔クセ〕地〽…同じ道にならんとて　シテ〽続いてこの川に身を投げて　地〽ともに土中に籠めしより、女塚にたいし

[3] 片桐洋一『中世古今集注釈解題』(2)、262～263頁

て、また男山と申すなり、その塚はこれ主は我、幻ながら
来りたり、跡弔ひてたび給へ、跡弔ひてたび給へ

じつは、この箇所も《女郎花》解釈上の問題点のひとつなのです。ここは「女塚」「男塚」のことを言おうとしているところですから、下線部の「女塚にたいして」のあとは「また男塚と申すなり」とあるべきところです。それが不思議なことに、「また男山と申すなり」と、突然「男山」が出てくるのです。この「男山」は文脈的には「男塚」と解するのが自然ですから、ここはたんに「男塚」のことを「男山」と言っていると解しておけばよいのかもしれません。しかし、そう解すると大きな矛盾にぶつかります。というのは、すでに述べたように、前場の「男山山上の段」のあとの問答では、「女郎花」の「謂れ」によって生まれた地名である「男山」は八幡山（＝男山）のこととしているからです。したがって、もし、右の「また男山と申すなり」の「男山」が山麓の「男塚」であるとすれば、《女郎花》は前場と後場で大きな矛盾を呈していることになります。この点はどう考えたらよいのでしょうか。

結局、これら2カ所の「男山」を整合的に把握しようとすれば、右の傍線部は、「妻と同じように土中に葬って以来、女塚にたいして、この八幡山を男山と呼ぶようになったのです。その頼風を葬った塚（男塚）はこれです」と解釈するしかないように思います。つまり、山麓の「女塚」「男塚」の由来を語る文句のなかに、頼風夫婦の悲劇によって八幡山が「男山」と呼ばれるようになった由来が挿入されているということです。そうだとすると、ずいぶん複雑な文章ということになりますが、ここがこのような文章になったのは、《女郎花》においては、頼風が「男山」に葬られたとする伝承と、頼風の墓を「男塚」であるとする伝承とが、やや曖昧なままに混在していることによるのではないかと思います。それは、さらに言えば、《女郎花》がふまえた頼風女郎花説話において、夫婦の墓所についての伝承がいささか錯綜していることによるのではないかと思うのです。

そもそも、《女郎花》の典拠とされている『古今和歌集序聞書三流抄』では、頼風夫婦の墓は八幡山（＝男山）山中と八幡川のほとりの「女塚」となっています。これにたいして、《女郎花》では、

「男山」を頼風に由来する山名だとする一方で、夫婦の墓は山麓にある「男塚」と「女塚」だともしているのです（男塚・女塚の場所が山麓であることは詞章中２カ所に明記されています）。この点では《女郎花》と『古今和歌集序聞書三流抄』とは設定を異にしているわけですが、『伝頓阿作古今序注』や『古今栄雅抄』（『謡曲拾葉抄』所引）などの頼風女郎花説話をみると、頼風の墓の場所は「男塚」という名で、「女塚」とともに山麓にあるとされています（現在の「男塚」「女塚」の場所も山麓です）。つまり、《女郎花》が頼風の墓を山麓の「男塚」としているのは、明らかに『伝頓阿作古今序注』や『古今栄雅抄』などの設定と一致しており、《女郎花》の典拠はかならずしも『古今和歌集序聞書三流抄』だけではないということにもなるのですが、それはともあれ、右の〔クセ〕の文句が「女塚にたいして、また男山と申すなり」と、いささか唐突な表現になったのは、このような複数の伝承をふまえたためではないかと思うのです。

話がすこし複雑になってしまいましたが、要するに、《女郎花》はこのような伝承をふまえて、「男塚」「女塚」を頼風夫婦の墓とし、「男山」を頼風の事績にちなむ地名とする理解のもとに作られているわけです。ここで、あらためて「男山山上の段」にもどれば、それはこの物語の根幹をなす頼風をイメージさせるものとして前場に置かれていることになります。

なお、『古今和歌集序聞書三流抄』の頼風女郎花説話では、その時代を平城天皇の時代（806～806）としていて、「男山」という山名は、頼風が「八幡山」に葬られたために生まれたものとされています。これにしたがえば、山名としては「八幡山」のほうが古く、「男山」はあとから生まれたことになりますが、事実はその逆で、「八幡山」という山名は、古来「雄徳山」「牡山」（『日本書紀』）などと表記されていた「男山」に、貞観元年（861）に豊前宇佐から八幡宮が勧請されてから生まれた名称なのです。このように、女郎花にまつわる悲恋物語によって「男山」という山名が生まれたということは、歴史的には正しくないのですが、事実はともあれ、《女郎花》は「男山」についてのそのような理解をふまえて作られているのです。

4. 《女郎花》を読む

これで、《女郎花》についてのもっとも根本的な疑問をなんとか解決できたのではないかと思います。最後になりますが、この節では、これまで検討してきた《女郎花》における「男山」理解をふまえて、あらためて《女郎花》を通読し、各段の随所にこめられた趣向や工夫を整理して、全体の「作意」の把握につとめたいと思います。

第1段は、ワキの登場をその内容としています。ワキは九州の松浦潟から上洛しようとしている僧ですが、ワキを九州の僧としたのは、石清水八幡宮（男山八幡宮）が九州の宇佐八幡宮を勧請した社であることをふまえた趣向です。そのことはワキの文句にも「わが国の宇佐の宮とご一体なれば参らばやと思ひ候」とみえています。

第2段は、ワキが男山の山麓に咲き乱れる女郎花に感じて、それを1本手折ろうとする場面です。この「男山」と「女郎花」は「男」と「女」を連想させるものとして古歌にも多く詠まれていますが、この「男」と「女」はもちろん《女郎花》に登場する頼風とその妻を暗示しています。ただし、男山に女郎花が多いことは能の虚構ではないようで、『謡曲拾葉抄』が引く『古今栄雅抄』には「男山は女郎花の名所也」とあります。

第3段では、シテの花守の老人が現われて、僧が花を手折ろうとするのをとがめたのをきっかけに、花守と僧の論争が展開します。二人のやりとりは女郎花を詠んだ古歌や古詩をふまえた風雅なもので、ここで引用されている古歌は女郎花にちなんだものだけでも6首もあり、そのうち5首は『古今集』の歌です。二人のやりとりは、僧がなにげなく口にした『古今集』の女郎花の歌をきっかけにして、さいごは花守も僧が花を手折るのを許すことになるのですが、この「女郎花づくし」にはもちろん頼風の妻が暗示されています。いかにも能らしい風雅な問答ですが、ここには花守の本身である頼風の悔恨の情もさりげなく記されています。この段のさいごに、「なまめき立てる女郎花、なまめき立てる女郎花、うしろめたくや思ふらん、女郎と書ける花の名に、誰偕老を契りけん、かの邯鄲の仮枕、夢は五十のあはれ世の、ためしもまことなるべしや、ためしもまことなるべしや」とあるのがそれで、これは「この心細げに立っている女郎花に偕老を約束した人がいるようですが、偕老の契りなどというものは実際にはありはしないもので、所詮はあの〈邯鄲の五十年の夢〉のように、一時の仮枕をかわすだけに終わるものです」というほどの意味かと思います。

第4段は、この稿で問題にした「男山山上の段」です。「男山」という山名が頼風に由来するという『古今和歌集序聞書三流抄』の理解をふまえ、八幡宮が鎮座する男山山上の荘厳なさまを描くことによって頼風を暗示しようとしたものです。前段では「女郎花」で妻を、この段では「男山」で頼風を暗示しているわけですが、このような「男山」の荘厳なさまの描写は、あるいは邪淫の悪鬼に身を責められている頼風の救済を暗示しているとも解せます。「日もかげろふの石清水」とあって、このあたりから夕刻となります。

第5段では、花守によって、いま参拝をおえた「男山」は、じつは山麓の「女郎花」と深いかかわりがあることが明かされ、花守はその説明のために、さらに僧を山麓の「男塚」「女塚」へと案内します。頼風ゆかりの「男山」が「男塚」と対応し、頼風の妻を暗示する「女郎花」が「女塚」に対応するのですが、そのような関係は下掛り（金春系）のテキストによってわかることで、上掛り（観世系）のテキストでは、「男山」が頼風ゆかりの場所であることの説明がないために、「男山」から山麓の「男塚」「女塚」への展開がはなはだ要領をえないものになっています。《女郎花》における上掛り・下掛り間の詞章の異同はこの場面に集中していますが、上掛りテキストの改編は《女郎花》の「作意」の把握に大きな障害となってきたと言ってよいでしょう。

第6段では、花守が山麓の「男塚」「女塚」の前で、それが小野頼風夫婦の墓であることを僧に教え、さらに自分はじつはその「男塚」の主の小野頼風であると明かして月下の木陰に消えてゆきます。これで前場が終わりますが、このころにはあたりはすっかり暗くなっています。

第7段は、狂言の物語（居語り）を中心とするアイの段です。そこでは『古今和歌集序聞書三流抄』の頼風女郎花説話とほぼ同じ内容の物語が語られますが、そこでは頼風は八幡宮の神官と説明されているのが注意されます。シテの頼風の素性については、《女郎花》でも『古今和歌集序聞書三流抄』でも明確に説明されていませんが、そう考えるのが自然だと思います。貴人姿という後シテの装束もそれと矛盾はありません。

第8段は、ワキ僧が頼風夫婦の出現を待ちうける場面です。ここでのワキの謡は、「一夜臥す、牡鹿の角の塚の草、牡鹿の角の塚の草、陰よりみえし亡魂を、弔ふ法の声立てて、南無幽霊出離生死頓証菩提」というものですが、これはやはり「塚」を重要な要素とする《求塚》の待受ケと同文です。おそらくは《求塚》のほうが先行するものと思われますが、流用のわりには、《女郎花》にもよく適合しています。

第9段は、頼風夫婦の亡霊が登場する場面です。この後ジテの「おう曠野人まれなり、わが古墳ならでまた何物ぞ」と、ツレの「屍を争ふ猛獣は禁ずるにあたはず」も《求塚》と同文ですが、これはかなり陰惨な描写で、はたしてこの《女郎花》にふさわしいかどうか、いささか疑問にも思うところです。登場した頼風は「なつかしや、聞けば昔の秋の風」と生前どおりの秋風をなつかしんでいますが、それにたいして、妻は「うら紫か葛の葉の」と恨みをいだいていることが注意されます。

第10段では、頼風によって、夫婦のなれそめから、妻が放生川に身を投げて女郎花に化したこと、その女郎花が頼風に顔を合わせようとしなかったために、頼風も川に身を投げたこと、その夫婦の墓が「男塚」「女塚」であること、などが語られます。このように生前のできごとが仕方話的に演じられるのも妄執物の類型なのですが、女郎花に化した妻が頼風に顔を合わせようとしなかったことは、妻の頼風にたいする恨みを物語るもので、ここで、頼風はそうした思い出を悔恨をこめて語っているのだと解せます。

第11段は、「あら閻浮恋しや」という文句で、後ジテのカケリになります。これはもちろん、頼風の現世（閻浮）への執心を示している場面ですが、これまでに描かれた妻の恨みをふまえると、このカケリには、妻が死してなお恨みをいだいていることにたいする悔恨もこめられているとみてよいでしょう。むしろ、その悔恨こそが頼風の執心そのものなのではないでしょうか。

第12段では、頼風が死後地獄で受けている責め苦が描写されます。これも妄執物の能の類型ですが、ここにはもちろん《女郎花》なりの主張がこめられています。ここでは妄者の頼風は、「道もさかしき剣の山」の上に「恋しき人は見えたり」と、その山を登ろうとするのですが、「剣は身をとおし、盤石は骨を砕く」となります。そのあとは、「こはそもいかに恐ろしや、剣の枝のたはむまで、いかなる罪の、なれる果てぞや、よしなかりける、花の一時を、くねるも夢ぞ女郎花、露の台(うてな)や花の縁に、浮かめてたび給へ、罪を浮かめてたび給へ」という文句をもって一曲が終わるのですが、ここには、頼風が死後もこのような苦しみを受けるのも、「恋しき人」の恨みによることが示されています。「花の一時を、くねる」は、『古今集』の序文にいう「若く盛んな時代」の謂であるとともに、妻の女郎花が頼風に顔を合わせようとしなかったことをさしているようで、そのような生前の所業も所詮ははかない夢だとして、「女郎花」の「花」から「露の台や花の縁」に続けて、極楽への往生を願って、一曲がとじられるのです。

以上が《女郎花》についての筆者の読みです。ここには筆者の勘違いも多少はあるでしょうが、《女郎花》はほぼこのような作品なのではないでしょうか。

むすび

《女郎花》は、その《女郎花》という曲名や前場の女郎花をめぐるやりとりなどから、なんとなく死後に女郎花に化した妻を中心にした作品というイメージを持たれているかもしれませんが、みてきたように、《女郎花》は頼風の執心を描こうとした作品とみるべきでしょう。その執心はひろくいえば現世にたいする執心ですが、もっと厳密にいえば、それは妻を死にいたらしめ、偕老の約束をはたせなかったばかりか、妻が女郎花に化してなお恨みをいだいていることにたいする悔恨に由来する執心となります。このような《女郎花》の内容に注意すると、ここで想起されるのが、《女郎花》が《頼風》とも呼ばれていたことです。この《頼風》という曲名は、永正２年（1505）の金春大夫元安（禅鳳）の京都粟田口での勧進能の演目にみえているのですが、《女郎花》の内容に照らすならば、その曲名は《女郎花》より《頼風》のほうがはるかにふさわしいように思われます。あるいは本来の曲名は《頼風》だった可能性もあると思いますが、はたしてどうでしょうか。

なお、この《女郎花》以前に、田楽の名手の喜阿弥の作と思われる《女郎花》があったことが『申楽談儀』第九条の記事から知られています。この喜阿弥作の《女郎花》は散佚して、現在はその内容は十分には知りえませんが、現存する一部の詞章によると、頼風の妻を主人公にした作品のように思われます。そうだとすると、妻をシテにした古曲《女郎花》にたいして、夫の頼風をシテにしたところにも、新曲《女郎花》の「作意」が認められるのではないかと思います。

Ominameshi, A Reading: Toward an Understanding of the Author's Intent

Amano Fumio

A major problem one faces in attempting to grasp the intent of *Ominameshi* occurs in the fourth section of the play, which the *Yōkyoku taikan* states "does not provide a very suitable feeling" (*amari niahashiikan wo ataenai*). Considered within the play as a whole, this scene might even seem unnecessary; however, it is vital to the play and to understanding fully the play's intent.

The Otokoyama scene depicts the sacred area of the Otokoyama Hachiman Shrine at the top of the mountain and then shifts to the area of the graves of the woman and the man at the foot of the mountain. In the *nochiba* of the play, the spirits of the Yorikaze couple appear and the tragic tale of their love and ensuing suicides unfolds, along with the description of the sufferings endured by Yorikaze in hell. In the *mondō* between the *shite* and *waki* following this scene, we learn that the place name Otokoyama is derived from the tragedy of the Yorikaze couple. If we refer to the *Kokinchū*, the poetic source for the noh, we see that Otokoyama was named as the burial place of Yorikaze after he followed his lover into death. We can thus assume that since the noh *Ominameshi* takes Yorikaze himself to be the *shite*, the setting of Otokoyama is also essential. The inclusion of the Otokoyama section can thus be seen as most natural and key to understanding the authorial intention of the play.

By interpreting the Otokoyama scene in this way, I will suggest that *Ominameshi* not be read as centering around a woman appearing in the form of an *ominaeshi* flower, but instead that it be read as a play depicting Yorikaze's inability to fulfill his promise to be true to his lover until death and his regret at having led her to her death. Read as such, I would propose that there is a high probablility of the play originally being referred to, not as *Ominameshi*, but as *Yorikaze*.

能〈女郎花〉第4段の謡について

竹本幹夫

はじめに

Ominameshi Conference において、私が実際に担当したのは、下記に引用する謡のうち、後半の、〔段哥〕と私が呼ぶ一小段と、その後に続くシテのセリフ、「これこそ石清水八幡宮にて候へよくよくおん拝み候へ」（これがイワシミズ＝ハチマングウです。よくよくご礼拝なさい）までであった。しかしながら本稿では、この部分を含む一連の謡を分析し、あわせて能〈女郎花〉の成立を探るという考察の都合上、前掲のシテセリフは省略し、これらの前にある〔サシ〕〔下ゲ哥〕と私が呼ぶ二小段分もあわせて掲出した。この本文は、伊藤正義氏校訂の『謡曲集』上巻[1]所収の光悦謡本のそれを用いた。(参考のため現代語訳も付した。）ただし伊藤氏の校訂本に示された小段名には誤りがあるので、訂正した。すなわち伊藤氏が〔哥〕〔上ゲ哥〕〔哥〕とした三つの段落は、はじめの〔哥〕は〔下ゲ哥〕、〔上ゲ哥〕〔哥〕は〔段哥〕と呼ぶべきものである。

〔段哥〕とは、複数の小段の旋律を接合した、特殊な小段である。〈女郎花〉第四段の〔段哥〕は、〔上ゲ哥〕と〔クセ〕とを接合したものである。つまり〔上ゲ哥〕末尾の3句分（しるしの箱を納むなる、法の神宮寺、ありがたかりし霊地かな）の旋律を通常の〔上ゲ哥〕とは異なるものに変更し、その直後に〔クセ〕と呼ばれる小段の第二節と第三節とを接合した形である。あるいはこれを〔上ゲ哥〕〔クセ〕という二つの別小段として把握することも可能かと思われるが、この部分の特殊性を強調する意図から、〔段哥〕とした。

またここに掲げた光悦本は、17世紀初頭に刊行された観世流のテキストであるが、謡曲〈女郎花〉の現存する最古のテキストとほぼ

[1] 伊藤正義氏校訂『謡曲集』上巻、新潮日本古典集成、1983年

同文である。さらにその他の古い写本と比較しても、謡の役割分担も含め、やはりほぼ同文である。ここで私が古写本と呼ぶのは、金春流の最古本で、金春禅鳳の写本（薬師寺蔵）、禅鳳本に続く金春流の古本である『遊音抄』(1532頃、天理図書館蔵)、観世流系の最古本である観世小次郎元頼の写本（1559、熊本大学永青文庫蔵)、の三種類である。いずれも法政大学能楽研究所のマイクロフィルムを参照した。これらの本は文字遣いが難解で、伊藤氏の校訂を経たテキストの方が、作品を考察するには便利である。

【本文（付、現代語訳)】

〔サシ〕(ワキ) 聞きしに超えて尊くありがたかりける霊地かな、(シテ) 山下の人家軒を並べ、(シテ・ワキ) 和光の塵も濁り江の、河水に浮かむうろくずは、げにも生けるを放つかと、深き誓ひもあらたにて、恵みぞ茂き男山、さかゆく道のありがたさよ。

〔下ゲ哥〕(地謡) ころは八月なかばの日、神の御幸なる、お旅所を伏し拝み。

〔段哥〕(地謡) 久方の、月の桂の男山、月の桂の男山、さやけき影は所から、紅葉も照り添ひて、日もかげろふの石清水、苔の衣も妙なれや、三つの袂に影うつる、しるしの箱を納むなる、法の神宮寺、ありがたかりし霊地かな。巌松峙つて、山そびえ谷めぐりて、諸木枝を連ねたり。鳩の嶺越し来てみれば、三千世界も外ならず、千里も同じ月の夜の、あけの玉垣みとしろの、錦かけまくも、忝なしと伏し拝む。

〔サシ〕(ワキ) 聞いていた以上に尊くまたすばらしい神域だなあ。

(シテ) 男山門前の町々の人家は隣り合って何軒も続き、にぎわいを見せている。

(シテ・ワキ) 汚れた人間世界に下ってわれわれを悟りに導こうという神の誓いは、傍らを流れる川の水の濁りにも表れており、河面に姿を見せる魚類は、生きものを殺さずに放すという、この八幡大菩薩の慈悲の深さをまことにはっきりと示している。また神の社のある男山には植物が繁茂し、それは神の恵みにより永遠の繁栄が約束されているしるしである。私たちはこの男山の山上へと続く坂道を、神への感謝を込めて、さあ登ろう。

〔下ゲ哥〕(地謡) 今日は8月15日でまさに神の祭の日、神が山上の神殿からお出ましになり、祭の間だけお住まいになるという、ふもとの神殿を礼拝していると、

〔段哥〕(地謡)「久方の月の桂の男山」(天空の月のように光り輝く美男子を思わせる男山) という異名の通り、ちょうど空には月が上り、その光は澄み渡り、月の光に紅葉までもが照り輝いている。そして夕日も沈んで影を落とすと、この石清水の地面を衣のように覆う苔の緑色は、いっそう美しく深みを帯びる。

この苔は、その昔、この石清水の地にお遷りになるために、阿弥陀如来と日光月光の二菩薩が天下った、行教和尚の僧衣の袂を思わせる。その阿弥陀三尊の聖霊を、聖なる箱に納め、安置したというここ石清水八幡宮は、まことにすばらしい神域なのである。

山上には松の古木が岩に根を張り、山は高くそびえ、周囲は断崖となり、山にも谷にも色々な樹木が生い茂っている。

この男山の嶺に立つと、全世界が眼前にあり、千里のかなたまでもくまなく照らす月の光の下に、八幡宮の神殿の朱色の美しい垣根や、模様を浮き織りにした神前の掛け幕も見える。それらを見、神聖な神の御名を心に思い浮かべるだけでも、自然と信仰心が起こり、礼拝するのである。

1.〈石清水の謡〉が本来一連の内容であること

本稿で上記の謡の全体を問題にするのは、これらがもともと一連の内容であると考えられるからである。この一連の謡をいま仮に、〈石清水の謡〉と呼ぶことにする。

〈石清水の謡〉は次のように、〈女郎花〉の筋立ての中にはめこまれている。

石清水八幡宮参詣を志す僧が、八幡宮が鎮座する男山の麓で、野に咲く女郎花に眼を留め、ちょうど現れた土地の老人と、女郎花についての和歌を題材に会話を交わす。そしてその老人に案内されて、山上の石清水八幡宮を参拝することになる。以下、〔サシ〕で、まず石清水神社の門前に広がる町々を通り、山の麓を流れる放生川を渡って、神域への道を登る。次に〔下ゲ哥〕では、山のふもとの、

祭礼の日に神がお出ましになる神殿を礼拝する。〔段哥〕の前半では、日が暮れ、明るい月が出て、照り輝く周囲の景色にいよいよ信仰心を起こし、ようやく山上に着く。〔段哥〕の後半では、そこは眼下をはるかに見はるかす尾根で、やがて僧は、その場所にある神殿を礼拝する。この謡は、ようするに石清水八幡宮への行程を歌う謡として位置付けられており、三つの部分からなるこの謡の、どの部分が欠けても、僧は石清水八幡宮に到達できない。

〔サシ〕〔下ゲ哥〕〔段哥〕という構成は、いわゆる「まとまった一謡」の構成単位である〔サシ〕〔下ゲ哥〕〔上ゲ哥〕などに準じており、音楽的にも安定感のある構成である。最後に〔段哥〕が位置するのは、必ずしも一般的とはいえないものの、歌謡として、これだけで独立して鑑賞することも可能な形である。このことについては、次章に詳しく検討するであろう。

一方、この構成の各部分を見ると、〔サシ〕の冒頭は観阿弥時代の独立の歌謡である〈高野の古き謡〉の冒頭句を転用したものである。それに続く内容は、男山山下の門前町の繁栄と麓を流れる放生川、山上への坂道を紹介した、導入部である。次の〔下ゲ哥〕は、参拝者が山麓の一の鳥居の内側にある、頓宮と呼ばれる御旅所に詣でたことを述べるが、その末の「伏し拝み」は文意を終結させずに次文へと続けていく形でありながら、次の〔段哥〕冒頭の「久方の、月の桂の男山」とは文意がつながらず、一見は、ここに断絶があるかのように見える。

しかしながらこの部分全体は、音楽的には、前に〔サシ〕だけでもあった方が安定感がある。またそれぞれの小段の段落末尾の文句が、

> ありがたかりける霊地かな（サシ冒頭句）—ありがたさよ（サシ末句）—ありがたかりし霊地かな（段哥前半の末句）
>
> お旅所を伏し拝み（下ゲ哥末句）—忝なしと伏し拝む（段哥末句）

と類似している。わざとそのように表現を揃えているのであろう。しかも「ありがたかりける」から「ありがたさ」「ありがたかりし」と信仰心をより強調するかのごとく、直接回想表現へと変化させて

いるのも、意図的な叙述なのであろう。思うに、山上に近付くにつれて、信仰心が強まるという表現なのであろう。そして御旅所を伏し拝んだ後、月の出た男山山頂を仰ぎ見るというのが、〔段哥〕前半の設定ではなかろうか。〔段哥〕後半は、やはり参拝者の視点から、山上の眺望を述べている。以上のごとく、この一連の謡にはテーマの一貫性があり、主人公の視点も存在する。石清水八幡宮の参拝者が、その山下と山上との全体を称える歌謡とでもいうべき内容である。はじめに述べたように、一曲の筋立てとの関連でいえば、山下の町屋を過ぎて放生川を渡り、登山口から御旅所を経て、山上の八幡宮に到達するという、一連の行程を歌っていることになる。しかし謡の内容そのものに即していえば、実はそうとも言えない面がある。この問題についても次章に言及する。

2.〈石清水の謡〉が独立の歌謡であること

表章氏は、世阿弥の芸談の筆録である『申楽談儀』に見える、曲不明とされていた文句の典拠を発見された[2]。表氏により〈女郎花の古き謡〉と名付けられた、田楽役者喜阿弥作曲のこの謡は、能〈女郎花〉とは別曲の、独立の歌謡である。世阿弥の能楽論書『五音』上巻に冒頭句が引かれる〔サシ〕に続いて、「上ゲ哥クセ」と呼びたくなるような、上ゲ哥形式で始まりクセ形式で終わる一連の謡であると考えられている。この〈女郎花の古き謡〉を、ここで論じている能〈女郎花〉に先行する田楽の古い能の一部であると考える立場もあるが、そうではなく、宴席などで歌うために作られた田楽歌謡であるとする表氏の見解が、現在の定説である。さてその論文の中で、能〈女郎花〉の中にある〈石清水の謡〉について、表氏は次のように述べる。

> 前場は、歌問答が世阿弥好みの趣向であり、はめこまれている形の八幡宮を礼賛した謡（サシ〔掛ヶ合〕・下哥・上哥の形。観阿弥の「高野の古き謡」の影響が認められる）の文辞

2 「〈女郎花の古き謡〉考」『観世』1972年7月号

も世阿弥くさくて、少なくとも前場は応永以後の作である可能性が強い。

この指摘の重要な点は、この謡（表氏の「サシ・〔掛ヶ合〕・下哥・上哥」は誤解であろう。竹本がサシ・下ゲ哥・段哥と呼んだもの）が「はめこまれている形」であるとしていることである。本稿執筆に際して確かめたところ、表氏より、それは「〈女郎花〉の能以前に作られ、能を制作する際に取り入れられた、『独立の歌謡』であるという意味である」との教示を得た（実は表氏は、この見解を、Ominameshi Conferenceの直前にも口頭で述べておられた由である）。この主張は確かに説得力がある。それではこの〈石清水の謡〉の作者と、能〈女郎花〉全体の作者とは、別人なのであろうか。

実はこの謡は、内容的には恋の妄執物の能である〈女郎花〉の主題と、直接には関連せず、能の構想の上では、突出した印象なのである。主題とは無縁の石清水八幡宮への讃美を長々と歌うことが、〈石清水の謡〉に能一曲の内容とは異質の印象を感じる最大の理由である。

さらに私見を加えれば、この謡は時を8月15日に設定しているにもかかわらず、一曲全体の中では、それが何の意味も持っていないことも問題である。8月15日とは、舞台となった石清水八幡宮における、一年中で最大の祭礼である、放生会の日である。この日、神は明け方寅の刻（午前4時頃）に御旅所に遷り、夕方酉の刻（午後6時頃）に山上の神殿に戻る。陰暦8月15日は秋の最中で、一年で最も月の美しい夜である。この能にとっては、女郎花の季節である点は都合がよいけれども、放生会の当日というめでたい日の名月の夜に、愛の破綻ゆえに入水して果てた、男女の亡霊が登場すべきいわれはない。〈石清水の謡〉は男山山上への案内という点で、内容が前後の詞章と一見はうまく合っている半面、謡自体は放生会に参拝して石清水を称える内容なのに、能としては8月15日に舞台設定すべき必要性がないわけである。放生会の当日であることは、実はこの謡の〔下ゲ哥〕以外のどこにも説明がなく、むしろ放生会の当日でない方が、能の内容からは都合がよいほどなのである。従って能の一部としては、該当する〔下ゲ哥〕の部分は、放生会の当日ではないという設定にするために、「8月15日の放生会の日にもなれば、八幡大菩薩がお出ましになるはずの、御旅所を伏し拝んで」とでも訳さねばならなくなるのである。しかし「ころは八月半ばの日」とは、この日が8月15日であることをいう文言で、訳文としても、上の訳文は無理である。それに内容的には神を称える、祝言色の強いこの謡では、まさに祭の当日に御旅所を礼拝する設定である方が、ふさわしいのである。「祝言性の強さ」という点でも、この謡は〈女郎花〉全体の構想とは大きくかけ離れていることになる。

第二に、その前後で石清水八幡宮への誘いの文句と到着の由とが語られるにもかかわらず、〈石清水の謡〉自体には、山上への移動の様子が必ずしも明確に説明されていない。〈石清水の謡〉は、いわゆる道行文ではなく、男山全体を俯瞰した視点の謡であると考えることもできる。また謡の内容は、石清水八幡宮に初めて参拝するワキの僧の視点からの感想であり、その土地に居住している老人であるという設定の、シテの視点ではない。しかもそれは、この前後が、シテのセリフや演技に焦点を合わせた、いわゆる「シテ中心主義」を前提にして構想されていることと整合しない。なにしろ、この場面で謡にあわせて演技するのは、シテなのである。描かれる心情は明らかに参拝者であるワキの心情であるのに、ワキを案内するからという理由でシテが演技するのは、場面展開と演技との乖離という点で大きな疑問が残る。これも独立の謡物を無理にはめ込んだ結果なのではなかろうか。

第三に、〔段哥〕の後半部分について、本稿冒頭にも述べたように、伊藤氏はこれを〔哥〕とし、表氏は〔上ゲ哥〕の後半と理解しているようであるが、いずれも誤りである。この部分は、前半の〔上ゲ哥〕部分を切り離して考えれば、短小ながら音楽的には明らかに〔クセ〕であり、本来の作詞・作曲者は〔クセ〕としての音楽的効用（高音域の前半部に対して、低音域の謡を接続し、途中で高音域に戻す）をある程度は意識して作っていることが確実視される。(もちろん高音域で始まる〔上ゲ哥〕前半部に低音域の〔クセ〕が接合している点は、非常に特異である。これについては本稿の末にも言及する。) ところが〔クセ〕にしては短いため、能にはめこまれた段階では、能〈女郎花〉の作者はこれを〔クセ〕と意識せずに使った可能性がある。それはどういうことかというと、「鳩の嶺越し来てみれば」の一句は、明らかに「上ゲ端（アゲハ）」と呼ばれる高音部であり、本来ここはシテ

（もしくはワキ）が歌わねばならぬ部分なのである。にもかかわらず、この「上ゲ端」をシテが歌わないのは、作者が〔クセ〕のつもりで演出しなかったことによるのではないか。つまり独立の歌謡として、能のような役替えなしで、一人もしくは複数の歌い手により歌われていたものをそのまま用いたため、〔クセ〕にしては短小な謡のこの部分が「上ゲ端」であることに気付かず、そのまま地謡に歌わせてしまったと考えられるのである。なお本稿のはじめに掲げた三種の古写本でも、この部分は地謡のままである。おそらくは能の成立当初から、この部分は地謡として歌われてきたのであろう。これは、この謡の作曲者と、〈女郎花〉の能の作者とが別人である、何よりの証拠と考えられる。

そもそもこの能の作者は、曲舞音曲（ようするに〔クセ〕部分）の音楽的特質の把握に習熟していないらしく、一曲中に二つの〔クセ〕風の謡があるのに、いずれも不可解な処理を行っている。一つは上記の部分であるが、もう一方の後場の〔クセ〕も、後シテと後ツレによる掛け合いの懺悔物語に続くという変わった内容で、こうした場合は、対話の形式を継続すべく、〔ロンギ〕という小段で終結させるのが、普通のやり方なのである。しかもこの〔クセ〕は、末句が繰り返しになる。しかし中入の段に〔クセ〕が配置されるのでもない限り、〔クセ〕では通常末句を繰り返すことがないのである。〔クセ〕の末句に繰り返しのある例外的事例としてよく知られているのは、世阿弥時代の素人の作である〈浮舟〉の前場の〔クセ〕である。これはようするに、能〈女郎花〉の作者が、（素人ではなかったにせよ、）曲舞音曲の何たるかを理解していなかったことを示すものであろう。

3.〈女郎花の古き謡〉やその他の能との関連

〈女郎花の古き謡〉は、能〈女郎花〉と同じ頼風説話（『古今和歌集序聞書三流抄』などに見える女郎花伝説）を参照しており、独立の歌謡とはいえ、本曲との何らかの関わりを持っていた可能性がある。すでに表氏の前掲論文に指摘されているが、〈女郎花〉第三段の〔上ゲ哥〕「うしろめたくや思ふらん、女郎と書ける花の名に、たれ偕老を契りけん」(こんな花に親しむとは、良心に引け目を感じるのではなかろうか、「あそびめ」という名の花なんぞを、だれがいつまでも傍に置いておこうと思うものか)は、そのまま〈女郎花の古き謡〉に見える文句で、そこからの引用と考えられるから、能〈女郎花〉の作者は、〈女郎花の古き謡〉の存在を知っていたことになる。能〈女郎花〉は、〈女郎花の古き謡〉をある程度は意識しつつ、『三流抄』の頼風説話を作品の説話的構想の中心に据えて、新たに劇化を試みたものであろう。〈女郎花の古き謡〉が全面的に利用されていないのは、それがこうした謡物の特色ともいえる、説話性を拡散させた内容—頼風説話をも踏まえるものの、あくまで文飾の一部としての引用で、嵯峨野の女郎花を題材とする僧正遍昭の和歌などの他のエピソードをも引用し、物語的な一貫性のない、女郎花尽くしの世界を作り上げている—であったからではあるまいか。つまりは〈女郎花の古き謡〉は、独立の歌謡として完成度が高かったため、そのまま能の一部にはめ込むには中途半端で、かえって難しかったのであろう。しかしながら〈女郎花の古き謡〉からの引用は、この作者が田楽謡を含め広い取材圏を持っていたことを示している。

この能に先行する諸作品との関係を次に見てみよう。能〈女郎花〉は、後場に男女二人の霊が登場する能であるという点で、〈錦木〉〈通小町〉〈舟橋〉などとの類似が指摘されている。また〈女郎花〉のワキの待謡と後シテ登場の謡は、〈求塚〉の詞章の借用であることも指摘されている。これに加えて、能〈女郎花〉の前半で、女郎花の詩歌についてのシテとワキとの問答から、名所の謡ともいうべき〈石清水の謡〉へ続き、さらにその後で男塚・女塚への案内と進む構想は、能〈求塚〉の前半での、生田の名所問答と若菜摘みの段から求塚への案内へと進む構想と、よく似ている。ようするに〈女郎花〉は明らかに、〈求塚〉を意識して制作されているのである。

後シテ・後ツレの登場する〈女郎花〉の後場は、男女一対の幽霊が登場する、恋慕の妄執能の多くに共通する構想でもある。そして上記の能の内では、とくに〈舟橋〉に近い。〈錦木〉は男女の幽霊能であるが、破綻した恋の妄執物というわけではない。また〈通小町〉は、実は〈舟橋〉の構想の下敷きになった作品とも考えられるが、〈女郎花〉により近いのは、〈舟橋〉の方である。ただし〈女郎花〉が〈舟橋〉と違う点が二つある。その一つは〔クセ〕があることで、これはむしろ〈錦木〉に共通する点であるが、その形は〈錦木〉とは異なり、末句が繰り返しになる。これは前述の通り、世阿弥時代の〈浮舟〉にもある形で、前半の〈石清水の謡〉で〔段哥〕後半の上ゲ端をシテ謡にしないことと同様、作者が曲舞音曲に習熟していなかったことを示している。曲舞は観阿弥が能に取り入れ、世阿弥が理論的に完成したものであるから、世阿弥グループの作者であれば、このような〔クセ〕の用い方はしないであろう。ここから〈女郎花〉の作者は、世阿弥の薫陶を受けた人物ではないという推論が導かれる。

またもう一つは、両者の役造型の違いである。〈女郎花〉終曲部の地獄の描写は、『往生要集』に見える衆合地獄の描写を踏まえるらしいが、邪淫戒を破った者が堕（お）ちる衆合地獄の描写は、〈女郎花〉のような恋の報いとしては、実は不相応なのである。恋愛を「邪淫」とするのは能の一般的な傾向であるが、例えば〈綾鼓〉で描かれる「邪淫の鬼」（よこしまな愛欲心のためにみにくい鬼の姿に変貌した者）は、『今昔物語集』などでも知られる、愛欲の権化としての「紺青鬼」の系統の鬼である。なおその改作である〈恋重荷〉の詞章にある「衆合地獄」の場合は、地獄の名称が出るのみで、呵責のありさまはずいぶんと和らげられている。また〈求塚〉の菟名日処女の堕地獄は、恋の妄執の結果ではなく、殺生の報いという位置付けである。そして〈女郎花〉の主人公の位置付けは、恋の妄執に苦しむ主人公でありながら、〈求塚〉の菟名日処女のそれに非常に近い。

これらに対して、〈通小町〉や〈舟橋〉のように、男女二人の幽霊が、妄執にさいなまれつつ登場する場合がある。これらは幽霊能という構想の下で、恋の苦悩という主題を描くための方便としての「苦患」や「邪淫の悪鬼」という位置付けなのである。そもそも世阿弥の妄執物の鬼能における地獄の描写は、生前の業因の再現という演技を基本としており、恋の妄執においてはとくにそうである。恋という、和歌の事件にもなる優美な題材を主題とすることにより、鬼能の幽玄化（より正確には非鬼能化）を目指したのが世阿弥であった。この場合の幽玄化とは、登場する霊鬼に人間的な弱さを付与することである。人間的に悩み苦しむのが、こうした鬼たちの特色である。世阿弥の場合、とくに男女二人の霊が登場する能では、このような意味での幽玄能志向が強いのである。従って死後の苦しみを述べる場合でも、現世における恋の苦悩の方がより克明に描かれ、地獄の苦患の描写にはあまり具体性がない場合が多い。

この世阿弥的傾向に比較すると、〈女郎花〉は男女の霊の登場する恋の妄執物の能であるのに、犯罪的な行為のために堕ちる衆合地獄の様子が具体的に描かれるのは、きわめて不自然なのである。「邪淫」の報いとして、仏典に説かれるような地獄の苦患をそのまま描く〈女郎花〉の作者には、〈求塚〉のような作品と、〈通小町〉のような作品との、主題上の区別がつかなかったようである。〈女郎花〉で、〈求塚〉の後シテを踏まえたような人物造型をしたのは、作者の誤解もしくは能に対する考え方の相違と考えられる。したがってこれもまた、〈女郎花〉の非世阿弥的な傾向の現れであると結論できる。

おわりに

〈女郎花〉の能は、田楽の謡である〈女郎花の古き謡〉を引用し、その存在を念頭に置きつつ制作されているらしい。〈高野の古き謡〉や〈求塚〉など、観阿弥・世阿弥系の作品をも参照していることは、本曲が世阿弥よりは時代の下る、15世紀後半頃に成立したらしい作品であることを示している。さらに〈女郎花〉に取り入れられた〈石清水の謡〉の中心部分である〔段哥〕が、〈女郎花の古き謡〉や、〈源氏の謡〉（〈須磨源氏〉にある光源氏一代記の謡で、「上ゲ哥クセ」という名称で呼ぶ例もある）等と同じく、田楽謡の特色であるらしい〔上ゲ哥〕と〔クセ〕とを接合させた旋律型を持っていることは、問題である。このような特異な旋律を持つ二つの謡が、偶然にもその一方は〈女郎花〉に一部引用され、また他方は曲中にそのまま取り込れてたとは考えがたい。〈石清水の謡〉の作者については、例えば前掲の表氏の説では、「世阿弥」もしくはその亜流の可能性を示唆されているが、作曲上の特色からいえば、世阿弥的ではなく、むしろ田楽系統ということになるのではあるまいか。もちろん世阿弥の影響下にある作者が、田楽風の旋律を真似て〈石清水の謡〉を作詞・作曲した可能性も否定は出来ないが、「上ゲ哥クセ」系の旋律型が田楽の特色である以上は、この謡も時代は比較的下るものの、田楽系の謡と考えるのが自然であろう。一方〈女郎花〉が世阿弥系統の能ではなく、曲舞音曲にも未熟である点（なお田楽能の〈苅萱〉などでも特異な〔クセ〕があり、その作曲者である喜阿弥が曲舞音曲をきちんと理解していなかったらしいことは、『申楽談儀別本聞書』に見える）を合わせ考えると、能〈女郎花〉の作者は、田楽系統の能の影響を強く受ける立場にいたらしいことが、想定されよう。

男女二人の幽霊による掛け合い風の演技という、〈女郎花〉の後場の構想の基本は、〈舟橋〉〈通小町〉とも共通し、これは大和猿楽系統の妄執物の鬼能の類型に準じたものと考えられる。しかし〈舟橋〉が、田楽でも上演していた古作能 からの改作であることは、注意を要する。現行〈舟橋〉は世阿弥の改作で、どの程度まで田楽能の影響を反映した作品か不明であるが、〈舟橋〉が恋の妄執に沈む主人公を「邪淫の悪鬼」という視点で描こうとするのは、あるいは古い田楽能からの影響なのかもしれない。もちろんすでに述べたように、現行の〈舟橋〉では、恋の妄執の報いとして地獄の苦患を描こうとする傾向は、かなり抑制され、抽象化されている。しかしながら以下に掲げる〈舟橋〉の終曲部の詞章には、わずかながら、かつては具体的な地獄の苦患を描くものであったろう、原作の名残を認めうるかに思われる。下記の引用部分が、原作〈舟橋〉の詞章のままであるというわけではない。原作の古風で陰惨な叙述の雰囲気を、多少なりとも引きずっているのではないかと思うのである。

> 執心の鬼となって、共に三途の川橋の、橋柱に立てられて、悪龍の気色に変はり、程なく生死、娑婆の妄執、邪淫の悪鬼となつて、われと身を責め苦患に沈むを…
> （恋への執着のあまり鬼となって、二人とも冥界との間の三途の川の橋で、人柱にされてしまい、身は邪悪な龍の姿に変じ、そのままた生死を繰り返す身の上となり、現世への執心である邪淫の罪のために悪鬼となって、自分で自分の身を責めさいなみ、地獄の苦しみに沈んでいたのを…）

上記の引用文は、〈求塚〉や〈女郎花〉の地獄の描写に比べると、やや観念的で具体性のない苦患の描写であるが、やはり恋の報いとしては、あまりふさわしいとはいえない。これは〈女郎花〉との部分的な共通要素と見なしてもよいように思われる。

すでに述べたごとく、〈女郎花〉には、世阿弥系統の能の影響を受けた部分も確かに存在するから、その制作年代は、世阿弥の作風がかなり浸透した時代を想定せねばならない。そして能〈女郎花〉は本来は田楽の座で作られ、そこから大和猿楽に移入された能であったという可能性を考えたい。15 世紀後半という成立時期は、そうした想定との関わりの上でも、かなり蓋然性が高いのではあるまいか。

The *Utai* in the Fourth Section of *Ominameshi*

Takemoto Mikio

This paper deals with the composition of the noh play *Ominameshi* through a consideration of the *utai* in the fourth part of the play.

First, the paper introduces this *utai*, which the author refers to as "*Iwashimizu no utai*" and which praises the sacred Iwashimizu Hachiman Shrine. Because the three parts of the *utai* act in concert with each other, they may be thought of as forming a whole.

Second, the essay contends that the *utai* is an independent chant that was not originally part of *Ominameshi* and was not a play itself. The reasons for this contention are as follows: first, in the noh there is no reference to the restriction of the time period as from dusk to the moonlit night, but there is in the chant; second, in terms of content, the viewpoint is that of the priest, but it is the old man who performs the *utai*, so that the viewpoint and the performance do not conform to the needs of the play; and third, in terms of composition, the author of the play seems not to have understood the particular characteristics of this *utai*.

Finally, the paper points out that the noh *Ominameshi* was influenced by "*Ominameshi no furuki utai*," an independent *utai* of *dengaku* and that the "*Iwashimizu no utai*" also bears similar compositional characteristics to *dengaku*. In addition, it is clear that *Ominameshi* was influenced by Zeami's noh plays; however, it can also be seen as influenced by older pre-Zeami *oni* noh plays. In conclusion, the paper suggests the possibility that *Ominameshi* was composed by a group of performers of *dengaku* after Zeami; that is, by the Yamato Sarugaku group to which the successors of Zeami adhered.

Plates

1. 女扇、江戸時代、『古代能楽中啓扇』。Woman's fan with *ominaeshi*. From *Kodai nōgaku chūkei ōgi.*

2. 唐織、江戸時代、林原美術館。*Karaori* with *ominaeshi* pattern. Edo Period. Hayashibara Art Museum.

3. 繍箔、江戸時代、厳島神社。*Nuihaku* with *ominaeshi* pattern. Edo Period. Itsukushima Shrine.

4. 唐織、江戸時代、林原美術館。*Karaori* with autumn flowers including *ominaeshi* on a ground of alternating blocks of red and white. Edo Period. Hayashibara Art Museum.

5. 『女郎花』前場。 *Ominameshi* Act I. Both the *Shite* (old man) and the *Waki* (monk) wear plain *mizugoromo* over plain *noshime* kimono. Kanze actor Urata Yasuhiro. Photo: Ushimado Masakatsu.

6. 尉扇、江戸時代、豊橋魚町能楽保存会。 An old man's fan, *jō ōgi*, with ink drawing of Chinese sages. Edo period. Toyohashi Uomachi Noh Preservation Committee.

(Left) 7. 三光尉、河内作、江戸初期、豊橋魚町能楽保存会。 *Sankōjō*. Deep creases lend this mask a feeling of pathos. By Kawachi. Early Edo Period. Toyohashi Uomachi Noh Preservation Committee.

8. 朝倉尉、天下一若狭守作、江戸初期、内藤記念館。 *Asakurajo*. By Tenkaichi Wakase no Kami. Early Edo period. Naitō Memorial Museum.

(Left) 9. 笑尉、出目満永作、江戸初期、内藤記念館。 *Waraijō*. The laughing lips and rustic coloring mark this style mask as low in dignity. By Deme Mitsunaga. Early Edo Period. Naitō Memorial Museum.

10. 『女郎花』後場。 Yorikaze dressed as a low-ranking aristocrat in an unlined *kariginu*, *ōkuchi*, and *kazaori eboshi*. Kanze actor Urata Yasuhiro. Photo: Ushimado Masakatsu.

11. 男扇、江戸時代、『古代能楽中啓扇』。 Man's fan, *otoko ōgi*. Edo period. *Kodai nōgaku chūkei ōgi*.

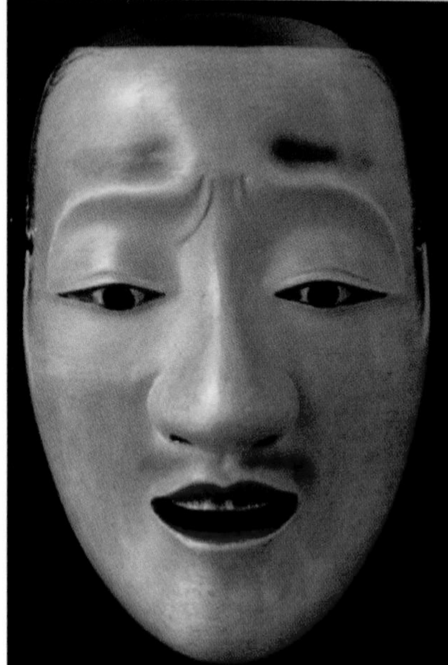

12. 中将、江戸中期、厳島神社。 *Chūjō* mask. Refinement appears in the thick eyebrows, gently down-turned eyes, light dusting of a mustache and gentle curve of the red lips exposing only the upper row of blackened teeth. By an unknown carver. Mid-Edo Period. Itsukushima Shrine.

13. 『通小町』。 *Kayoi Komachi*. Shii no Shōshō in *kariginu* with *yase-otoko* mask. Kanze actor Hashimoto Kōzaburō. Photo: Ushimado Masayuki.

(Right) 14. 痩男、是閑作、江戸初期、豊橋魚町能楽保存会。*Yase-otoko* mask used in *Kayoi Komachi*. By Zekan. Early Edo period. Toyohashi Uomachi Noh Preservation Committee.

15. 若男、友閑作、江戸初期、徳川美術館。 *Waka-otoko* mask, the standard choice of Hōshō and Kongō schools. A commoner, but of some refinement, *waka-otoko* masks may be close to *imawaka* or similar to *kantan-otoko* (Photo 16). By Yūkan. Early Edo Period. The Tokugawa Art Museum.

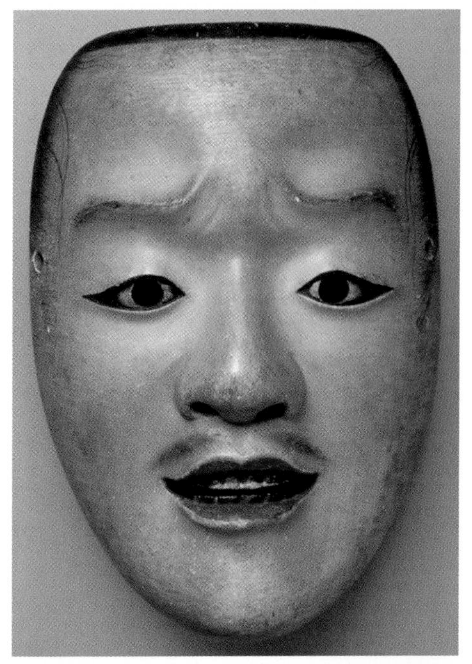

16. 邯鄲男、有閑作、江戸初期、内藤記念館 *Kantan-otoko* mask, one Kanze-school alternative for Yorikaze. In place of the drawn-in fuzzy eyebrows of the aristocrat *chūjō* (Photo 12), *kantan-otoko* retains his natural eyebrows. The muscular cheeks and terse lips suggest strength; the furrows between the eyebrows lend the face a degree of intense thoughtfulness. By Yūkan. Early Edo Period. Naitō Memorial Museum.

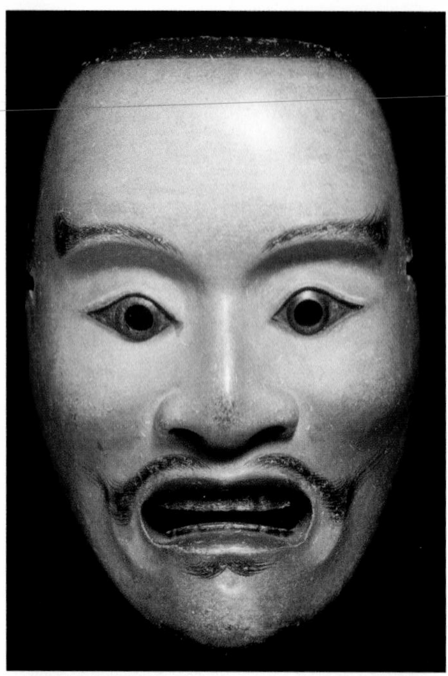

17. 怪士、江戸時代、内藤記念館。 *Ayakashi* mask. Rounded eyes, swerving eyebrows, similarly swerving mustache and rounded open lips bearing two sets of teeth, the upper set with gold tips echoing the metalic inserts in the eyes, all give this mask an other-worldly strength. By an unknown carver. Edo Period. Naitō Memorial Museum.

18. 鷹、江戸初期、内藤記念館。 *Taka* mask, suggested as a non-standard mask for *Ominameshi*. The diamond-shaped eyes and triangular creases above them create the troubled expression. Ears and a broad, open mouth distinguish this large version of *taka* from the smaller *kotaka* mask. By an unknown carver. Early Edo Period. Naitō Memorial Museum.

Ominameshi and Considerations of Costume and Mask

Monica Bethe

Lack of scenery on the noh stage places special importance on costume as imagery. Colors, patterns, and textures all play a role in establishing the atmosphere and may in addition reflect images integral to the verbal text. The shape of the garments, that is, their type defined by cut and tailoring, is decided by tradition and indicates the social status of the wearer, drawing on external reference to common practice: nobles wear round-collar cloaks, daimyo wear matched suits, and the like. The masks, worn for the *shite* and sometimes *tsure* roles, delineate the characters. One might say the combination of garments and mask embody the character, while the movement, song, and rhythms of the performance enact the character through the unfolding of the text.

In choosing garments and masks, the actor is guided not only by the traditions of his school, but also by his own sense of appropriateness, based on his understanding of the play within the context of the entire repertory of noh. For reference, he may look to other noh with similar themes, structures, mood, song or choreography in order to find parallels that suggest refinements in costuming. He considers both what the piece shares with other noh of the same type and what distinguishes the specific noh play from others. Parallel plays help provide guidelines for both costuming and modulation of tempo during a performance.

Based on thematic and structural parallels with other plays, the early twentieth-century noh scholar Nogami Toyoichirō placed *Ominameshi* among the "attachment pieces" (*shūshinmono*).[1] *Shūshinmono* depict ghosts who suffer in hell from excessive attachment and appeal for prayers to relieve their pains or grant them salvation. In

[1] At the end of Volume 6 of his *Nōgaku zensho* (Tokyo: Sōgensha, 1942-44), 237-53, Nogami Toyoichirō classifies all of the noh plays by thematic categories, based not only on the story content, but also on performance elements, such as the type of dance or mask. See page 240 for *Ominameshi*.

Ominameshi, Yorikaze, the *shite* in the second act, performs a short scene in which he descends into lover's hell, which is probably the justification for including this play among the *shūshinmono.* A state of excessive attachment, however, might rather be accorded to the woman (*tsure*) in the play, who, disappointed by Yorikaze's neglect, threw herself in a river and died. Shimazaki Chifumi also listed *Ominameshi* as a "male" *shūshinmono,* along with *Funabashi, Kayoi Komachi,* and *Nishikigi.*[2] Other *shūshinmono* that share with *Ominameshi* the theme of a woman drowning herself due to love attachment, but which center on the woman *shite*, are *Motomezuka* and *Ukifune.*

The classification of *Ominameshi* as a *shūshinmono* is, however, not entirely obvious. The general atmosphere of the play, with its preponderance of poems, is more refined than most attachment pieces. In addition, the title "*Ominameshi*" immediately brings to mind elegant plays that go by plant names, such as *Kakitsubata* (iris), *Saigyō zakura* (cherry tree), and *Yugyō yanagi* (willow). Despite the major difference that these plays represent the plant on stage as a *shite* figure while *Ominameshi* does not, the dominant role of the plant image is shared. In *Ominameshi* it is expressed through poetry and the imagery of the *ominaeshi* flower being an impersonation of the drowned woman, for it grows at the site of her grave and is the same yellow as her robe. The actor may choose to heighten this flower image through costuming, as detailed below.

From reading the text of *Ominameshi* one might seriously wonder where the main focus is—on the flower, the drowned woman, or the man who must come to terms with her death. The allotment of roles, however, makes the focus absolutely clear. The main role goes to the ghost of the man, Yorikaze.[3] It is therefore his costume and mask that help define the play. The woman, whose story bridges the center of the play, from the end of Act I through the interlude and the *kuse* of Act II, has been marginalized to a *tsure* role with few lines and little real action. Her costume is a standard norm. Chart 1 shows the costume types prescribed for each role in the play.

[2] Among these male *shūshinmono*, thematically more distant plays include *Akogi, Utō, Fujito*, and *Matsumushi.* See Shimazaki Chifumi, *Restless Spirits from Japanese Noh Plays of the Fourth Group* (Cornell, East Asia Series, 1995), 15.

[3] Non-canon versions of *Ominameshi*, both noh and other genres, cast the *shite* as a woman, so this is a conscious choice of the playwright. See Matisoff article page 173.

Chart 1

Roles in *Ominameshi* and their standard costumes

waki	traveling priest	*noshime*, *mizugoromo*, *sumibōshi*
maeshite	guardian of the flowers	*noshime*, *mizugoromo*, old man's fan, old man's mask
kyōgen	man of the place	*atsuita*, *kataginu*, *hakama*
nochizure	woman	red *karaori* in *kinagashi* draping, woman's fan, *ko-omote* mask
nochijite	ghost of Yorikaze	*atsuita*, unlined *kariginu* (or *chōken*), *ōkuchi*, *kazaori eboshi*, man's fan, male mask

Imagery and Costuming

The *ominaeshi* flower that gives the play its title blooms in early autumn. Somewhat similar to Queen Anne's lace, it has a spherical multi-centered head and stick-like stalk. A field of *ominaeshi* flowers swaying in the wind can appear like a ripple of yellow waves, while individual *ominaeshi* among other wild flowers add touches of ornamental yellow. This flower provides a focus for the action of the play. In addition to being the topic of an exchange of poems in the first act, when the implications of the characters for its name 女郎花 (maiden or damsel flower) are highlighted, the *ominaeshi* takes on special significance from the story told towards the end of the first act, of how an *ominaeshi* grew up from a grave of a woman who drowned herself from neglected love and how this flower then seemed, to the woman's lover, to reject his advances by turning away (*kuneru*) every time he approached. At the end of the noh play the lover, Yorikaze ("approaching wind"), comes to terms with this act of turning away and seeks salvation through the flower and its association with the sacred lotus.[4]

An actor wishing to create a visual expression of this central flower image on stage might do so through his choice of colors or design patterns. In noh, explicit reading of the costume imagery can be considered too obvious and overdone, but evocation of season (such as through designs including autumn flowers) is important, and visualization of poetic elements on a subtle level is encouraged. In this play, with its male main role combined with a focus on a female flower, to mirror the poetic focus in the costume by including the flower as a design motif on the woman's garment might serve to sharpen the imagery. Similarly, to clothe the male figure in colors evocative of the flower might echo the central image of the play in addition to representing his character. Therefore, some actors have proposed costuming the *shite* in the second act in yellows and yellow-greens, suggesting the colors of the *ominaeshi* flower.[5] These greens

[4] The association that links *ominaeshi* with the lotus is that they are both flowers that can be dedicated to the Buddha. See page 425 in Edward Kamens, "Dragon-Girl, Maidenflower, Buddha: The Transformation of a Waka Topos, 'The Five Obstructions,'" *Harvard Journal of Asiatic Studies* 53:2 (1993): 389–442.

[5] Conversations with Takabayashi Kōji and Izumi Yoshio, 1995.

and yellows hark back to the Heian-period layered color combinations (*kasane iro*) that dictated the seasonal interpretations through clothing of the aristocracy. One called "*ominaeshi*" combines white and yellowish-green.[6] A *kariginu* of millet yellow would highlight the image of the yellow garb of the drowned woman and the yellow flower that sprang from her grave, while one of pale green would suggest the flower through the *kasane iro* association.[7]

Since the *ominaeshi* is one of the "seven autumn flowers" (*aki no nanagusa*) representative of the season and depicted often in art, it appears in various forms on fans (Photo 1[8]) and a number of types of robes, such as gold leaf, stencil-dyed under robes, brocaded women's robes (*karaori*; Photos 2 & 4), and embroidered satin robes (*nuihaku*, Photo 3). Within this seasonal context, it is entirely appropriate for the *tsure* in the second half of *Ominameshi* to wear a *karaori* (brocaded robe) with *ominaeshi* flowers in its pattern or to carry a fan including a depiction of *ominaeshi*. Indeed, the standard robe of *tsure* women, not only in *Ominameshi*, is a red *karaori*. Typically these *karaori* are either "spring" or "autumn" robes, the latter often bearing designs of the seven autumn flowers. It is by propitious chance that such a design is particularly suited to this play.

Defining the *Shite* Role through Costume and Mask

While the colors, patterns, and textures work to create the scene, setting season and mirroring imagery, the types of robes and masks define the role in terms of social status, occupation, fate, and personality. For the modern actor, tradition dictates the general scope, a tradition that relies on paradigms of correlation and association, which sometimes, as in the case of *Ominameshi*, may contain contradictions.

[6] For discussion and illustration of layered colors, see Nagasaki Seiki, *Kasane no irome* (Kyoto: Kyoto Shoin, 1988), 47.
[7] It must be remembered that the choice of color of the garment is up to the actor. Not all actors would choose to garb Yorikaze in the colors of the flower. A common choice is blue, appropriate to Yorikaze's low court rank.
[8] From Kongō Iwao, ed., *Kodai nōgaku chūkei ōgi* (Kyoto: Happōdō, 1971).

The Old Man in the First Act

The selection of costume and mask for the first act is comparatively straightforward and falls within established rules. The standard costume for the guardian of the flowers (*shite* in the first act) designates him as a commoner, an old man, as might appear in the first act of fourth or fifth category plays (Photo 5).[9] It is distinguished from costumes for old men who have greater dignity or higher status by the absence of the voluminous *ōkuchi* (divided skirts) and by the type of mask.

The color of the collar of the undermost garment in a noh costume reflects social hierarchy: navy blue for rustic workers, white for the nobility. The guardian of the flowers wears pale blue, a step above navy, which is at the bottom. His plain-color *noshime* (plain-weave box-sleeve kimono) also suits low-ranking old men, as does his plain-weave, solid-color *mizugoromo* (wide-sleeve jacket). The colors chosen tend to be navy blue for the *noshime*, and brown for the *mizugoromo*.[10] The guardian of the flowers carries an old man's fan (*jō ōgi*, Photo 6), which he never opens. Typically this has an ink painting of Chinese sages on it.

Nothing stands out in this costuming of the first act; the character can assume an identity slowly. The first half of *Ominameshi* is primarily verbal: a contest of poetry connoisseurship, a tour of Iwashimizu Shrine, and a narration of the story behind the "female" and "male" tombs of the drowned woman and Yorikaze. Very little action accompanies the verbal imagery. The simplicity of the costume allows for concentration on sound and text.

The mask for the old guardian of the flowers represents an old man of lower class, a working man. Masks of this type are distinguished from, on the one hand, masks of dignified old men worn by gods in the first act of a noh, and, on the other, masks of old men used in the

[9] Fourth and fifth-category old men roles include the fisher in *Akogi,* the hunter in *Utō,* and Minamoto no Tōru in *Tōru.*

[10] The Kanze school notes the possibility of substituting a *noshime* with small checks, but the lowly old man in *Ominameshi* would never wear an *atsuita* with woven checks, because woven patterns are of older origin and considered more noble than the easily-produced dyed patterns, according to Fujishiro Tsugio, *Shashin de miru nō no shōzoku* (Tokyo: Wanya Shoten, 1972), 40–5.

second act where a god performs a dance. Chart 2 compares the features and expressions of the various kinds of old men's masks. Noteworthy is that the greater the dignity, or *kurai,* of the role, the less realistically the hair is portrayed. Implanting hair for the mustache lends the mask a greater realism and humanity, as opposed to godliness. Similarly, opening the lips wide to expose both upper and lower teeth is less dignified.

Chart 2

Types of old men's masks by rank or dignity (*kurai*)

	dignified god	dancing god	commoner
names of mask types:	*kojō* *akobujō*	*maijō* *shiwajō* *ishiōjō*	*asakurajō* *waraijō* *sankōjō*
features			
eyebrows	painted	painted	painted
mustache	painted	painted/implanted hair	implanted hair
beard	implanted hair	implanted hair	implanted hair
teeth	only upper	only upper/ both sets	upper & lower
expression:	placid, wise	distinct personality differ by school	earthy, cruder

Traditions vary among the five schools of noh as to which of the commoner old men's masks should be worn in *Ominameshi* (see Chart 3). Kita, Kongō, and Komparu all use *sankōjō* (Photo 7), a mask with deep creases lining the cheeks and eyebrows and a somewhat worn expression. Kanze and Hōshō allow the actor a choice, including *sankōjō, asakurajō* (Photo 8), which has fewer wrinkles, softened contours, and an open expression, and *waraijō* (Photo 9), whose lips are pulled back in a leer and eyes have a bitter-sweet glint. To choose *asakurajō* lends the guardian more pathos, while to wear *waraijō* emphasizes his menial tasks. The choice of mask for the first act would probably be considered in light of the choice of mask for the second act, a more complex topic.

Chart 3

Masks used for the guardian of the flowers in *Ominameshi* by school

Kita, Komparu, Kongō	*sankōjō*	middle to low dignity (*kurai*)
Hōshō	*sankōjō* or *asakurajō*	gentler expression, middle dignity
Kanze school	*asakurajō* or *waraijō*	lowest dignity

Yorikaze in the Second Act: Costume and Mask

Ono no Yorikaze, *shite* in the second act of *Ominameshi,* is presumably a member of the lower aristocracy. Although there is no clear evidence that a man called Ono no Yorikaze existed in real life, his historical reality is not impossible. He may in fact have been a minor member of the Ono family, who had connections to the Iwashimizu area.[11] The elements of Yorikaze's costume (Photo 10) correspond to his social station. Most schools use the broad-sleeved, round-collared, unlined *kariginu* (hunting cloak). The gauze weave (*ro*) of the cloak lends it a diaphanous lightness and is embellished with designs woven with thin strips of gold or silver leaf paper. The designs are often large and spaced, though they may be smaller and fill the space more evenly. Common designs are court patterns (*yūsoku monyō*), like vertical undulating lines, (*tatewaku*) or naturalistic patterns, like flowers with dew or clumps of grasses. The *kariginu,* belted with an embroidered satin sash (*nuimon koshiobi*), is an aristocratic garb, such as is worn by the retainer of Emperor Takakura, Nakakuni, in *Kogō*, and by the courtier Minamoto no Tōru in *Tōru.*[12] While the elegant, luxurious Tōru combines this unlined *kariginu* with *sashinuki* (courtier's pantaloons) and an *uikammuri* (crown), marking him as an upper aristocrat, Yorikaze wears *ōkuchi*

[11] Sakakura claims that the Ono family was connected with the Iwashimizu area. Sugiura Yoshirō, et al. "*Ominameshi arekore*" *Kanze* (July 1966), 15.

[12] Other characters who wear unlined *kariginu* include the *shite* in *Yugyō yanagi,* the *tsure* in *Sumiyoshi mōde*, and the *waki* in *Yuya, Hibariyama*, and *Aizomegawa,* as well as a number of child actor roles.

(broad divided skirts) and a *kazaori eboshi* (black lacquer hat), representative of lower ranks of the aristocracy.[13] Underneath these outer garbs, Yorikaze wears an *atsuita* (brocaded kimono) without red, a common undergarment for a wide variety of older male roles, and an inner collar of light blue (lower rank) or white. The colors of the *atsuita* are faintly visible through the gauze *kariginu*. Yorikaze carries an *otoko ōgi* (man's fan, Photo 11). This typically has either an ink drawing or a painting of, say, a bamboo fence on a gold or silver ground.[14]

In general *kariginu* costumes require the mask of a courtier, such as *chūjō* (Photo 12), or its variant *imawaka*. Indeed, the Kita and Komparu schools designate *chūjō* for the role of Yorikaze, while Kanze and Hōshō schools list *chūjō* as an alternative mask (see Chart 4). The gentle, sensitive expression of this mask, with its slight smile graced by a light mustache, with its broad sculpting of the area around the eyes, topped by high, curving bone ridges and fluffy painted eyebrows, and with its light coloring, is highly refined. *Chūjō* was devised to express the elegance of Heian court life, such as is shown in lyric plays like *Tōru*. A mask of this refinement seems incongruent with the mood of a *shūshinmono* and, in particular, unsuited to express the tortures enacted at the beginning of the *kiri* section of the play describing how Yorikaze unsuccessfully scales the sword-branch trees of hell in lust for the woman at the top (see LaFleur article).[15] The relative importance of this scene to the play as a whole is the key point in the variety of performance interpretations.

[13] *Kazaori eboshi* is listed by Kawabata as an Edo-period variant of the *tate-eboshi*, a tall lacquer hat worn from the Heian period on. Kawabata Sanehide, *Nihon fukushokushi jiten* (Tokyo: Tōkyōdō Shuppan, 1969), 44. Since the word appears in noh texts (Shii no Shōsho is described as donning a *kazaori eboshi* in *Kayoi Komachi*), this late dating may be wrong. The top of the hat is folded to the left (everyday) or the right (when attendant on the emperor), as if blown over by a strong wind, and secured with a cord. High nobility wear straight *tate-eboshi*, but those under the sixth rank wear bent *kazaori eboshi* as a norm. In the noh, *kazaori eboshi* are worn by the *shite* in *Utaura*, and by the *tsure* in such plays as *Shoson*, *Genjo*, and *Sōshiarai Komachi*, as well as by the *waki* in *Kokaji*. Generally it is combined with unlined *kariginu*.

[14] The man's fan, *otoko ōgi*, is typically used for unmasked male roles in fourth category plays.

[15] Konishi shares this view. Konishi Jin'ichi, "Sakuhin kenkyū 'Ominameshi'" *Kanze* (July 1966): 10–1.

Chart 4

Masks used in *Ominameshi* according to school traditions

Kanze	*waraijō/asakurajō*	*kantan/chūjō/imawaka*
Hōshō	*sankōjō/asakurajō*	*waka-otoko*
Komparu	*sankōjō*	*chūjō*
Kongō	*sankōjō*	*waka-otoko*
Kita	*sankōjō*	*chūjō*

The other main use of the *chūjō* mask is for warrior-courtiers, such as Tadanori and Kiyotsune. The costume for these roles includes a sweatband that covers the forehead and thereby obscures the delicate area of the mask above the eyes so as to create the impression of a stronger, more masculine face. Similarities in the structure of *Ominameshi* and of typical warrior plays include their both having a *kakeri* dance and a passage where the *shite* describes a descent to hell. Even though the warrior's hell is a very different place from the hell of needle mountains and sword-blade trees, the mood of the *kakeri* in *Ominameshi* is similar to that of warrior pieces.[16] This fact, according to the Kita actor Takabayashi Kōji, is probably the reason why the Kita school dresses Yorikaze in a costume similar to a warrior's, thereby justifying their use of the *chūjō* mask.[17] Instead of the *karig-inu*, the Kita school uses a *chōken* (a loose broad-sleeved cloak) with one sleeve slipped off the shoulder, rolled up, and tucked into the *ōkuchi* at the back, leaving the right sleeve of the *atsuita* underrobe exposed. The body panels of the *chōken* are securely bound at the waist.[18] The only differences between the Kita costume for Yorikaze and for warrior-courtiers are that Yorikaze does not carry a sword,

[16] There are two standard styles for performing the short *kakeri*, one for warriors, and one for madwomen. Mimetic variants on the *kakeri* also exist, such as the hunting scene in *Utō* and the fishing scene in *Akogi*.

[17] Conversation, November 17, 2000. Takabayashi said that the Kita school reasoning is often based more on performance elements, such as the type of dance, here the short and unsettled *kakeri*, rather than a graceful long instrumental dance (which would be suited to a *kariginu*), than on the status of the character. In the Kita school costuming Yorikaze's status is made explicit only by the type of hat he wears.

[18] The use of a *chōken* with the right sleeve off the shoulder actually follows an old tradition. Shimotsuma Shōshin writing in 1596, states in his *Dōbusho* (Comments on Noh Plays) and his *Nōdensho* (Noh Traditions) that the costume for Yorikaze is a *chōken* over *ōkuchi* and a *kosode*-style garment. In the former book he suggests as masks *heita*, *chūjō*, *kantan-otoko*, or a red *waka-otoko*; in the latter book he leaves out the possibility of the *heita* mask.

and that he wears a *kazaori eboshi* in place of a *nashiuchi eboshi.* This somewhat military costuming works well with the Kita dance style, often described as more "military" because of its broad, expansive gestures. The costuming also allows for a dynamic rendering of the final hell scene.

In other schools, the choice of the elegant courtier's *chūjō* mask is more likely to invite the actor to play the second act with a restraint atypical of the intense confrontation often found in *shūshinmono.* Such underplaying may be desirable: minimization of the hell scene would then be a part of a long process of trivialization in this noh.[19] In the first act poems are quoted, but not comprehended; flowers are desired, but forbidden; permission is granted, but ignored; love vows are made, but forgotten; promises are given, but misinterpreted, leading to the drowning of the woman. Belated sympathy is felt by the lover, but rejected by the flower (taken to be the woman's spirit) turning away. His subsequent drowning is initiated as a vindication, but is ultimately represented as groundless overreaction.

A comparison with the second half of *Kayoi Komachi* clarifies the extent of the anti-intensity in *Ominameshi* (Score 1). Both noh open their second part with a female *tsure* approaching a priest engaged in praying for a dead soul. The woman is followed by a man, who also rises from the realm of the dead. The man detains the woman, they argue, the woman moves toward the priest, and the man recounts his story with increasing intensity. During his narration (mostly sung by the chorus), in a moment of realization, the tempo changes, the melody smoothes out, and grievances are forgotten or forgiven in a desire to receive salvation through the prayers offered. Despite similarities in overall choreographic outline, however, the effect of both performances is entirely different. *Kayoi Komachi* expresses a raging antagonism, hurt feelings, and gross misunderstandings that melt into a resolution almost by magic. Wig and mask mirror the intensity

[19] The hell scene is minimized in performance in more ways than just the choice of mask. The rhythm is less intense and less erratic than in, say, *Fujito* or *Nishikigi.* The movements enact the words, but lack the sharp dynamics seen in most other hell scenes. In fact Shimotsuma Shōshin writing in the late 16th century calls the play a love piece. He suggests that the *kuse* be performed very quietly to express this love, and though the movements he outlines for the hell scene are mimetic, he does not indicate they should be done with intensity.

(Photo 13): wild black hair (*kurogashira*) cascades down the back and shaggy locks obscure the face; sunken eyes in the bony skeletal face of the *yase-otoko* mask (Photo 14) flash with the thwarted passions of the underworld.

In contrast, Yorikaze sports flowing locks (*kurotare*), and an elegant mask. To use a standard *shūshinmono* mask of a suffering ghost, like *yase-otoko*, for Yorikaze, would distort the play by overemphasizing the importance of the hell scene, which after all is only nine lines and takes only a couple of minutes to perform. Unlike Shii no Shōshō in *Kayoi Komachi*, Yorikaze lacks infatuation: his affections are cool. He is able to ignore his love and chides her for overreacting (Act II, *dan* 2, *kakaru* segment *"sukoshi chigiri no sawari aru. Hito ma o mokoto to omoi keru ka"*). It is true that in a moment of self-pity and self-recrimination he drowned himself, but in the final scene of the play he negates even this expression of affection by questioning his own powers of interpretation. This act of reconsideration leads him to a desire for enlightenment and is implemented in performance by changes in music and dance style. Shifting from the strident dynamic mode (*tsuyogin*) to the melodic mode (*yowagin*), Yorikaze asks through the chorus, "What type of sin deserves this torture?" (*ikanaru tsumi no nareru hate zo ya yoshi nakari keru*), then changing rhythm from the pulsing *ōnori* to the softer *hiranori*, the answer comes "Even the temporary bending of the flower was but a dream" (*hana no hitotoki o kuneru mo yume zo*). Displacing the shifts in rhythm and in mode by a line (Kanze school), rather than having them occur at the same moment, as they do in *Kayoi Komachi*, helps to dampen the effect by blurring the moment Yorikaze turns to enlightenment (see Score 2 for details).

In trying to find a suitable mask for Yorikaze, the Hōshō and Kongō schools turn to using the mask of a commoner: *waka-otoko* (Photo 15). A commoner's mask would normally, however, require a *happi* jacket rather than a *kariginu*, and is therefore inconsistent with the prescribed costume for the play.[20] Perhaps because of this inconsistency, the Kanze school leaves the choice of type of mask up to the

[20] One other play, *Utaura*, has the *shite* combine a commoner's mask (*waka-otoko*) with the courtier's *kariginu*.

actor: either a similar commoner's mask (*kantan-otoko*, Photo 16), or one of the courtier masks (*chūjō* or *imawaka*).

It is the psychological variation inherent in the *kantan-otoko* mask that probably forms the basis for choosing it. In its original conception, the *kantan-otoko* mask represents the Chinese commoner whose troubled mind leads him to travel in search of enlightenment. After dreaming he was king for fifty years, he awakens to accept the reality of his life and return to his native village. The mask must express both the confusion of an introvert and the clarity of one enlightened. Tilt the mask down, and the thick taut cheeks, concentrated stare, and lines between the eyebrows converge into an expression of questioning bewilderment; tilt the mask up and an openness erases the shadows of doubt about the eyes. The breadth of expressive potentiality, the sense of being disturbed but not vengeful, make this mask a good choice.

The Hōshō and Kongō school's choice of the *waka-otoko* mask takes a middle line. This "young man" mask represents a commoner, but it comes in two variations, one more like *kantan-otoko*, the other more like *imawaka*. The Hōshō mask has the gentle mustache of the aristocratic *imawaka* mask, but rounder eyes and rising curved lines between the eyebrows are similar to those of *kantan-otoko*. Nakamura Yasuo quotes an early Edo-period document describing the Kongō *waka-otoko* as "younger than *chūjō* and weak," but he himself feels it is somewhat "stronger than *kantan-otoko* and most suitable for *Ominameshi* and *Utaura*."[21]

Thus, the extent to which the *shite* actor of one of the schools that allows a choice in mask wishes to emphasize the aristocratic status of Yorikaze, or his weak-willed character, will be reflected in his choice of mask. A middle line that comes close to fulfilling both aspects is the *imawaka*-like *waka-otoko* mask.

The present-day choices all cast Yorikaze in human guise. The choices reflect differences in status and in personality, but none, for reasons discussed above, reinforce the hell scene, even though it is this scene that seems to be the main argument for classifying

[21] Nakamura Yasuo, *Nō men: bi, kei, yō* (Kyoto: Kawara Shoten, 1996), 141. *Utaura* also has a short hell scene, but is not an "attachment" play.

Ominameshi as a *shūshinmono*. A look at the masks used for other *shūshinmono* with similar themes of lovers' troubles clarifies the underlying incongruity between this classification of *Ominameshi* and the modern mask tradition.

Funabashi shares the theme of drowning lovers.[22] In *Funabashi* the ghost of the lover, a nameless commoner, wears a *happi* jacket (as opposed to Yorikaze's *kariginu*) and colored *ōkuchi* (or *hangiri*) divided skirts. Essentially the same costume is worn by the lover in *Nishikigi*, which shares with *Kayoi Komachi* the theme of a man frustrated in his attempts to gain the acceptance of a woman he desires. Masks for such ghosts of commoners are typically chosen from the *ayakashi-mikazuki* group.[23] These include *ayakashi* (Photo 17), *mikazuki, chigusa-otoko, shinkaku,* and *awa-otoko*. Though differing in details, all of these masks have metallic eyes, reflecting an unearthly abode, stark features, and an atmosphere of intensity. They lack, however, the skeletal features suggesting weakness and severe suffering in hell characteristic of *yase-otoko.*

Konishi Jin'ichi, writing on *Ominameshi,* discusses the inappropriateness of certain lines and of the hell scene to the general mood of the play, and poses the question of a mask capable of expressing these passages within the context of the play as an entirety.[24] After rejecting the idea of the middle-aged warrior mask (*heita*) reserved for successful warriors, he suggests an *ayakashi* mask. In particular, he refers to a comment the actor Kanze Hisao made when speculating on an appropriate mask for the old version (no longer performed) of

[22] The lovers in this play meet secretly by passing over a pontoon bridge, but when their disapproving parents find out, they cut the ropes that bind the bridge, and inadvertently incur the death of the lovers.

[23] *Ayakashi* masks began as variants of the *mikazuki* type, used for vigorous gods (e.g. *Takasago, Yumi Yawata*), but in the late 16th century came to be used also for revengeful warriors (*Ikarikazuki, Funa Benkei*) due to a trend towards deifying dead samurai. This latter use was expanded to vengeful ghosts in general in the Edo period. The specific mask used in the Mid-Edo period for such ghosts as appear in *Funabashi* varied according school: Kanze—*mikazuki,* Hōshō—*ayakashi*, Komparu—*shinkaku,* Kita—*togō.*

[24] Konishi, op. cit., 10-1.

Unrin'in.[25] Hisao suggested interpreting the old *Unrin'in* as a *shūshinmono* by using *taka* (Photo 18), an *ayakashi-mikazuki* style mask, for the role of Mototsune. This jealous brother pursued his sister when she ran off with Narihira and managed to return her to the capital by "gulping her up like a demon." Konishi thinks *taka* would also be a good choice for *Ominameshi,* because the expression of the mask is more disturbed than that of *chūjō,* not as tormented as that of *yase-otoko,* and less vengeful than a standard *ayakashi.* In particular, the triangular creases that converge in the furrows between the eyebrows of this mask lend it a troubled expression.

To recapitulate, costuming the main role in the second act of *Ominameshi* challenges the actor to make interpretive decisions. He can cast Yorikaze as an aristocrat, clothing him in a *kariginu* and masking him with *chūjō,* but this will necessitate a very refined rendition of the hell scene, atypical of *shūshinmono.* It will, however, give Yorikaze an elegance not unsuited to the flower imagery integral to the play. Alternatively, the actor can lower the social rank of Yorikaze and choose a commoner mask that reflects more indecisiveness if he feels this is an important part of Yorikaze's character, but he thereby sets up a slight incongruity with the *kariginu* costume. Finally, the actor might step out of the present-day practice and choose a more typical *shūshinmono* mask of the *ayakashi* type, but this might, conversely, place excessive emphasis on the brief hell scene and create too much of a mood contrast with the first act. Whatever the mask chosen, the actor may further opt to heighten the flower imagery of the play through his choice of the designs and colors of the costume.

[25] Texts for both old and revised versions of *Unrin'in* appear in Yokomichi Mario and Omote Akira, *Yōkyokushū 1* in vol. 40 of *Nihon koten bungaku taikei* (Tokyo, Iwanami Shoten, 1960), 154–6. They have been translated by Earl Jackson in Karen Brazell, ed., *Twelve Noh and Kyōgen Plays* (Cornell, East Asia Series, 1988), 39–61. While the first act is essentially the same in both versions, the second act of the earlier version enacts intense jealousy, and that of the new version displays the delights of courtly life. As the old version (in Zeami's hand) was scrapped for the new version, it is impossible to know how it was actually costumed. Kanze Hisao is interpreting it as a *shūshinmono* by suggesting the *taka* mask.

Score 1
A Comparison of Two Shūshinmono Entrance Scenes

Ominameshi

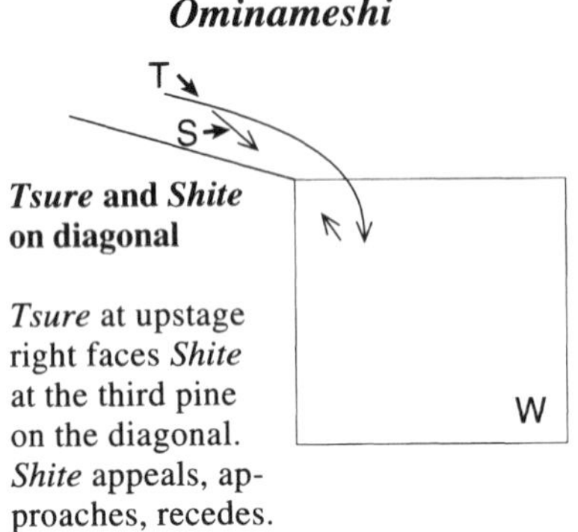

***Tsure* and *Shite* on diagonal**

Tsure at upstage right faces *Shite* at the third pine on the diagonal. *Shite* appeals, approaches, recedes.

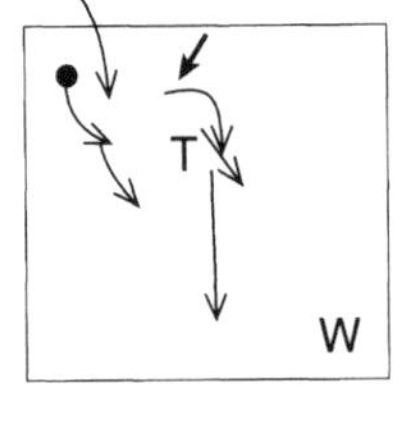

Appeal to *Waki* for prayers
Side by side, *Tsure* at upstage center, *Shite* at upstage right, step forward to ask for prayers. They are told to relate their story. *Tsure* advances and kneels to enact drowning.

***Tsure* joins *Waki* to watch *Shite* narration.**

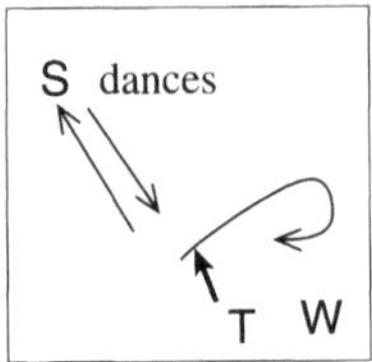

Kayoi Komachi

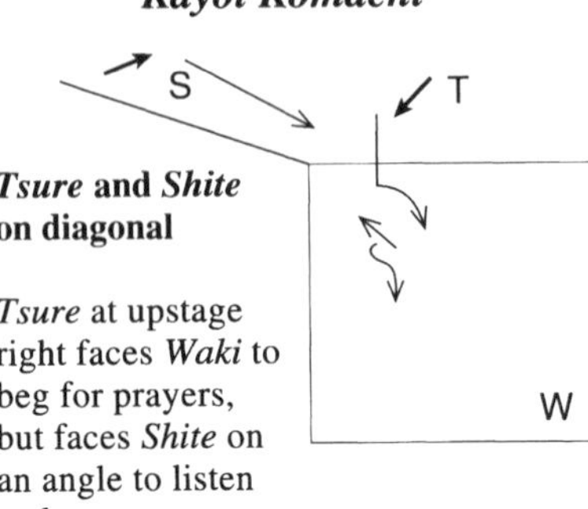

***Tsure* and *Shite* on diagonal**

Tsure at upstage right faces *Waki* to beg for prayers, but faces *Shite* on an angle to listen and argue.

S
T
W

Appeal to *Waki* for prayers
Tsure approaches *Waki* for prayers. After beckoning her to stop, *Shite* enters stage and grabs her sleeve. She evades him; both are side by side facing *Waki*.

***Tsure* joins *Waki* to watch *Shite* narration.**

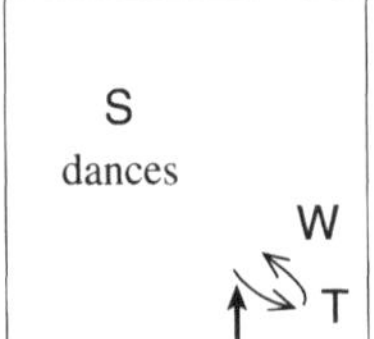

Score 2
Kakeri Dance and Final Scene of *Ominameshi*

Kita School

Key	
——	= forward movement
- - -	= backing movement
0	= stamps
Δ	= kneeling

Kanze School

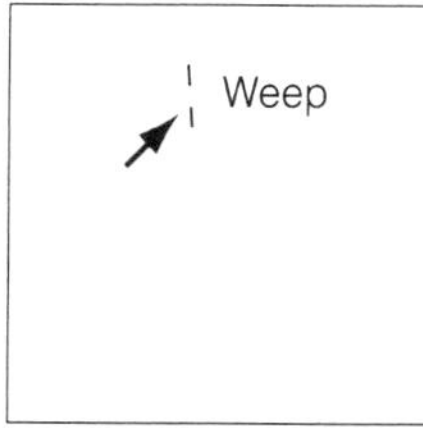

Issei (unmatched) (sung full, expansive)

あら閻浮恋しや
How I miss the world of men!

- ***cry pattern, go to upstage center***
- *cry pattern, go to upstage right*

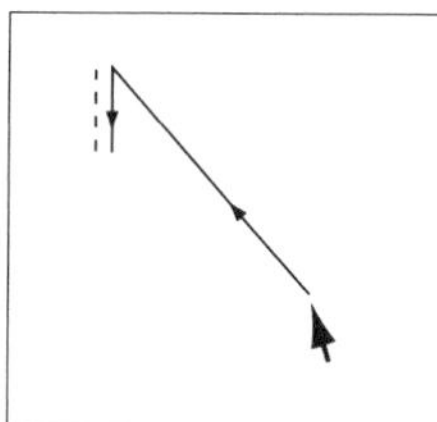

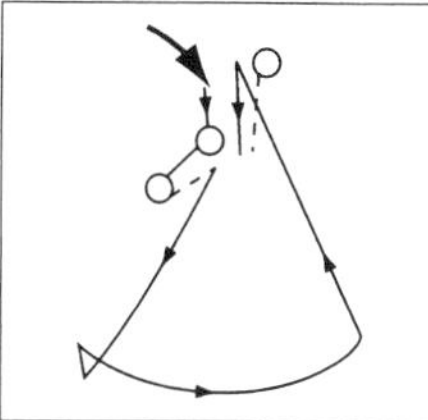

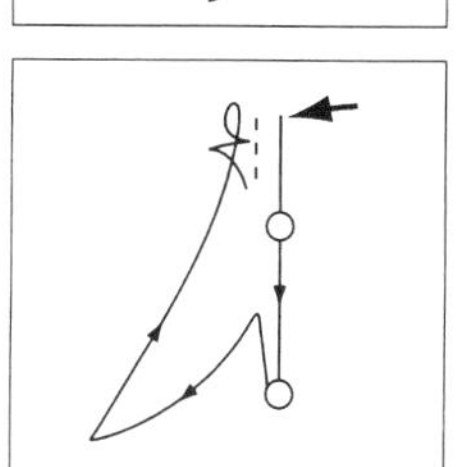

Kakeri
Short dance enacting the *shite*'s nostalgia, and functioning as a bridge to the following hell scene.
(section 1)
Hand drums play uneven, free rhythm patterns quickening in anticipation of the break, when the *shite* stamps,
(section 2)
quickening again before the end of the dance. Flute adds embellishment.

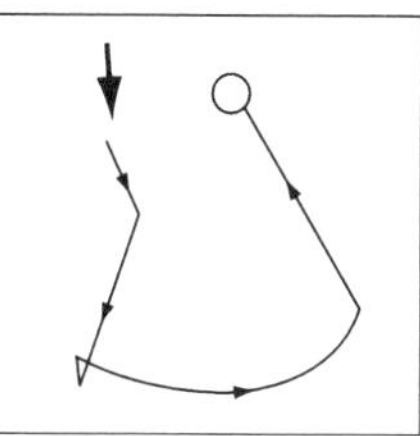

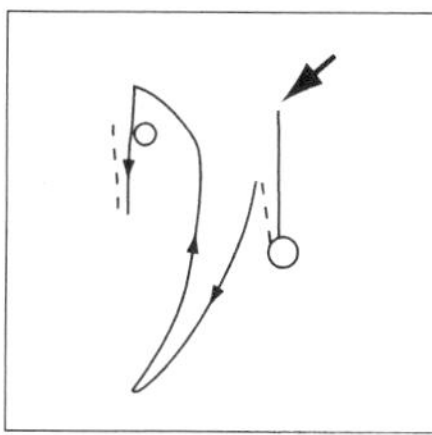

Kita School		*Kanze School*
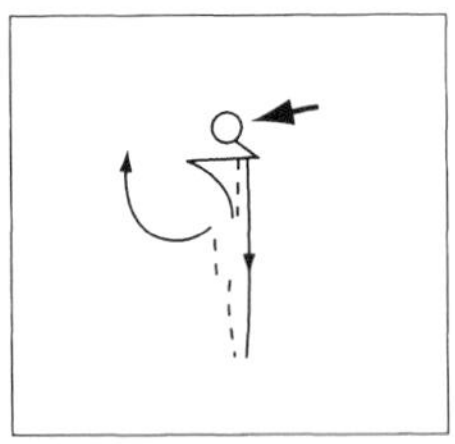	***Noru*** (*tsuyogin*) (sung energetically, rhythmically) 邪淫の悪鬼ハ身を責めて Demons of my immorality close in on me. · ***stamps, left, right, point, open*** · *standing at upstage right*	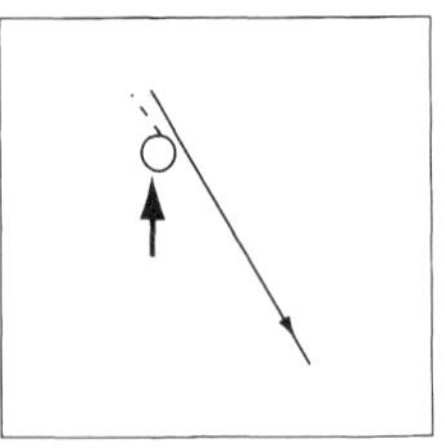
Movements broad. Rhythm quickens.	邪淫の悪鬼ハ身を責めて Demons of immorality hound me. · ***go to center, point, open*** · *3 stamps turning right, point*	*Movements sharper. Rhythm quickens.*
Approaches the mountain.	その念力の Lusty desire's · ***backing point*** · *go to stage center*	*Stamps intensify terror. Approaches mountain and looks around.*
	道も嶮しき path is steep. · ***circle right*** · *look around*	
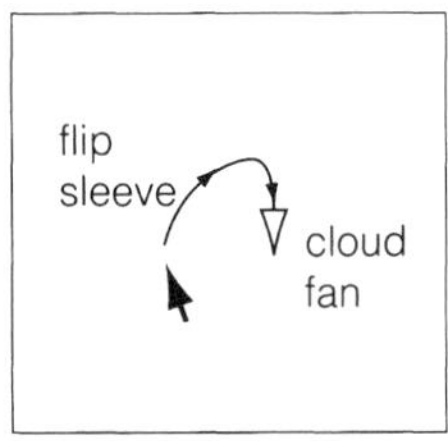 	剣の山の On Sword Mountain · ***at upstage center, flips sleeve*** · *look up to front, circling arm*	
At Sword Mountain he spots his love on top, expessed by flipping the sleeve, then by looking up with the fan extended in the cloud-fan pattern.	上に恋しき人ハ見えたり at the top my love is visible. · ***cloud-fan pattern, kneel, look up*** · *stamps to front, twirl to right, kneel facing front, cloud-fan pattern*	*Approaching Sword Mountain, he views his love on top, extending and raising his fan in the cloud-fan pattern.*

Kita School

fan to
chest

Large gestures = climbing; bringing fan to chest = being pierced; staggering back in S curve = being beaten.

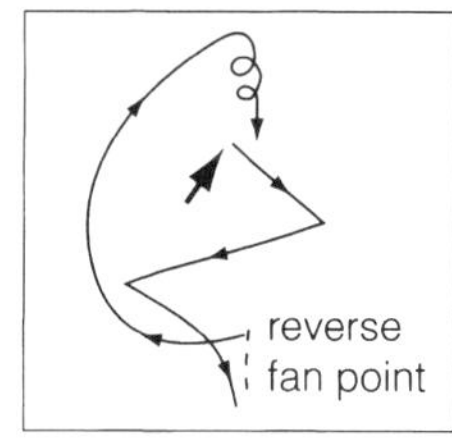

Activity underscores the energy of the song. The **shite** ***points at the sword-branch tree and in ever smaller, faster circles gives a sense of frenzy.***

嬉しやとて
Ecstatic
· ***stands***
· *rise on right knee*

行き登れば
I climb up.
· ***go forward, stepping point to left then right***
· *kneeling steps indicate climbing*

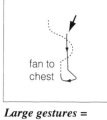

剣ハ身を通し
Swords pierce my body.
· ***backing brings fan to chest***
· *stand, turn beating chest with fan, kneel facing bridge*

磐石ハ骨を砕く
Stones beat my bones.
· ***back up in "S" figure***
· *stand, 7 stamps*

こハそも如何に恐ろしや
Truly this is frightening.
· ***large zigzag (→left→ right)***
· *go to upstage right, mist-fan pattern*

剣の枝の
For the sword branches
· ***circling fan, go to down stage center***
· *go to downstage center*

撓むまで 如何なる罪の
to bend, what (weighty) sin
· *point and circle right*
· ***reverse fan and point***

なれる果てぞや
ran rampant?
· ***right to upstage center, double circlets, point***
· *to upstage center, pointing go to center, open*

Kanze School

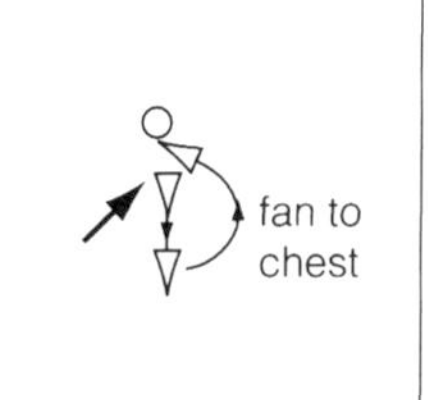

Kneeling steps = climbing; fan to chest = being pierced; kneeling = weakness; stamps = sound of being beaten.

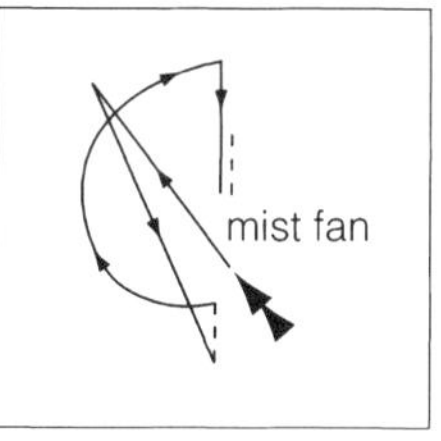

Rushing to downstage is followed by a shift to the softer melodic mode on "what sin..." and is accompanied by quieter movements.

Kita School

Kanze School

Kita chant shifts to both melodic mode and congruent rhythm (**hiranori*****) on "a trivial one."***

由なかりける
A trivial one.
· ***slow, deliberate open pattern***
· *pivot right, circle both arms in flap-fan pattern*

花の一時を
The flower's momentary
· ***6 stamps***
· *6 stamps*

Kanze shifts to congruent rhythm and smooth singing on "the flower's...."

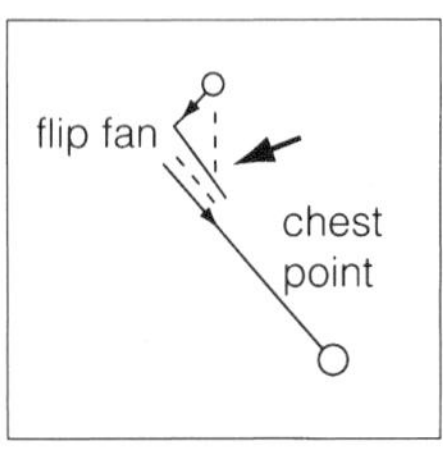

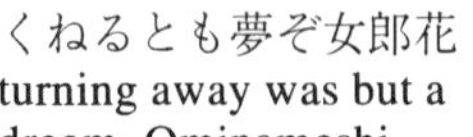

turning away was but a dream. Ominameshi
· ***flip fan, broad point turning to* waki/tsure**
· *point from chest to* waki/tsure

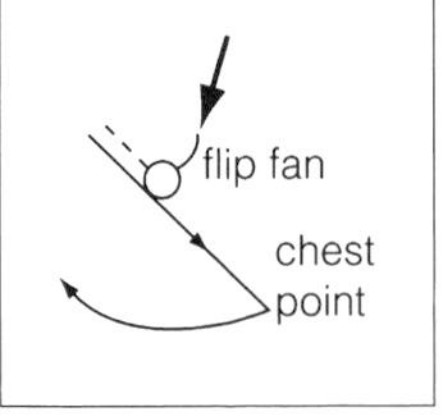

***Stamps aid the transition to calmer rhythm and mood. Chest point is an appeal to the* waki/tsure,**

On your dewy calyx,
· ***chest point going to* waki *spot***
· *half open*

linked with the sacred lotus
· ***stamps***
· *circle right*

Flip fan underscores the sense of realization. Stamps reinforce new rhythm. Chest point presents his realization to the waki/tsure.

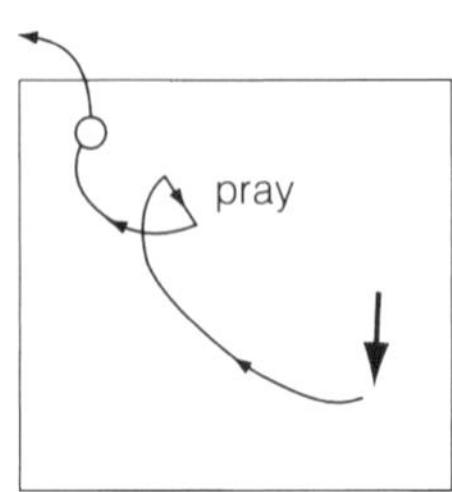

浮かめて賜え給え
flat me plase
go to upstage R, face waki, pray, open
circle to upstage R

罪を浮かめて (slower, quieter) 賜え給え
erase my sins, I plea
open fan , face curtain, stamps, exit
pray, face crtain, stamps, exit

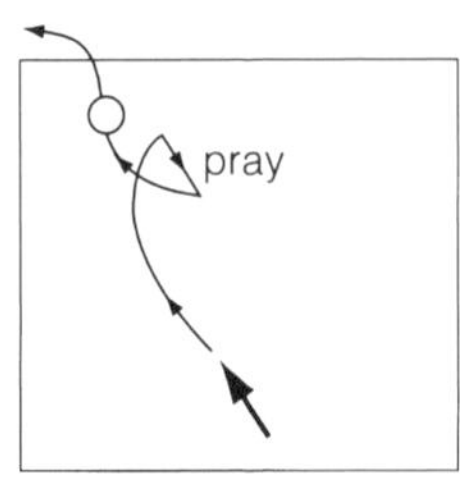

The closing sequence follows an appeal with the prayer pattern

The closing sequence follows an appeal with the prayer pattern

『女郎花』における面と装束

モニカ・ベーテ

能における装束の使い方は伝承と形式によって、すでにある程度まで決められている。そこで演者はその決められた範囲の中で、装束と面を通し曲の解釈を行なうのが常である。特に『女郎花』においては、シテ方は後ジテが付ける装束の選択によってその曲の解釈そのものが左右されるほど影響を持っている。流儀による決まりで観世、宝生流が狩衣と中将の衣装で現れる頼風は優雅な公家の姿となるが、これが「邪淫の悪鬼」で始まるノリ地と似つかわしくなく、控えめな舞の表現となり、押さえられた地獄に落ちるこの場面によって、逆に女郎花の花の雰囲気とその重要さは表出され易く思われる。

しかし喜多流では、逆に「カケリ」と地獄の場面によって狩衣ではなく修羅物のごとき長絹を用い、ノリ地を大きく舞っている。さらに貴族の面の替わりに庶民の面、若男や邯鄲男などを使う選択肢も金剛流、宝生流、観世流にある。この場合、頼風の迷う心をよく現しつつも、しかし貴族の衣装である狩衣と庶民の面は少々合致しないように思われる。現代の訳者や文学者が古い風習を学びながら流儀における伝承や形式からはなれ、他の執心物の面の使い方にも暗示を受けて、怪士系の鷹の面をという案も出したことがある。しかし、これも地獄の情景を強調するだけである。曲全体を考えると、この9行をそこまで拡大解釈してもよいだろうか。初期の『女郎花』にかえり得るか、またはそれから遠く離れるのか、歴史的な研究はまだまだ不足と言える。

この論文では、上の問題をもとに前場、後場の『女郎花』の装束と面について論考し、舞台の動きの図や舞う人の型付けによって異なる解釈を解明する。また、特に女郎花の花のイメージが曲全体に関わることから、この女郎花の花の姿や象徴を、装束の色合いや文様によって表現する可能性を具体的な例で探る。

'97女郎花学会に参加したことなど

観世流能楽師
鵜沢　久

1997年10月にピッツバーグで行なわれた女郎花の学会に参加したことは、色々な意味で私にとって印象深い思い出となっている。一番最初にこの事を言うのは、私事で恐縮ではあるが、同じ年、1997年2月16日に父が他界した。幼少より稽古を受けた、能という道においての師の一人であり、大先輩でもあり、日常を共にしながら、父から得た有形、無形の能に関するあらゆる教えは、今、何ものにもかえがたい私の血であり、肉となっている。高齢（83才）であったし、予期しない事ではなかったにしても、私には、初めて経験する身近かな者の死であった。気持ちの整理をつけるよりも先にその時の私にとっては、目前にある大事な事を乗り越えながら日が過ぎ、落ち着かぬままの渡米となった。今、考えれば機中も含めて、ピッツバーグでの数日間は、それまでの目の回るような忙しさから離れて、我と我が身を考える貴重な時間だった。あの頃はまだ父の私に対する思いに胸をはせては、あふれる涙に自分の情けなさを思い、しかし、ここまで自分が拓いてきた道でもあるのだと思い直し、父もそうだったように、頼れるのは自分だけだと自らを励ましていた。

前置きがかなり長くなってしまったが、そんな中であのピッツバーグの小さな劇場で、すぐ前にお客さま、そして三方とり囲まれての半能「女郎花」は、面白い経験で、思い出深いものだった。初め、スメサースト先生は、紋付、袴だけでもよいということだったが、せっかくならという事で、装束と面を持参する事となった。ツレは娘（光）にさせたが、ワキはいなかったから、ちょうどエマート先生が、一緒だったので、彼に紋付、袴でワキ座に座ってもらい、テープをかけ、女郎花の後半を演じた。大変せまい楽屋だったので、装束をつけるのは、かなり大変だったが、舞台は、精一杯の装置をして下さった。小さな橋掛に松も置いて。床は黒のビニールのシートのようなものを敷き、これはかなり摺り足をしても板のような感触で悪くはなかった。テープだったので、シテ．ツレ．ワキの役の謡がテープと重なって、それぞれの声を出す為に見ている人は変に思ったかもしれないがしかたがない。しかし、シテの謡いから、地謡になる所での拍子は、なかなか合わせるのが難しかった。三番目物のような曲だと、わりに、テープをかけたままでも、何とか舞えるようにも思うが（曲にも、部分にもよるが）この曲のように、複数の役のものが言いかわしたり、シテもある思いを動作と共にする事が割に多いことはやりにくかったし、思いも出しにくかった。けれど、そのような事は、それはそれで、わかっていたことでもあるので、致し方ないとして、この曲についてのことを少し述べる。先にことわっておくが今回は、女郎花全曲を演じたわけではないので、全体としてのこの曲の表現については、感じたことを話すことはできない。

しかし前半部分について思い出すのは、昔、先輩の方の稽古の時の寿夫師の言葉と、その後の先輩の舞台を自分が見た印象である。それは、ワキを伴なって男山八幡宮の嶺から眼下にみる景色と、シテのたたずむ風情は、むせる粟の如く咲く女郎花の群生、その色と匂いと共に、その舞台から私に充分それらを想像させたことである。

後半は今回演じたわけだが、ともかく面は邯鄲男、単狩衣に、風折烏帽子という公達のような姿でありながら、その詞章は、おお広野人稀なりという求塚の後シテの詞と同じであったり、翔の後は、邪淫の悪鬼は身を責め、剣の山に恋する人を見つけて登れば、剣は身を通し磐石は骨を砕く、というように凄惨なものである。これをみても、出立ちは、少し強めな、例えば怪士のような系統の面に、黒頭をつけ、着るのは、袷狩衣とか袷法被かそういう方向性の方がやりやすいのではないかと思った。しかし、最後の場面で花の一時もくねるも夢そ女郎花、となり、観世流の場合は、ヨワ吟にもなり、罪をうかめてたび給へと曲は終わることもあり、又一曲を通じて、和歌が大事な要素にもなっているし、又、この男のもつ弱さややさしさを表現するには、やはり強すぎる出立ちでは合わないだろうとも思う。いづれにしても、何か中途半端な、あまりやりやすい能ではないし、演じるのが難しい能であろう。私は多くはみていないが少なくとも過去には、この能の舞台を面白いと思ったことはなかった。しかし今回演じてみて、面白い能になるかもしれないと思った。さては我が妻の女郎花になりけるよと…又立ち退けば元の如し、という部分は謡も型もとてもよい所で私はここが好きである。又ここから拍子を踏んでゆく所もなかなか心地よい。いつか私も一番全部を演じてみたいと思っている。

この男の虚しさとその時の自分の虚しさをまったく異質ではあっても今、私はそれを考えている。私がピッツバーグでの女郎花学会に参加し、半能「女郎花」を演じさせていただいたことをスメサースト先生御夫妻と、前年に亡くなられた父と私と長い間おつき合いくださり、スメサースト先生との出会いを導いて下さった，島崎千富美さんに深く感謝申し上げたい。

2000.5.4

Reflections on Participating in the 1997 *Ominameshi* Conference

Uzawa Hisa
Kanze School *Shite* Actor

Participating in the *Ominameshi* Conference at the University of Pittsburgh in October 1997 was a deeply moving experience for me. On a personal level, I should note that my father passed away on February 16, 1997. Having practiced noh from a young age with someone who acted as my teacher and mentor, and also sharing daily life together, the tangible and intangible teachings I gained in noh are now an inseparable part of my blood and my life. At eighty-three years old, my father had lived a long life so his end was not unexpected, but for me it was the first death of someone close. Before I was able to collect myself emotionally, I simply had to overcome the necessary tasks that lay before me. I then found myself going abroad to Pittsburgh without ever having fully prepared myself. As I think back on it now, this period, including the time spent on the airplane and the several days in Pittsburgh, allowed me to distance myself from my oppressively busy schedule and provided me with an invaluable period in which to reflect and to consider where I stood. At the time, I was still filled with thoughts of my father, and my tears were a reminder of my unhappiness. However, by reconsidering how I had laid out my own path, just as my father had done before me, I was able to reassure myself that the one person I could rely on was myself.

This preamble has grown lengthy, but it was with this state of mind that I performed at the small Pittsburgh theater, with the audience in front and surrounding me on three sides. Performing half of the noh *Ominameshi* was both an interesting and a memorable experience for me. When Professor Smethurst first asked me to perform, she told me that a formal kimono and *hakama* would be sufficient, but we decided to bring along costumes and masks for the occasion. The *tsure* was played by my daughter, Hikari, and since we were missing a *waki*, Professor Emmert, who was also attending the conference, dressed in a formal kimono and *hakama* and sat in the place of the *waki*. Using a prerecorded cassette tape for musical accompaniment, we performed the latter half of *Ominameshi*. Putting on the costume in the small dressing room was an ordeal, but much effort had gone into appropriately outfitting the stage. A pine tree was placed near the small *hashigakari*. The floor was covered in a sheet of plastic material that felt similar to a plank floor, even when movements involved considerable sliding of the feet. Since we used a cassette tape, the *utai* of the *shite*, *tsure*, and *waki* roles had to be layered with that of the tape and may have appeared strange to the audience as each person chanted over the tape. It took considerable practice to time my *shite* role to fit the rhythm of the chorus section. Although it depends on the play and the section of the play, for the most part the movement for third-category plays can be timed to a cassette tape without much difficulty. However, with this play, in which multiple characters converse and the thoughts of the *shite* often concur with actions, it was difficult to time and to express fully the thoughts of the *shite*. But these were concerns that I was aware of before performing and could not be avoided, so I will turn to a discussion of the noh play. Since I did not perform the entire noh, my observations on expression in the play will be limited to the latter half.

I recall a senior student of noh being instructed by Kanze Hisao, as he practiced a section from the first half of the play, and my impression after seeing the student perform the play. I could imagine the color and scent of the *ominaeshi* flowers, blooming in profusion like steamed millet, viewed by the *shite* accompanied by the *waki* at the peak of Otokoyama at the Hachiman Shrine.

It was the latter half that I performed this time, with a *kantan-otoko* mask, unlined hunting cloak (*kariginu*) and a black lacquer hat (*kazaori eboshi*). Although this is the costume of an aristocrat, the speech, "rarely do people pass through this vast plain," performed after entering, is the same as that of the *shite* in the noh *Motomezuka*. Following the *kakeri* there is the gruesome passage, "the devils of infidelity torture my body . . . climbing Sword Mountain where I spy my beloved, swords pierce my body and boulders crack my bones." Based on these two sections, it might seem easier to perform using a strong entrance in an *ayakashi*-type mask, a long black wig (*kuro-gashira*) and a lined hunting cloak or monk's robe. However, the final scene reads "bending away for a moment, the *ominameshi*, but a dream," and is performed by the Kanze school in the melodic mode (*yowagin*), ending with the phrase, "deliver me from my sins." *Waka* poetry is an important element throughout the entire noh and a strong entrance would not be suitable for expressing the weak or gentle nature of the man. In any case, this noh is hard to grasp and difficult to perform. I have not seen many performances, but never did I consider *Ominameshi* an interesting play. I thought that performing *Ominameshi* this time would make the play more interesting to me. I particularly came to enjoy the speech and movement in the [final] section "my wife has turned into an *ominameshi* . . . then stands up as before." The next part in which the foot is stamped to the rhythm also has a very nice feel to it. I hope one day to perform *Ominameshi* in its entirety.

Although the despair of the man and my own despair were of a very different nature, I can now see the similarities. I would like to express my deepest gratitude towards Professor Mae and Richard Smethurst, who made it possible for me to participate in the *Ominameshi* conference in Pittsburgh and to perform the half noh *Ominameshi*, as well as to my late father to whom I am ever indebted, and to Shimazaki Chifumi who first introduced me to Professor Smethurst.

May 5, 2000

Appendix

○露の臺―露臺といふ成語を借りて、臺を花の縁で極樂の蓮華臺の意に取り做した。

花の一時を。くねるも夢ぞ女郎花。露の臺や花の縁に。浮かめてたび給へ罪を浮かめてたび給へ

「露の臺や」と常座へ行きてワキに合掌し、直して留拍子を踏む。

女郎花も蓮も同じく花ですから、縁のあるものとして、極樂の蓮華臺に生まれられるやうに成佛させて下さい」

といつて退場。

〔考異〕

諸流（五流）

著しい異同はない。

古諸本（光悦本）

【一】ワキ「これは九州……この秋（光度）思ひ立ち……　ワキ「急ぎ候程に……宇佐の宮と御一體なれば（にて御座候ほどに）……眺めばやと存じ（光思ひ）候ても……色を飾り露を含み（光ん）て……　【二】シテ「なう（光〳〵）その花な……　ワキ「さて御身は（光そも）如何なる人なればこれほど咲き亂れたる（光おほき）……　シテ「げにげに……手向と思ふべけれど（光も）……　シテ「いやさればこそ……その御喩へ（光歌）を……　シテ「おう（光あゝ）　【三】ワキ「この野邊の……未だ（光ナシ）八幡宮に……　シテ「この尉こそ唯今（光ナシ）山上する……

【四】シテ「これこそ石淸水……はや日の暮れて（光ナシ）候へば（光程に）御暇申し候べし（光ナシ）……　シテ「あら何ともなや……徒事にて候（光そや）女郎花（光男山）と申すこそ男山につきたる（光女郎花の）謂れにて……　シテ「これなるは男塚又（光ナシ）……　ワキ「さてその……名字は如何なる人やらん（光名をはなにと申候そ）

○同じ道—同じ冥途。

【八】

○閻浮—閻浮提の略。この世。

○邪婬の惡鬼—邪婬の惡業を責め立てる鬼。

○劍の山—往生要集に「又復獄卒取二地獄人一置二刀葉林一見二彼樹頭一有二好端正嚴飾婦女一。如レ是見已卽上二彼樹一。樹葉如レ刀割二其身肉一。次割二其筋一。如レ是勝二割一切處一。已得レ上レ樹、已見二彼婦女一復在二於地一。以二欲媚眼一上看二罪人一作二如レ是言一。念レ汝因緣我到二此處一。汝今何故不二來近一我。何不レ抱レ我。罪人見已欲心熾盛。次第復下、刀葉向レ上、利如二剃刀一。如レ前遍割二一切身命一。既到レ地已而彼婦女復在二樹頭一。罪人見已而復上レ樹」

○劍の枝の—金葉集和泉式部の歌に「地獄の繪に、劍の枝に人の貫かれたるを見てよめる」と詞書して「あさましや劍の枝の撓むまでこは何のみのなれるなるらん」とあるに據つた。

じ浮世に住まぬまでと同じ道にならんとて

シテ『續いてこの川に身を投げて（と正面先にて下に居り）

地『ともに土中に籠めしより女塚に對して（と立ち）又男山と申すなりその塚はこれ、主はわれ幻ながら來りたり。跡弔ひてたび給へ跡弔ひてたび給へ（と脇正面にてワキへ向き）

【八】

地『あら閻浮。戀しや（と袖にて面を掩ひながら常座へ行き）

〔カケリ〕

地（キリ）『邪婬の惡鬼は。身を責めて。邪婬の惡鬼は身を責めて。その念力の。道もさかしき劍の山の。上に戀しき。人は見えたり嬉しやとて。行きのぼれば。劍は身を通し磐石は骨を碎く、こはそもいかに恐ろしや。劍の枝の。撓むまで。如何なる罪の。なれるはてぞや。よしなかりける。

女の後を慕つて、この川に身を投げ、同じく土中に埋められたので、女塚に對して、こちらを男山とも申すのです。その塚はこれで、その塚の主は私で、幻の姿で現れて來たのです。どうぞ後世を弔つて下さい」

【八】

頼風「あゝこの世がなつかしい」

〔カケリ〕にその心持を示し、

頼風「死んだ後は、邪婬の惡業の爲に、惡鬼に身を責められて、險しい劍の山の上に、戀しい人の姿が見える、あゝ嬉しいと思つて、女を思ひ込んだ力で、その山へ登つて行くと、劍は身を刺し通し、磐石で身を碎くのです。何といふ恐ろしいことでせう。劍の枝に刺し通されるまでの、恐ろしい罪の報いを受けたのです。思へば、女郎花がちよつとすねて見せるといふのも、つまらない夢でした。でも、

ツレ『泣く泣く死骸を取り上げて。この山本の土中に籠めしに

シテ「その塚より女郎花一本生ひ出でたり。頼風心に思ふやう。『さてはわが妻の。女郎花になりけるよと。なほ花色もなつかしく。草の袂もわが袖も。露觸れそめて立ち寄れば。この花恨みたる氣色にて。夫の寄れば靡き退き又。立ち退けばもとの如し

地『ここによつて貫之も。男山の昔を思つて女郎花の一時を。くねると書きし水莖のあとの世までもなつかしや(としをる)

シテ次の謠に合せて舞ふ。(舞クセ)

【七】

地クセ『頼風その時に。かのあはれさを思ひとり。むざんやなわれ故に。よしなき水の泡と消えて徒らなる身となるも。偏にわが科ぞかし。若か

の塚から女郎花が一本生えて出ました。さてはわが妻が女郎花になつたのだと思つて、やはりなつかしく思はれ、この草に置く露を女の袂の涙と思ひ、わが袖と觸れ合はさうと、その草のもとへ立ち寄ると、花は恨めしさうな樣子をして、自分が近寄ると退き離れ、自分が立ち退くと、またもとのやうになります。この樣なことを申してゐますと、かの貫之が、男山の昔を思ひ出して『女郎花が一寸ねて見せる』と書いたことまで偲ばれて、なつかしいのです」

【七】

頼風「その時、私は妻の心持を察し、あゝ可哀想なことをした。果敢ない身を水に投げて死んでしまつたのも、全く自分の罪だ。一層のこと、自分もこの世を棄てて、同じ冥途へ行かうと決心して、また

○草の袂も—女郎花の葉に置く露を女の袖の涙に見立てたのである。

○貫之—紀氏。醍醐天皇頃の歌人。古今集撰者の一人で、その序の筆者。〔蟻通〕〔草子洗小町〕參照。

○男山の昔を—古今集の序に「男山の昔を思ひ出で、女郎花の一時をくねるにも、歌をいひてぞなぐさめける」とあるをいふ。尤も原文の「男山の昔」とは前掲「今こそあれわれも昔は」の歌についていつたのを、ここでは貫之が男塚女塚の昔語を思ひ起していつたもののやうに附會してゐる。

【七】

○むざん—無慙。罪を犯して慙ぢないこと、轉じて氣の毒なこと。

○歸らば連れよ―娑婆に歸らば連れて行けとの意。葛の葉の裏返るといひかけた
○妹背の波―波は歸るの緣で出し、下の消えを呼び出す料とした。
○消えにし魂の―魂を玉に玉の緒を女郎花にいひかけた。
○花の夫婦―花やかな夫婦女郎花に通はせた。
○人ま―人の往來の絶え間男の暫く通つて來なかつたことをいふ。
○放生川―男山の麓を流れる川。
○あへなき―はかなき。

シテ『歸らば連れよ。妹背の波

地『消えにし魂の。女郎花。花の夫婦は現れたり（とシテ常座、ツレ大小前へ行き）。あらありがたの。御法やな（とワキへ合掌）

ワキ『影の如くに亡魂の。現れ給ふ不思議さよ

ツレ『わらはは都に住みし者。かの賴風に契りをこめしに

シテ「少し契りのさはりある。人まを眞と思ひけるか

ツレ『女心のはかなさは。都を獨りあくがれ出でて猶も恨みの思ひ深き。放生川に身を投ぐる

と謠ひながらツレ正面先へ行き下に居て投身の心を示し、立ちてワキの上に行きて下に居る。

シテ「賴風これを聞きつけて。驚き騒ぎ行き見れば（と正面先へ出で）。『あへなき死骸ばかりなり（としをりながら常座に歸り）

賴風「いや夫婦だ、娑婆へ歸るのならば、連れ立つて行かう」

といつて、僧の前に現れ、

二人「亡くなつた女郎花の夫婦が現れて來ました。ありがたいお經でございます」

僧「影のやうに、幽靈の現れて來たのは、實に不思議なことだ」

妻「私は都に住んでゐた者で、あの賴風と契りを結んだのでございますが……」

賴風「暫く差支があつて行かなかつたのを、もう全く緣の絶えたもののやうに思ひ込んで……」

妻「淺はかな女心に、都を獨りうかれ出て、深く恨めしう思ひ、この放生川に身を投げました」

賴風「私はこれを聞いて驚き騒ぎ、行つて見ると、もはや果敢ない死骸となつてゐたので、泣きの涙で死骸を取り上げて、この麓の土中に埋めました。すると、そ

【五】
○牡鹿の角の―新古今集柿本人丸の歌「夏野行く牡鹿の角の束の間も忘れず思へいもが心を」を引き、束を塚にいひかけた。
○出離生死―生死の迷界を脱離して、速かに菩提を證得せよとの意。

【六】
○曠野人稀なり―九相詩「野外人稀何物有、爭レ屍猛獸不レ能レ禁」を引いた。
○うら紫か葛の葉の―恨むを紫にいひかけ、恨むの緣で葛と續けた。葛の葉は風に裏返り易いから、うらみると續け慣はした語。

狂言「御逗留にて候はば重ねて御用仰せ候へ
ワキ「頼み候べし
狂言「心得申して候
といひて狂言は引く。

【五】
ワキ上歌(待謡)『一夜臥す。牡鹿の角の塚の草。牡鹿の角の塚の草蔭より見えし亡魂を。弔ふ法の聲立てて。(正面へ向き合掌して)南無幽靈出離生死頓證菩提(といひて直す)

【六】
出端の囃子にて、後ジテ小野頼風、面邯鄲男・黒垂・金緞鉢巻・風折烏帽子・襟白・着附厚板・單狩衣・白大口・腰帶・扇の裝束、後ヅレ頼風の妻、面連面・鬘・鬘帶・襟赤・着附摺箔・色入唐織着流の裝束にて、ツレを先に立てて出で、ツレは直に舞臺に入りて常座に立ち、シテは橋懸一の松に留まりて、
後ジテ『おう曠野人稀なり。わが古墳ならで又何物ぞ
後ヅレ『屍を爭ふ猛獸は。禁ずるに能はず
シテ『なつかしや。聞けば昔の秋の風
ツレ『うら紫か葛の葉の

【五】
後段
旅僧はこゝに一夜寢て、かの塚の草蔭から現れ出た亡魂を弔はうと、誦經して、
僧「――『南無幽靈、生死を出離して、頓に菩提を證せよ』
(幽靈よ、生死の迷界を離れて、速かに成佛せよ)と讀經する。

【六】
旅僧が讀經して、假寢してゐると、その夢に、後ジテ小野頼風、後ヅレ頼風の妻が現れ出る趣で登場。
頼風「おうこの廣い野原に往來する人とてはなく、わが古墳の外に何物もない」
妻「その塚も、猛獸がわれ一と爭つて來て、屍を喰ひ散らすのをとめることは出來ませんし……」
頼風「あゝなつかしい。聞けば昔のわが妻の聲だ」
妻「いえ、あなたにはお恨みがあるだけです」

狂言「さる程に女郎花の子細と申すは。古この八幡に。小野の頼風と申す御方の御座ありしが。訴訟の事候うて。永々御在京なされ候が。とある女と契り給ひ。この所へ御下向の時御申し候は。後より迎へを參らする間。御下向候へと御約束なされしが。頼風はよろづ暇なき御身なれば。左樣の事を忘れ給ひ。御音づれもなく候間。かの女尋ねて來り。その由申し候に。折節頼風は山上に御座ありて。御留守の事なれば。内よりあらけなく返事を申す間。さては頼風の御心變り行きたり。この上は都に歸りてもせんなしとて。放生川へ身を投げ空しくなり給ひて候。あたりの者ども驚き騷ぎ。取り上げ申す折節。頼風山上より御歸りあり。立ち寄り御覽あるに。都にて契り給ひし御方なれば。先非を悔い給へど返らぬ御事なれど。そのまゝ野邊の土中に築き込み。女塚と申し候。又頼風も程なく空しくなり給ふ間。同じく塚に築き込み。男塚と申し候。又女郎花と申すは。かの女性の身を投げし時。山吹色の衣を召されしを。そのまゝ土中に築き込み候が。その上より生ひ出でたる草なれば。女郎花と申して。この山の名草にて候。まづ我等の承り及びたるはかくの如くにて候が。何と思し召し御尋ねなされ候ぞ。近頃不審に存じ候

ワキ「懇に御物語り候ものかな。尋ね申すも餘の儀にあらず。御身以前にいづくともなく老人一人來られ候程に。卽ち言葉を交はして候へば。色々古歌などを詠まれ。男塚女塚を敎へ。頼風夫婦の事を身の上のやうに申され。そのまゝ姿を見失うて候

狂言「これは奇特なる事を承り候ものかな。總じてこの山下に。左樣の老人は御座なく候が。さては頼風の御亡心現れ給ひ。御言葉をかはし給ふと存じ候間。暫くこの所に御逗留あり。重ねて奇特を御覽あれかしと存じ候

ワキ「近頃不思議なる事にて候程に。暫く逗留申し。ありがたき御經を讀誦し。かの御跡を懇に弔ひ申さうずるにて候

がなり。申さねば又なき跡を。誰か稀にも弔ひの。たよりを思ひ頼風の。更け行く月に木隠れて夢の如くに、失せにけり夢の如くに失せにけり

シテ「木隠れて」と右へ廻りて常座にて開き、静かに中入。

風の……」といつて、更け行く月の木蔭に夢のやうに消え失せてしまつた。

◎老人退場する。

○思ひ頼風の―思ひ寄るを頼風に、風の吹くを更け行くにいひかけた。

【問】

【問】 狂言山下の者、着附段熨斗目・長上下・腰帯・扇・小刀の装束にて名乗座に出で、

狂言「かやうに候者は。八幡の山下に住居する者にて候。承り候へば。女郎花の盛りの由申し候間。参りて見申さばやと存ずる。（ワキを見て）いやこれに見馴れ申さぬ御僧の御座候が。いづ方より御出でなされ候ぞ

ワキ「これは九州松浦潟より出でたる僧にて候。御身はこの邊の人にて渡り候か

狂言「なか〳〵この邊の者にて候

ワキ「さやうにて候はばまづ近う御入り候へ。尋ねたき事の候

狂言「畏つて候。（舞臺の眞中に出で下に居て）さて御尋ねなされたきとは。いかやうなる御用にて候ぞ

ワキ「思ひも寄らぬ申し事にて候へども。古この所に於て。頼風夫婦の御事につき様々子細あるべし。御存じに於ては語つて御聞かせ候へ

狂言「これは思ひもよらぬ事を承り候ものかな。我等もこの邊には住居仕り候へども。左様の事委しくは存ぜず候さりながら。初めてお目にかゝり御尋ねなされ候事を。何とも存ぜぬと申すもいかゞにて候へば。凡そ承り及びたる通り御物語り申さうずるにて候

ワキ「近頃にて候

○千里も同じ—和漢朗詠集白樂天の詩句「三五夜中新月色、二千里外故人心」を借りた。
○朱の玉垣—月夜の明きといひかけた。
○御戸代—神前の御戸帳。
○かけまくも—口にかけて申すも忝い。御戸帳に錦を掛くといひかけた。
【四】
○何ともなや—何ともいひやうのない程驚いたとの意
○男塚女塚—男山の南十町許り志水町の東の田の中に女郎花塚があり、その左にあるを女塚、右にあるを男塚といふ。もとより謡曲以後の假託である。
○小野の頼風—謡曲作者の假作名であらう。

きたる謂れにて候か
シテ「あら何ともなや（とワキへ向き）。前に女郎花の古歌を引いて。戯れを申し候も徒事にて候。女郎花と申すこそ。男山につきたる謂れにて候へ。又この山の麓に。男塚女塚とて候を見せ申し候べし。こなたへ御入り候へ
シテ正面へ二三足出で、ワキも少し出づ。シテ正面の方に向き、
シテ「これなるは男塚。（目附柱の方に向き）又こなたなるは女塚。（ワキへ向き）この男塚女塚について女郎花の謂れも候。これは夫婦の人の土中にて候
ワキ「さてその夫婦の人の國はいづく。名字は如何なる人やらん
シテ「女は都の人。男はこの八幡山に。『小野の頼風と申しし人
地上歌『恥かしや古を（ワキ元の座に歸り）。語るもさす

關係があるのです」
翁「これは驚き入つた。今更そのやうな事をお尋ねなさるやうでは、先程から古歌を引いて戯れを申したことも無意義であつた。女郎花は勿論この男山と深い關係があるのです。なほ又この山の麓に、男塚・女塚と申すのがありますから、お見せしませう。こちらへお出でなされ」
といつて、山の麓へ下りた心で、
翁「これが男塚で、又こちらにあるのが女塚です。この男塚・女塚について、女郎花の物語もあります。これはもと夫婦の人を埋めた塚です」
僧「して、その夫婦はどこの國の人で、名字は何と申します」
翁「女は都の人で、男はこの八幡山に住む小野頼風といつた人です。いや、このやうな昔話をするのはお恥かしいが、と申して、お話しなければ、誰もその亡き跡を弔つてくれる人もなし……實は私が頼

○久方の月の桂の男山—續古今集卜部兼直の歌。下句「さやけき影は所からかも」久方のは月の枕詞。月の異名を桂男といふので、桂の男山と續けた。○日もかげろふの—紅葉の色、月の光で日光もかげる程光を失ふといひかけて、石の枕詞「かげろふの」に轉じた。○苔の衣—僧の衣。苔は石の緣語。○三つの袂—三衣即ち袈裟大和國大安寺の行教和尚が貞觀元年宇佐八幡に參籠した節、その衣に阿彌陀三尊の影が映じた靈夢を見て、男山に八幡を勸請したといふ故事(今昔物語に見ゆ)をいふ。夫木抄衣笠内大臣の歌に「石清水すみはじめけん月影の三つの衣に影ぞうつりし」○しるしの筥—御神體勸請の筥。八幡御垂跡のしるしであるから、行教和尚の袈裟を筥に納めて勸請したといふ。○神宮寺—神社に附屬した寺。○鳩の嶺—男山の別名。○三千世界—三千大千世界の略。一切世界の意。

を伏し拝み(と二人とも下に居て合掌)。上歌「久方の。月の桂の男山。(二人立ちワキは脇座に歸り)。月の桂の男山。さやけき影は所から(とシテ右の方を見廻し)。紅葉も照り添ひて日もかげろふの石清水。苔の衣も妙なりや。三つの袂に影うつる(常座へ歸り)。しるしの筥を納むなる。法の神宮寺ありがたかりし靈地かな。巖松峙つて。山聳え谷廻りて諸木枝を連ねたり(と見上げ見下し)。鳩の嶺越し來て見れば(と正面先へ出て見上げ)。三千世界もよそならず千里も同じ月の夜の(見廻し)。朱の玉垣御戸代の。錦かけまくも。忝しと伏し拝む(と常座に歸る)

【四】

シテ「これこそ石清水八幡宮にて御座候へよくよく御拝み候へ。はや日の暮れて候へば御暇申し候べし(と右へ廻り歸る心)

ワキ「ならなら女郎花と申す事は。この男山につ

御せられるお旅所を拜し、

翁「場所柄とて、(あたりの景色を見て、)この男山では月の光も清く、紅葉の色も一入濃く、日の紅さにも勝るばかりで、この石清水はほんとに結構な所です。それからあの彌陀三尊の尊影のお映り遊ばされた袈裟を收めた御筥を納めた神宮寺も、誠にありがたい靈地です。山の岩根には松が聳え、峯から谷へかけて、色々な木の枝が生ひ繁つてゐる。かうして鳩の嶺へ來て見ると、全世界が一眸の中に集まつてゐて、隈なく照らす月の光が、赤い玉垣に映えた神々しさ、ほんとにこの山に鎭座まします神樣は、ありがたいことです」

と拜する。

【四】

翁「これが石清水八幡宮です。よく御拜なさい。はや日も暮れたから、私はこれでお暇します」

僧「もうし、この女郎花は男山とどういふ

も眞なるべしやためしも眞なるべしや

【三】

ワキ「この野邊の女郎花に眺め入りて。未だ八幡宮に參らず候

シテ「この尉こそ唯今山上する者にて候へ。八幡への御道しるべ申し候べしこなたへ御入り候へ

シテ・ワキともに舞臺の眞中に出で正面に向きて、

ワキ『聞きしに超えて貴くありがたかりける靈地かな

シテ『山下の人家軒を竝べ

シテ ワキ（向合ひ）『和光の塵も濁江の。河水に浮かむうろくづは。げにも生けるを放つかと深き誓ひもあらたにて。惠みぞ繁き男山。榮ゆく道のありがたさよ（と謡ひて正面に直し）

地下歌『頃は八月半ばの日。神の御幸なるお旅所

【三】

僧「實は私はこの女郎花を眺め入つて、まだ八幡宮へお參りしないで居るのです」

八幡宮の神前に連れ立つて行つた態で、舞臺は八幡宮前となる。

翁「この老人もこれから山上する所です。丁度よい所です、私が御案内しませう。こちらへお出でなさい」

僧「これは評判に聞いてゐたのにもまして、結構なありがたい神境ですな」

翁「山下にはあのやうに人家が立ち竝び、神境を流れるあの川には、生きた魚を放つ放生會と申す儀式が行はれ、神德のあらたかな神樣で、神の御惠みによつて、世の中の愈々榮えて行くのは、誠にありがたいことです」

といつて二人は、八月十五日神輿の渡

【三】

○和光の塵—和光同塵の意神佛が衆生濟度の爲に德光を和らげて世塵に交はり、衆生と緣を結ぶこと。

○うろくづ—魚類。

○生けるを放つ—毎年八月十五日にこの八幡山下の放生川に魚を放つ神事をいふ。この事「放生川」に作らる。

○男山榮ゆく道—古今集讀人知らずの歌「今こそあれわれも昔は男山榮ゆく時もありこしものを」を借りた。

○神の御幸—神輿の渡御。

○忍ぶの摺衣―忍び隱すを信夫にいひかけ、摺衣を着飾る心で女郎と續けた。信夫は岩代國にあり忍摺の名産地。
○摺衣―草を摺つてその汁で模樣を染めた衣。
○女郎と契る草の枕―前掲源順の詩句及び續後拾遺集安藝の歌「女郎花よるなつかしく匂ふかな草の袂もかはすばかりに」に據つた。
○女郎花憂しと見つつぞ行き過ぐる男山にし立てりと思へば―古今集布留今道の歌。
○なまめき立てる―古今集僧正遍昭の歌「秋の野になまめき立てる女郎花あなかしがまし花も一時」を引いた。
○うしろめたくや―古今集兼覽王の歌「女郎花うしろめたくも見ゆるかな荒れたる宿にひとり立てれば」を引いた。
○誰偕老を契り―前掲、源順の句。
○邯鄲の假枕―蜀國の盧生といふ者が楚國邯鄲の旅宿で枕を借りて眠り、粟飯一炊の間に五十年の榮華の夢を見たといふ故事を指す。この事〔邯鄲〕に作らる。

なと。深く忍ぶの摺衣の。女郎と契る草の枕を。ならべしまでは疑ひなければ。その御喩へを引き給はば。出家の身にては御誤り

ワキ『かやうに聞けば戯れながら。色香にめづる花心。「とかく申すによしぞなき。暇申して歸るとて。『もと來し道に行き過ぐる（正面へ二足出づ）

シテ「おう優しくも所の古歌をば知ろしめしたり。『女郎花憂しと見つつぞ行き過ぐる。男山にし立てりと思へば

地下歌『優しの旅人や。花は主ある女郎花。よし知る人の名にめでて。ゆるし申すなり一本折らせ給へや（とワキへさし）。上歌『なまめき立てる女郎花。なまめき立てる女郎花。うしろめたくや思ふらん。女郎と書ける花の名に誰偕老を契りけん。かの邯鄲の假枕。夢は五十のあはれ世のためし

きと人に語るな』（わしがはまり込んださと人にいふな）と深く隱したのです。とにかく、その名に戯れて、女郎と契るといつたのに違ひないのだから、この歌を喩へにお引きなさるのは、御出家として御心得違ひでせう」

僧「さう仰しやれば、戯れとはいへ、色香をめでるといふことになつて、かれこれ申すも詮ないことです。ではお暇して歸りませう。もと來た道を行き過ぎませう」

翁「おゝ、これは風流な、この男山についての古歌を御承知ですな。――『女郎花憂しと見つつぞ行き過ぐる、男山にし立てりと思へば』（この女郎花は美しい花だが、男山に立つてゐるのを見れば、夫を持つてゐるのであらうから、殘念ながら見過して行かう）

といふ歌を。ほんとにお僧はやさしいお方だ。いかにもこの女郎花は主ある花ですが、いえ構ひません、優しい御賞翫が嬉しいから、さし上げませう、一本お折り下さい。いやこの女郎花は、なまめかしい姿で立つてゐますが、淋しい野にゐては、不安心にも思ふことでせう。女郎といふ名に戯れて、友白髪の契りを結ぶといつた人もあります。さういへば、この花の粟色から思ひ出したことですが、邯鄲の枕に五十年の榮花を夢みたといふこともほんとでせうかしら」

○かの菅原の神木にも―新古今集神祇に「建久二年の春の頃、筑紫へ罷りけるものの、安樂寺の梅を折りて侍りける夜の夢に見えけるとなん」と詞書して、「情なく折る人つらしわが宿のあるじ忘れぬ梅の立枝を」とあるをいふ。安樂寺は菅原道眞の廟所、神木はそこにある飛梅をいふ。〔老松〕參照。

○折りとらば手ぶさに穢る立てながら三世の佛に花奉る―後撰集僧正遍昭の歌。但し原歌の初句「折りつれば」とある。手ぶさは手、三世の佛は過去現在未來三世の諸佛。

○僧正遍昭―俗名良峯宗貞左近衞少將藏人頭となつたが、仁明天皇の崩御を悲しんで出家し遍昭といつた。六歌仙の一人。

○名にめでて折れるばかりぞ女郎花―古今集僧正遍昭の歌。下句「われ落ちにきと人に語るな」

て候

ワキ「たとひ花守にてもましませ。御覽候へ出家の身なれば。佛に手向と思しめし一本御許し候へかし

シテこの間に舞臺に入り常座に立ちて、

シテ「げにげに出家の御身なれば。佛に手向と思ふべけれど。かの菅原の神木にも折らで手向けよと。その外古き歌にも。『折りとらば手ぶさに穢る立てながら。「三世の佛に花奉る』などと候へば。殊更出家の御身にこそ。なほしも惜しみ給ふべけれ

ワキ「さやうに古き歌を引かば。何とて僧正遍昭は。名にめでて折れるばかりぞ女郎花とは詠み給ひけるぞ

シテ「いやさればこそわれ落ちにきと人に語る

野の花守です」

僧「たとひ花守でお出でなさらうと、私は御覽の通りの出家ですから、佛への手向と思つて、一本お與へ下さい」

翁「なる程、御出家の事なれば、佛に手向けたいとお思ひなさるのは御尤もですが、あの菅原天神も、神木の飛梅を手折らないで、そのまゝ手向けにせよとお詠みなされ、その外古歌にも、――『折りとらば手ぶさに穢る立てながら、三世の佛に花奉る』（この美しい花を折つてお供へしようとすれば、折る手で穢れる恐れがあるから、折らないで、この儘で、諸佛にお供へ致します）とも詠まれてあるのですから、御出家は殊更折るのをお惜しみ下さる筈だと思ひます」

僧「そのやうに古歌をお引きなさるが、それならば、僧正遍昭は何故『名にめでて折れるばかりぞ』（女郎花といふ名前が面白いので、折つたまでだ）と詠まれたのです」

翁「いや〳〵、僧正遍昭は女郎花を折つたのをよくないと思へばこそ『われ落ちに

○古歌にも詠まれたる―後に引いてゐる古今集布留今道の歌「女郎花憂しと見つつぞ行き過ぐる男山にし立てりと思へば」を指す。
○家づと―家への土産。

【二】

○花の色は蒸せる粟の如し―本朝文粹巻一源順の詠ニ女郎花一詩に「花色如ニ蒸粟一、俗呼爲ニ女郎一、聞レ名戯欲レ契ニ偕老一、恐惡ニ衰翁首似一レ霜」（和漢朗詠集にも收む）を引いた。
○多かる花に―古今集小野良材の歌「女郎花多かる野邊に宿りせばあやなくあだの名をやたちなん」を借り、種々花の多いのに、何故女郎花の一本を手折るかとの意に用ゐた。

桂林雨を拂つて松風を調む。「この男山の女郎花は。古歌にも詠まれたる名草なり。これも一つは家づとなれば。花一本を手折らんと。この女郎花のほとりに立ち寄れば

と脇座へ行く。

【二】

シテ老翁、面朝倉尉・尉髮・襟淺黄・着附小格子・茶絓水衣・腰帶・扇の裝束にて幕より出でながら、

シテ（呼掛）『なうその花な折り給ひそ。花の色は蒸せる粟の如し。俗呼ばつて女郎とす。戯れに名を聞いてだに偕老を契るといへり。『ましてやこれは男山の。名を得て咲ける女郎花の。多かる花にとりわきて。など情なく手折り給ふ。あら心なの旅人やな

ワキ「さて御身は如何なる人にてましませば。これほど咲き亂れたる女郎花をば惜しみ給ふぞ

シテ「惜しみ申すこそ理なれ。この野邊の花守に

竝べたやうであり、向ふの林から訪れてくる風の音は琴を彈いてゐるやうだ。その中でも、男山の女郎花といへば、古歌にも詠まれた名草で、故鄕へのよい土産だから、一本折り取らう」

といつて、女郎花のもとへ立ち寄る。

【二】

僧が將に女郎花を折らうとすると、シテ老翁（實は小野賴風の靈）が登場して、

翁「もうし、その花をお折りなさるな。その女郎花といふ花は、昔の人に『花の色は蒸した粟のやうに黃色で美しく、俗に女郎と名づけられてゐる。その名前に戲れて、この花と偕老の契りを結ばう』などといはれたものです。殊にこゝは男山で、女郎花には特別の緣故があつて咲いてゐるのに、外の花が澤山あるのを取りもしないで、何故情の心もなく女郎花を折らうとせられるのです。ほんとに考のない旅人だ」

僧「一體あなたはどういふ方なれば、このやうに澤山咲いてゐる女郎花をお惜しみなさるのです」

翁「惜しむのがあたりまへです。私はこの

○不知火の―筑紫の枕詞。末を知らぬといひかけた。

○山崎―攝津國三島郡にあり、淀川を隔てて男山を望む。

○石清水八幡宮―山城國綴喜郡男山にある。貞觀元年行教和尚が宇佐八幡を勸請した宮で、應神天皇・神功皇后・玉依姫の三座を祀る。

○わが國の宇佐の宮―宇佐八幡宮は豐前國宇佐郡宇佐にある。今官幣大社。ワキの出生地と同じ九州であるから、わが國のといつた。

○野草花を帶び―詩句らしいが、出所未詳。

ワキ道行『住み馴れし。松浦の里を立ち出でて。松浦の里を立ち出でて。末不知火の筑紫潟いつしか後に遠ざかる。旅の道こそ、遙かなれ旅の道こそ遙かなれ

「末不知火の」と右の方に向きて二三足出で、またもとに歸りて旅の心を示し、道行濟みて正面に向き、

ワキ「急ぎ候程に。これははや津の國山崎とかや申し候。(右の方に向き)向ひに拜まれさせ給ふは。石清水八幡宮にて御座候。わが國の宇佐の宮と御一體なれば。參らばやと思ひ候。(正面の方に向き)又これなる野邊に女郎花の今を盛りと咲き亂れて候。立ち寄り眺めばやと存じ候

といひて舞臺の眞中に出で、

ワキ『さても男山麓の野邊に來て見れば。千草の花盛んにして。色を飾り露を含みて。蟲の音までも心あり顏なり。野草花を帶びて蜀錦を連ね。

僧「住み馴れた松浦潟を出發し、筑紫潟を次第に遠ざかつて、かうした長旅をすると、いかにも果ての知られない遠々しい氣持がする」

と旅の心持を謠つてゐるうちに、舞臺は攝津國山崎となる。

僧「旅を急いだので、はやこゝは攝津國山崎とかいふ所です。向ふに拜まれるのが、石清水八幡宮です。この宮はわが九州の宇佐八幡宮と御一體だから、參詣しませう」

と男山の麓へ來た態で、

僧「おゝこの野原には女郎花が今を盛りと咲き亂れてゐる。あそこへ行つて眺めませう」

といつて野邊に近寄つた態で

僧「さて〳〵この男山の麓の野に來て見ると、色々の草の花盛りで、みな露を含んで色とり〴〵に面白く、草の間に鳴く蟲の音までが、いかにも風雅な趣である。この草花の美しいことは恰も蜀江の錦を

郎花となつたこと、頼風もその心根を憐んで女の跡を追ひ、かくて男塚・女塚に築きこめられたことを語り、今邪婬の悪鬼に責められてゐる様を示して、僧の回向を乞ふ。

【出典】古今集の序に、

男山の昔を思ひ出で、女郎花の一時をくねるにも、歌をいひてぞなぐさめける。

とあるを骨子として、能作書にいはゆる、名所舊跡に事寄せた作り能を構想したものである。藻鹽草に、

平城天皇の御時、小野頼風といふ人、男山に住みけり。京の女と契りしのち、かの女八幡へ尋ね行きて、頼風がことを問ふ。家なるもの答へていふ、「この程はじめたる女房ましますが、そこへ行き給ふ」と答ふ。この女怨めしく思ひて、八幡の川の端に山吹重ねの衣ぬぎ捨てて、身を投げ死にけり。その衣朽ちて女郎花生ひ出でたるなり。

とあるが、この書は謡曲以後のもので、本曲から出た傳説を記したものに過ぎない。

【概評】〔通小町〕〔定家〕〔船橋〕などと同様、男女邪婬の妄執を描いた曲であるが、この事はキリに少しばかり寧ろ唐突に述べてゐるだけで、類曲中、呵責の程度の最も輕いものといふべきであらう。第二節に古歌を多く引いてゐるのは、本曲創作の動機が那邊にあつたかを察せしめるだけで、別段わづらはしい感じを起さしめないが、第三節に男山八幡の縁起を説いてゐるのは、この曲柄には餘り似合はしい感を與へない。後段第六・七節は本曲の主想で、叙述も甚だ滑かに行つてゐる。

【一】

前段

舞臺は初め九州松浦潟で、ワキ九州松浦潟の僧登場。

僧「私は九州の松浦潟から出て來た僧です。私はまだ都を見たことがないので、この秋思ひ立つて都に上るのです」

と見物人に自己紹介をし、

【一】

名乗笛にて、ワキ松浦僧、角帽子・着附無地熨斗目・絓水衣・腰帯・扇・數珠の装束にて舞臺に入り名乗座に立ち、

ワキ「これは九州松浦潟より出でたる僧にて候。われ未だ都を見ず候程に。この秋思ひ立ち都に上り候

【一】

○松浦潟—肥前國唐津灣の總名。

女郎花（をみなめし）

觀（寶春剛喜）

解説

【能柄】四番目　複式夢幻能

【人物】ワキ　松浦僧、前シテ　老翁（小野頼風の靈）、狂言　山下の者、後シテ　小野頼風、後ツレ　頼風の妻

【所】山城國　男山

【時】秋（八月）

【異稱】〔頼風〕ともいつた。

【作者】能本作者註文には世阿彌の作、二百十番謠目錄には龜阿彌の作とす。粟田口勸進猿樂記に永正二年四月十六日〔頼風〕を演じたこと、言經卿記に文祿四年三月三十日本曲を註釋したことが見えてゐる。

【梗概】九州松浦潟の僧が都見物に出て立ち、やがて男山の麓に來る。折から秋のこととて千草の花の咲き亂れてゐる中に、殊に女郎花の一際美しく咲いてゐるのを見て、一本折り取らうとすると、一人の老翁が現れ出てこれを留める。そして互に古歌を引いていひ爭つた後、老翁は僧を石淸水八幡に案內し、又男塚・女塚を敎へて、自分がその男塚の主小野頼風であると告げて消え去る。僧がその跡を弔つてゐると、やがて頼風とその妻の亡靈が現れ出て、頼風と契りを結んだ都の女が男の中絕えを恨んで放生川に身を投げ、その亡魂が女

佐成謙太郎著

謡曲大観

第五巻

東京　明治書院

めること。「邪婬の悪鬼となつて　われと身を責め苦患に沈むを」（《舟橋》）に同趣。
一〇〈邪婬一途の欲心によって〉。
一一 現行観世流はサカシキ、宝生、喜多流などサガシキと発音。『日葡辞書』にサガシイ。
一二「剣の山」は『宝物集』等に見える。「刀山剣樹」に同じ。『往生要集』に八大地獄のうち第三衆合地獄を「またふたたび獄卒、地獄の人を取りて刀葉の林に置く。かの樹の頭を見れば、好き端正厳飾の婦女あり。かくの如く見已りて、即ちかの樹に上るに、樹の葉、刀の如くその身の肉を割き、次いでその節を割く。かくの如く一切の処を劈き割いて、已に樹に上ることを得已りて、かの婦女を見れば、また地にあり。（中略）かくの如く無量百千億歳、自心に誑かされて、かの地獄の中に、かくの如く転り行き、かくの如く焼かるること、邪欲を因となす」と説く。
一三「地獄の絵に剣の枝に人の貫ぬかれたるを見てよめる　あさましや剣の枝のたわむまでこは何のみのなれるなるらん」（『金葉集』雑、和泉式部）。
一四〈「ほんとにつまらぬことをしたものだ、花盛りのひと時、「くねる」女郎花に心をとられたのも今は夢〉。
一五〈極楽の蓮の台に坐れるよう、女郎花も蓮も同じ花の縁によって成仏させて下さい〉。「露の台」は「花の台」と言うべきところを、「蓮ノ台ヲ女郎花ノ露ニナゾラヘ」（『謡抄』）た表現。

12

【カケリ】（閻浮恋しさの心）

〔ノリ地〕地へ九邪婬の悪鬼は（足拍子を踏み）身を責めて（以下謡に合せて働く）邪婬の悪鬼は　身を責めて　一〇その念力の（正面先へ出）道も一一嶮しき（見返り）一二剣の山の（正面を見上げ）上に恋しき（足拍子）人は見えたり（飛返り膝をつく）（扇を高く掲げ）嬉しやとて（にじり寄り）行き登れば（扇を胸に当て右左の膝をつく）剣は身を通し　磐石は骨を砕く（立って数拍子）（常座へ行き）こはそもいかに（扇を前へ下ろし）恐ろしや　一三剣の枝の（正面先へ出）撓むまで（扇を指して舞台を回り）へいかなる罪のなれる果てぞや　一四由なかりける（扇を打合せ）

〔歌〕地へ（数拍子）花の一時を（ワキへ扇で指し）くねるも夢ぞ女郎花　一五露の台や花の縁に（舞台を回り）（常座でワキに向い合掌）浮かめて賜び給へ（脇正面を向いて）罪を浮かめて賜び給へ（袖を返して留拍子）

一 〈草は露を帯びて泣くように見えるが、私もまた涙に袖が濡れ、露に濡らしつつ、ちょっとさわろうとして傍へ寄ると〉。女郎花の草葉に置く露を袂の露(涙)に見立てた。
二 紀貫之は、『古今集』仮名序に「男山の昔を思ひ出でて女郎花の一時をくねるにも、歌を言ひてぞ慰めける」と書いている。
三 「女郎花の一時をくねる」は、花の咲くのが一時に過ぎないのを皮肉る、の意であるが、頼風説話では「女郎花ノ男ヲクネリタリシ事ヲ、女ノ物クネリ(恨みすねる)スルニ云ヒナシテ書ケルナリ」(『三流抄』)と解する。
四 「水茎の跡」は筆跡。ここは『古今集』仮名序のこと。
五 〈彼女の哀れな心を理解して〉。
六 〈ふびんなことよ、私のせいで、死ななくてもよいのに水の泡と消えて、空しく死んでしまったのも、ただもう自分の罪だ。辛いこの世に住み永らえぬに越したことはない。同じ冥途に赴く身となろうと〉。
七 「と」は、宝生流以外「ぞ」。底本に同じ古写本もある。
八 「閻浮提(えんぶだい)」の略。人間の世界。
九 邪婬戒を破ったため地獄に堕(お)ち、邪婬の悪鬼となって、自分自身の妄想によりわが身を責 11

生(オ)ひ出でたり　(物思う風情で)頼風心に思ふやう　へさてはわが妻の女郎花になりけるよと　なほ花色(ハナイロ)も懐(ナツ)かしく　草(一)の袂(タモト)もわが袖も　(左袖を出して見つめ)つゆ(露・)触れ初(ソ)めて立ち寄れば　(正面先に出)この花恨(ウラ)みたる気色(ケシキ)にて　夫(オット)の寄れば靡(ナビ)き退(ノ)き　また立ち退(ノ)けばもとのごとし　(舞台を小さく回って真中に立って女郎花を指す)

〔歌〕(数拍子を踏み)地へここによって貫之(二ツラユキ)も　男山(オトコヤマ)の昔を思つて　(舞台を回り)女郎花のひと時を　くねる(三)と書きし水茎(四ミズグキ)の　あとの世までも(跡・後)　(涙を押える)懐かしや

〔クセ〕(真中で正面を向いたまま)地へ頼風その時に　かの(五)哀れさを思ひ取り　(足拍子)無慙(六ムザン)やなわれ　(以下謡に合せて働く)ゆゑに　由(ヨシ)なき水の泡と消えて　徒(イタズ)らなる身となるも　ひとへにわが咎(トガ)ぞかし　若(シ)かじ憂(ウ)き世に住まぬまでと　同じ道にならんと(七)て　シテへ続いてこの川に身を投げて　(足拍子を踏んで膝をつく)(立ち上り)地へともに土中(ドチウ)に籠(コ)めしより　(常座で扇を左肩にかいこみ脇正面を見)女塚に対して　また男山と申すなり　(正面の山上を見上げ)(正面へ出て下を見こみ)その塚はこれ主(ヌシ)はわれ　幻(マボロシ)ながら来たりたり　(ワキを見つめ)跡弔(アトトム)らひて賜(タ)び給へ　跡弔らひて賜び給へ

〔詠〕地へあら閻浮(八エンブ)恋しや　(涙を押えながら常座へ行く)

六〈曠野に人影稀にして、わが古墳以外に何物もない。死屍を争いむさぼる猛獣は止めだてしようもない〉。『九相詩』第六、噉食相「外野人稀何物有、争レ屍猛獣不レ能レ禁」に基づくか。《求塚》にも見える。 9

七〈懐かしいこと、風の音を聞くと、それは昔の秋風と同じだ〉。

八〈恨めしいよ、娑婆に帰るなら一緒に連れて行け、妹背の仲だから〉。「葛」「恨む」「かへる」「秋風」など縁語（『連珠合璧集』）。また夫婦の仲を川にたとえて「妹背の川」（歌語）ということから、「川波」の意で「返る」と縁語の「波」を用いた。

九「玉の緒」（命）を隠して言う。 10

一〇 亡魂が、女郎花と化した女とその夫の夫婦ゆえ「花の夫婦」と言う。「女郎花トアラバ…花のすがた」（『連珠合璧集』）。

一一 僧の回向の読経。

一二〈少しばかり逢瀬に差支えがあって、訪れに絶え間のできたのを、まことの心変りと思ったためか〉。「人間」は、人のいない間の意。

一三〈ふらふらとさまよい出て〉。

一四〈今さら取り返しのつかぬ死骸だけである〉。

【出端】でツレとシテが登場　ツレは常座　シテは一ノ松に立つ

［（サシ）］シテ（正面へ向き）〽おう六曠野人稀なり　わが古墳ならでまた何物ぞ

ツレ〽屍を争ふ猛獣は禁ずるにあたはず

［（一セイ）］シテ〽七懐かしや　聞けば昔の秋の風

地〽八（恨・裏・うら紫）うらむらさきか葛の葉の

シテ（ツレへ向き）〽（返・帰）かへらば連れよ妹背の波

［ノリ地］地〽（シテは数拍子を踏み）消えにしたまの　九（緒・女郎花）をみなめし　一〇花の夫婦は　（常座へ行き）現はれたり　（ワキへ向いて合掌）あらありがたの　一一御法やな　（ツレは大小前でワキへ向く）

［掛ケ合］（シテとツレは正面を向く）ワキ〽影のごとくに亡魂の現はれ給ふ不思議さよ

ツレ（ワキへ向き）〽わらはは都に住みし者　かの頼風に契りを籠めしに

シテ（正面を向いたまま）「一二少し契りの障りある　人間を真と思ひけるか

ツレ〽女心のはかなさは　（正面先へ出）一三都を独りあくがれ出でて　なほも恨みの思ひ深き　（ツカツカと正面先へ出て見こみ）放生川に身を投ぐる　（膝をついて投身の体）

シテ（ツレの投身の辺りを見）「頼風これを聞きつけて　驚き騒ぎ行き見れば　（一四 涙を押えて常座に戻る）〽あへなき死骸ばかりなり

ツレ（脇座辺に着座して）〽泣く泣く死骸を取りあげて　この山もとの土中に籠めしに

シテ「その塚より女郎花一本

一　土中に埋められていること。　6

二　小野頼風と女の説話（次頁第10段）は、『三流抄』に基づく。解題参照。

三　〈昔の事を語るのも、どんなものかと憚(はばか)られるが、話をしないとまた、亡き跡を誰かに稀にでも弔(とむら)ってほしいと思っている、その便宜もなくなってしまうと思い寄るままに、頼風と名乗った人は〉。

四　「夏野行く牡鹿の角の束の間も忘れず思へいもが
心を」（『新古今集』恋五、人麿）に基づき、初
句を「ひと夜臥す」に改めて、「牡鹿の角の」　7
までが「束」に音通の「塚」の序。以下三行、　8
《求塚》と同文。

五　亡霊供養の文。〈どうか幽霊よ（悟りを開き）生死の迷いを離れてすみやかに成仏せよ〉。「南無幽霊成等正覚、出離生死頓証菩提」（《求塚》）とも。

たこの山の麓(フモト)に　男塚女塚(オトコヅカオンナヅカ)とて候ふを見せ申し候ふべし　こなたへおん入り候へ[二]

〔問答〕シテ　足を運んで正面を見やり「これなるは男塚(オトコヅカ)　また脇正面を見て　こなたなるは女塚(オンナヅカ)　この男塚女塚につきて女郎花(オミナメシ)の謂(イワ)はれも候　ワキへ向き　これは夫婦(フウフ)の人の土中(ドチュウ)にて候

ワキ　シテへ向き「さてその夫婦(フウフ)の人の国はいづく　名字(ミョオジ)はいかなる人やらん

シテ「女は都の人　男はこの八幡山(ヤワタヤマ)に　へ小野(オノ)[二]の頼風(ヨリカゼ)と申しし人

〔歌〕地　面を伏せ　へ恥づかしやいにしへを[三]　面を上げ　語るもさすがなり　ワキへ向き　申さねばまた亡(ナ)き跡を　誰(タレ)か稀(マレ)にも弔(トム)らひの　便(タヨ)りを思ひよりかぜの（寄・頼風・風）　ふけ行（吹・更）　舞台を回り　く月に木隠(コガク)れて　常座で正面を向き　消え失せた体で中入り　夢のごとくに失せにけり　夢のごとくに失せ(ウ)にけり

〔問答・語リ〕　アイが登場　女郎花を見に来てワキと会い　所の謂れを語る

〔上ゲ歌〕　脇座に着座のまま　ワキ　へひと夜臥す(ヨフ)　牡鹿(オシカ)[四]の角(ツノ)のつかの草（束・塚）　牡鹿(オシカ)の角(ツノ)の塚の草　蔭(カゲ)より見えし亡魂(ボオコン)を　弔(トム)らふ法(ノリ)の声立てて

正面を向き合掌　〔誦〕ワキ　へ南無(ナム)[五]幽霊出離生死頓証菩提(イウレイシュツリショオジトンショオボダイ)

（膝まずいて合掌）伏し拝み

（シテはその場に立ち）
〔上ゲ歌〕地へ 久方の[一三] 月の桂の男山 月の桂の男山 （山を見やり）さやけき影は所から 紅葉[一四]も照り添ひて （以下謡に合せて動き）日もかげろふの石清水 苔[一五]の衣も妙なれや 三[一六]つの袂に影うつる 璽の箱を納むなる 法の神宮寺[一七]

（ワキへ向く）ありがたかりし霊地かな

〔歌〕地へ 巌松峙つて （高く山を見上げ）山そびえ谷めぐりて （左右を見廻し）諸木枝を連らねたり 鳩[一八]の嶺越し来て見れば （正面先へ出 下を広く）三[一九]千世界も外ならず （見渡し）千里も同じ月の夜の あけの玉垣みとしろの 錦かけまくも 忝けなしと伏し （常座でワキを向く）拝む

〔問答〕シテ （正面を向き）「これこそ石清水八幡宮にて候へよくよくおん拝み候へ はや日の暮れて候へば おん暇申し候ふべし （会釈して帰りかける）

ワキ「のうのう女郎花と申す事は [二〇]この男山につきたる謂はれにて候ふか

シテ「あら[二一]何ともなや （足を止めてワキへ向き）さきに女郎花の古歌を引いて戯れを申して候ふも[二二]徒ら事にて候 男山と申すこそ女郎花の謂はれにて候へ[二三] ま

一三〈月の光が冴えわたるのは、月の桂の男山という所柄ゆえで〉。『続古今集』神祇、卜部兼直の歌。末句「所からかも」。月の異名「桂男」を「男山」に言いかけ、「桂」と「紅葉」、「月」と「日」を対に用いた。

一四〈紅葉もその光にいっそう輝きを増し、ために日の光も顔色を失うほどのここ石清水〉。「かげろふ」は「石（清水）」の枕詞。「石清水」が「苔」の序。

一五「苔の衣」は僧衣のこと。「三つの袂」（「三衣」は僧衣の総称）と縁語。

一六 行教和尚が宇佐参詣の砌、神告を受け、衣に弥陀三尊が移り給い、男山へ移座した。「此の袂にやどり給ひし三尊は、当社の正殿のうしろの壁に赤き縄をひきてかけ奉るとも申し、御璽の筥に納め奉るとも云へども、両説未レ定」（『八幡愚童訓』乙本）。

一七 神社所属の寺をいうが、ここは石清水八幡そのものをいう。石清水は八幡権現大菩薩を祀り、石清水八幡宮寺とも称する神仏一体の信仰形態。

一八「鳩の嶺」は男山の異称。「鳩トアラバ…嶺、八幡山」（『連珠合璧集』）。

一九〈全世界も視野の中にあり、千里隈なく照らす月の夜の明るさに、朱の玉垣や錦の御戸帳もはっきり見え〉。「御戸帳」は神前の掛け幕。

二〇〈この男山に関係する謂れがあるのですか〉。

二一 しょうもない、の意。相手の無理解への失望。

二二〈何をしたことやら、無意味なことだった〉。

二三〈女郎花の謂れを表わすものです〉。

一〈あでやかに立っている女郎花は人目が気がかりなことだろう〉。「秋の野になまめきたてる女郎花あなかしがまし花もひと時」（『古今集』誹諧歌、遍昭）。「女郎花トアラバ、うしろめたく」（『連珠合璧集』）。『古今集』秋上、兼覧王の歌による）。古《女郎花》（解題参照）に、以下「契りけん」まで同文が見える。

二〈花の名は女郎花と書くので偕老を契る、と言ったのは誰だったか〉。『和漢朗詠集』（二四八頁注七参照）をふまえる。

三〈蒸せる粟と言えば、邯鄲の枕に五十年の栄花を夢見たはかなさの先例も、偕老の契りのそれと 4
全く同様だ〉。《邯鄲》参照。

四〈何ですって〉。

五 山頂の寺社に参ること。「参上山上」（『明月記』）。

六 以下「霊地かな」まで《高野巻》（『五音』所引《高野》にも）に同じ。

七 和光同塵の意。二二五頁注八参照。

八 男山の麓を流れる放生川をさす。「水の濁りも神徳の、誓ひは清き石清水の」（《放生川》）。

九 放生会には鱗類（魚類）を放生川に放流する。

一〇〈いかにも生き生きとして、放生会の功徳よと思われ、神の深い御誓願がはっきり現われていて〉。

一一「今こそあれわれも昔は男山さかゆく時もありこしものを」（『古今集』雑上）。

一二 八月十五日は放生会で、神輿の巡行がある。途中一時神輿を安置する所が「お旅所」で男山山麓にある。

愛でて　許し申すなり（ワキへ左手を差し出し）　一本折らせ給へや

〔上ゲ歌〕（正面を向き）地へなまめき立てる女郎花[一]　なまめき立てる女郎花　後ろめたくや思ふらん　女郎と書ける花の名に[二]（以下謡に合せて舞台を一巡）　誰偕老を契りけん　かの邯鄲の仮り枕[三]　夢は五十路のあはれ世の　例もまことなるべしや（常座で正面を向く）　例もまことなるべしや

〔問答〕（シテへ向き）ワキ「この野辺の女郎花に眺め入りて　いまだ八幡宮に参らず候

（ワキへ向き）シテ「なにといまだ八幡宮へおん参り候はぬとや[四]　この尉こそ山上[五]する者にて候へ　八幡へのおん道しるべ申し候ふべし（正面へ）こなたへおん入り候へ（出てワキとニ同道の体）

〔掛ケ合〕（正面を見て）ワキへ[六]聞きしに超えて尊くありがたかりける霊地かな

シテへ山下の人家軒を並べ（向き合って）

シテ ワキへ和光[七]の塵も濁り江[八]の　河水[九]に浮かむ鱗類は　げにも生けるを放つかと[一〇]　深き誓ひもあらたにて　恵みぞ茂き男山[一一]（坂・栄）　さかゆく道のありがたさよ

〔下ゲ歌〕（両人正面を向き）地へころは八月なかばの日[一二]　神の御幸なる　お旅所を

（常座でワキへ向き）シテ「げにげに出家のおん身なれば　仏に手向けと思ふべけれど
も　かの一三菅原の神木にも折らで手向けよと　そのほか古き歌にも
へ一四折り取らば手ぶさに穢る立てながら　「三世の仏に花奉るなどと
候へば　一五ことさら出家のおん身にこそ　なほしも惜しみ給ふべけ
れ　ワキ「さやうに古き歌を引かば　何とて僧正遍昭は　一六名に愛
でて折れるばかりぞ女郎花とは詠み給ひけるぞ　シテ「一七いやされ
ばこそわれ落ちにきと人に語るなと　一八深くしのぶ（忍・信夫）の摺り衣の　女郎
と契る草の枕を　並べしまでは疑ひなければ　そのおん譬へを引き
給はば　出家の身にてはおん誤り　ワキへ「一九かやうに聞けば戯れな
がら　色香に愛づる花心　「とかく申すに由ぞなき　暇申して帰る
とて　（歩み出す体）へもと来し道に行き過ぐる　（ワキへ向いて）シテ「おうやさしくも所の古
歌をば知ろしめしたり　へ二〇女郎花憂しと見つつぞ行き過ぐる　男山
にし立てりと思へば
〔歌〕（正面を向き）地へやさしの旅人や　花は二一主ある女郎花　二二よし（・由）（ワキへ向き）知る人の名に

「折らで（折らないで）手向けよ」は「なさけなく折る人つらしわが宿のあるじ忘れぬ梅の立枝を　この歌は建久二年の春のころ、筑紫へまかれりける者の、安楽寺の梅を折りて侍りける夜の夢に見えけるとなん」（『新古今集』神祇）に基づくか。

一四〈折り取ったなら人の手に触れて穢れるから、生えているままに、三世（過去・現在・未来）の諸仏に花を供え奉る〉。下掛り「折りつれば」。『後撰集』春、遍昭の歌（初句「折りつれば」「手に取れば」など）。

一五〈俗人ならぬ出家の御身なら、いっそう手折ることをお控えなさるべきだ〉。

一六『古今集』秋上、遍昭の歌の上句。

一七〈いえ、だからこそ下句を「われ落ちにきと人に語るな」と深く秘匿されたので〉。「落ちにき」は、「落馬」に「堕落」の意を掛けた。

一八〈深く忍んで女郎と契り、枕を並べたことまでは確かなことだから〉。「しのぶの摺り衣」は、「信夫摺」を掛けて「女郎」の序。「草」は「女郎花」と縁語。

一九〈このように伺うと、冗談口をたたいたのも花の色香を愛でての風流心からだが、これ以上はとやかく申すすべもない〉。僧が言い負かされたことを認めた。

二〇『古今集』秋上、布留今道の歌。

二一　夫を持っている意。男山に咲いていること。

二二〈よろしい、古歌の故事由来を知っていることに免じて〉。「よし」は許可の意に由縁の意を掛け、「名に愛でて」は注一六の表現を借る。

〔サシ〕 ワキ（真中へ出て）「さても男山麓の野辺に来て見れば　千草の花盛んにして　色を飾り露を含みて　虫の音までも心あり顔なり　野草花を帯びて蜀錦を連らね　桂林雨を払つて松風を調む

〔□〕 ワキ「この男山の女郎花は　古歌にも詠まれたる名草なり　これもひとつは家苞なれば　花一本を手折らんと　この女郎花のほとりに立ち寄れば

〔問答〕 シテ（幕から呼掛けながら登場）「のうのうその花な折り給ひそ　（橋掛りを歩み）花の色は蒸せる粟のごとし　俗呼ばつて女郎とす　戯れに名を聞いてだに偕老を契るといへり　（ワキへ向き）（正面の男山を向き）へましてやこれは男山の　名を得て咲ける女郎花の　多かる花にとりわきて　など情けなく手折り給ふ　（ワキへ向く）あら心なの旅人やな

ワキ（歩み来るシテへ向い）「そもいかなる人にてましませば　これほど咲き乱れたる女郎花をば惜しみ給ふぞ　シテ「惜しみ申すこそ理りなれ　この野辺の花守にて候　ワキ「たとひ花守にてもましませ　ご覧候へ出家の身なれば　仏に手向けと思し召し　一本おん許し候へかし

一 歌枕。山頂に石清水八幡宮がある。
二〈草花が色とりどりに咲き、露を帯びて〉。 2
三〈風流を解する風情である〉。
四〈野の草は花を咲かせて蜀江の錦を展べたように美しく、桂の林は風が吹いて、雨のしずくを吹き払う音が松風のように聞える〉。詩句か、未詳。
五 注一六・二〇の歌など。
六〈その花を折ってはなりません〉。以下、古歌による花争いは、《雲林院》などにも見える一類型。
七「花色如蒸粟、俗呼為女郎、聞名戯欲契偕老、恐悪衰翁首似霜」（『和漢朗詠集』女郎花）に基づく。
八〈俗に女郎花と称する〉。女郎花を女に擬すことは、漢籍以来の伝統的表現。「俗」は、現行の観世・金剛流はゾク、古写本や宝生・喜多流はショク。 3
九〈女郎という名を聞くだけで戯れに共白髪の契りを結ぶ〉。
一〇〈男山という名の場所に咲いている女郎花なのに〉。すでに男と契りを結んでいる、の意。
一一〈他にもたくさん咲いている花の中で、とりわけこの女郎花を、どうして無情にも手折ろうとなさるのか、ほんとに思いやりのない旅人だよ〉。「女郎花トアラバ…多かる」（『連珠合璧集』）。『古今集』秋上、貞文の歌による）。
一二〈お見かけどおり、出家の身ですから〉。
一三「菅原の神木」は、飛梅のこと（《老松》参照）。

1

【名ノリ笛】でワキが登場　常座に立つ

〔名ノリ〕ワキ（正面へ向き）「これは[一]九州松浦がたより出でたる僧にて候　われいまだ都を見ず候ふほどに　この秋思ひ立ち都に上ぼり候

〔上ゲ歌〕ワキ（正面を向いたまま）へ住み馴れし　松浦の里を立ち出でて　松浦の里を立ち出でて　[二]末しらぬひ（知らぬ・不知火）の[三]筑紫がた　（以下歩行の体）いつしかあとに遠ざかる　旅の道こそ遥かなれ　旅の道こそ遥かなれ

〔着キゼリフ〕ワキ（正面へ向き）「急ぎ候ふほどに　これははや[四]津の国山崎に着きて候　[五]向かひに拝まれさせ給ふは　[六]石清水八幡宮とかや申し候　[七]わが国の[八]宇佐の宮とご一体にてござ候ふほどに参らばやと思ひ候　（正面先を眺め）またこれなる野辺に女郎花の今を盛りと咲き乱れて候　立ち寄り眺めばやと思ひ候

一「松浦」は佐賀県松浦郡の地名。歌枕「松浦潟」に通わせた。

二「末知らぬ」に「筑紫」（九州の総称）の枕詞「不知火」を言いかけた。

三「筑紫潟」は歌枕ではないが、「松浦潟」との縁で用いている。

四 山崎は京への西の入口にあたる。山城の国（京都府）で「津の国」（摂津）ではないが、国境に近いための誤解らしい。

五 石清水八幡宮は、山崎からは淀川を隔てた対岸に位置する。

六 貞観二年、行教和尚が、九州の宇佐から男山（現京都府八幡市）に遷して祀った。二五一頁注一六参照。

七「わが国」は、ワキ僧にとっての国、つまり九州。

八 宇佐八幡宮。欽明天皇の御代に肥後の国（熊本県）菱形の池に顕現し、後に豊後の国（大分県）宇佐に鎮座。

登場人物

前シテ　老　人　笑尉（朝倉尉）・絓水衣・無地熨斗目

後ジテ　小野頼風の霊　邯鄲男・風折烏帽子・黒垂・単狩衣・白大口

後ツレ　小野頼風の妻の霊　小面・唐織

ワ　キ　旅　僧　角帽子・絓水衣・無地熨斗目

ア　イ　所の男　長上下

備　考

＊四番目物、略二番目物。太鼓あり。

＊観世・宝生・金春・金剛・喜多の五流にある。

＊底本役指定は、シテ・後シテ、ツレ、ワキ、二人（シテ、ワキ）、同、地。

構成と梗概

1　ワキの登場　九州松浦の僧（ワキ）が都への途中に石清水八幡へ参詣する。

2　ワキの詠嘆　僧は男山に咲く女郎花を眺め、手折ろうとする。

3　シテ・ワキの応対　老人（前シテ）が呼びかけながら現われ、花を手折ることの是非を古歌で応酬する。

4　ワキ・シテの応対　老人は僧を八幡宮へ案内する。霊場の叙景と縁起。

5　シテ・ワキの応対　僧は女郎花の謂れを問い、老人は男塚・女塚へ案内する。

6　シテ・ワキの応対、シテの中入り　老人は小野頼風夫婦の塚を教え、弔いを頼んで木蔭に消える。

7　アイの物語り　所の男（アイ）が僧に女郎花の謂れを語り、供養を勧める。

8　ワキの待受け　僧の読経弔問。

9　ツレ・後ジテの登場　頼風の妻の亡霊（ツレ）と頼風の亡霊（後ジテ）が現われ、閻浮を懐かしむ。

10　ワキ・ツレ・シテの応対、シテの物語り　女が女郎花となった謂れを語り、回向を頼む。

11　シテの立働き　閻浮への執心。

12　シテの立働き、結末　冥途での邪婬の責め苦を示して、救済を懇請する。

新潮日本古典集成

謡曲集

上

伊藤正義　校注

新潮社版

Index

Compiled by the contributors

CORNELL EAST ASIA SERIES

4 Fredrick Teiwes, *Provincial Leadership in China: The Cultural Revolution and Its Aftermath*
8 Cornelius C. Kubler, *Vocabulary and Notes to Ba Jin's* Jia: *An Aid for Reading the Novel*
16 Monica Bethe & Karen Brazell, *Nō as Performance: An Analysis of the Kuse Scene of* Yamamba
17 Royall Tyler, tr., *Pining Wind: A Cycle of Nō Plays*
18 Royall Tyler, tr., *Granny Mountains: A Second Cycle of Nō Plays*
23 Knight Biggerstaff, *Nanking Letters, 1949*
28 Diane E. Perushek, ed., *The Griffis Collection of Japanese Books: An Annotated Bibliography*
32 A. Ronald Walton, *Tone, Segment, and Syllable in Chinese: A Polydimensional Approach to Surface Phonetic Structure*
36 Miwa Kai, tr., edited & annotated by Robert J. Smith & Kazuko Smith, *The Diary of a Japanese Innkeeper's Daughter*
37 J. Victor Koschmann, Ōiwa Keibō & Yamashita Shinji, eds., *International Perspectives on Yanagita Kunio and Japanese Folklore Studies*
38 James O'Brien, tr., *Murō Saisei: Three Works*
40 Kubo Sakae, *Land of Volcanic Ash: A Play in Two Parts,* revised edition, tr. David G. Goodman
41 Zhang Xinxin, *The Dreams of Our Generation and Selections from Beijing's People,* eds. & trs. Edward Gunn, Donna Jung & Patricia Farr
44 Susan Orpett Long, *Family Change and the Life Course in Japan*
48 Helen Craig McCullough, *Bungo Manual: Selected Reference Materials for Students of Classical Japanese*
49 Susan Blakeley Klein, *Ankoku Butō: The Premodern and Postmodern Influences on the Dance of Utter Darkness*
50 Karen Brazell, ed., *Twelve Plays of the Noh and Kyōgen Theaters*
51 David G. Goodman, ed., *Five Plays by Kishida Kunio*
52 Shirō Hara, *Ode to Stone*, tr. James Morita
53 Peter J. Katzenstein & Yutaka Tsujinaka, *Defending the Japanese State: Structures, Norms and the Political Responses to Terrorism and Violent Social Protest in the 1970s and 1980s*
54 Su Xiaokang & Wang Luxiang, *Deathsong of the River: A Reader's Guide to the Chinese TV Series* Heshang, trs. Richard Bodman & Pin P. Wan
55 Jingyuan Zhang, *Psychoanalysis in China: Literary Transformations, 1919-1949*
56 Jane Kate Leonard & John R. Watt, eds., *To Achieve Security and Wealth: The Qing Imperial State and the Economy, 1644-1911*
57 Andrew F. Jones, *Like a Knife: Ideology and Genre in Contemporary Chinese Popular Music*

58 Peter J. Katzenstein & Nobuo Okawara, *Japan's National Security: Structures, Norms and Policy Responses in a Changing World*
59 Carsen Holz, *The Role of Central Banking in China's Economic Reforms*
60 Chifumi Shimazaki, *Warrior Ghost Plays from the Japanese Noh Theater: Parallel Translations with Running Commentary*
61 Emily Groszos Ooms, *Women and Millenarian Protest in Meiji Japan: Deguchi Nao and Ōmotokyō*
62 Carolyn Anne Morley, *Transformation, Miracles, and Mischief: The Mountain Priest Plays of Kyōgen*
63 David R. McCann & Hyunjae Yee Sallee, tr., *Selected Poems of Kim Namjo*, afterword by Kim Yunsik
64 HUA Qingzhao, *From Yalta to Panmunjom: Truman's Diplomacy and the Four Powers, 1945-1953*
65 Margaret Benton Fukasawa, *Kitahara Hakushū: His Life and Poetry*
66 Kam Louie, ed., *Strange Tales from Strange Lands: Stories by Zheng Wanlong*, with introduction
67 Wang Wen-hsing, *Backed Against the Sea*, tr. Edward Gunn
68 Brother Anthony of Taizé & Young-Moo Kim, trs., *The Sound of My Waves: Selected Poems by Ko Un*
69 Brian Myers, *Han Sŏrya and North Korean Literature: The Failure of Socialist Realism in the DPRK*
70 Thomas P. Lyons & Victor Nee, eds., *The Economic Transformation of South China: Reform and Development in the Post-Mao Era*
71 David G. Goodman, tr., *After Apocalypse: Four Japanese Plays of Hiroshima and Nagasaki*, with introduction
72 Thomas P. Lyons, *Poverty and Growth in a South China County: Anxi, Fujian, 1949-1992*
74 Martyn Atkins, *Informal Empire in Crisis: British Diplomacy and the Chinese Customs Succession, 1927-1929*
75 Bishop D. McKendree, ed., *Barbed Wire and Rice: Poems and Songs from Japanese Prisoner-of-War Camps*
76 Chifumi Shimazaki, *Restless Spirits from Japanese Noh Plays of the Fourth Group: Parallel Translations with Running Commentary*
77 Brother Anthony of Taizé & Young-Moo Kim, trs., *Back to Heaven: Selected Poems of Ch'ŏn Sang Pyŏng*
78 Kevin O'Rourke, tr., *Singing Like a Cricket, Hooting Like an Owl: Selected Poems by Yi Kyu-bo*
79 Irit Averbuch, *The Gods Come Dancing: A Study of the Japanese Ritual Dance of Yamabushi Kagura*
80 Mark Peterson, *Korean Adoption and Inheritance: Case Studies in the Creation of a Classic Confucian Society*
81 Yenna Wu, tr., *The Lioness Roars: Shrew Stories from Late Imperial China*
82 Thomas Lyons, *The Economic Geography of Fujian: A Sourcebook*, Vol. 1
83 Pak Wan-so, *The Naked Tree*, tr. Yu Young-nan

84 C.T. Hsia, *The Classic Chinese Novel: A Critical Introduction*
85 Cho Chong-Rae, *Playing With Fire,* tr. Chun Kyung-Ja
86 Hayashi Fumiko, *I Saw a Pale Horse and Selections from Diary of a Vagabond,* tr. Janice Brown
87 Motoori Norinaga, *Kojiki-den, Book 1,* tr. Ann Wehmeyer
88 *Sending the Ship Out to the Stars: Poems of Park Je-chun,* tr. Chang Soo Ko
89 Thomas Lyons, *The Economic Geography of Fujian: A Sourcebook,* Vol. 2
90 Brother Anthony of Taizé, tr., *Midang: Early Lyrics of So Chong-Ju*
91 Chifumi Shimazaki, *Battle Noh: Parallel Translations with Running Commentary*
92 Janice Matsumura, *More Than a Momentary Nightmare: The Yokohama Incident and Wartime Japan*
93 Kim Jong-Gil, tr., *The Snow Falling on Chagall's Village: Selected Poems of Kim Ch'un-Su*
94 Wolhee Choe & Peter Fusco, trs., *Day-Shine: Poetry by Hyon-jong Chong*
95 Chifumi Shimazaki, *Troubled Souls from Japanese Noh Plays of the Fourth Group*
96 Hagiwara Sakutarō, *Principles of Poetry* (Shi no Genri), tr. Chester Wang
97 Mae J. Smethurst, *Dramatic Representations of Filial Piety: Five Noh in Translation*
98 Ross King, ed., *Description and Explanation in Korean Linguistics*
99 William Wilson, Hōgen Monogatari: *Tale of the Disorder in Hōgen*
100 Yasushi Yamanouchi, J. Victor Koschmann and Ryūichi Narita, eds., *Total War and 'Modernization'*
101 Yi Ch'ŏng-jun, *The Prophet and Other Stories*, tr. Julie Pickering
102 S.A. Thornton, *Charisma and Community Formation in Medieval Japan: The Case of the* Yugyō-ha *(1300-1700)*
103 Sherman Cochran, ed., *Inventing Nanjing Road: Commercial Culture in Shanghai, 1900-1945*
104 Harold M. Tanner, *Strike Hard! Anti-Crime Campaigns and Chinese Criminal Justice, 1979-1985*
105 Brother Anthony of Taizé & Young-Moo Kim, trs., *Farmers' Dance: Poems by Shin Kyong-nim*
106 Susan Orpett Long, ed., *Lives in Motion: Composing Circles of Self and Community in Japan*
107 Peter J. Katzenstein, Natasha Hamilton-Hart, Kozo Kato, & Ming Yue, *Asian Regionalism*
108 Kenneth Alan Grossberg, *Japan's Renaissance: the Politics of the Muromachi Bakufu*
109 John W. Hall & Toyoda Takeshi, eds., *Japan in the Muromachi Age*
110 Kim Su-Young, Shin Kyong-Nim, Lee Si-Young; *Variations: Three Korean Poets*; Brother Anthony of Taizé & Young-Moo Kim, trs.
111 Samuel Leiter, *Frozen Moments: Writings on* Kabuki, *1966-2001*
112 Pilwun Wang & Sarah Wang, *Early One Spring: A Learning Guide to Accompany the Film Video* February

113 Thomas Conlan, *In Little Need of Divine Intervention: Scrolls of the Mongol Invasions of Japan*

114 Jane Kate Leonard & Robert Antony, eds., *Dragons, Tigers, and Dogs: Qing Crisis Management and the Boundaries of State Power in Late Imperial China*

115 Shu-ning Sciban & Fred Edwards, eds., *Dragonflies: Fiction by Chinese Women in the Twentieth Century*

116 David G. Goodman, ed., *The Return of the Gods: Japanese Drama and Culture in the 1960s*

117 Yang Hi Choe-Wall, *Vision of a Phoenix: The Poems of Hŏ Nansŏrhŏn*

118 Mae J. Smethurst, ed., *The Noh* Ominameshi: *A Flower Viewed from Many Directions*

FORTHCOMING

Joseph Murphy, *The Metaphorical Circuit: Negotiations Between Literature and Science in Twentieth-Century Japan*

S. Yumiko Hulvey, *Sacred Rites in Moonlight: Ben no Naishi Nikki*

Charlotte von Verschuer, *Across the Perilous Sea: Japanese Trade with China and Korea from the 7th to the 16th Century*, Kristen Lee Hunter, tr.

Pang Kie-chung & Michael D. Shin, eds., *Landlords, Peasants, and Intellectuals in Modern Korea*

Fan Pen Chen, *Visions for the Masses: Chinese Shadow Plays from Shaanxi & Shanxi*

Ann Lee, *Yi Kwang-su, the Novel* Mujŏng, *and Modern Korean Literature*

Joan R. Piggott, ed., *Capital and Countryside in Japan, 300-1180: Japanese Historians Interpreted in English*

Brett de Bary, ed., *Deconstructing Nationality*

Kyoko Selden & Jolisa Gracewood, eds., *Modern Japanese Literature Readers*
Vol. 1 Stories by Tawada Yōko, Nakagami Kenji, and Hayashi Kyōko
Vol. 2 Stories by Natsume Sōseki, Inoue Yasushi, and Tomioka Taeko

Richard Calichman, *Takeuchi Yoshimi: Displacing the West*

Judith Rabinovitch and Timothy Bradstock, *Dance of the Butterflies:* Kanshi *(Chinese Poetry) from the Japanese Court Tradition*

To order, please contact the Cornell University East Asia Program, 140 Uris Hall, Ithaca, NY 14853-7601, USA; phone 607-255-6222, fax 607-255-1388, ceas@cornell.edu, www.einaudi.cornell.edu/eastasia/CEASbooks

SB/8-03/.7M pb